THE COMPLETE ILLUSTRATED
BREEDER'S GUIDE
TO MARINE AQUARIUM FISHES

Produced and distributed by
T.F.H. Publications
One T.F.H. Plaza
Third and Union Avenues
Neptune City, NJ 07753
www.tfh.com

ISBN 1-890087-71-8

Printed and bound in the United States of America

Library of Congress Cataloging-in-Publication Data
available upon request

Design by Alesia Depot & James Lawrence
Color separations by Digital Engine, Burlington, Vermont

Co-published by
MICROCOSM LTD.
P.O. Box 550
Charlotte, VT 05445
www.microcosm-books.com

FRONT COVER

Clockwise from top left: Yellowhead Jawfish (*Opistognathus aurifrons*) male mouthbrooding eggs, photograph by Scott W. Michael; Picasso Clownfish (*Amphiprion percula*) at ORA, photograph by Matthew L. Wittenrich; Orchid Dottybacks (*Pseudochromis fridmani*) at ORA, photograph by Matthew L. Wittenrich; Banggai Cardinalfish (*Pterapogon kauderni*) pair, photograph by Alf Jacob Nilsen/Bioquatic Photo.

BACK COVER

Top: Percula Clownfish (*Amphiprion percula*) spawning pair, photograph by Alf Jacob Nilsen/Bioquatic Photo;
CENTER: Orchid Dottybacks (*Pseudochromis fridmani*) at Florida Institute of Technology, photograph by Matthew L. Wittenrich;
BOTTOM: Tank-bred Comet (*Calloplesiops altivelis*) at C-Quest, photograph by Scott W. Michael.

THE COMPLETE ILLUSTRATED

BREEDER'S GUIDE

TO MARINE AQUARIUM FISHES

MATTHEW L. WITTENRICH

WITH A FOREWORD BY MARTIN A. MOE, JR.

PRINCIPAL PHOTOGRAPHERS
MATTHEW L. WITTENRICH, ALF JACOB NILSEN, SCOTT W. MICHAEL

ILLUSTRATIONS BY JOSHUA HIGHTER

MICROCOSM

tfh

PROFESSIONAL
SERIES™

CONTENTS

Modes of Reproduction   Page 22

Spawning   Page 88

Math & Motivation   Page 278

PART TWO: SPECIES GUIDES

ACKNOWLEDGMENTS

It is impossible to imagine creating such a book without the constant support of family, friends and fellow aquarists. Through years with enormous amounts of saltwater seeping through the floors, electric bills higher than most small businesses, aquariums and equipment spread throughout the house, live worms in the refrigerator and an occasional fire, my parents Michael and Dawn Wittenrich and my sister Fawn constantly supported me.

Anyone who enters the realm of breeding marine aquarium fishes becomes instantly grateful for the pioneering work of Martin A. Moe, Jr., Frank Hoff, Thomas Frakes and others who helped unravel mysteries of captive reproduction and thrust the hobby where it is today. Bill Addison of C-Quest Hatcheries, Jeff Turner and Kevin Gaines, both with Oceans, Reefs and Aquariums, and Nick Nevid of Proaquatix should be commended for their trail-blazing success in raising numerous species of marine aquarium fishes.

To Martin Moe, especially, my sincere thanks for all your inspiring books on marine husbandry and breeding and your graciousness in agreeing to write a foreword to this work.

This book has taken shape over a number of years, and the list of people to whom I am indebted has grown significantly. Many people have contributed greatly to my understanding of the underwater realm and have influenced my thoughts and provided innumerable ideas and suggestions. These include Mark Meekan, Andrew Halford, Andrew Heyward, Max, Rachel, Cathy and Tarene (Australian Institute of Marine Science), Stephan Simpson (University of Edinburgh), Phil Munday (James Cook University), Kevan Main, Mike Nystrom, Nicole Rhody, Dave Jenkins (Mote Marine Laboratory), John Scarpa, Leroy Creswell (Harbor Branch Oceanographic Institution), Stephen Tettelbach, Larry Liddle, Howard Reisman, Andy Rhyne, Sandra Shumway (Southampton College), Anthony Gill (Arizona State University), Hong Yan (National Taiwan Ocean University), Ferdinand Cruz, Tomas Cabagay, Burt Malieri, Andy, Thoc and Frank, Mark Carra (Pet World), David Boruchowitz (*Tropical Fish Hobbyist*), Phil and Matt Bumgarner and Matt Hines (Trident), Whit Hazelton (Proaquatix), Howard Browman (Austevoll Research Station), Bob Fenner, Aaron Kaminski, Todd Gardner, Dave Georger, Jarod Miller, John Chiemilowic, Pat Mills, Melissa Rice, Jamie Hill, Linda Giampavolo, Laura Cousin and Ryan Black. Special thanks to Vince Rado of ORA for arranging my photography at their facilities.

I am deeply indebted to my editor and publisher, James Lawrence, and the team at Microcosm for bringing my dream to reality. For design: Alesia Depot; for yeoman's work in copyediting: Mary Sweeney, Janice Heilmann and Judith Billard; for photography, Scott W. Michael of Coral Realm and Alf Jacob Nilsen of Bioquatic Photo; and to Kathy Lucas, Kevin Pomeroy, Rose Lucas and the staff of Digital Engine in Burlington, Vermont for their invaluable help with color images and production.

Finally, my advisor, Ralph Turingan, and lab mates at Florida Institute of Technology, J. R. Kerfoot, Tom Samarco, Eleanor Aurrellado, Vutheary Hean, Justin Anto, Ronald Malio, Sarah Jones and Alexandra Didoha deserve special recognition.

—*Matthew L. Wittenrich*
Melbourne, Florida

Captive breeding comes of age: Picasso Clownfish, a genetically stable color morph of the true Percula Clownfish (*Amphiprion percula*) introduced by Oceans, Reefs & Aquariums.

A QUIXOTIC DREAM

Marine Fish Breeding: Once an Impossible Notion

THE PAST

The year was 1972. Marine aquarium keeping, in the infancy of its modern form, was barely 10 years old. An arcane appendage of the freshwater aquarium world, the marine hobby of the time was saddled with the technology of the late fifties and sixties: rust-prone tanks with metal frames and slate bottoms, under-gravel biological filters, pale fluorescent lights, paltry water circulation driven by airstones, and bleached coral skeletons for decor. A few species of hardy marine fishes were available and these were the only observable life to be found in most of these stark early marine aquariums.

The idea of breeding marine aquarium fish had been alive for years but until then had never been realized. One of the deterrents was a lack of fundamental understanding of the marine environment. Marine aquarium keeping sprang out of the established ideas and technology of the freshwater hobby. Most aquarists in the 1950s and sixties were not biologists, much less marine biologists, and their understanding of aquatic ecosystems was grounded in the freshwater environment. In freshwater, almost everything happens on the bottom. Fish spawn and little fish grow up in the same general areas as the adults, most plants and invertebrates are benthic (on the bottom), few float or swim very far, and although plankton exists, it is not the critical biological factor that it is in the marine environment. The bottom basically contains the entire biological ecosystem, including fish reproduction, which can be adequately replicated and managed within the confines of an aquarium.

In contrast, the ecosystem of a marine environment is only partially present on the bottom. Most marine organisms, including almost all marine fish, depend on the shifting, flowing world of the plankton (a soup of marine life forms of all sizes, including microscopic phytoplankton and zooplankton) for sustenance and for distribution of eggs and larvae. The plankton hosts these larvae for extended periods, feeding them and distributing the late larvae to areas where they can metamorphose and survive.

An understanding of this ecological dichotomy was not common in the early days of the marine aquarium hobby, and most early attempts at breeding marine fish centered on the benthic environment established in a typical marine aquarium. Such attempts were doomed to failure since few marine fish produce offspring that are competent to survive the early larval period in a benthic environment.

Success in breeding marine ornamental fish was not found until biologists began to work seriously at spawning and rearing these fish with an understanding of the essential nature of the planktonic environment in the reproductive scheme of marine organisms. It was necessary to develop an environment to provide an adequate substitute for the physical, chemical, and nutritional factors essential to planktonic fish larvae. This could better be provided in a tank separate from the little piece of oceanic bottom that maintained the broodstock. Matthew Wittenrich discusses all of this well in Chapters 8 and 9 of this book.

The history of breeding and commercial production of marine ornamental fish began in the early 1970s. At that time, spawning and rearing saltwater aquarium species (now known as marine ornamentals) was considered, for the most part, impossible. There had been

Martin Moe in his home breeding laboratory in the Florida Keys where he is currently working with the Longspined Sea Urchin, *Diadema antillarum*.

some success in rearing a few marine fish, one or two at a time, at marine laboratories and public aquariums, but production of commercial numbers of marine aquarium species was but a quixotic dream.

The dream was realized, however, in late 1972, and I can tell you how it happened. I was there.

After working as a fishery biologist for the State of Florida for almost 10 years, I took a job in 1969 with a fledgling aquaculture company whose goal was to develop the technology for rearing pompano, a commercially valuable subtropical marine fish with delectable eating qualities. Finding a first food for the just-hatched pompano larvae was one of the major challenges, but we did it.

The key to our success was a very small and easily cultured marine rotifer that was then in use at Scripps Institution of Oceanography in La Jolla, California where they were studying plankton dynamics. We thought that this rotifer might be useful in feeding larval pompanos, and we obtained a starter culture from Dr. Ruben Lasker. This experiment led to success and large-scale production of juvenile pompano.

I left that job in 1971 to return to a doctoral program at the University of South Florida. During that first year my academic ambitions waned, and my thoughts turned to propagation of marine tropical fishes. After some research, the first species I focused on was the Common or Ocellaris Clownfish (*Amphiprion ocellaris*). It was well-suited to aquaculture: it was content to live in a small territory and was a demersal spawner with relatively large eggs and larvae. It was also in great demand in the hobby, a market—maybe thanks to "Nemo"—that has yet to be fully satisfied.

I built a small hatchery in my garage in the Florida Keys and bought a few adult clownfish. The first spawn came in November of 1972, and that resulted in eight juveniles. I thought it a good initial success. Production soon rose into the hundreds, and I was actually selling juvenile clownfish in early 1973 for the grand sum of 35 cents each.

The die was cast, my fish-farming fever rose, and I started a little company, Aqualife Research, to try to make commercial production of tank-raised marine aquarium fish a reality. I never did finish that doctoral program.

As with most things in the scope of human endeavor, once something is shown to be possible, interest and effort becomes more intense and technology advances rapidly. Soon a number of other aquarists, hobbyist and professional, bent their attention to breeding clownfish. Frank Hoff and Tom Frakes, working for Aquarium Systems, joined the fledgling industry in 1974 just down the block from my Aqualife Research hatchery, and we competed for quite a few years. Then Chris Turk, who worked for me at various times and places in his youth, started a clownfish hatchery with Sea World in California, and for a number of years these three companies were the only commercial breeders of ornamental marine fish.

Commercial propagation of marine ornamental fish is one of those things that look great on paper, but the reality is painfully different. A litany of things can, and will, go wrong. The old witticism—"You can make a small fortune breeding marine ornamental fish as long as you start with a large fortune"—has been proved true time and again.

By the mid 1990s, all three of the first-generation of commercial marine ornamental fish hatcheries had passed from the scene. But new hatcheries, some large and some small, some in the US and others in various foreign countries, answered the siren song with multitudes of impossibly colored, incredibly valuable, little marine fish crowded into tanks of crystal-clear saltwater. Some of these hatcheries still exist and some have faded under the technical and financial realities that aquaculture presents. Still, the potential to breed marine aquarium species is alive and well and many of us still get feverish at the thought of being the first to propagate a new species.

THE PRESENT

The field has changed considerably since those early years. We have a better understanding of how to create and manage large and small marine aquariums, and reef tanks populated with live coral and formerly difficult-to-keep fishes. Captive, micro-scale approximations coral reef ecosystems, once an impossible dream, are now commonplace. Aquarium equipment specially designed for marine aquarists—all-glass and acrylic tanks, high-intensity lights, efficient filters, protein skimmers, saltwater pumps and hi-tech wavemakers, specially formulated marine foods, sea salt mixes and chemicals, along with many other innovations—are now in the category of "off the shelf" rather than having to be adapted from the freshwater world.

Strangely enough, once it became possible to maintain and culture photosynthetic corals through vegetative fragmentation (growing new colonies from cuttings), coral culture quickly surpassed the much older efforts to breed marine fish. The reason for this goes back to that dichotomy of the marine ecosystem with benthic and planktonic environments, separate, yet vitally biologically entwined.

Although vegetative coral culture can be accomplished on a benthic substrate, successful culture of marine fish with planktonic larvae demands creation of an adequate substitute for both the benthic and planktonic marine environments. Only a relatively few hobbyists in the world are now willing and able to do this. This book will certainly help many other hobbyists to venture into this demanding, but very rewarding branch of the marine aquarium hobby.

The explosion of the reef tank, coral-culture branch of the marine hobby has also had the interesting effect of increasing the demand for small, colorful fish with intriguing behavior that are adaptive to reef tanks—precisely the type of fish that are most easily cultured. These species, such as clownfishes, gobies, and dottybacks are small as adults, spawn readily in the confines of an aquarium, and can be reared through the larval stages with equipment and techniques that can be applied in Chicago as well as Hawaii. These fish have been and are the mainstay of current commercial marine ornamental marine fish hatcheries. However, despite the 35-year history of marine fish culture, only 2 to 10 percent of the current marine fish market in numbers and in species are tank-reared.

The current dynamics of marine ornamental fish culture are driven by scarcity, price, and protective environmental laws. These factors function together both economically and emotionally to increase the value of marine ornamental fish, and concomitantly make tank-raised fish more competitive. Clownfish are undoubtedly the most common tank-reared species. In fact, clownfishes, particularly *Amphiprion percula* and *Amphiprion ocellaris*, are becoming available in various genetically stable color morphs, a development that mirrors the early culture of the Crucian carp (goldfish) in China 1,500 years ago and the discus during the last century, as well as many other species of freshwater aquarium fish. I thought that this might develop when I first bred this species back in 1972 and I'm glad I lived to see it begin.

There are two reasons why there are so few species of tank-raised marine ornamental fishes in the aquarium trade. The first and most significant is that it is not easy to culture marine fishes, especially to develop the skills necessary to be successful. Only a few species lend themselves to culture far from the sea, and it is expensive in both time and dollars

to engage in this pursuit for either fun or profit. The technology to culture some of the most-prized species—angelfish, tangs, and butterflyfish for example—is still in development, the culture of these species by hobbyists is still the impossible dream. The second, most important to a commercial venture, is that only a few species enjoy the extensive market demand, ease of culture, and high stable price to support the effort and expense of commercial culture.

The big news, however, is the growing number of hobbyists who have the passion and drive to rear marine fish in small home hatcheries. The techniques for rearing clownfish are now well known and many hobbyists now do so. Books by Wilkerson, Hoff, myself, and now Wittenrich have described the basic technology for hobbyists. But perhaps the driving force for this development is the Internet, the information that is available at the click of a mouse, and the new ability of breeders to share experiences, information, and even fish through personal contacts where geographical distance is a minimal factor. And one of the most important parts of this development is that these new and passionate breeders of marine ornamental fish are not constrained by the commercial value of the object of their endeavors. No, they can work with whatever species captures their interest: Emerald Clingfish, or Royal Grammas, or blennies, or dragonets, or obscure gobies, whatever their interest determines and through that work advance the future of the whole field of marine fish culture.

THE FUTURE

Ahh, the future . . . Soon we'll be able to take a clipping from a fin and create vast numbers of cloned angelfish of unimaginable beauty and hardiness, then keep them in fantastic contained ecosystems controlled by technology we can't imagine. Or maybe not . . .

The future has ways of developing along positive and negative pathways we can't foresee. Predictions are rarely accurate. Biology does not change, but the technology through which we manipulate biology is constantly evolving. I think (barring total catastrophe, which, by the way,

The marine aquarium as a window on nature, a living link between farflung tropical coral reefs and the millions of people who will never see them in person.

food fish will surely lend critical information to its ornamental cousin. Technology allowing, the culture of marine fish will follow to some extent the history of the culture of freshwater fish, but it will take much longer, and people who accomplish it will be more knowledgeable and dedicated to an important mission.

It is not possible to protect and preserve things that are not known, and not revered. A wetland, for example, is not likely to be protected from filling and development, or a coral reef from destructive fishing, pollution and climate change, unless the public is aware of the beauty and essential value of that ecosystem to human life. The marine aquarium hobby is a beacon, a focus, a guidepost, a candle in the dark, a bellwether, and a critical outreach pulpit for the relatively small number of us who love and care for the ocean's creatures—to educate the many who do not know and do not care, at least not yet. Everyone who keeps a marine aquarium is, in one way or another, an ambassador from the oceans and reefs to all of humanity.

We know what to do: preserve what can be preserved, fight to control pollution, prevent senseless ecological destruction, live with a small carbon footprint, and most important, curtail and reverse production of greenhouse gasses. Some of us believe that breeding marine fishes is part of the solution, and now we have Matthew's important new book as guidance and inspiration.

—*Martin A. Moe, Jr.*

is not impossible) that we will deepen our understanding of the biology of marine fish reproduction and early life history in the years ahead, and through that understanding, develop better methods for successful breeding of many species of marine fish.

The highest value fish, of course, such as pygmy angelfish, will be the object of the most intense research, and we will see a number of these species enter the commercial trade in the not-too-distant future. I think that eventually we will see commercially available live foods for the early larvae. Food organisms of the proper nutritional constitution and free from bacterial and environmental toxins that are reared and processed in large quantities and available to hobbyists just as live brine shrimp, rotifers, and some copepods are today. Water quality and bacterial control (not only the prevention of bad bacteria but also the enhancement of good bacteria) will be an important factor in development of the aquatic environment for the culture of marine fish larvae, and the commercial farming of marine

*Martin A. Moe, Jr. is the author of **Breeding the Orchid Dottyback: An Aquarist's Journal, The Marine Aquarium Handbook: Beginner to Breeder** and other titles. He lives and continues his breeding research in Islamorada, Florida.*

Ocellaris Clownfish (*Amphiprion ocellaris*) pair spawning in a home marine aquarium. The smaller male will guard the clutch of sticky eggs (see arrows) attached to the live rock until hatching.

CHAPTER 1

A BREEDER'S JOURNEY

Discovering a passion for amateur aquaculture

I set up my first saltwater aquarium at the age of 12, and that same year my father, an active SCUBA diver, helped me get my first dive certification. Our family spent several weeks in Florida each year, and my freshly acquired diving skills helped me observe the jewels of my newfound fascination in their natural surroundings. I was embarking on something that must have given my parents reason to pause for years to come.

According to a logbook I kept, by the age of 14 I had overrun my bedroom with 26 aquariums dedicated to breeding, trading and selling various species of freshwater fish. I had tanks on the top bunk, the floor, my dresser, and desk—everywhere I could squeeze in one more aquarium for breeding. I stripped my clothes from the closet to make room for shelves holding 10-gallon tanks that I divided in half in order to be able to raise anabantoids. I bred and sold cichlids, tetras, barbs, catfish, killifish, piranhas and myriad others, but nothing kept my attention for long. I can still see the astonished look on the clerks' faces at the local fish shop when I pulled the pile of change from my corduroys to pay for my fish-of-the-week. My father and I soon joined a local fish club and I became even more firmly hooked. I went to fish auctions only to set up more aquariums to bring more potential broodstock home.

Throughout my years in grade school and high school I spent more time researching fish than studying math. Whenever possible, I managed English papers and class projects to revolve around some aspect of fish biology or behavior. I wrote short articles for the local fish club newsletter on fish reproduction and had some of them reprinted in a Canadian publication. My first article appearing in

Tropical Fish Hobbyist magazine had been an assignment for a high school English class.

Marine breeding started almost as an afterthought. I maintained a 40-gallon saltwater aquarium as a display tank to offset the stark bare-bottom scheme of my breeding tanks. I had gained considerable knowledge of freshwater fish husbandry and reproduction and then, in the marine community tank, a pair of Ocellaris Clownfish (*Amphiprion ocellaris*) spawned. According to everything I had heard, this was not supposed to happen. "Impossible!" I thought. " Marine fish aren't supposed to spawn in aquariums."

FAIL FIRST, THEN SUCCEED

I found myself frustrated at the lack of published information on spawning and raising marine fishes. I could not locate a single piece of literature on the topic of raising clownfishes. Granted, published reports did exist, but in my youth (and before the Internet) I lacked the essential networking skills to find them. I attempted to raise the first spawn the same way I would a freshwater cichlid. It did not work.

Undaunted, I excitedly tore down the freshwater tanks and began feverishly setting up saltwater aquariums. I purchased clownfish, damsels, angelfish, gobies, lionfish and anything else I thought was unusual or appealing. Before long, the spills of saltwater onto the floor forced me to move my battery of aquariums into the basement. I built my own protein skimmers and wet-dry filters along with individual siphon boxes on 53 aquariums and plumbed them into a central filtration system. I still had no clue as to what I was really doing, but I was excited. No one I approached was able to offer advice or insight and most gave a snide look when confronted by a boy wanting to know how to raise captive-bred marine fish.

Before long I came across some literature citing the need for rotifers and microalgae to feed larval marine fishes. My old standby, newly hatched *Artemia* or brine shrimp, was too large as a first food for most marine species. As soon as I discovered this, I ordered cultures of rotifers and microalgae

from Florida Aqua Farms. It took me 14 spawns of clownfish eggs and many months of trial, error and tinkering with rotifers and phytoplankton before I raised my first nine clownfish past metamorphosis. I was 15 at the time.

As soon as I turned 16 I got a job at a local pet shop. It was, I found, a terrific place to experiment with new species. Weekly shipments of saltwater fish allowed me to observe the reproductive habits of different species. Fish such as dwarf angels and triggers that the boss told me had to be kept separate from each other spiked my curiosity.

When I knew the coast was clear, I began putting every individual of a given species into the same aquarium to observe their behaviors toward one another. There were, I confess, battles and some fish ended up the worse for wear, but I ended up with pairs of gobies, angelfish, damsels and butterflies that spawned regularly as a result. The lesson I learned was that marine fish live to eat and reproduce, and being in an aquarium won't stop them if their keeper provides the right conditions.

I acquired more aquariums, learned to drill glass, taught myself the fine arts of plumbing and filtration and ended up with a fish room housing more than 68 marine tanks. From a rundown trout hatchery I obtained dozens of round fiberglass tubs and plumbing system parts that turned into ideal larval rearing and juvenile grow-out vessels.

This, in conjunction with my newfound knowledge of rotifer and microalgae culture as well as lots more trial and error, allowed me to raise most species I attempted. I gave up many things to work with these fishes and it has taken some time to make up for my lack of interest in other social areas.

Today, boyhood passion has become a life in marine biology and research into reef fish culture. I have refined my ways and no longer raise *Artemia* in gingerale bottles. I've had the great fortune to have graduated to professional-grade university and commercial aquaculture facilities. Most surprisingly, the ability to breed and raise marine fishes in captivity has begun to take on new significance as the future availability of wild-caught coral reef species is becoming ever more uncertain.

Marvelling at the concentration of species diversity, the author inspects a tankful of freshly caught reef fishes being displayed for sale in the Cartimar pet market in Manila, Philippines.

CAPTIVE CULTURE: WHY WE NEED IT

Many observers believe that bans on collecting coral reef fishes are drawing ominously closer, and the marine aquarium hobby is facing the fact that it must find alternative means of sustainability.

The demand for marine aquarium fishes has increased steadily over the last two decades as a direct result of new equipment, improved husbandry techniques and better foods that are allowing many more marine enthusiasts to be successful.

With an estimated two million marine aquarists worldwide, concern is mounting over the sustainability of fish populations and coral reef habitats. Slightly more than 1,000 different species of reef fishes are collected for the aquarium trade, with an average of 27 million specimens caught each year, according to a report by Edmund Green of the UN Environmental Programme in 2002.

A great many threats face today's oceans, most of them much greater than fish collecting for the aquarium trade. Coastal development and pollution play a significant role in the degradation of near-shore waters and the decline of coral reefs. Capture fisheries aimed to supply food have long been responsible for the depletion of fish stocks. Some food fishermen in developing countries resort to destructive practices such as dynamiting reefs or dumping large quantities of cyanide into the ocean to stun fishes. Finally, the ominous rise in sea temperatures caused by global warming is a phenomenon that many scientists believe could lead to the worldwide decimation of coral reefs within the coming century.

The aquarium trade has long drawn criticism from certain conservation groups that point to the collection of fish, corals and live rock as a contributing cause to the poor condition of many coral reefs. They point to damaging collection techniques, such as the use of sodium cyanide (NaCN), and the high mortalities often associated with shipping and handling. While there can be no doubt that coral reef habitats are in trouble in many areas, the real impact of collectors and the marine aquarium hobby remains poorly studied and surrounded by controversy. It is certainly minor compared to climate change, pollution from deforestation and shoreline development. In fact, many supporters of the aquarium trade claim the hobby can be sustainable and an integral component of reef conservation.

Still, in view of all the threats that face reef environments, marine aquarists have an obligation to be stewards of

Filipino aquaculture worker with a small Copperband Butterfly caught as a settlement-stage larva and raised to market size.

these precious resouces and to make informed decisions about the fishes and invertebrates they buy and keep. A marine aquarium is a window on an exotic tropical world and an excellent tool for learning about coral reefs and the life forms that make them so captivating. An informed marine aquarist can be part of the solution, not a contributor to the problem.

WILD HARVEST VS. AQUACULTURE

Today less than 10 percent of marine aquarium fishes available to the consumer are captive-raised, as opposed to greater than 90 percent of the freshwater species sold. Aquaculture has a real potential to alleviate some of the stresses facing coral reef environments, but it does raise some difficult questions.

Wild-capture fisheries supplying the marine ornamental trade provide thousands of jobs throughout the supply chain. Most notably, fishers or collectors in rural coastal areas of developing countries such as Indonesia and the Philippines have few income-generating alternatives to the money they can earn by collecting aquarium animals. These earnings often support entire family units, and without them many fishermen might be forced to resort to drastic measures such as dynamite fishing to supply their families with food. By encouraging sustainable collection, entire villages in undeveloped areas can become stewards of their local reefs and protect them from destructive threats.

Millions of people throughout the world rely on the productivity of coral reefs to maintain a livelihood. Impoverished countries rely directly on coral reefs for daily survival, while others rely indirectly on its wealth through tourism and recreation.

Unfortunately, if environmental forecasters are correct, global changes in weather and even the chemistry of the oceans could spell doom for many, if not most, reef areas in the coming century.

While encouraging sustainable collection practices of wild fishes is important to maintain socio-economic benefits in poor tropical countries, there can be no question as to the urgent need to develop aquaculture technologies for marine aquarium species.

Securing the knowledge of the life histories of coral reef fishes and demonstrating the ability to culture them in captivity will offer some security in protecting bio-diversity in the coming years. At the same time, captive breeding can offer alternative livelihoods should the fisheries collapse or wild harvests be banned.

Indeed, the farming of giant clams (*Tridacna* spp.) and many species of corals in Third World countries is a success story in the making. The clams, once fished to the brink of economic extinction, have made an amazing comeback, and the sale of captive-grown corals from Pacific Island countries is increasing dramatically.

In 1992 the Convention on Biological Diversity adopted an international treaty with three main goals:

1) Conservation of bio-diversity.

2) Sustainable use of a country's resources.

3) Fair and equitable sharing of benefits arising from (exported) genetic resources.

The objectives of the Bio-diversity Treaty are to develop national strategies for the conservation and sustainable use of each country's bio-diversity. The agreement covers all ecosystems, species, and genetic resources. It sets principles for the fair and equitable sharing of benefits arising from such bio-diversity, most notably those destined for commercial use.

The treaty has acquired 188 signing parties, with the United States a notable hold-out as of this writing in 2007. This treaty has unique implications in aquaculture, as companies operating on a commercial scale are often far-removed from the areas where cultivated species originate. There is opposition by the commercial aquaculture industry to the notion that some economic benefit should return to these countries of genetic origin.

Wild-caught Ocellaris Clownfish: should countries of origin get royalties on their genetic exports?

Freshwater Lessons

We need only look at the freshwater aquarium hobby for a view of how things can change. The keeping of freshwater fishes in home aquariums really began to grow when books and magazines started to reveal the successful techniques for their care. Demand for livestock spiraled, fed in part by the new possibilities of using air freight to get wild-caught fish quickly—and alive—from the tropics to places where they could be displayed and sold.

Very little was known about their reproduction at the time, and virtually all specimens were collected from the wild from rivers, streams, and lakes in Central and South America, Africa, and Asia. Before long, species such as the Bala Shark (*Balantiocheilos melanopterus*), Tiger Barb (*Puntius tetrazona*), several species of loaches (*Botia* spp.), and the beautiful Golden Dragon Arowana (*Scleropages formosus*) had been seriously overfished and were reported to be commercially extinct in areas where they had been abundant.

It did not take long, however, for aquarists to begin breeding and raising freshwater fishes—both commercially in ponds and at home within the confines of hobbyists' aquariums. As time went on, the demand for interesting fishes grew and the percentage of amateurs raising aquarium fishes increased. Today, many groups of fishes such as killifish and many unusual cichlids would not be available in the trade if it were not for dedicated private breeders. As the captive breeding of freshwater fishes increased, a marked shift from collection to culture took place, greatly alleviating pressures on wild stocks. To be sure, wild collection is likely to continue. For example, those species not suited to mass culture such as Cardinal Tetras (*Paracheirodon axelrodi*) are still collected from the wild and provide a large economic benefit for Brazilian fisherfolk, who self-enforce sustainable harvests and protection of local waters.

In many instances, however, captive propagation is essential. Human encroachment is a constant threat to aquatic habitats and has driven many species to extinction. The Tecopa Pupfish (*Cyprinodon nevadensis*) is one example. The native California hot springs occupied by this pupfish were channeled to facilitate building construction; exotic gambusias were introduced to control mosquitos; groundwater use was accelerated and pollution increased, ultimately leading to the complete demise of the lovely Tecopa Pupfish, which was declared extinct in 1970. Several other species of pupfish, such as *C. longidorsalis*, survive only in captivity as their native habitats have been destroyed. Although the ocean is a massive expanse of water, throughout history humans have demonstrated the ability to drive fish stocks to commercial extinction. Captive breeding may be one answer when wild stocks are threatened.

Banggai Cardinalfish is a spectacular fish, easily bred in the home aquarium, yet possibly threatened with overcollecting in its limited wild range.

PIONEERING EFFORTS

Even though we've known for decades that some coral reef fishes can be successfully raised in captivity, aquarium enthusiasts have had very little practical advice on how to breed most species. Experimental rearing of reef fishes was successful as early as the 1930s, while commercial techniques were found for many species in the 1950s. Among the pioneers who deserve credit for cracking the codes of breeding and rearing clownfishes and other species are Martin A. Moe, Jr., Frank Hoff, Tom Frakes, and Bill Addison.

Still, even today, commercial-scale production methods exist for only a handful of marine aquarium species. Successful future production seems probable in a large number of species, but many others seem only a remote possibility. While much of the progress with commercial marine aquarium fish production is cloaked in secrecy, aquarium enthusiasts are playing a crucial role in freely sharing their observations on behavior, feeding, growth and reproduction of marine fishes.

Many aspects of reproduction and larval husbandry remain unknown for a variety of fish families, and dedicated home and public aquarium aquarists are those most likely to observe and report important new information.

In my view, there is a real need to encourage captive propagation outside the commercial, profit-driven enterprises. Such facilities have limited capacity for research and the economics of developing new species rarely permit any deviation from production. Breakthroughs in breeding new species are certain to come much faster with the increased participation of amateur and home-scale experimenters.

Additionally, many species of marine aquarium fishes are not suited to commercial culture. The reproductive modes of such species as the Royal Gramma (*Gramma loreto*) make production difficult in large, consistent numbers. Royal Grammas are ideally suited to hobbyist culture. They are justifiably popular fish and are always in high demand, but are likely never to be mass-produced.

Many species of fish in both the freshwater and marine aquarium hobbies fluctuate in their availability. Driven by ebbs and flows of wild populations and by market forces and catch limits, the market for many marine fishes could be better assured by captive breeders. Rare fishes that fetch high prices also present great opportunities to determined experimental breeders. Many examples of expensive species that are rarely collected from the wild exist in the marine aquarium trade. Basement breeders have the potential to become key players in supplying these rare fishes to the marketplace. (Public aquarium biologists are actively working on breeding rare and threatened marine species, but they are usually prevented from supplying stocks to the aquarium trade, even when they have surpluses.)

Perhaps the largest difference separating the freshwater and marine aquarium trades today is the lack of home-based saltwater breeders. When I first became interested in propagating marine fishes, the almost total lack of information was daunting. This is still the number one reason aquarists are hesitant to attempt culturing marine fishes.

In fact, there are countless spawning events in saltwater aquariums every year, but relatively few people try to save the eggs or rear the larvae. This could all change if fishkeepers become more aware of culture techniques and if culturing supplies and equipment are more readily available.

Consider that there are over 2,000 known species of gobies, most of them marine, but less than a dozen are reared on a commercial scale. Most of them would prove just as easy as the first, and the only reason they haven't been captive-bred is that no one has tried. Inspired? Be observant and watch fish at local pet shops. Look for possible signs of courtship, research the species' requirements, set up some aquariums and raise them. Be the first to bring a new species through spawning and rearing in captivity. Marine aquarists of the future will be indebted to you.

TO YOUR SUCCESS

This book is the culmination of many years of trial and error and is the product of my experiences and biological observations in homebased and commercial aquaculture, as well as scientific collaborations with some of today's leading marine fish propagators. I offer this as a practical guide to give you the confidence and knowledge needed to successfully propagate marine aquarium fish in captivity.

One word of warning: As I learned in my boyhood experiments, you will need to be committed to succeeding and willing to learn all you can about the reproduction and life history strategies of the species that attract your interest.

The aquarium hobby is one based largely on opinion and anecdotal science, rather than laboratory tests and controlled experiments. Techniques and methodology that one aquarist swears by may not work for another.

The smartest breeders, however, constantly gain from the experiences of others. This book is intended as a guide. Your culture techniques are sure to evolve, and there are certain to be important breakthroughs in the equipment and foods available. Experimentation will be key in making things work in your own breeding efforts.

Small-scale marine fish hatcheries operated by hobbyists may have a nice potential for earnings, but getting beyond more than modest profitability can be a long and difficult road. This book is about the challenge and tremendous satisfaction to be found in breeding marine fishes at home rather than a business manual. A sense of passion is what first drives most hobbyists to raise these fishes, and it is in that spirit that I have compiled this guide. I believe that curiosity is a tremendous motivator, as is doing something most people still think is impossible.

I wish you luck and success as you make your own discoveries and bring your first batches of captive-bred marine fish to viable size. I hope that you will share your findings with others and, in embarking on your own extraordinary venture, help contribute to the future of responsible marine aquarium-keeping and even the healthy future of coral reefs and the incredible fishes they give us.

Demersal-spawning Black Clown Goby (*Gobiodon albofasciatus*) female laying eggs (see arrows) on a cleared patch of staghorn coral (*Acropora* sp.) Coral or clown gobies spawn readily in the aquarium.

CHAPTER 2

MODES OF REPRODUCTION

The Amazing Sex Lives of Coral Reef Fishes

Reproduction is a central theme in the life of any wild organism. For a coral reef fish, eating, avoiding being eaten and perpetuating the species are the order of the day. Given the unique and competitive circumstances in which these reef fishes live, modes of reproduction have evolved to provide truly unique solutions to the challenge of ensuring that one generation successfully creates the next.

Although the world's oceans cover much of the earth's surface, coral reef fishes cluster in a tiny fraction of it. Geographically bound in a belt hugging the equator, coral reefs are arguably the most intricately balanced ecosystem on the planet; nowhere else can one find so many diverse creatures living in such close proximity. On certain reefs in the Great Barrier Reef system, over 1,500 species of fishes inhabit a common area. More than 80 species have been found on small patch reefs only a few yards in diameter in the Caribbean.

Each species of fish living on a reef has evolved to occupy a well-defined niche within the ecosystem which has resulted in a variety of survival traits that allow each species a chance to thrive. Whether a fish spends most of its time in open water or tucked safely in protective thickets of stony coral, it has developed a reproductive strategy to maximize success despite the presence of countless hungry predators and the physical realities of strong tides, currents and seasonal weather patterns. The reproductive modes of marine fishes are extremely diverse and for the would-be breeder, they are a crucial factor in determining the success of captive propagation.

There are two broadly distinct modes of egg dispersal among marine fish families: *Demersal Spawners* and *Pelagic Spawners*.

DEMERSAL SPAWNERS

Anyone who has come up through the ranks of freshwater aquarium-keeping will be familiar with demersal spawning, perhaps best illustrated by the fiercely parental cichlids.

Demersal spawning fish produce eggs that are designed to remain in a defined area where they are typically guarded until hatching occurs. Some produce eggs that are adhesive and attach to a solid surface, as do the various clownfishes or anemonefishes. Others produce a gelatinous ball of eggs placed in a cave as do the dottybacks and comets. Some groups, such as the grammas, lay individual eggs placed in a nest site within a cave. Perhaps the most fascinating are the mouthbrooders like the jawfishes and cardinal fishes that produce an egg mass that is orally incubated.

The great majority of demersal eggs are protected in some form by the parents. Typically only the male partakes in brood-care duties. Since demersal spawning fish guard their eggs and do not expose them to predation in the water column, spawning can occur at any time during the day or night. Early morning and afternoon are preferred spawning times for many demersal spawning species. In many cases, the parent standing on guard does not eat for days or weeks while it protects the eggs. Typically, once hatched, the larvae of demersal spawners drift up into the water column to join a myriad of other planktonic life forms.

Throughout the reef world, there are exceptions to these general methods. For example, the Sharpnose Puffer (*Canthigaster valentini*) is a demersal spawner that offers no protection to its eggs but the eggs and larvae of this species are highly unpalatable to other fishes.

For many beginning marine fish breeders, the demersal spawners may present the best opportunity for success in their first attempts at captive reproduction.

PELAGIC SPAWNERS

Pelagic spawners produce small eggs containing one or more oil globules that aid in buoyancy. Eggs are shed into the water column and become pelagic; that is, they float in

A pair of Clark's Clownfish (*Amphiprion clarkii*) that spawn regularly in a community reef aquarium. Smaller male is at front.

the upper water column at the mercy of the seas.

Pelagic spawning fishes generally release buoyant eggs at the height of a spawning ascent. Following an elaborate courtship, male and female rise up into the water above the reef or lagoon floor, simultaneously releasing eggs and sperm at the height of the ascent. Spawning ascents are performed to shed eggs high in the water column, above the reef structure, to avoid the predatory mouths of other fishes found on the reef and to assist the eggs in their upward migration.

Much chaos and confusion abounds during pelagic spawning, and the parents themselves will often eat a portion of their own eggs. Pelagic spawning fishes are typically larger and stronger swimmers than demersal spawning fishes or are equipped with some form of protection. The chance of succumbing to predation is high during courtship and spawning as most energy and attention is focused on reproduction.

Smaller species such as cowfishes and trunkfishes have protective body armor, while the lionfishes sport venomous spines that make them an unpalatable snack.

Dusk and early evening is the usual time of spawning among the pelagic spawning fishes. These are transition periods on the reef. Diurnal species are seeking refuge in the protective crevices of the reef for the coming of night and nocturnal species are preparing for their debut. This is the time when eggs are least likely to be preyed upon.

It is generally true that pelagic spawning fishes produce many times the number of eggs of demersal spawners, but these highly vulnerable eggs spend more time in the plankton (the incredibly diverse collection of tiny animals—known as *zooplankton*—and plant life—known as *phytoplankton*), where the chance of predation is increased. Demersal spawners lay far fewer eggs, but offer parental protection.

When the eggs of demersal spawners hatch, they are much more advanced, competitive larvae than the larvae of pelagic spawners. The numbers of demersal and pelagic larvae that survive to make their way back onto a reef theoretically even out, as fish populations historically remain relatively constant.

LARVAL DIFFERENCES

Eggs of pelagic spawners hatch an average of 24 to 36 hours after they have been shed into the water column. The very tiny fishes that hatch are known as pro-larvae. These lar-

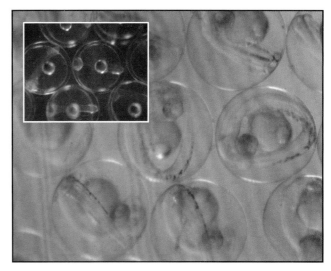

Large eggs of demersally spawned dottyback eggs compared to much smaller pelagic, free-floating reef basslet eggs (inset).

vae possess few characteristics, lacking pigmented eyes, a digestive system or mouth, and with only a rudimentary finfold, a precursor to actual finnage. They simply float around in the water column feeding off their yolk sac for another day or two before a functional gut, mouth parts and pigmented eyes develop. Pro-larvae are extremely vulnerable to predation during this period.

Demersal larvae develop in the egg until pigmented eyes and fins have developed. Larvae are more competitive at this stage and have little remnant yolk. The larvae that result from demersal eggs are *phototactic*—able to recognize and move toward light. They usually break free from their egg cases a few hours after nightfall and move towards plankton-rich surface waters attracted by the dim light of the moon. Hatching at night reduces the chance of predation on their journey to the surface.

Both types of larvae develop in the surface waters of the ocean. Marine fish are unique in having a *bipartite life cycle*—larvae and adults live considerably different lives. The larval cycle is spent in the open ocean, whereas a successful adulthood depends on being near the protection of the seafloor.

Coral reefs are highly populated and competitive areas

Classic pelagic spawning in the Barred Hamlet (*Hypoplectrus puella*), casting their tiny, bouyant eggs to the open seas.

with a high concentration of potential predators ready to swallow small larvae. The eggs and larvae, therefore, are cast away into the open ocean where the odds are better that they will develop enough to avoid predation until they are big enough to settle onto a protective reef. The open ocean is the safest haven for undeveloped larvae. Food organisms abound and predators are fewer. The larvae feed on other planktonic organisms until they metamorphose into juvenile fish and *recruit* or settle back down to bottom, preferably a complex *benthic* structure such as the coral reef.

How reef fish recruitment works is the subject of much debate. To simply pass one's offspring into the colossal ocean with no guarantee that any would ever return seems an unlikely evolutionary scenario for survival of a species. It seems an insurmountable task for a fish no larger than a pencil eraser to find its way to a suitable environment. Remarkably, these tiny larval fish somehow find their way back from the open ocean to coral reefs, lagoons, mangrove swamps and the sand flats they inhabit as juveniles and adults.

A long-standing theory as to how this occurs is known as *passive recruitment*. If the currents and gyres where the eggs were shed happen to return the newly transformed fish to a suitable reef structure at precisely the same time the fish are ready to settle, it would recruit to that reef.

This model has since been refined, as it is now clear that juveniles are using navigational cues to actively swim to reef structures. The exact cues that post-metamorphosis larvae use to find structures remains unclear, but many theories abound.

Researcher Dr. Stephen D. Simpson of the University of Edinburgh has coined an explanation he calls "the song of the pied piper" which suggests that a reef structure has a distinct underwater sound signature. The local population of snapping shrimp and vocal fish produce sounds that can be heard from long distances. Any snorkeler or diver that has descended on a coral reef has surely heard these sounds which make reefs so noisy.

Reef sound is known to attract a number of settlement stage reef fishes and is regarded as a major cue in recruitment.

Chemical cues of reefs and surrounding areas are likely important as well. Water from different reefs and different habitats such as lagoons and mangroves produces differences in amino acid and other chemical signatures that may attract larvae. In any case, post-metamorphosis fish are no longer viewed as passive particles at the mercy of the currents.

Most larvae do not make it to adulthood. Many will be eaten while in the plankton, while masses of others will be swept into waters where survival is impossible. For instance, in New Jersey, New York and even further north in New England, there is an annual arrival of juvenile reef fishes from the Caribbean, carried by the Gulf Stream into waters that will turn frigid and deadly as fall and winter weather arrives.

By the time a pelagic stage fish is ready to settle from

LIVE-BEARING
Bythitidae - Livebearing Brotulas

DEMERSAL:
POUCH BROODERS
Solenostomidae - Ghost Pipefishes
Syngnathidae - Seahorses &
Pipefishes

DEMERSAL:
MOUTHBROODERS
Apogonidae - Cardinalfishes
Opistognathidae - Jawfishes
Plesiopidae - Longfins*
Trichonotidae - Sand Divers

DEMERSAL:
BROOD TENDERS
Balistidae - Triggerfishes
Blenniidae - Blennies
Chaenopsidae - Tube & Pike
    Blennies
Gobiesocidae - Clingfishes
Gobiidae - Gobies
Grammatidae - Grammas
Labrisomidae - Weed Blennies
Microdesmidae - Dartfishes &
Wormfishes
Monacanthidae - Filefishes
Pomacentridae - Damsels & Clown
    fishes
Pseudochromidae - Dottybacks
Tetraodontidae - Puffers & Tobies
Tripterygiidae - Triplefins

DEMERSAL:
LACK PELAGIC PHASE
Batrachoididae - Toadfishes
Pholidichthyidae - Convict Blenny
Plotosidae - Eel Catfishes

A pair of Green Mandarin Dragonets in a classic pelagic spawning ascent. Released eggs (arrow) will rise and float away in the ocean currents.

EGGS IN GELATINOUS MASS
PELAGIC LARVAE
Antennariidae - Frogfishes
Caracanthidae - Coral Crouchers**
Ogcocephalidae - Walking Batfishes
Scorpaenidae - Scorpionfishes &
    Lionfishes*

PELAGIC EGGS & LARVAE
Acanthuridae - Surgeonfishes
Anomalopidae - Flashlight Fishes
Aulostomidae - Trumpetfishes
Bothidae - Lefteye Flounders
Callionymidae - Dragonets
Carangidae - Jacks
Centriscidae - Shrimpfishes

Cirrhitidae - Hawkfishes
Chaetodontidae - Butterflyfishes
Cheilodactylidae - Morwongs
Dactylopteridae - Helmut Gurnards
Diodontidae - Porcupinefishes
Echeneidae - Remoras
Ephippidae - Spadefishes &
    Batfishes
Haemulidae - Grunts
Heterocongridae - Conger Eels &
    Garden Eels
Holocentridae - Squirrelfishes &
    Soldierfishes
Labridae - Wrasses
Lutjanidae - Snappers & Fusiliers
Malacanthidae - Tilefishes
Monocentridae - Pineapple Fishes
Monodacytlidae - Monos
Mullidae - Goatfishes
Muraenidae - Moray Eels
Nemipteridae - Spinecheeks
Ophichthidae - Snake Eels
Ostraciidae - Trunkfishes
Pegasidae - Sea Moths
Pempheridae - Sweepers
Pinguipedidiae - Sand Perches
Pomacanthidae - Angelfishes
Platycephalidae - Flatheads
Priacanthidae - Bigeyes
Sciaenidae - Drums & Croakers
Serranidae - Dwarf Seabasses,
Hamlets, Anthias, Groupers,
    Soapfishes, Reef Basslets
Scaridae - Parrotfishes
Siganidae - Rabbitfishes
Soleidae - Soles
Synodontidae - Lizardfishes
Tetrarogidae - Waspfishes
Zanclidae - Moorish Idol

*Not all genera and species conform.   ** Reproductive mode not certain.*

the plankton, it has developed remarkable physical attributes that can power it against local currents to the direction it perceives as offering a safe haven. This process remains largely unstudied and is a controversial issue among fisheries biologists. Whatever the eventual findings may be, the odyssey of larval reef fishes into the deep blue sea and back to shore is certain to remain one of nature's wonderments.

NATURAL SPAWNING SYSTEMS

When attempting to breed a particular species of marine fish in captivity it is important to take every aspect of the fish's life history into consideration. In addition to knowing the mode of egg release, it is essential to know the number of fish required for successful spawning.

A pair of Blackbarred Convict Gobies (*Priolepis nocturna*) spawning in a halved flower-pot. Many gobies form long-term pair bonds and spawn repeatedly together.

To breed Hippo Tangs (*Paracanthus hepatus*) requires two things not commonly available to a home-based aquarist: a very large aquarium and a school of tangs. If two Hippo Tangs are placed in the same aquarium, the odds are against spawning. Some fish are haremic in nature. One or more males control a group of females which they defend and mate with. In some species, if conditions facilitating harem formation are not favorable, the male will settle for a relationship with one female that may be long-term or last only for the duration of spawning.

Many spawning systems that have evolved in marine fish families are difficult to replicate in the cramped quarters of the average aquarium. It is important to understand these natural spawning systems and manipulate certain aspects of the environment so that spawning is possible with the number of broodstock available.

MONOGAMY & LONG-TERM BONDING

Few marine fish establish truly monogamous pairs that remain together for life. The butterflyfishes (Chaetodontidae) are the best example of monogamy. Target Gobies (*Signigobius biocellatus*), the various Sleeper Gobies (*Valenciennea* spp.), Dragon Gobies (*Amblygobius* spp.), Firefishes (*Nemateleotris* spp.), and some large angelfishes (Pomacanthidae) may also establish monogamous pairs. The term monogamy is used when one male and one female remain together for the duration of many spawnings.

Long-term pair bonding is the term applied to most marine fishes that form male-female pairs, as they may change partners several times throughout their lifetimes.

Butterflyfishes form pairs at an early age and typically remain together for life. Pairs can be observed traveling over the reef in search of food and rarely venture far from one another's side. When one member strays too far out of range, the other darts around in a frantic search for its lost mate. If one is lost or a victim to predation, only then will the other seek a new mate.

Target Gobies have a truly affectionate pair bond and will establish a small territory around a cave and rarely stray more than a few body lengths from each other. If a member of the pair becomes lost, killed, or collected, it is not uncommon for the survivor to refuse food and slowly waste away.

Banggai Cardinalfish (*Pterapogon kauderni*) as well as other cardinalfishes establish individual pair bonds within an existing school. Being nocturnal, the school congregates during the day around the sheltered spines of sea urchins with each male-female pair resting quite close to the other. When a school is observed for prolonged periods, these pairs are easily seen within the whole of the school. When night falls, the fish spread out in search of food and reestablish pairs when dawn approaches. Cardinalfishes are capable of producing sound and it is theorized that vocalization is important in communication and pair recognition.

Fish that spawn in isolated pairs will prove the easiest to spawn in captivity. Those that form monogamous or long-term pair bonds may prove difficult to pair, although spawning will become cyclic once initiated.

HAREM SPAWNERS

Harem spawning is a dominant spawning system in marine fishes. A dominant male of the species controls a group of females. The number of females within the male's harem is directly related to his body size and energy expended to control, protect, and spawn with the harem.

These harems may be rather obvious as in some species of wrasses. A male Bluehead Wrasse (*Thalassoma bifasciatum*) for example, is often three times larger than the females in his harem. The vigilant male keeps a close watch over the harem, which often takes the form of a large writhing ball, maintained that way by the male.

In other species, the members of the harem may be spread out over a wide range across the reef. With the onset of the spawning season, the male makes trips around the reef and spawns with receptive females. Species that maintain this sort of haremic lifestyle usually stake out some sort of territory. Males maintain a large peripheral territory, protecting the females from competing males. Within the male's territory, females also stake out smaller domains, which are guarded from neighboring females. The degree of territoriality extends primarily to conspecifics, and other fish are allowed entrance, provided they are not competing for food. Some species maintain harems throughout their lives, while others form haremically polygamous relationships only for the act of spawning.

Controlling a harem presents a great risk for males. During the spawning season, males are busy defending females and the spawning site from invading fish and other males while also trying to court and spawn with receptive females in his harem. These species are generally pelagic spawners that rise high into the water column to shed eggs and sperm. Much confusion and chaos abounds at this point, and the male is vulnerable to attack by predators. To cope with the dangers associated with the male's role, females within the harem form a hierarchy. If something happens to the male, the dominant female begins to transform into a male. This dominant female will begin controlling the group before a noticeable difference in size or color appears.

BREEDING ASSEMBLAGES

Large pelagic marine species such as surgeonfish (Acanthuridae) are often more immune to predation and make use of their size and stature to migrate to optimal spawning grounds. Preferred spawning areas for most breeding assemblages are in the forereef area which is exposed to the high-energy incoming waves. Here, fish that may have migrated from long distances congregate for the sole act of spawning. The strong currents on the forereef transport eggs to offshore locations quickly so they are not exposed to egg-eating predators on the reef. Both sexes migrate to these locations and mating generally occurs in temporary spawning pairs. Groupers (Serranidae) and snappers (Lutjanidae) are also well known for performing large spawning migrations. Such large aggregations are prone to overfishing. Fisheries authorities in some countries are moving to protect their known spawning locations.

PROMISCUITY

It seems that many small, site-attached fish such as damsels and dottybacks, practice a promiscuous spawning style. Males actively court and spawn with any female that may be available. In many instances, the male may brood several clutches of eggs deposited by different females in the same locality. These fish do not typically demonstrate any cyclic pattern of mate choice. They may spawn with many partners during a given spawning season and may or may not spawn with similar mates again. Males are indiscriminate in their choice of mates, while females tend to be slightly choosier in their decisions, trying to be persuaded by a member of the species demonstrating desirable traits to be carried on. Promiscuity seems predominant in small fish with a high risk of predation. Mate choice is often simplified in captivity and since no pair bonds are established, two heterosexual fish in reproductive condition should spawn. These fish often tolerate members of their own species only for the sole act of spawning and otherwise maintain rigid territorial boundaries outside the reproductive season.

GONOCHORISTS

Some marine fish are of a predetermined sex. These fish are known as gonochorist. As soon as the fish hatches from its egg case, it contains either male or female genetic material. These fish are not capable of sex reversal and often pose a problem to captive-breeding efforts. Pairs are formed through trial and error since few marine fish species exhibit any signs of *sexual dimorphism* or external differences between the sexes.

Fish that are genetically sexed to be male or female usually form long-term pair bonds at an early age and remain together for a long time. Since the fish remain in heterosexual pairs, there is no need for the fish to change sex. Butterflyfish have been observed pairing at lengths of only $1\frac{1}{2}$ inches. Goldenhead Sleeper Gobies similarly pair up at early ages. When attempting to spawn these fishes, differences in color, size, or other physical features may be the only clues to matching a pair. Triggerfishes, lionfishes, filefishes, puffers, boxfishes and butterflies are a few examples of fish with genetically fixed sexes. Gonochorism may help explain why so few have been spawned in aquariums.

HERMAPHRODITISM

Hermaphroditism in its purest form is simple enough to understand: one organism has both male and female reproductive organs.

In the natural world, however, it is not always so simple, often involving complex and intricate life history strategies that become increasingly difficult to fathom. The many forms and functions of sex change in marine aquarium fishes can be especially complex.

Hermaphroditism is widespread throughout the animal kingdom. Fishes, in fact, provide the most widely recognized examples of sex-changing organisms. More than 18 families of *teleost* or bony, ray-finned fishes are known hermaphrodites.

For the marine fish breeder, hermaphrodites are best broken down into two main categories, simultaneous hermaphrodites and the more common sequential hermaphrodites. Simultaneous hermaphroditism is straightforward. One individual of a given species possesses both male and female reproductive tissue within the gonads and can act

Sex change is one of the key survival tools for many species of marine fish, including these Maroon Clowns (*Premnas biaculeatus*), which are protandrous hermaphrodites. The smaller, submissive male can transform itself if the female dies or is lost.

as either sex during a single spawning event. Physical adaptations usually prevent self-fertilization from occurring. Typically, simultaneous hermaphrodites undergo lengthy and elaborate courtship rituals apparently to identify the sexual function of each individual before the actual spawning event. Some species will spawn, and then spawn again a short time later with the same partner posing as the opposite sex. Simultaneous hermaphrodites are a minority among marine aquarium fishes and are best represented by hamlets and smaller members of the Serranidae family such as the Belted Sandfish (*Serranus subligarius*).

Sequential hermaphroditism involves an individual acting as one sex during the early portion of its life and eventually, if conditions are appropriate, changing sex. During sex change, the sex cells of prior sexual function degenerate while those of future sexual function proliferate. Protogynous hermaphrodites are sequential hermaphrodites that undergo sex change in the female to male direction.

Protandrous hermaphrodites are sequential hermaphrodites too but sex change occurs in the male to female direction. The various classes of hermaphrodites and non-hermpahrodites are as follows:

Protandrous Hermaphrodites

Protandrous hermaphrodites begin their lives as males and eventually, if social conditions permit, reverse sex into functional females. Clownfish are the best examples of protandrous hermaphrodites, although some dottybacks (*Ogilbyina* and *Cypho* spp.) exhibit this form of sex change. Most species that practice this sort of sex reversal live in some sort of harem, or social hierarchy. The most dominant fish in the group develops into a mature and dominating female. The next individual in the pecking order becomes the functional male. Any other fish living in the group are either submissive males, or in the case of clownfish, asexual individuals with no sex at all. These asexual members of the hierarchy await their chance to become either male or female based on the social structure of the group. If the dominant female dies, the functional male will transform into the dominant female. Among the asexual or submissive fish a pecking order is established, the most dominant of these becomes the functional male.

It is the social status of the fish that determines its sex. In captivity, two juvenile fish in the same aquarium will duke it out to determine which will dominate and mature with female sexual functions. Since resources are limited, the submissive member will ultimately become a male. It is important to place juvenile fish in the same aquarium, as it is not clear whether fish can revert back to their original sex once a sex reversal has taken place. With clownfish, a large individual is obtained and assumed female. A small juvenile placed in the aquarium will become the functional male based on social status and continued dominance displays from a residing female.

Perhaps the most advantageous characteristic of some coral reef fishes is their ability to change sex under altering social conditions.

African Pygmy Angelfish pair (*Centropyge acanthops*): as practicing protogynous hermaphrodites, any two juvenile angelfishes should form a male-female pair.

Protogynous Hermaphrodites

Protogynous hermaphrodites are the exact opposite of protandrous hermaphrodites. They begin their lives as females and mature into functional males. In at least some species, all males originate from females that have reversed sex. No individual begins life as a male; they must first take on the role of a female. Once transformed and fully developed, they are called *terminal males*.

Fish that are born males are usually smaller and less colorful than terminal males. Protogyny is the most common form of sex reversal among representative marine fish. Most wrasses, groupers, dottybacks, anthias, some gobies and angelfishes practice protogyny. Pairing these fish is similar to that of protandrous hermaphrodites: place two or more younger specimens together (or one large and one small fish) and the resulting fish will end up being of different sex and status within the social hierarchy.

Bi-Directional Sex Change

It was once assumed that sequential hermaphrodites had the potential to change sex only once during their lifetime. That is, if an individual began life as a female it could later in life change to a male. It was assumed that protogynous hermaphrodites could not revert to the original female sexual function.

This theory of sequential hermaphroditism has since been proven wrong. The most widely recognized examples are gobies of the generas *Gobiodon* and *Paragobiodon* as well as hawkfishes (Cirrhitidae) and most recently, dottybacks

(Pseudochromidae). Coral-dwelling gobies are primarily protogynous hermaphrodites. They begin their lives as females and change sex to become males later in life if social conditions are appropriate for such change to occur. If, however, the female dies or disappears, the male is capable of reverting sex to prior female sexual function (Munday et al. 1998).

This finding is extremely important in the realm of hermaphroditism, especially in marine fishes. In the case of the coral-dwelling gobies, this bi-directional sex change is an apparent adaptation of survival. These fish occupy a very specialized niche within the branches of *Acropora* and *Pocillopora* corals. They almost never leave the protection of the branching corals. With this in mind, the fish have only two options to survive and reproduce: travel in search of a mate or wait until a recruit of the same species settles in or near the coral head. This weighted decision is full of risks and costs. If the risk of leaving the protection of the coral in search of a new mate is greater than that involved with lost reproductive opportunities waiting for a mate, the fish will remain in male reproductive function. When a recruit settles in the coral head, protogyny dictates that the new fish will begin its life as a functional female, thus a pair is formed. If, however, the cost of remaining in the coral head, waiting for a mate, is too great a cost in terms of reproductive success, the male can leave in search of a new mate. If a solitary female is found a successful pair is formed. If another solitary male is found the newcomer will become the submissive fish in the coral head and revert to its original female sexual function.

Bi-directional sex change is not easily observed in these species. It is assumed that it is an evolutionary adaptation to keep reproductive success high to aid in species survival. Protogyny is commonplace in these fishes, but it is not known to what extent bi-directional sex allocation is used.

There are many rules governing sex change in marine fishes. Many factors contribute to controlling sex change, although the main driving force seems to be social hierarchy. When two hermaphroditic fish of the same sexual function are placed in confinement or separated from conspecifics, a hierarchy is formed. In social hierarchies containing several to many individuals of a given species, sex change sometimes occurs in all but the dominant fish, depending on social pressure.

Finally, many marine fish species have a social threshold binding sex reversal. In groups such as *Anthias*, sex change will only occur when the proper ratio of males and females is present. Other species routinely undergo sex change when maintained in isolation, such that isolated protandrous species will become female and protogynous species will become male.

Bi-directional Juveniles

In at least some species of aquarium fishes, it appears that bi-directional juvenile gonads allow sex changes that transform a young fish directly into male or female without first acting as the opposite (submissive) sex. It was once thought that the Royal Gramma (*Gramma loreto*) was a protogynous hermaphrodite. This assumption was based largely on extreme size differences between the sexes. After intensive examination of gonadal cells, it was deemed that *G. loreto* possesses bi-directional gonads allowing it to coordinate its sex based on the surrounding social structure it has settled into (Asoh and Shapiro 1997).

Many species of reef fishes are known to exhibit bi-directional gonads. Butterflyfishes and some gobies, for example, maintain long-term pair bonds and are not known to change sex. The Yellowhead Sleeper Goby (*Valencienna strigatus*) is virtually always found in pairs in the wild. Even newly recruited juveniles of a few centimeters in length are found in pairs. It is obvious that the fish are not sexually mature at this size, and it is doubtful that the pairs are genetically fixed male and female at this stage. The chances of males and females coming into contact at such a young age, with hardly any isolated individuals being observed, suggests a gonad that is virtually asexual and ready to go either way. This allows any two juvenile fish to pair off and then determine sexual gender. The same is true for many species of butterflyfish. This trait offers unique advantages under controlled culture conditions. If gonochorist species exhibiting bi-directional juvenile gonads are paired before sexual maturity, a heterosexual reproductive pair is usually obtained. (In a sense, science is confirming the long-held advice of freshwater breeders: to be sure of getting a mated pair, buy five or six juveniles of the same species and raise them together.)

ANATOMY BASICS

Both the testes of males and ovaries of females are encased in a tissue membrane. Several epithelial layers all with different functions exist in this membrane. The outermost membrane has the simple duty of holding form to the gonad and identifying it as such. The innermost layer of the gonad contains a labyrinth of thin membranes extending toward the center. This is the origin of sex cells. Primordial cells form in the epithelial layer of the gonad and remain there until hormonal signals cause them to mature into functional sex cells.

These primordial cells are deemed *spermatogonia* in males and *oogonia* in females. Spermatogonia give rise to dividing cells, eventually forming tailed sperm. Oogonia develop into *oocytes*, which are typically given a number designation as to their stage of development. Hydrated eggs are the last stage of this process of *oogenesis* or egg formation.

During sex change in sequential hermaphrodites, the sexual tissue of prior sexual function degenerates. Degeneration of the actual sex cells begins first, followed shortly by a regrouping of sexual tissue to form the necessary tubules and delivery ducts needed for the transportation of future sex cells. Proliferation of sex tissue of future sexual function occurs simultaneously as the other tissue is broken down. Timelines to complete sexual function vary dramatically.

Masked Gobies (*Coryphopterus personatus*) reportedly complete protogynous sex change in roughly nine days (Cole and Robertson 1988) yielding a functional male. Other species require up to 200 days.

In many species, a remnant band of tissue representing prior sexual function exists at the perimeter of the gonad. Some species and specimens within a species, however, lack any discernable signs of prior sexual function, limiting assumptions on the occurrence of sex change in that species. Remnant tissue of prior sexual function is one explanation for the occurrence of bi-directional sex change in a species. It is possible that under hormonal signals this tissue can proliferate accompanied by the degeneration of present tissue and assume the original sexual function.

The most plausible explanation for the occurrence of bi-directional sex change rests in the epithelial layer of the gonad. When the two primordial cell types of males and females are placed side by side they seem indistinguishable. Many scientists believe that these cells are in fact the same. Perhaps the term "*gonia*" is better suited to both cell types. It is believed that, as primordial cells, they have the ability to adopt either sexual function based on hormones received from the blood.

If this does in fact prove true, bi-directional sex change is more easily understood. Hormones in the blood are released in the presence of environmental and social stimuli. Primordial gonia then undergo the changes needed to assume the proper sexual function. The genetic makeup of a species will be the ultimate limiting factor controlling the ability of the species to undergo bi-directional sex change.

The discovery of bi-directional sex allocation opens the door to a world of still unanswered questions. If several species of marine fishes have demonstrated the potential to change sex in both directions, what is to say that many other families are not capable of such acts? It should be noted that several species within the Amphiprioninae or clownfish family have shown no inclination toward bi-directional sex change. In these species protandry seems to be concrete and the female function terminal.

Captive-bred Ocellaris Clownfish (*Amphiprion ocellaris*): protandrous hermaphrodites, meaning that any young two fish should become a male-female pair when housed in isolation.

A netful of prospective broodstock: Orchid Dottybacks ready for market. Captive-bred stock, whenever available, offer an ideal start for beginning marine breeders.

CHAPTER 3

BROODSTOCK BASICS

Choosing & Housing Your Breeders

The term broodstock is used to define the fish used for spawning. These are sexually mature, usually paired, fish whose eggs and larvae are collected and reared. The term broodfish, brooders and breeders are used synonymously to define such parental stock. Establishing a breeding pair or group in your care is the first step toward success in home propagation of marine fishes, and is both challenging and fascinating. With luck, this broodstock will reward you with many spawns and many hundreds or thousands of viable offspring.

Ideal traits in broodstock vary from species to species and are difficult to summarize. Individuals should be the best representatives of the species you can find and possess every characteristic that makes the species desirable including attractive coloration, size and the right personality. The most important aspect of broodstock selection is health, starting with the fishes' degree of acclimation to aquarium life.

If spawning is to be successful in captivity, fish must feel completely comfortable in their surroundings, both inside and outside the tank. If the fish display a fear of humans that cannot be overcome, they are likely to fail as broodstock. Many wild fish will exhibit extreme stress during the acclimation period, and the slightest disturbance outside the aquarium will send them streaking for cover. Eventually, most captive fish acclimate to these disturbances and regain security in their environment.

A good example of this is the freshwater discus (*Symphysodon* spp.). When first imported, wild discuses are extremely shy and reluctant to spawn . Overcoming their fear of humans is crucial to successful spawning. Over time and through hand-feeding, these broodstock eventually become acclimated to captivity and will spawn. This holds true for marine fish as well. Adjusting wild fish to handfeeding can become an exhausting task, but often proves invaluable for difficult species. Wild clownfish, such as Saddlebacks (*Amphiprion polymnus*) and the Maldive or Blackfin Clownfish (*A. nigripes*) are particularly finicky and stress easily in captivity. Slowly learning to eat from their keepers hands will eventually bring timid species begging at the glass for food and spawning prolifically.

Healthy fishes exhibit vibrant color, a lusty appetite and a vigorous attitude. A fish that comes to the glass upon approach is a sure bet and should be chosen over an individual of the same species cowering in the corner of the aquarium. The eyes of the fish should be clear and the body and belly smooth and well rounded. Know the characteristics to look for in the species intended as broodstock. Good underwater photographs of wild specimens are especially useful. Look for robust, vibrant individuals that show interest in human approach.

The size of initial broodstock fish should be based on the sex-reversal capabilities of that species (*see pages 166-276*) and the number of individuals available. It is generally best to buy juvenile fishes and raise them to maturity. In this way the fish will receive more attention than if they were allowed to mature elsewhere. They are intended to become valuable breeding stock and ought to be treated as such. Good water quality and proper feedings of high quality foods will ensure that they mature with vigor. Warmer tank temperatures of about 80°F and frequent feedings of high-quality foods will speed the process.

If the fish you are attempting to breed are capable of sex reversal, it is best to obtain the smallest individuals possible. It may take longer to establish spawning pairs, but the time spent is well worth the end result. If the fish are too old and have reached a terminal sex, chances are against pair formation if the sex-changing capabilities are limited. If broodstock availability (or your budget) is limited for the species you have targeted, try to obtain one large individual and one as small as possible. This will increase your chances of ending up with a male-female pair. If they have not already matured sexually, the release of pheromones and direct aggression by a large, dominant fish will generally stimulate a smaller, submissive individual to change sex (or in some species to maintain sexual function while the dominant individual changes sex). Certain species exhibit classic juvenile coloration that eventually shifts to adult colors upon sexual maturation. This can be a useful guide when identifying broodstock.

The ability of marine fishes to change sex can be both mystifying and problematic at times. For example, even well-established pairs can be destroyed if separated for any length of time. At one point I separated pairs of Neon Dottybacks (*Pseudochromis aldabraensis*) to stop them from spawning. After only 14 days of separation, females initiated sex change into males and chaos resulted when the pairs were reunited.

SUREFIRE STARTER STOCK

Starting with captive-bred fish may be the easiest route to breeding for newcomers . A well-established reality in captive propagation is that tank-raised stock are more disease-resistant, better adapted to aquarium feeding, much less fearful of humans and, most importantly, have not been subjected to the same shipping and handling stresses as their wild counterparts.

Captive bred offspring are, in fact, much easier to induce to spawn. They were born and raised in the ever-changing environment of captivity and are thus not affected by normal captive conditions. However, the decision to buy captive-bred broodstock is a matter of debate. Questions have arisen as to the genetic degradation of successive generations of captive-bred fishes. Many forms of terrestrial and aquatic organisms have been domesticated and inbred for centuries, and intentional inbreeding can bring out certain desirable traits in a species or breed. If two captive-raised fish are obtained from the same hatchery and allowed to spawn there is little chance of any genetic degradation occurring within limited generations.

Orangepeel Dottybacks (*Pseudochromis tonozukai*) going through their pair-formation rituals. In this sexually dichromatic species, the male is a distinct orange. Bonding occurs when the female accepts the male's advances and enters his PVC cave.

The ideal approach is to obtain captive-bred offspring from different hatcheries or match captive-raised individuals with wild representatives. This ensures a mix in the gene pool and still holds the advantage of easy spawning. Somewhere down the road it will be necessary to bring in a few wild fish to mix up the gene pool of captive-bred lineages, but this is hardly an immediate concern for beginning breeders.

It may help to know that freshwater fishes were once difficult to breed. When first imported, discus and angelfish were extremely difficult to spawn. Today, "domesticated" freshwater angels and discus present few problems to prospective hobbyists. Once marine fishes are raised through many generations, a similar trend should be observed.

PAIR FORMATION

Given the widespread occurrence of hermaphroditism in marine fish families, pair formation in captivity would seem a sure thing. In practice, however, pair formation is often an extremely difficult and frustrating process. Many approaches can be taken to encourage pair formation, each

Female Flame Dottyback (*Cypho purpurascens*) emerges from a suspended basket in the broodstock tank. She has been allowed to acclimate in a protected space for a number of days before a small exit hole was cut, allowing her access to the male.

with its own benefits and disadvantages. The different techniques available to a home breeder are often limited by budget constraints or by the number of specimens available to be paired.

Most marine aquarium fish are ideally paired from an early age. By isolating two individuals in an aquarium as juveniles or subadults, a heterosexual pair is almost guaranteed. Young fish that are not yet sexually mature work best for this task. Under nature's rules of social dominance, if you have only two fish of one species, one will be dominant and one submissive.

In protogynous hermaphrodites (the majority of pseudochromids, some gobies and dwarf angels) the larger more aggressive individual will assume the sexual function of the male while the submissive individual will become a functional female.

Protandrous species (members of the *Ogilbyina* genus and the clownfishes) will yield a larger, dominant female and a functional, submissive male.

While this method is not foolproof, given the territorial and often aggressive nature of reef fishes, it does offer the best chance of success. Juvenile fishes are no more placid than adults and in some cases aggression may be fierce in juveniles given their hierarchal battle for dominance (the emerging dominant fish may harass the smaller fish until it must be rescued or it succumbs). To help buffer this aggression during pair formation, it always helps to add a number of PVC fittings, flowerpots or similar structures as caves and retreats in the aquarium. Submissive fish usually cower near the surface as the dominant fish often stakes out the entire aquarium floor as its domain. Mounting PVC structures that penetrate the surface or hang near the surface, can give the submissive fish a place to feel more secure.

PVC caves and other devices also provide visual barriers. In bare tanks the sexes have no choice but to be in constant visual presence of one another. This can cause extreme aggression by the dominant fish. If not juveniles or subadults, fish of noticeable size difference should be chosen as candidates. The size will dictate the hierarchy and limit the battle for dominance. Hiding places are still essential.

The downfall to this method of pairing is the time required for the fish to reach sexual maturity and begin spawning. This can range from a few weeks to many months depending on the age of the fish. If you have the time and future broodstock specimens are available at a small size, starting with young fish is the best route.

Unfortunately, finding small or young fish of a given species is sometimes difficult if not impossible. Often, the only species readily available in small sizes are those already being reared in captivity. If very small or young fish can't be had, the size difference between the potential mates you acquire becomes an extremely important factor in pair formation.

This is often a method of trial and error. Placing a larger specimen with a smaller specimen in an aquarium containing sufficient hiding structures will often yield a sexually active pair. Since the dominant sex generally achieves a larger average body size, its sexual function can be assumed as the terminal sex. If the dominant sexual function has not yet been attained, it should quickly ensue with the addition of a smaller specimen. The sexual function of smaller individuals is difficult to predict. This is where the trial and error comes in. The smallest individual available should be used in such pairing trials (as long as it is not obviously weak or a substandard speciment).

Many species of interest are not commonly available at local aquarium stores. Typically, you might find one specimen of a given species per aquarium store. The length of time the specimen has been isolated from members of its own species will usually determine its sexual function. If the specimen is large and has been isolated for some time, chances are good it has reached its terminal sexual function. If only large specimens are available, it is best to purchase only one fish and await the arrival of a smaller specimen.

Another common method used in pairing marine fish is to introduce several to many individuals of a given species into the same aquarium with plenty of hiding places. In a large aquarium (at least 30 gal. for small species, more for bigger fish) several conspecifics can safely be housed together. It is best to obtain at least four specimens for pairing and spawning to commence quickly and successfully. Such arrangements usually yield more than one functional male in protogynous species. Males will actively defend a territory centered around a spawning site while females generally occupy PVC lengths hung near the surface of the aquarium. This method restricts the interaction and aggression individual females receive from overbearing males and spawning is more frequent as there are typically more females available. Protandrous species can be spawned in similar fashion, but a larger tank is required, as the dominant females will restrict the movement of the male. Males must be offered some retreat from aggressive females so that a spawning site can be maintained.

DIVIDED PAIRING

Pair formation is most readily and safely accomplished in an environment that allows prospective mates to interact visually, but not physically. This method of separation is most often used with adult pseudochromids. Put simply, a broodstock aquarium is separated so prospective mates cannot physically interact.

The most common approach to this method is through the use of breeder baskets. Breeder baskets are commonly used to isolate pregnant livebearers in a freshwater community aquarium. Generally, these baskets are available in two basic forms. The more widely available of the two is a simple plastic frame supporting a mesh bag. Stainless steel flaps are bent over the aquarium glass to hold the basket at the surface. Another type of breeder basket has an acrylic front panel to aid in making visual observations. The remainder of the basket is a course plastic mesh that more readily allows water exchange. Either type will work for its intended purpose. (Other types of acrylic holding boxes may be used, as long as good water circulation can occur.)

The submissive fish is placed in the breeder basket while the dominant fish is granted freedom in the remainder of the tank. In these situations, only one or two lengths of PVC or similar objects should be placed in the aquarium to act as a spawning site. A short length of PVC placed in the breeder basket will help the submissive fish feel more secure. Visual stimuli will result in the two fish interacting often. The dominant fish will rarely leave the breeder basket in which the submissive individual has been placed. Dominant fish often charge the submissive individual and display aggressive postures. Submissive fish placed in the basket act as if the basket were not there by cowering in the corner or fleeing to the opposite side.

This method has two main advantages. First, it allows the two fish to interact without harm to either one. Pair formation in the absence of separation often yields a severely beaten or dead fish. Second, it allows the submissive fish, most often the female, a chance to feed unhindered in an attempt to boost protein intake and thus egg production. The sooner eggs are available within the ovaries the sooner spawning will occur.

Given time, the aggressive displays will subside and the submissive member will no longer flee the attention of the dominant individual. When this occurs some weeks later, the breeder basket can be lowered in the water column slightly or a small hole cut in the side of the basket to allow only the smaller individual access. In this way the smaller submissive member of the pair can leave the safety of the basket to interact with the dominant specimen. If some weeks pass before this is done the ovaries are often

well rounded with eggs and the fish is capable of spawning. This greatly increases the chance of successful spawning. Over the course of a few weeks the submissive fish will also associate the breeder basket with safety. The lowered location in the water column allows the submissive individual to leave the basket to interact with the dominant specimen. Should the dominant fish prove overbearing, the submissive partner will duck back into the basket. Spawning generally occurs within a few weeks.

Breeder baskets may prove too small for the isolation of larger species. Eggcrate panels sold as light diffusers can be used to divide an aquarium containing large dottybacks, such as *Labracinus* or *Ogilbyina* species, and are also useful in pairing clownfish with marked size differences. A hole is easily cut in the eggcrate to allow the smaller individual access to the larger, dominant fish while offering a safe retreat in the event aggression gets out of control. This proves ineffective for most smaller dottybacks and gobies, as both sexes can squeeze through the openings. An alternative is to erect a wall with the plastic grid used by needlepointers. This material is available at most craft stores and is usually sold in 8 x 10-inch sheets. Cable ties are used to fasten this grid to a section of eggcrate cut to size. Attaching this grid to eggcrate will give it rigidity.

The area of the aquarium sectioned off should be comparatively small. A corner of the aquarium is best in most cases. The submissive fish needs a safe retreat while eggs develop in the female, but the goal is to have the two interact by installing a shorter divider or a window cut in the plastic grid. In species exhibiting extreme size dimorphism (difference between the sexes) a hole can be cut in the divider only large enough for the smaller individual to fit. Should the dominant fish's aggression become a threat, the smaller fish can simply retreat behind the safety of the divider.

BI-DIRECTIONAL PAIRING

The recent discovery of bi-directional sex change within marine fishes such as certain dottybacks opens up many possibilities for captive pairing. Species capable of bi-di-

Wild broodstock Spinecheek Gobies (*Oplopomus oplopomus*) collected by the author for a captive-breeding program in the Philippines.

rectional sex change theoretically should be relatively simple to pair, as any two fish regardless of sex or age should form a functional heterosexual pair. The submissive fish rather than the dominant fish is the one that is forced to undergo sex change in species capable of such processes.

Sex change in the reverse direction is physiologically expensive, thus the battle for dominance is often extreme. The need to keep the would-be pair separate but in close, visible proximity must be stressed. Two fish of the same terminal sex will fight extensively. If not separated, death to one is a more common result than sex reversal. The best approach is similar to that mentioned above. The two fish are allowed visual contact for several weeks through a divider. After a while the basket or divider is opened slightly to allow interaction but also an escape path for the submissive fish. Protogynous sex change averages 30 days in most marine fishes. We know that bi-directional sex change takes longer—in most cases on record, roughly double the

time needed for sequential sex change. In one case, for example, an investigation of the duration of time required for bi-directional sex change in two species was reported to be nearly 90 days.

Males from two spawning pairs of both *Pseudochromis cyanotaenia* and *P. aldabraensis* were isolated in 10-gallon aquariums. In their new circumstances, one male of each forced pair assumed a controlling role. After three months the submissive former male of each pair deposited an egg mass in the dominant male's spawning shelter.

PAIRS VS. TRIOS

Pair spawning is the most common route to spawning any fish in captivity, but it is possible and recommended in some species to maintain trios.

Keeping trios in spawning aquariums has many advantages over pair spawning. With pairs, isolated females have no escape from threats initiated by the male. As the sole female and only other living organism in the aquarium, the female is the main target of the male's attention. With trios, the male divides his attention between the two females. This diffuses the pressure on the females, and they are less likely to be beaten and tattered. For harem spawners such as blennies of the genus *Meiacanthus* and *Petroscirtes*, multiple females are recommended.

Egg production is effectively increased when multiple females are maintained in the spawning aquarium. Usually the females will spawn at staggered intervals. In dottybacks, when one female spawns the male becomes aggressive defending the brood of eggs within his cave. In the wild, males probably do not spawn with multiple females while guarding a brood of eggs, that is, multiple clutches of eggs are not deposited together. In captivity, however, males will often spawn with multiple females and tend several clutches of eggs at the same time. Trios can produce more larvae than do isolated pairs. Successful spawning lasts longer and stress and aggression are limited.

Zan Didoha secures a
nest of South Sea Devil
Damsel (*Chrysiptera
taupou*) eggs in a rear-
ing tank at the Florida Institute of Technology,
Melbourne, where the
author does his re-
search.

CHAPTER 4

THE BREEDING ROOM

Housing & Husbandry for Broodstock

Before breeding marine fishes, you must have mastered the basics of keeping a healthy saltwater aquarium. It is beyond the scope of this book to
provide a detailed examination of the many types and methods to establish
and maintain a modern marine aquarium. There are many books available to guide
you (*see Sources, page 286 and Further Reading, page 302*).

With few exceptions, most of the marine aquarium fishes included in these
pages are well-suited to life in the aquarium. Many species that are good candidates for home breeding will readily adapt to aquariums no more than 10 gallons
in capacity. A testament to this fact is the ease with which so many species are
successfully spawned in inexpensive, standard 10-gallon tanks.

The system chosen to spawn and raise marine fishes is a matter of objectives. For
many hobbyists whose sole intent is to spawn and rear a few clownfish, little more
than two or three aquariums and some extra space in the family room is all that is
needed.

A more serious approach would be to dedicate one room to the purpose of
spawning and raising marine fishes. This involves several to many aquariums,
usually connected to a central filtration system. If the latter is chosen, a decision
must be made as to the number of species that will be targeted and the number of
offspring desired. How many pairs of a certain species do you want? An entire fish
room could be dedicated to one species. Several broodstock pairs could be maintained and hundreds of juveniles could result. Alternately, in the same-size fish
room, numerous broodstock pairs of different species could be spawned and raised.

Before any decision is made as to what type of aquariums will be required, you

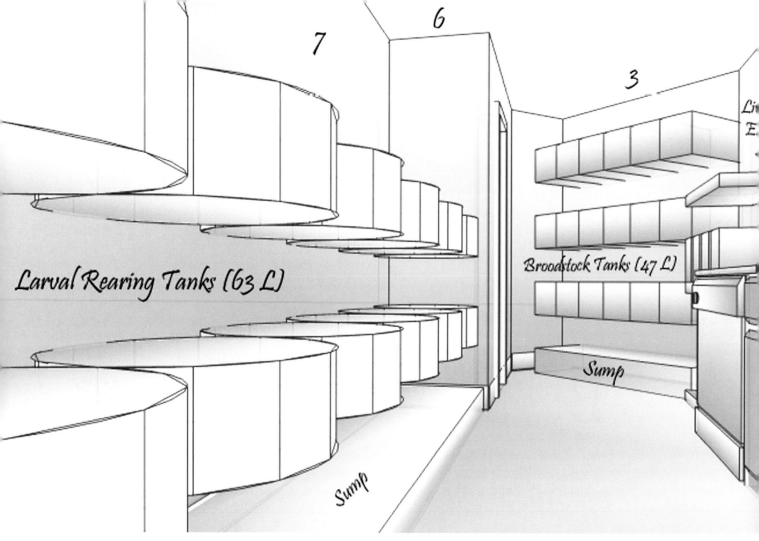

7

6

3

Larval Rearing Tanks (63 L)

Broodstock Tanks (47 L)

Sump

Sump

Li
E

Plan for a small-scale experimental hatchery built by the author at the University of Edinburgh. Key elements in a breeding room are separate areas for broodstock tanks, larval-rearing tubs, and an area for live food culture and enrichment.

must first determine which species you wish to work with and how many pairs you want to obtain. If multiple species are your dream, what are they? Although hobbyists with fish on the brain 24 hours a day can usually find room for one more aquarium, space should be a primary consideration when designing a small-scale system.

Aquariums intended for the sole purpose of spawning marine fish need not be elaborate. Modern day reef aquariums with live corals and intense lighting regimens are not needed, nor are most things typically associated with marine aquariums like coral gravel and live rock. In most cases,

aquariums intended for this purpose are bare glass with little more than a few PVC or other shelters scattered over the bottom.

The main idea to keep in mind when establishing such an aquarium is ease of maintenance. Spawning marine fish require large amounts of food, fed several times per day. The aquarium floor must be easily siphoned and maintained to assure proper water quality. The exact placement and size of the spawning shelters used is species-specific and will vary— as will the size of the spawning aquarium. Detailed descriptions are given in the species description section.

The Spawning Tank

The broodstock tank, in which spawning takes place, should be kept as simple as possible. My preference for spawning tanks came by chance.

I heard by word of mouth that an aquarium store was going out of business and was selling all their aquariums at a very low price. I was looking to set up a central filtration system and figured this would be the most inexpensive means of obtaining aquariums with pre-drilled holes. When I went to pick them up, the only tanks available were 20-gallon "high" aquariums with pre-drilled holes and bulkhead fittings. At first I had no interest in these tanks, but as time went on and I began to spawn and rear more species of fish I found many advantages to these aquariums.

While working with dottybacks (Family Pseudochromidae), for example, pair formation is often a major obstacle. Males, and to a certain extent females, become quite aggressive toward one another before a first spawn has commenced. Usually after the first spawn, aggressive displays subside. The added height of "high"-style aquariums allows the female to flee the male's attention should he become overbearing. Cut lengths of PVC hung at the surface can act as shelter for the female. The dominant male patrols the bottom of the aquarium while the female is safe above the male's territory.

In some species, such as the Splendid Dottyback (*Manonichthys splendens*), males routinely choose spawning shelters that are located off the bottom, sometimes suspended near the surface. In these instances, the female will avoid the male's attention by remaining on the bottom of the tank. Clownfish also seem calmer in higher aquariums. This is especially true for the larger species, such as Clark's (*Amphiprion clarkii*), the Tomato (*A. frenatus*) and Maroon (*Premnas biaculeatus*) Clownfishes.

The size of the spawning aquarium varies with the fish in question, but several aspects remain the same no matter the species. More details will be given in the species descriptions, but some general guidelines can be given here. The social structure and natural history of the species of fish as well as its adult size will determine the size and shape of the aquarium chosen for conditioning and spawning.

Aquarium Size

The spawning aquarium need only be large enough for the fish to feel comfortable. For some species that are site attached, such as clownfishes, living in the confines of sea anemone in the wild, smaller aquariums are perfectly suitable for spawning as the fish are not used to swimming long distances. A pair bond is formed and the two fish rarely leave one another's side.

Other species that maintain larger territories or do not maintain a territory at all and simply wander over the reef will require larger aquariums. Some promiscuous fish that do not form pair bonds will scrap and possibly harm one another when not in spawning condition; they, too, will require a larger spawning aquarium. It is recommended that the fish be offered as large a tank as possible in which to spawn. Clownfishes are often spawned in 55-gallon aquariums and dottybacks are usually spawned in 40-gallon "breeder" aquariums. While this is ideal and has long proven a hobbyist standard, it is not essential.

The average breeding aquarium would be a 20-gallon "high". This is my average, and other active marine breeding enthusiasts have their own views on this subject. Most marine species available that are likely candidates for captive breeding projects will do so in tanks of 10 and 20 gallons in capacity. Accounts of commonly bred species and the minimum-size spawning aquarium requirements are listed on page 174. From my own experience and that of various other acquaintances, 10 to 20 gallon aquariums can be used for virtually all species. Most clownfishes, dottybacks, gobies and blennies will spawn in aquariums of this size, assuming compatible heterosexuals are present and ideal water conditions are maintained.

It is worthwhile mentioning that, as spawning aquariums are typically bare, biological filtration is limited to external media. Smaller aquariums not connected through a central filtration system can suffer from the heavy bio-load of frequent feedings used for conditioning. Larger aquariums will prove necessary if isolated spawning aquariums are maintained. Central filtration systems greatly increase total water volume and buffer potential water quality problems. Hence small aquariums such as 10-gallon tanks can be maintained in series with little worry of water deterioration. If you plan on having non-linked broodstock tanks, 40 to 55-gallon aquariums may be easier to maintain.

Glass aquariums are the best for spawning purposes. Many aquariums designed as living room centerpieces have permanent glass or acrylic top panels that limit access by the aquarist. It is important to be able to reach all corners of the aquarium easily. If the bottom of the aquarium cannot be easily reached without auxiliary tools or taking off your shirt, it is wise to choose a different aquarium. Many times the behaviors or reproductive modes of the breeders will warrant a deep tank. Many species of seahorse require tanks that are at least 36 inches deep in order to successfully mate. Pelagic spawners, too, require sufficient depth. In most cases, however, surface area is more important than depth as it will increase the amount of gas exchange that occurs, improving oxygen saturation, redox potential, and breakdown of nitrogenous waste.

The best approach to breeding most species is with a bare aquarium and a suitable spawning site such as a ceramic tile or plastic tunnel (the appropriate spawning site for each species is given in the species descriptions). Bare aquariums are easier to clean. The wastes that accumulate on the bottom of the aquarium are more easily seen and siphoned out when there is no gravel or other decorations in the way.

I have noted that bare aquariums tend to persuade more fish to spawn. It seems as if there is nothing else to do, so the fish compromise and spawn. I once maintained a pair of Sebae Clownfish (*A. sebae*) in a 75-gallon reef tank hoping they would spawn. The fish frolicked in a Haddon's Carpet Anemone (*Stichodactyla haddoni*) for over a year. The fish showed no signs of reproductive behavior until I moved the pair to a 30-gallon aquarium with nothing more than a flowerpot for shelter and amusement. They spawned within three months. The only structures that should be present

Simple broodstock system assembled by the author with 15-gallon tanks and a 55-gallon sump tank with central filtration.

in the spawning aquarium are those intended as spawning sites or shelter.

Because the aquarium will be bare, the bottom exterior should be painted with a black or blue paint. This will prevent the void bottom space that often makes fish feel insecure. Painting the bottom also prevents light reflecting upwards. The back and sides are usually painted as well to give a further sense of security to the breeders.

The spawning aquarium should be placed at waist level or higher. When pairs are placed closer to the floor with a view of passing human legs, they often seem skittish and reluctant to spawn. When placed higher than waist level, the fish usually greet the keeper at the front glass and beg for food. The spawning aquarium should be kept out of highly trafficked areas. In fact, broodstock tanks are best placed in a fish room where the only person they normally see is their keeper. This goes a long way in making the fish feel more at ease. If a fish room is not available, place the tank in the corner of a quiet room where the fish can still be enjoyed, but will not be bothered by constant commotion outside the tank. Do not take this advice lightly: when I advise people on broodstock setups, I always stress that one of the major reasons spawning attempts fail is the location of the broodstock tank. Give your breeders some privacy and they will be much more likely to reward your efforts.

Polyculture

While it is advised and in most cases essential for broodstock pairs to be isolated to induce spawning, it is possible with some fish to place more than one species of broodstock in the same aquarium. Broodstock aquariums are normally set up as monocultures. This means that one broodstock pair of one species is maintained in an isolated aquarium with no other fish present. This offers the fish privacy and reduces the risk of unpredictable forces affecting the spawning of broodstock.

However, advanced and novice marine fish breeders alike can run out of space for newly acquired broodstock. If only a few isolated spawning aquariums are maintained or there are too few aquariums hooked up to the central filtration system to house all desired broodstock pairs, it is possible to house them in the same aquarium with few complications. In this way the broodstock aquarium is used more efficiently.

In order to successfully house more than one broodstock pair of marine fish in the same aquarium several criteria must be met. First, only one pair of a given species can be housed in the same aquarium to prevent interference with the breeding cycle or even unwanted sex-change events. Species forming monogamous pairs such as clownfishes and

gobies will generally fail to spawn when placed with conspecifics outside the pair. Severe aggression arises and one pair often ends up dead.

Similarly, fishes of the same family should not be placed together. This means only one pair of clowns, gobies or dottybacks should be placed in the same aquarium. Reproduction is hindered when similar fish with similar body shapes, behaviors and/or reproductive modes are placed in the same aquarium. Different species from the same family often have very similar reproductive strategies and, when placed together, battles over spawning sites and territories become a problem.

The key to maintaining a polyculture is to add two species of fish that are as dissimilar as possible. It is best to attempt polyculture only with fish that are known to be hardy and easily spawned. If the fish are shy and retiring, they should be given their own aquarium. It is important to offer adequate shelter and spawning sites for each species. It is also important to pick compatible species that are of different colors. Oftentimes, especially with dottybacks, fish of similar color or habits will be attacked.

Neon gobies and clownfishes are perhaps the most common species used in polyculture. Orchid Dottybacks and clownfishes also work well. Both examples can successfully coexist in tanks as small as 15 to 20 gallons. The clownfishes spawn on ceramic tiles placed vertically against the tank walls, while gobies and dottybacks utilize PVC pipes and other configurations placed on the tank floor. Use caution and watch the fish interact. Individuals of a given species often lash out at unsuspecting fish. While a species as a whole may be considered peaceful, exceptions are possible and not all representatives of the species will follow the rules.

NITROGEN-CYCLE CONTROL

The mechanisms responsible for nitrification in closed systems are perhaps the most important aspects of aquarium keeping. Biological filtration is the most important means of filtration within any body of water—be it an aquarium or roadside puddle. Naturally occurring bacteria will quickly colonize every available surface area within the aquarium creating a thin bio-film. It has been estimated that up to 30% of the total nitrification occurring in closed systems occurs passively on tank walls, within the substrate, on and within filter tubes, etc. The remaining nitrification must occur in a filtration unit specifically designed for such duties.

Fish regularly secrete ammonia (NH_3) and carbon dioxide as part of their metabolic activity. That is, ammonia and carbon dioxide are excreted to the surrounding environment as fish respire and secrete waste in the form of liquid urea and feces. Heterotrophic bacteria present within substrate matter, within filter systems and occurring passively on tank walls also contribute to ammonia loads by breaking down organic debris, detritus and excess food present in the system.

Ammonia is the largest threat to marine fishes and proves the most lethal molecule created through the nitrogen cycle. Ammonia exists as two distinct forms that are at equilibrium in water. The relationship between un-ionized or free ammonia (NH_3) and ionized or toxic ammonia (NH_{4+}) is a function of pH. At higher pH values, such as those found in marine aquariums, a higher ratio of un-ionized (NH_3) ammonia is present. Un-ionized ammonia (NH_3) is much more harmful to fishes as the molecule is able to pass through the epithelial membrane of the gills. The ionized form of ammonia (NH_{4+}) represents a larger molecule that is prevented from entering the body by its size proving less harmful to fish.

Ammonia is the first step in the nitrification process and is the agent responsible for triggering the cycle's activity. In a sterile environment such as a newly established marine aquarium, fish literally swim in their own urine and must tolerate peaks of ammonia since there are no bacteria present within the system to remove or convert this substance to less toxic by-products.

The first few weeks of establishing a marine system are vital. Regular advice warns that only a few, hardy fish should be added to the system and fed lightly to avoid excess levels of ammonia. As ammonia levels rise due to fish metabolism and uneaten food matter, *Nitrosomonas* spp. nitrifying

bacteria begin colonization and convert the ammonia to nitrite (NO_2), the first key part of aerobic nitrification.

As ammonia is converted to nitrite by bacteria, nitrite rises to peak levels, and stimulates a second group of beneficial nitrifying bacteria to colonize. *Nitrobacter* spp. is triggered to colonize by the presence of nitrite, but its growth is hindered by excess levels of ammonia. This inhibition of growth is the reason nitrite levels peak only after the ammonia spike has fallen. In essence, a see-saw pattern between ammonia and nitrite occurs. Nitrite is still a highly toxic chemical that must be broken down by the process of nitrification. The chemical signal of nitrite is similar to that of chloride salts, which are actively pumped through the gill membranes of fish. The fish is tricked in a sense to pump in toxic chemicals. Nitrite is rendered less toxic at high specific gravity values. At a specific gravity of 1.026 fish are tolerant of slightly higher levels of nitrite.

Limiting Nitrate Build-Up

Nitrate (NO_3) is the end product resulting from nitrification. Harmful only at extreme levels (>100 ppm), nitrate is best removed from the system by partial water changes. It is possible to break the bonds of the nitrogen and oxygen, yielding harmless nitrogen gas that will escape the system as a regular part of gas exchange. This process of denitrification relies on anaerobic denitrifying bacteria utilizing the oxygen and releasing the nitrogen into the system.

In reef tanks, de-nitrification systems are ideal as there are generally only low levels of nitrate generated. In marine fish breeding, there is a constant addition of waste products through frequent feedings that are much heavier than normally seen in reef aquarium keeping. Nitrate levels can easily become elevated in such a system and must be dealt with by water changes. Denitrification systems capable of handling such a high bio-load are typically large and difficult to maintain. Live rock and similar porous material is an ideal choice for partial denitrification. Perhaps the most economical method to limit nitrate build up in recirculating seawater systems is through the use of live macroalgae such as

Central filtration systems with oversize biological filtration and skimming capabilities make broodstock maintenance simpler.

Caulerpa spp. or the very hardy *Chaetomorpha linum*. Given adequate light levels these green macroalgaes grow extremely fast, utilizing available nitrogen for growth. As nitrogen products are used during metabolic growth, these products are effectively removed from solution and incorporated into the growing tissue of the plant, which can be harvested periodically (and sold or composted).

It is important to realize the relevance of this cycle in closed systems. Waste products are constantly being secreted in a limited water volume supported only by filtration systems supplied by the aquarist. Mechanical filtration traps suspended particulate matter floating free in the water column. If these particulates are decaying or otherwise fouling and adding to the waste generated by the system, it makes sense to trap them. But, once trapped in filter media, these particulates continue to foul and break down, adding ammonia to the system. In my view, chemical filtration is a greatly over-emphasized mode of filtration. Ion-exchange resins and activated carbon all hold their place in terms of filtration, but must be carefully applied to fit the system. It makes sense to keep the design simple. Rather than relying on man's inventions to rid the aquarium of unwanted waste, I prefer to let nature take its course with naturally occurring organisms such as beneficial bacteria and macroalgae. Chemical filtrants have a limited life and once saturated can no longer rid the aquarium of wastes.

Foam blocks and other re-usable filter pads are ideal media in isolated aquariums and central filtration systems because they support immense colonies of nitrifying bacteria and act as both biological and mechanical filtration. By trapping suspended particulates, the block is a perfect site for bacteria to break down waste products. Once saturated with organic detritus, the foam blocks can be rinsed and re-installed in the system. These types of media should never be thrown out or replaced unless they actually begin to degrade. The filter media found in some filters on the market today encourage regular disposal of biological filtration cartridges. By doing this, the whole filter is effectively thrown out, suddenly depleting the bacterial population of the system. Notice such aquariums becoming cloudy right after the cartridges have been replaced. If using such a filter, pick a design with two or more cartridges and replace them on a rotating basis, never disposing of all media in one cleaning session.

The best means of filtering a broodstock tank or a central system dedicated to breeding marine fish is to use a combination of three or more filtration methods to ensure good water quality even if one malfunctions. Biological filtration and regular partial water changes are the keys to maintaining healthy broodstock.

An ample wet-dry filter filled with bio-media is needed to handle the large quantities of organic wastes generated in broodstock and rearing systems.

FILTRATION

When choosing a filtration model best-suited to the needs of broodstock aquariums, think biological. Since there will be no gravel or other objects in the broodstock aquarium to harbor the beneficial nitrifying bacteria, some sort of filtration unit that offers biological filtration must be provided outside the aquarium. Central water systems are easily fitted with various filtration units. Three types of filtration exist for the marine aquarium: biological, mechanical, and chemical. Biological filtration relies on colonies of nitrifying bacteria to utilize oxygen and break down waste products transforming them into relatively harmless byproducts (nitrates), which are then removed by regular partial water changes. This is the most natural method of filtration and in many instances the only method I utilize. Mechanical filtration is a simple method that relies on the removal of suspended particulate matter from the water column. Usually mechanical and biological filtration go hand-in-hand, as most materials used to harbor colonies of nitrifying bacteria will remove suspended particulate matter. Chemical filtration is just that. Chemicals are added to the water to remove or trap, usually by binding or adhering, waste products. The most common form of chemical filtration relies on charged ions attracting and binding waste products as in activated carbon or "charcoal."

With the vast array of filter gadgets on the market there is no shortage of choices and plenty of confusion about what is really necessary. Foam fractioners (skimmers), ozone reactors, ultraviolet sterilizers, wet-dry filters, and fluidized bed filters are only a handful of commonly available filtration units available to marine aquarists. While these can be very useful, they are often expensive. When a small-scale marine fish hatchery is put together, money is one thing that seems to flow like water from a burst pipe. It is best to conserve this precious commodity wherever realistically possible. Filtration in a central water system occurs in one common area, the sump. The sump is the common pool into which the water from all aquariums flows. Water drains by gravity into the sump and is pumped back to the aquariums from this point. The sump is where the filters and heaters will be placed.

Wet-Dry Filters

Also known as trickle filters, wet-dry filters have long been a popular form of biological filtration for marine aquariums. The concept and construction of these filters is relatively simple. They have many advantages for filtering broodstock aquariums, especially their ability to fully oxygenate water that enters the reaction chamber. The water is pumped to the top of the wet-dry filter and slowly trickles down through the filter media, typically plastic bio-balls that offer large amounts of surface area, and eventually returns to the sump where it is pumped back to the aquariums. The term "dry" is applied to this filter due to the fact that the medium is not submerged in water. Water is merely allowed to cascade over and through it. In this fashion the nitrifying bacteria that have established colonies on the surface of the media are living under a very thin layer of water that spreads out over a large surface area and increases the rate of oxygen saturation and gas exchange. The colonies of nitrifying bacteria are aerobic, utilizing oxygen to convert or oxidize waste products. This results in a very fast and efficient means of biological filtration.

Filter media is the most important area of consideration with these filters. Virtually every manufacturer of aquarium hard goods has come out with a new filter media that claims to be superior—balls, blocks, linguini-like masses of plastic ribbon and many others. Surface area is the most important aspect of the medium, along with a tendency not to trap detritus. A good medium will have large amounts of surface area and a moderate amount of void space or ample air exposure. The hard surfaces are the home base for nitrification. The void space is important for gas exchange. If there is too little void, gas exchange will be hindered and the medium may become clogged.

Water that is fed to the trickle filter must run through a pre-filter to prevent clogging. If any particulate matter works its way into the chamber it will begin to decay. If enough debris gets lodged in the bio-media, water quality will deteriorate. If a properly maintained pre-filter is present (and cleaned at least weekly) the filter will rarely need service.

For the aquarist with a central water system, a high-capacity wet-dry filter can easily be constructed using

Small central sump for a few broodstock tanks centralizes protein skimming, heating, water chemistry monitoring and pumping in one compact unit.

nothing more than a 30-gallon rubber trash can, some pieces of pipe, a few tools, and the proper media. A stand is constructed to hold the trash can above the water level of the sump and the bottom of the trash can is fitted with a large bulkhead or a couple of glued-in pipes fitted as low as possible in the chamber to act as a water outlet. The choice of media can be creative. I have used everything from my mother's old hair curlers to recycled fishing line and plastic gutter-guard and plastic scraps. Many manufacturers sell bio-balls and plastic scrap for this purpose (*See Sources.*). The entire chamber is filled with the material of choice. The top of the trash can is then inverted and a battery of holes drilled into the surface of the lid. This modified drip plate is the means by which the water is spread out over the medium. The flow of water being pumped to the drip plate should be enough to cover the highest holes so the water drips through evenly. This can be difficult to adjust but spray bars will help spread the water over the media. Spray bars, constructed of $\frac{1}{2}$ inch PVC pipe with capped ends will help spread the water over the media. Depending on the amount of space available, number of aquariums, number of broodstock pairs, and the amount of food being fed, a series of these filters can be plumbed to the sump.

Ultraviolet Sterilization

The hole in the ozone layer above the earth is the best example of what UV can do. For years, the hole has been getting larger and larger and what this is doing to life here on earth is extremely worrisome to environmental scientists, who believe that higher UV levels may be linked to increased skin cancer rates and the extinction of tropical frogs and toads. Organisms on earth have no means of reflecting high amounts of ultraviolet radiation so if exposed to high levels of UV wavelengths for a prolonged period of time, cells perish.

The killing power of UV has been put to good use by aquarium manufacturers who have used it to create a filtration system to limit the number of pathogens and free-floating bacteria in aquarium water. The average (uncrowded and not overfed) marine aquarium does not absolutely require UV sterilization, but the security of having it to control a disease breakout often warrants the investment. Broodstock aquariums are rarely overstocked, but the fish in them are fed large amounts of food. As long as regular water quality maintenance is undertaken, a UV sterilizer is not necessary. It is a good investment if the money is available.

Crowded conditions such as in larval rearing tanks and grow-out tanks are prime candidates for a UV sterilizer. These tanks are packed full of fish and fed often, a recipe for a bacterial invasion. *Vibrio* and other bacteria are common pathogens that attack juvenile fish in cramped quarters; UV is effective in ridding a system of these and other waterborne pathogens.

Protein Skimmers

Also known as foam fractionators, these are very effective, highly recommended filters for any central water system. I was amazed the first time I saw the waste in the collection cup of a protein skimmer —a rich, thick, dark brown goop extracted from the seemingly clear aquarium water. No filter pad on the market removes junk like that. Protein skimming is a natural occurrence that anyone who has ever strolled a beach on a windy day or walked along a rocky shoreline has observed. The brown foam that swirls around in small eddies is a result of protein skimming on a large scale. A well-designed protein skimmer is worth its weight in gold but be sure to choose a reliable model rated for the amount of water in your system.

There are many types of protein skimmers available to marine aquarists: co-current, counter current, venturi, down-draft, and many more added each year. Counter-current, venturi and down draft models are superior to co-current models.

A counter-current protein skimmer pumps water into the top of a contact chamber through a reaction chamber and exits at the bottom. Fine bubbles, created with a wooden air diffuser, rise from the bottom of the contact chamber. The bubbles traveling up and the water traveling down cause the water to swirl violently in the chamber. Organic molecules, amino acids, fatty acids and a variety of other pollutants adhere to the surface of the tiny bubbles and congregate at the top of the contact chamber forming a stable layer of foam. When this layer of foam grows large enough, it pushes its way up a riser tube, where it eventually falls out into a collection cup. Here, the foam dissipates and anything that was adhering to the surface falls off. The longer the contact time between the water and the bubbles the more waste will be created.

Venturi protein skimmers are operated with one inlet. A water pump is fitted with a venturi valve that feeds air into the rushing water. A mass of tiny bubbles is constantly fed into the reaction chamber. Properly designed venturi protein skimmers are an ideal choice for central systems. They are often built wider rather than higher, conserving

Dissolved organic wastes can build to dangerous levels in a broodstock system unless skimmers are used constantly.

space. The venturi valve rarely needs maintenance compared to the monthly replacement of wooden air diffusers in counter-current models and they allow a better turnover rate.

Fluidized Bed Filters

Fluidized bed filters were developed in aquaculture facilities to cope with high densities of fish. Although their design varies, the concept is quite simple. An acrylic or PVC tube is filled with fine sand. It is usually hung on the back of an aquarium or sump or is freestanding within the sump. The tube is either sealed at the bottom or both ends to form a pressurized chamber. Water is pumped to the bottom of the tube, forced upwards through the sand and exits an outlet at the top of the tube. The sand grains allow for an enormous amount of surface area for nitrifying bacteria to colonize. As the sand grains and water swirl in the tube, bacteria are fed and some scrubbed loose from the surface of the sand. This ensures that new nitrifying bacteria are continuously growing on the surface of the sand. Young, rapidly growing colonies of nitrifying bacteria are much more efficient at transforming waste products to nitrates. The constant grinding of the sand ensures the bacteria stay in a state of exponential growth. These filters have proven valuable to public aquariums or central water systems with high waste output from high densities of fish. Dangerously high ammonia levels will be reduced to unreadable levels in a few hours when a seeded fluidized bed filter is added. Fluidized bed filters have become very popular with home aquarists of late although those for the aquarium hobby differ dramatically from the huge units used in commercial aquaculture.

Live Rock

Live rock is not just a decoration for reef aquariums but can be an extremely useful addition to broodstock systems. Live rock is collected from the vicinity of a coral reef and consists mostly of aged coral rubble (branches or masses of reef-building coral skeletons) of varying sizes. It varies in quality depending on location from which it was collected. The surface of the rock is often brilliantly colored with calcareous algae, macroalgae, sponges, and even small corals. Burrowing organisms such as worms and crustaceans create a labyrinth of caves and tunnels through the rock, often giving it a very porous nature. On the exterior of the rock and in the open pores where water circulation makes oxygen available, aerobic nitrifying bacteria can be found in large numbers. These bacteria perform the nitrification that is present in virtually any biological filter. An interesting benefit to live rock is that it also harbors live anaerobic

Caulerpa-filled algae filter works to extract nitrogenous wastes naturally from system water. With a bed of live sand, this unit also serves as a refugium where small crustaceans such as amphipods and copepods can multiply without predation by fishes.

denitrifying bacteria in its deep recesses that break down nitrate molecules.

Live rock is an excellent addition to the sump of a central water system. At times I have relied solely upon it to filter the water of low-density broodstock systems. It is best, however, to rely on live rock as an enhanced source of natural filtration. The bottom of the sump can be covered with cured live rock that is void of organisms that require high light levels. Room light is usually enough to keep certain algae species alive, but a fluorescent light can improve the growth of these plants and also the nitrification of wastes. Live rock is not without disadvantages. The burrowing organisms within the rock secrete waste and when packed tightly together drastically reduce flow rates through the rock. Over time nitrogenous wastes can build up in crevices of the rock. Weekly or monthly purging of the rock will keep these wastes from becoming harmful.

Live rock should not be added directly to broodstock aquariums, as many demersal spawners will place their eggs on or within the rock. For species such as dottybacks, whose eggs must be removed for hatching, the rock makes this task extremely difficult. Gobies will find the tiniest of holes to spawn in, and removal of the fish or the spawn becomes a daunting task.

Macroalgae Filters

Much debate and alarm have been raised about the destruction of wetlands, mangrove forests, seagrass beds and saltmarshes. These habitats are vital to the survival of coral reefs. Terrestrial waste products leach into ground water where they eventually reach the shoreline. As the water trickles past the roots and leaves of these plants, most of the waste products such as nitrates and phosphates are stripped from the water. This concept can be used to filter aquarium water as well.

Many plant filters have been created for use in freshwater aquariums. There is no single-best design for these filters, but the concept is simple. Plants are to grow either fully submerged in the sump (aquatic species) or propped up so their roots penetrate the water's surface and strip ammonia, nitrogen, phosphates and other toxins from the water. Freshwater tanks are easily filtered with a great variety of plants. Fitting a marine aquarium with a plant filter is more difficult, since relatively few plants can tolerate seawater. There are a few plant candidates for such filters that may or may not be suited to every marine enthusiast. These filters require a lot of space and may not fit in a small fish room.

These natural filters should not be the sole means of filtration, but are worth the time to set up. The easiest way to benefit from plants is to place a handful of *Caulerpa* or *Chaetomorpha* in the sump over some live rock, give it some light and allow it to flourish. These aquatic macroalgaes rapidly if supplied with the right conditions. The faster the plants are allowed to grow, the more waste products they will remove from the water. Frequent pruning will ensure waste removal and facilitate new growth. More elaborate systems can be set up, but simplicity of maintenance is a key issue in selection. Algae turf scrubbers remove ammonia, nitrates and phosphates, but are not easy to acquire and can be difficult to maintain.

Caution should be taken with plant filters as pH and dissolved oxygen levels may be drastically altered by the addition of a mass of photosynthesizing plants. Drastic changes can be prevented with a timer to light plants only at night or when the aquariums are unlit.

Activated Carbon

Activated carbon has advantages in both broodstock aquarium and juvenile grow-out vessels. This material is created by exposing carbon grains to high temperatures and pressures, resulting in a very porous material that functions much like a sponge. Activated carbon works in two ways to remove organic molecules from the water column. It traps organic compounds in its pores and chemically bonds polar organic molecules to the surface of the carbon grain.

Activated carbon can be used in a variety of ways depending upon the type of set-up being used and the room available. The best results occur when water is forced through the carbon so that no water has a chance to by-

The macroalga of choice in many algae filters, *Chaetomorpha linum* grows rapidly and extracts dissolved wastes efficiently.

pass it. Carbon can be placed in mesh bags and positioned under the water inlet to the sump or in an inline chamber. Inline chambers can be created from PVC pipe fitted with reducers and tubing and supplied with a piece of foam at both the inlet and outlet to keep the carbon in place. Canister filters can also be filled with activated carbon and fitted on the sump. Bags of carbon simply placed in the sump will take up organic molecules, although at a much slower rate.

THE ISOLATED SPAWNING TANK

An isolated spawning tank is how most beginners experiment with marine breeding, and it is essentially a modified display aquarium. One tank of the appropriate size for the desired species is established and given its own filtration system, heating and light source, and maintenance schedule.

Choosing a filtration unit for such an aquarium should be taken seriously. Most species require no gravel in the spawning aquarium and complications often arise when

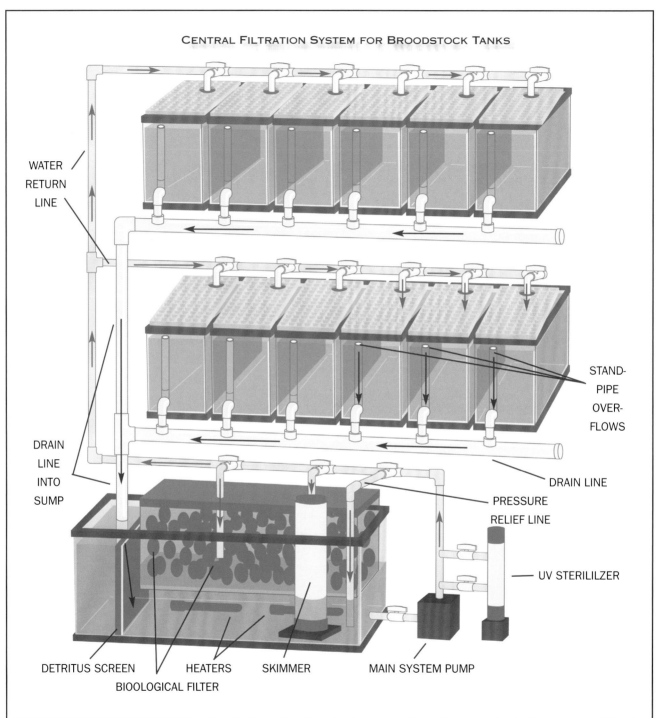

CENTRAL FILTRATION SYSTEM FOR BROODSTOCK TANKS

WATER
RETURN
LINE

STAND-
PIPE
OVER-
FLOWS

DRAIN
LINE
INTO
SUMP

DRAIN LINE

PRESSURE
RELIEF LINE

UV STERILILZER

DETRITUS SCREEN   HEATERS   SKIMMER   MAIN SYSTEM PUMP

BIOOLOGICAL FILTER

COMPACT BROODSTOCK SYSTEM described by the author, featuring two rows of breeding tanks plumbed into a central filtration system with biological filtration, skimming, heating and UV-sterilization all clustered around a simple aquarium sump.

gravel beds get filled with detritus. However, in isolated aquariums the gravel usually plays a major role in filtration. Acting as a biological filter, the surface area of the gravel becomes colonized with beneficial nitrifying bacteria.

In spawning tanks devoid of gravel, effective biological filtration must be provided to compensate for the lack of gravel. There is no such thing as too much biological filtration, only too little. Self-contained, hang-on-the tank power filters and canister filters offer many workable choices. Care must be taken to choose a model powerful enough to cope with heavy broodstock feedings. Many small and low-powered outside power filters are impractical for spawning aquariums. The filter box, which holds the filter media must be large enough to support ample amounts of media and must force all the water through the media, not allowing any water to escape without being filtered. For a 20-gallon breeder aquarium, you might opt for a power filter rated for a 50 to 70-gallon tank to give a margin of safety.

Most such filters that use a slide-in media cartridge are not suitable. The cartridge is a mechanical filter that traps uneaten fish food and fish waste. Carbon is usually added in the cartridge. While the carbon does work to a certain extent, it may not adequately filter the water. The carbon usually falls to the bottom of the cartridge rather than being dispersed evenly throughout. Water takes the path of least resistance and will flow around the carbon. As a result, few waste products are absorbed. By the time nitrifying bacteria adhere to the surface of the filter cartridge it is replaced with a new one and the benefits of them are lost. (If you choose one of these power filters, be sure to pick a model with multiple cartridges so that they can be replaced on a rotating basis.) In my view, the best choice is one which offers a vertical water flow pattern, so the water is forced up or down through the filter media.

Manufacturers recommend certain media be used in their filters to offer the best performance. It is best to only use those filtration mediums that offer the most biological filtration and skip any exotic chemical beyond activated carbon. Foam blocks are a great choice for biological filtration as they offer ample amounts of surface area as well as trapping suspended debris. Fit as many foam blocks as possible in the space available. In both canister filters and outside power filters, foam blocks can be squeezed to fit.

Maintaining these filters is a simple task. The foam blocks are acting as the filter and should never be thrown out unless they begin to deteriorate. Every week or so the foam blocks should be removed and rung out in saltwater to remove all trapped material. (The foam blocks must be rinsed in saltwater not fresh water so the beneficial bacteria are not harmed.)

Another choice of filtration for a marine spawning aquarium is a sponge filter—an internal filter operated by an airlift attached to an air pump. These filters offer a vast surface area for nitrifying bacteria to colonize and as a result effectively reduce waste products.

Central Filtration Systems

My definition of a tank is any vessel that holds water and is used to house fish. This definition is meant to be broad because when designing and building a central filtration system, glass aquariums are not the only choice. Many influences affect tank selection. Factors such as available space, hardware and tools, carpentry and plumbing skills, purpose of the tanks, and price will influence what type of tank to use.

Glass Aquariums

Glass aquariums come to mind when we think of fish tanks. Every pet shop carries affordable all-glass aquariums in the size ranges used in most home-scale marine breeding. For the purpose of a central filtration system, a hole must be drilled through the glass to act as a drain for water. Tanks with a pre-drilled hole are available at specialty aquarium stores and pet shops can order them. This is especially true for aquarium stores geared toward reef aquarists. If there are no such stores in your area contact an aquarium distributor or manufacturer. Often a specialty glass shop will have experience in drilling glass aquariums.

However, with a little patience, you can drill the holes yourself. Glass aquariums have many advantages. Viewing the inhabitants and painting the external side panels and bottom are easy. They can be placed directly next to one another with little wasted space. They are probably the most aesthetically pleasing of all possible tanks. Also, they are fish-safe with no worry of introducing contaminants and fish-ready when you buy them—a benefit if set-up time is a major consideration. However, glass tanks are delicate.

Economical tanks of any size can be constructed with sheets of glass, acrylic, or plexiglass and aquarium-safe pure silicone sealant. It is beyond the scope of this book to give aquarium building instructions, but you can ask your local fish shop for advice or look for instructions on the Internet.

Plastic Tanks

Although they come in different configurations than conventional aquariums, plastic storage containers or prefabricated tanks are ideal for spawning marine aquarium fishes. They are made by many different manufacturers and are available at many supermarkets, hardware and department stores. They are usually wider, come in a variety of sizes and shapes and offer a larger surface-area-to-volume ratio. Plastic containers have many advantages for aquarists establishing a fish room on a central filtration system since they are easily drilled with a basic power tool and holesaw attachment. They are usually available in dark colors that make painting unnecessary, are stackable and easily transported, and are usually quite economical.

But there are drawbacks. Soft plastics will sometimes degrade and leak contaminants into the water. Although I have never had a problem with this, it is a fact to consider. The quality of plastic used to make the container will usually determine if it will be suitable to house fish. The harder the plastic, generally the better.

To convert plastic storage containers into a suitable habitat for both the aquarist and the fish, a viewing window must be installed. Acrylic, including the Plexiglas brand, is available from a variety of sources and different manufacturers. Local plastic specialty shops may have piles of scrap plastic, with the protective paper still intact, left over from other jobs and available at a fraction of the price. Generally, ¼ inch works well for all applications. Acrylic, not glass, must be used for the viewing window. As the tank is filled with water, the sides will bow from the water pressure. If glass is used, the pressure of the flexing walls will surely crack it or break the silicone seal. Acrylic is easily drilled and has a certain amount of flexibility.

The viewing window should have at least a one-inch frame on all sides. A small hole is drilled in the side of the container to accommodate the blade of a jigsaw which is then used to cut out the remainder of the window. The corners can either be rounded or square, although rounding them is both easier and more aesthetically pleasing. A piece of clear acrylic sheet is cut to fit tightly inside the container, extending beyond the edge of the window opening by an inch or more. The acrylic is positioned and marked for the location of the bolt holes that will be drilled though the acrylic and into the container. If the container is smaller than 20 inches wide on a side, eight bolts will suffice, at each corner and midpoint. If the container is larger than this, bolts should be placed every three to five inches.

Stainless steel, aluminum, and plastics can be used for this application. Saltwater is very corrosive and most fasteners will eventually degrade. The bolts will be sheathed in silicone, making them waterproof and corrosion-proof.

After the holes are drilled, a bead of silicone is spread evenly over the inside of the frame of the hole cut in the container. The acrylic viewing window is then laid in place and the bolts fastened. Silicone is used to cover the bolts. Twenty-four hours later, this indestructible tank is ready to use.

Another very useful application of plastic tanks is in housing pelagic spawning species. Square or rectangular tanks are not suitable for these species, as the eggs must be collected soon after spawning. A circular flow of water created from a return pipe and a siphon box fitted to the tank create an ideal egg collector. Pelagic spawners often fail to reproduce in shallow tanks as they cannot complete or initiate a spawning assent. Fifty-gallon plastic drums are

Simple 16-tank broodstock system using inexpensive 15-gallon glass tanks for spawning, 50-gallon sumps and fluorescent shop lights for illumination.

acrylic can be used for the viewing window. With a frame or a routed groove, a bead of silicone is spread around the opening before clamping or sliding the viewing window into place inside the tank, so that water pressure forces it against the tank wall.

Prior to installation of the viewing window, the tank is waterproofed using either fiberglass resin or two-part marine epoxy paint. Marine epoxy paint is available in many colors. Two coats should both seal and color the inside and all exposed edges of the tank. If clear fiberglass resin is used, the plywood should be painted with black paint before the resin is spread over it. Care should be taken to cover the corners and joints with waterproofing material.

commercially available from a number of sources. Fitted with acrylic windows and specialty plumbing, these tanks are suitable for angelfishes and basslets. The return line to the tank is placed on the bottom of the tank and water is allowed to rise to the bulkhead drain at the top in a circular and upward flow, bringing eggs to the collector.

Plywood Vessels

Plywood tanks of any size are a great choice for anyone with basic woodworking skills and tools. They also can be drilled very easily with little worry of cracking. But they are heavy, and in the end may be more expensive than glass aquariums.(Some tank builders also think of them as less prone to catastrophic failure than home-built glass aquariums.)

A four-sided box is constructed using $^{3}/_{4}$-inch plywood (marine grade or at least with two smooth sides). Drywall screws are suitable for constructing smaller tanks while bolts or progressively larger screws will be required for larger tanks. A frame is constructed using 1 x 1-inch lumber, 2 x 4s or any lumber that will create a fastening point for the acrylic or glass viewing window. Aquarists with a router can place the viewing window in a routed groove rather than a frame. Since the plywood should not bow, glass or

Drain Methods

Because a central filtration system relies on water entering and exiting the broodstock tanks, it is important to have a reliable means of draining water from tanks to the sump. This is where holes drilled in the tank are important. Whether or not a standpipe is needed depends on where the hole is drilled. (A standpipe is a vertical tube, open at the top, into which water can flow continuously and be carried out of the tank by gravity.) There are many different methods that can be used to accomplish this task. We will examine each part separately and then piece them together.

Holes are easily drilled with a hole saw in plywood, acrylic and plastic tanks and in glass tanks with an acrylic pane. A sharp hole saw is particularly important when cutting a hole through acrylic or plastic. A paddle bit can be used to drill through wood, but tends to slip and drills a sloppy, often oval-shaped hole in soft material. Hole saws have a circular toothed ring attached to a drill bit. The center bit holds the saw steady, creating a clean hole with no slipping.

When placing holes in plastic tanks, a small drill bit, any size smaller than the actual hole desired, is used to drill a hole through the plastic in the area desired. Then, using a propane torch or heat gun, the plastic around the hole is slowly heated by waving the flame across the surface. Do not aim the torch at any one spot for too long, as this will melt the plastic and cause the hole to widen. When the plastic is hot, the PVC, CPVC, or bulkhead fitting is pressed against it and turned back and forth, slowly pushing through the plastic. In this way a perfect hole is created for the diameter of the fitting being used. Also, the plastic will be bent inward slightly allowing the sealant more surface area to adhere to, and it gives the fitting on the other side more plastic to bite into.

Glass tanks require a little more work if they do not have a pre-drilled hole. In order to successfully drill through glass, a diamond-tip drill bit,

The author installing drains and return water lines in a small-scale breeding facility at the University of Edinburgh, Scotland. Note flexible hose from tank to drain line.

or brass tube bit must be obtained. Diamond-tip bits are a bit more expensive, but with proper care they will last long enough to drill a hundred or so holes. Brass bits must be used in combination with a grinding medium and are not as reliable as diamond-tip drill bits. Diamond drill bits used for large diameter holes such as those needed for aquariums are of tube or core types, resembling a hole saw without the central drill bit. A $\frac{3}{4}$-inch core bit works well with $\frac{1}{2}$-inch PVC male threads and a $1\frac{1}{4}$-inch core bit will be required for $\frac{3}{4}$-inch PVC fittings.

A wall of putty should be molded into place roughly an inch or two outside the area designated for the hole to create a dam to hold a puddle of water around the drill bit, keeping it cool. A drill press is not essential to drill glass aquariums, but definitely helps. Hand drills are a bit more difficult, but with practice they are equally efficient. If a hand drill is used, a hole must be started with a stencil—a flat piece of lumber with a similar size hole placed over the

aquarium glass as a guide. Apply very little pressure and make sure the bit is traveling straight. Once the glass has been scored the wood stencil can be removed. It is often a good idea to practice drilling holes through glass on an old aquarium to gain a feel for cracking thresholds and pressure as well as the various speeds of the drill being used. Drilling glass is easy —assuming the drill or press is run straight. If the drill is tweaked to the side, a crack or clam-shell-type breakage is a sure bet.

Hole Placement

There are many locations in the tank to place the drain hole, but think carefully before drilling any holes or buying pre-drilled tanks. Consider how much room is available in the fish room and on the stand that will support the tanks. Holes placed in the bottom are most common, as concealing the plumbing needed to return the water to the sump is easy. But this design requires a bit more room underneath the tank than those with holes placed elsewhere. Usually, a length of PVC pipe is laid out under all the aquariums and water from each tank then drains into this pipe and then to the sump. If the tanks are to be stacked in rows of more than three, it is best to place the holes in the front or sides as space will become limited very quickly. Also, drainage holes on the bottom will require a standpipe, which is simply a piece of pipe extending from the bulkhead placed in the bottom to the top where the desired water level is to be maintained.

Holes are also commonly placed near the top of one corner of the back pane of glass. This placement is good for those with limited space between tank rows and does not require a standpipe. A bulkhead is added and is usually fitted with a nipple on the outside of the tank. A length of flexible tubing is attached to the nipple and fed into a drain line or is run directly into the sump. Some room will be required behind the tanks so they cannot be placed flush against a wall.

Holes can also be drilled on the sides of the aquarium. If space is lacking behind and in front of the tanks, but lots of room is available along the sides, drain lines can be fed down between the tanks. The tanks will not be placed directly next to one another and plumbing will be visible. This is not the most aesthetic option, but functional.

Finally, the drain can be installed in the front of the aquarium. Since the hole is drilled in the side of the tank that will face out, more tanks can fit on one rack. The hole is usually placed near the bottom with a 90-degree elbow for the standpipe that controls the water level. Although more functional than attractive and some viewing access to your broodstock is sacrificed, this is an excellent design and perhaps the best. It allows easy access to clogs in the pipes. The tanks can be butted right up against the back wall and all the plumbing is in front. Leaks or damaged portions are easily spotted.

Standpipes

Standpipes are used when the hole is placed in or near the bottom of the tank. A straight piece of PVC or CPVC pipe

is cut to an appropriate length to maintain the desired water level of an inch or two below the top of the tank. Plastic mesh, such as that used to guard gutters, is cut in lengths of roughly two inches by four inches, rolled up and inserted into the pipe to prevent fish from plunging into the sump. Standpipe screens should be installed even for big fish to prevent large materials from clogging and flooding the tank. If something accidentally falls into the tank, it will become lodged in or near the standpipe. Screens should be periodically removed and scrubbed or replaced because food, feces and other material become lodged there and the water level will rise.

Often, if the standpipe is constructed of small diameter (anything less than 1-inch) pipe or the turnover rate is high, water swirling into the standpipe creates a vortex that can make a high-pitched, aggravating noise. A larger diameter standpipe in the tank or a lesser flow rate will eliminate the noise. For 10 to 20-gallon tanks, a $^3/_4$ to 1-inch diameter drain should suffice, but bigger tanks need $1^1/_2$ to 2-inch diameter standpipes.

A further advantage to using standpipes rather than bulkhead fittings in the upper reaches of the tank is easy drainage of tank water by removing the standpipe from its slip fitting. All the water will drain quickly to the sump. If the tank needs maintenance, this method beats draining the tank with a siphon. (The sump volume must be large enough to handle the excess water.)

Bulkheads

I use the term bulkhead to describe the fittings that create a waterproof seal on the inside and outside of the tank around water entry and exit holes. Manufactured bulkheads are available in most sizes, but the price for the 50 or so bulkheads needed to plumb a central filtration system adds up quickly. A bulkhead is a male fitting with a large rib and a fitted rubber O-ring that goes on the inside of the tank and fits through the hole. A threaded nut is then screwed on from the outside to create a waterproof seal. They are made of high density molded plastic and are usually supplied with a screen for the inside and an elbow for the outside. The outside hole will accommodate PVC pipe if one wishes to plumb it with pipe rather than flexible tubing. There are other options for the cost-conscious hobbyist.

Plastic Pipe Fittings

PVC and CPVC fittings are inexpensive and easy to work with. Commonly used diameter fittings are $1/2$-inch for small tanks, $3/4$-inch for medium to large tanks, and 1-inch for larger tanks or those requiring a higher turnover rate. PVC fittings are available in many more sizes and variations and are the choice for most fish room plumbing. Do not try to mix PVC and CPVC, as they are not compatible. Male and female fittings are available and are ideal for this application. It doesn't matter what fitting goes on the inside or outside but male fittings are generally placed on the inside of the tank with the male threads protruding out of the aquarium through the drilled hole. A rubber O-ring is placed tightly around this fitting, on the inside and compressed between the bulkhead flange and the wall of the tank. (Some bulkheads may have O-rings inside and out.) The female fitting is then gently screwed on from the outside. Pliers or a wrench can be used to tighten the fitting only if hand tightened fittings are obviously not snug. This should be done slowly and carefully so the glass does not crack. When the O-ring is tight against the glass and the fitting, a waterproof seal will result. Silicone can be added around the seal before tightening to ensure a waterproof seal. O-rings can be purchased from hardware stores or made from a few stacked pieces of bicycle tubing or garden hose.

PVC and CPVC fittings used to create a waterproof seal are available in a variety of different styles but you want a slip-fit, not threaded, style for the interior of the tank, where the standpipe will be placed. The outside fitting can either be threaded on both sides or threaded on one side and a slip fit on the other, depending on the situation and the desired drain method. If the water is to drain directly from the tank into a larger drainpipe a slip fit is better. If, however, the drain pipe is situated more than a foot away from the bottom of the tank a threaded fitting will allow a nip-

ple to be added which can then be connected to flexible tubing to deliver the water to the drain pipe. Here is an example: a $3/4$ inch fitting with male threads on one side and female threads on the other side is pushed up through the outside of the tank. Then, a $3/4$-inch fitting with female threads on one side and a slip fit on the other side is placed on the inside, an O-ring added that is screwed down onto the male threads coming up through the hole. The standpipe is slipped into place. A $3/4$-inch nipple with male threads is then screwed into the female threads of the outside fitting. Flexible tubing is pushed over the nipple and fed down to the drainpipe.

Drainpipes

The water from each tank can be delivered to the sump by individual pipes or tubes, but that increases the potential for leaks and decreases the potential to uniformly filter the water. In most multi-tank breeding rooms, a larger-diameter drainpipe is placed below a row of tanks to collect the water from tanks in that row and then down to the sump. I will mention only a few methods of draining the water from the tank that work for me and are the least likely to cause flooding.

The number of tanks in a given row and the volume of water each is turning over, determine the diameter of the drainpipe. On average, a 2-inch diameter PVC drainpipe works well. Three and 4-inch drainpipes can be used, but are not necessary unless there are more than 10 or 15 tanks in a row. It is best to place the drainpipes directly below the tanks running along the rack of tanks to the sump.

You do not need a watertight fitting when connecting each tank to the drain. A hole saw is used to drill a hole in the drainpipe below each bulkhead fitting. The hole diameter should be cut to fit a short length of PVC approximately $1^{1}/2$ inches in diameter. When this piece is pushed into the hole, a collar is created. The bottom portion, along the horizontal waterflow pattern, of the short length of PVC pushed into the drainpipe should be drilled on both sides with a large drill bit or notched out with a jigsaw to allow drain water to flow past easily. The collar is an effec-

Simple drain system collecting overflow water from the stand-pipes in a rack of tanks feeding into a central sump below.

turn to the sump. This method of returning the water from the tank to the sump allows the aquarist the option of utilizing only one drainpipe placed below the lowest row of tanks. Flexible 1-inch clear vinyl tubing can be used to feed the water from the top row of tanks to this drainpipe. The drainpipe used for this method should be at least 3 inches in diameter due to the amount of water being drained into it, and it should have a slight slope in its positioning, downward toward the sump to speed water flow.

A simpler but less watertight approach calls for one nipple to be placed on the bulkhead under the tank and a length of flexible tubing connected. The drainpipe is drilled with holes close to the diameter of flexible tubing and the flexible tubing is simply pushed in place. This is not a waterproof seal nor is it guaranteed that the tubing won't pop out and cause a leak. When this method is used, one drainpipe can be placed below each row of tanks or one drainpipe below the lowest row can be used. Be sure the flexible tubing is secured and is not likely to be dislodged and cause a flood.

Along the same lines as the previous example, the drainpipe can be placed in front of the row of tanks or behind them. If the bulkhead fitting is placed on the side, the front, or the back of the tanks, a PVC or CPVC elbow can be used and connected to a length of PVC or CPVC pipe that will go directly into the drainpipe. This is a good method of returning the water. The holes in the drainpipe can be cut to the diameter of the pipes leading out from the bulkhead. A close fit is already established and a bead of silicone will waterproof it. One drainpipe per row of tanks will be required. (*See accompanying photographs.*)

Sump

Plastic storage containers, large aquariums, rugged "structural foam" Rubbermaid water troughs used for livestock and plastic garbage cans are all ideal containers for the sump, the central reservoir and service area for your system. The function of the sump is to afford enough room for returning water and to house the filtration equipment. It also increases the total water volume, helping keep a bal-

tive means of butting the drainpipe as close to the tank as possible. When the stand is built, chances are good that wood or other building material will limit how close the drainpipe can be placed to the tank. The collar reduces the chance of leaks between the tank and the drainpipe. One disadvantage of this method is that it limits the volume of water that can be forced through the drainpipe without leaking. If the standpipe is removed to drain the tank rapidly, the drainpipe may overflow with the sudden increase in flow through the pipe.

When the drainpipe is not placed directly under the tanks, two options are available. The first and better of the two is to place a threaded nipple on the bulkhead fitting under the tank. Then, drill an appropriate size hole in the drainpipe, thread it, and place a similar nipple on the drainpipe after sealing it with Teflon tape. The two nipples are connected with a length of flexible tubing and the chance of the drainpipe flooding is almost zero due to the fact that the drainpipe is sealed with no open ends, except for the re-

Broodstock tanks (20-gallon) at the Florida Institute of Technology using the author's design recommendations, with a centralized filtration system using a shallow sump with a pool liner on the floor level. Note moveable standpipes, used to adjust water levels.

anced system. The sump should be large enough to cope with the amount of water above the standpipe in every tank connected to the system. If a power failure occurs and the return pump shuts down, the sump must be able to handle all the draining water or it will end up on the floor.

When cleaning tanks, standpipes can be lifted and the tanks allowed to drain directly into the sump. The sump must be large enough, then, to hold the minimal operating water and the water from drained tanks. When choosing a sump be sure it is large enough for the intended volume of water and all the equipment it needs to hold. This is the key requirement of a good sump, along with being leakproof and made of an inert material that will not degrade under the effects of saltwater. Home-built plywood boxes and metal watering troughs can be used if they

are well-sealed with two-part marine epoxy paint. Pond liners are an excellent choice for larger systems as they can be fitted in nearly any position or place and can be fitted to flow over and around obstructions such as lumber studs. Careful attention should be paid to minimizing the number of wrinkles, especially around corners, as they accumulate debris.

Return Pump

Choosing an ideal return pump to deliver water from the sump—through a maze of PVC pipes—to a battery of aquariums several feet off the floor can seem intimidating if you are not a fluid mechanic or civil engineer. The right pump is, in fact, a crucial link in any central filtration system. Determining a desired flow rate and velocity at a given height can often lead to complicated equations which can leave many aquarists with a headache long before they figure out what size pump to buy.

There are many models of internal and external water pumps that make ideal return pumps for centralized systems. Virtually all readily available models suited to small-scale systems are centrifugal pumps with three main components: the impeller, the casing, and the motor. The impeller is coupled to the motor either magnetically or through a sealed shaft. Impellers directly connected to the motor through a sealed shaft are prone to failure in corrosive salt environments leading to leaks and possibly metal contamination. Pumps with magnetic-drive impellers are more popular as they are completely sealed. Many models are not suited to saltwater applications and it is important to check for metal components such as screws and shafts before selecting a pump. My favorite small-scale return pumps are the various sizes of Danner Mag-Drive pumps. These are inexpensive and perform efficiently both inside and outside the sump and are saltwater-safe.

Flow Rate

Water pumps are typically measured in flow rate; smaller pumps are measured in gallons per hour (GPH), while larger pumps are rated in gallons per minute (GPM). In central filtration systems we are most interested in pumping X amount of water at Y amount of head. This can be quite difficult to determine as the labyrinth of PVC should be designed to distribute water evenly through a number of outlets. In general, as the pumping height or head increases the flow rate decreases. A pump that is rated at 700 GPH may only pump 250 GPH at a head of seven feet. Each pump designed for specific applications will exhibit different relationships between height and flow rate. Most manufacturers include a performance chart which illustrates this relationship. Performance curves are also available for many popular hobby pumps on-line.

As water moves upward and forward within a pipe, the flow rate drops as friction creates resistance. Friction loss also occurs within pipe fittings such as elbows, Tees, unions and ball valves. These losses are usually minor, but when added together they can take a substantial toll on the overall flow rate. The velocity of the water (measured in feet/sec) has a direct relationship with friction loss. As velocity increases so too does friction loss. Increasing the diameter of the pipe reduces the velocity and thus also reduces friction loss. Increasing the diameter of the return line can deliver nearly double the amount of water at a given head due to the reduced friction loss.

Ideally, suitable pumps are determined by elaborate calculations and graphs that plot the intersection between the performance curve of the pump and the system curve of your plumbing and head requirements. Several spreadsheets and software programs have been designed to calculate the needed flow rate within a system. A useful spreadsheet developed by Sanjay Joshi, Nathan Paden, and Shane Graber is available from Advanced Aquarist Online. (*See Sources.*) If in doubt, the owner or manager of a local aquarium shop often has first-hand experience and can provide good advice.

Some general rules apply: The plumbing of the system and the rating of the return pump should be designed to turn over the entire volume of water three to six times every hour. I know of many successful hobbyists who operate on different turnover rates, so this figure is not sacrosanct. Many hobbyists prefer to use smaller-diameter return-line piping (e.g. ½-inch) to boost the velocity of water entering the tanks. The increased velocity increases the overall water movement in the tank to keep uneaten food and fecal matter suspended in the water column until it exits the tank and flows to the sump. Increasing the velocity will require a stronger pump.

To make a simple estimate of pump rating needed, first calculate the total water volume of each tank in the system and multiply this figure by the number of times you want the tank volume to turn over. For example, if we wanted the turnover rate to be six times per hour in a 10-gallon tank, we would estimate a flow rate of 60 GPH. If we had 10 tanks connected to this system, we would require 600 GPH of flow. Using this total flow we can now estimate the required pump based on the performance curve at a given height. Remember, that friction losses and other losses were not calculated so a slightly larger pump will be required. If you are also running other equipment (such as a skimmer or UV filter) off the main pump, this will also diminish the volume of water reaching the tanks. Generally it's best to use a dedicated pump to feed a protein skimmer. For most hobby-scale breeding rooms, avoid large pumps rated in horsepower and try to choose a model near or slightly over what your system requires. Large pumps can dramatically alter the water temperature of your system.

Return Lines

The return line used in most applications of home-based breeding systems should be ³/₄- to 1-inch in diameter. Return lines larger than these are ideal for buildings full of tanks and large pumps, but for the average aquarist with no more than 100 aquariums ³/₄-inch PVC or CPVC pipe is best. If the return line diameter is too large, pressure will be lost and the top row of tanks will receive very little flow.

The plumbing attached from the pump to return the water is simple. One vertical pipe brings the water to a horizontal feeder pipe running above each row of tanks. (*See diagrams and photographs.*) Each tank has a ball valve to control the water flow. Gate valves are available, but are not as accurate as ball valves.

The most important aspect of return lines is a bleed valve to adjust water pressure on the pump. (Backpressure will severely shorten its life.) The bleed valve is placed in the sump not too far away from the pump itself. A T fitting is placed off the main line and is fitted with a ball valve and some extra lengths of pipe to feed the water back into the sump. The bleed valve helps regulate the flow and prevents backpressure on the pump. When all the valves in the tanks are adjusted to the proper flow, if a slight humming sound is heard in the pump body, there is backpressure occurring on the pump and the bleed valve should be opened slightly. Also, when you close valves for maintenance, the bleed valve allows water to exit back into the sump without causing too much backpressure. If you have oversized your main system pump, a bleed valve is especially important-

PUTTING IT ALL TOGETHER

Putting all the parts together for the first time can seem a bit intimidating. First off, an appropriate area must be chosen in which to build the system. Spare rooms are ideal, but the basement is better since water will be spilled from time to time, and the temperature is more easily controlled. In many areas around the world the temperature gets too hot in the summer time and the tanks will overheat. It is best, although not essential, to devote an entire room to the purpose of spawning and raising marine fish. In this way the space can be heated with a small room heater rather than having to run and monitor multiple aquarium heaters. Larval rearing tanks, algae and rotifer cultures, *Artemia* hatcheries and any other tank not connected to the central system, will be heated separately.

If you are starting small and can't devote a whole room to aquariums, a spare wall is really all that is needed. If the family room is where it must fit, so be it.

The tank stand can be quite stylish with varnished hardwood and swinging doors to conceal all the plumbing, or it can be made from cinder blocks or exposed two-by-four lumber. The latter method is typical, as this is to be a breeding operation and not a family room showcase. The tanks will need maintenance quite often, so the more basic the construction, the easier it will be to clean, feed, remove spawns and so on. Diagrams are included here as guides but nothing is set in stone. The tanks can be placed in a single row against a long wall or stacked in several rows to save space or to suit your budget and personal preferences.

After the stand is up, the plumbing can be installed. Before the tanks are placed on the stand, the drain pipes and return lines should be fitted in place. Return lines and plumbing fittings should always be glued together with PVC cement but do not glue parts past the ball valve that feeds each tank, however. (This provides more flexibility if you move or change tanks in the future.) The ball valves themselves may not need gluing if the slip fit is tight enough. This will save the valves, should the system be torn

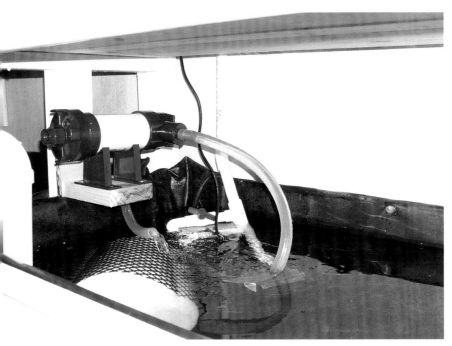

UV sterilizer positioned over a large sump constructed with a lumber frame and lined with black pond liner. Ultraviolet radiation kills common marine parasites.

constantly and slowly replaced. (Some hobbyists feed all such replacement water from a reverse osmosis filter or RO/DI unit to keep any tap water contaminants out of their tanks.)

Diagrams are included to illustrate the basic scheme of central water systems. These systems can vary according to each aquarist's specifications, budgets and space limitations. The sizes of the aquariums will differ according to the species of fish raised and the amount of room available.

In a properly planned fish room, three separate central systems are usually established to accommodate spawning, larval rearing and grow-out. In general, the broodstock and larval tanks are small, and juvenile grow-out tanks are large.

Seeding New Systems

As marine fish begin spawning, the space allotted to raising the offspring is inundated with aquariums and tubs of various sizes. As the need arises to establish more aquariums, keeping track of the nitrification cycle will save much time and headaches. Often, an aquarium or system must be established quickly to accommodate a batch of juveniles or newly acquired broodstock.

Quickly seeding or maturing an aquarium that is not part of a central filtration system is an extremely useful trick of the trade. Many aquarists seed new aquariums by adding one or two fish and starting the nitrogen cycle from the beginning. This is fine if time is of no consequence, but more often than not it is. Many people add a few cups of gravel from an established aquarium or a few small pieces of live rock. While these methods introduce vital microorganisms, they do not process the amount of waste generated by numerous fish.

Dedicated aquarists should maintain several extra foam blocks or similar filter media running in a mature system, should a situation arise that calls for a new aquarium or

down at a later date. Drain lines can either be sealed with PVC glue or silicone sealant. Since there is no pressure on the drain pipe, silicone will work fine to form a waterproof seal. The tanks are now placed on the stand and the bulkhead fittings attached to the drainpipe.

One or more plastic garbage cans or inert plastic vats should be obtained for the purpose of mixing synthetic seawater. The vessel should be filled with freshwater and the sea salt mixed in. The water is then poured or pumped into the sump. (A powerhead pump with vinyl hose is useful in mixing and pumping water from the mixing vessel.) The main system pump is now turned on until the sump is nearly empty. More water is mixed and added to the sump until all the tanks are full and the sump water level is correct.

All future water added to the system should be introduced via the sump. This gives the new water a chance to mix with that of the system before it enters the tanks with living organisms. The sump can also be fitted with a float valve and freshwater feed so that water lost to evaporation is

rearing vessel. An outside power filter is a useful tool for seeding new tanks. By loading the new filter with foam blocks that have been running on an established system for weeks or months, ammonia and other wastes secreted in the new water will be reduced. Squeezing a well-seeded foam block into the new tank, trapped particulates and all, is another effective way of adding vital microbe populations.

If it can be spared (as from a water change), half the volume of the new tank should be added using old water, or rather, that from an existing system or aquarium. The goal is to maximize the beneficial microorganism population as quickly as possible in the new aquarium.

When mature water and a mature filter are placed in a new aquarium, the nitrogen cycle is off to a good start. Ammonia generated by the fish will be secreted in the water column where it will pass through the filter media in the power filter. The existing nitrifying bacteria populations will break down the waste and an effective cycle is established. The tank walls and any substrate will require a few weeks to fully colonize, but as long as feeding is limited, such a system is fully capable of handling the load generated by a group of young, tank-raised fish or new broodstock.

Quarantine

When several breeding pairs of marine fish are being housed within a centralized system, it is of utmost importance to screen everything that goes into these tanks.

Every fish that is to be placed in this central system of tanks should first be quarantined to eliminate the possible spread of disease. Once the fish are acclimated to the broodstock system and have begun spawning, outbreaks of disease will become rare.

New broodstock candidates should be placed in a separate aquarium or central system for a period of 30 days. This time allows them to become adjusted to localized water conditions and living conditions. It also gives the aquarist time to observe the fish for possible signs of infection and disease. If, after 30 days, the fish are disease free, they can be added to the main broodstock system. With an isolated broodstock tank, quarantine is not necessary.

Martin Moe installing a new home breeding room, with a variety of tank sizes all connected to central filtration systems.

PHOTOPERIOD & ILLUMINATION

Spawning aquariums are simple. They are devoid of most aquascaping and aesthetics used in display aquariums. High-tech lighting is not required. In most cases, simple lids are constructed of plastic egg crates used in overhead lighting fixtures, and no direct illumination is provided to the individual aquariums. To run just one spawning aquarium for an isolated broodstock pair, an inexpensive plastic molded canopy with fluorescent strip light will provide adequate illumination.

In the case of several or many aquariums connected to a central filtration system, no direct illumination is necessary. Instead, room lighting will often suffice. Depending on the size of the room, one to many fluorescent lighting fixtures are mounted directly to the ceiling. Ordinary hanging or ceiling-mounted shop lights sold at hardware stores adequately serve the purpose of illumination. These can be suspended over a rack of tanks, but strong lighting over the aquarium is not important. Only enough light to view the fish is necessary.

Photoperiod (the hours of daylight) is important. The cycle of light and darkness, along with temperature, are the main controlling forces driving hormone production and spawning seasons in wild populations of marine fish. In captivity these environmental factors can be manipulated to create an ideal spawning environment.

To simulate the long summer days of the tropics, a photoperiod of 12 to 16 hours of light seems ideal for most marine aquarium species. Slight variations in this scheme do little harm as long as they are controlled and maintained constantly with an automatic timer connected to the light fixture. Fish may cease to spawn if the photoperiod varies from day to day.

Commercial marine aquaculture facilities have used light manipulation to regulate the spawning rhythms of several commercial species such as red drum and striped bass. By manipulating day and night cycles over a period of days or a few weeks, often greatly reducing the day length, seasonal changes can be artificially represented in a short time. This triggers the fishes' pituitary glands to produce reproductive hormones and trigger spawning. Largely unexplored in marine ornamental aquaculture, light manipulation has the potential to exploit seasonal spawners.

Light Intensity

Light intensity is a term generally associated with the keeping of live corals, but it also has its place in the marine fish breeding arena. While the actual spectrum of light provided is not generally important, the amount of light is. Direct overhead illumination is not necessary and when multiple aquariums are connected through a centralized filter, lights often become a nuisance too near the aquarium surface. Overhead room lighting is typically all that is needed. To keep costs down, opt for inexpensive 6500K daylight fluorescent bulbs. If your budget allows, use full-spectrum or daylight bulbs for a more pleasing view of your fishes.

It is interesting to note that certain species seem susceptible to a bleaching phenomenon when not provided enough light. I have observed two Red Sea species, *Pseudochromis fridmani* and *P. springeri*, develop dull blotches on the center of their bodies when maintained in dark conditions for prolonged periods of time. The overall color of these specimens continually faded until they died some weeks later. Some forms of protozoan parasites are encouraged by these conditions, and it is possible that the condition could have been corrected with proper light since fish of the same species living elsewhere within the same centralized water system remained healthy.

TEMPERATURE

As with any marine aquarium, the temperature of the water must be set and controlled to stay within limits depending on the geographic origin of the species. Erratic fluctuations of temperature must be avoided.

As most marine aquarium fish originate in tropical locations in the Indo-Pacific and Caribbean, a temperature range of 76°F to 80°F (24°C to 27°C) is ideal. Many species spawn best at temperatures near the lower range around 76°F (24°C), while others prefer warmer water up to 82°F (28°C). Admittedly, the range in values is small and most species will spawn in any of the above-mentioned temperatures. In warmer water, the metabolic rate of the fish is increased. They will consume more food, become more active and often spawn more readily.

Fish such as Ocellaris Clownfish (*Amphiprion ocellaris*), Orchid Dottyback (*Pseudochromis fridmani*), Yellowhead Jawfish (*Opistognathus aurifrons*) and the Greenbanded goby (*Elacatinus multifasciatum*) maintain reliable spawning cycles at 80°F. The resulting eggs are robust with good hatch rates and reliable larval survival. When water temperature is decreased to near 76°F, reproductive cycles stagger and egg development is prolonged by roughly 24 hours or more.

Curiously, in some species such as the Orchid Dottyback, larvae hatch out significantly larger at 76°F than at 80°F. Prolonged incubation can result in larger larvae that are sometimes easier to rear. Neon Dottybacks (*Pseudochromis aldabraensis*) suffer reproductive dysfunction at higher temperatures and larvae experience higher mortality. Similarly, I have observed Tomato Clownfish (*Amphiprion frenatus*) eggs fail to develop normally at higher temperatures and experience erratic hatching. Ocellaris Clownfish (*A. ocellaris*) seem to suffer the opposite effect and hatch erratically at lower temperatures. Initiating a spawning rhythm is often a simple task throughout a wide temperature range; however, embryology and larval development are strongly determined by water temperature.

Temperature control in isolated broodstock tanks is best maintained by high-quality submersible heaters. In a central water system, it is a good idea to place two or more heaters in the sump in case one fails. In a dedicated breeding room, it is often more efficient to heat the room rather than each individual aquarium or system. In this way all the water in the room is maintained at the same temperature, making egg and water transfers physiologically less taxing.

It is advisable to keep detailed records of temperature fluctuations occurring in the spawning aquariums. Daily records often reveal possible temperature influences or problems associated with spawning. If you are experimenting with different temperatures in different, isolated tanks, an individual heater will be needed for each tank, with the room kept at a base temperature of around 76°F.

OXYGEN

Dissolved oxygen levels are extremely important in broodstock systems and in rearing vessels. Not only does the broodstock require oxygen to remain alive and healthy, but the beneficial nitrifying bacteria present on filter media and most surfaces within the aquarium also utilize oxygen to carry on their all-important functions of nitrification (the breakdown of waste products). Within the confines of broodstock aquariums, a lot of food is added to facilitate spawning. If a sufficient population of nitrifying bacteria is not present or the level of dissolved oxygen is low, the organic matter will not be broken down quickly, leading to the deterioration of aquarium water and stress to the inhabitants.

During every aspect of the reproductive cycle, the energy needs and metabolism of the broodstock is very high, making it of utmost importance to maintain high levels of dissolved oxygen. Often, the conditioning of broodstock creates a stressful environment. When dissolved oxygen levels are low, the fish will likely exhibit an increased respiratory rate most often accompanied by clamped fins. The water may be yellowish from the high levels of dissolved organic waste present. A partial water change is one immediate corrective action you can take. The addition of fresh saltwater will increase dissolved oxygen levels, allowing nitrification to continue the breakdown of the organic waste. This is, however, only a short-term solution.

Dissolved oxygen is important for more than respiration and nitrification. Many aquarists have heard the term redox or oxygen reduction potential, a measurement of the ability of water to break down waste molecules. Keeping redox high (as measured by an electronic redox meter) insures that waste molecules are broken down rapidly and not allowed to accumulate.

Long-term solutions to correcting low dissolved oxygen or redox levels are easily applied to most broodstock aquariums. The simplest method is fitting the tank with a small internal powerhead or airstone. The powerhead will help circulate the water and with the venturi valve open slightly, create a stream of fine bubbles and be very efficient in maintaining the desired level of dissolved oxygen. A protein skimmer will also help increase oxygen levels.

Oxygenation is especially important for a central filtration system. Water from the sump is pumped into the broodstock aquariums through a labyrinth of pipes and valves. Most aquarists place the inlet below the water sur-

Pristine conditions over a coral garden in Australia's Great Barrier Reef: crystal-clear water, low in dissolved wastes, well-oxygenated and with stable temperature, salinity, and day length—nature's model for ideal marine breeding and rearing aquariums.

face but this allows little surface agitation and subsequently little gas exchange occurs in the individual aquariums. It is best to keep the inlet a few inches above the water surface. One easy way to help with oxygenation is to heat the end of the PVC return line with a heat gun, and then clamp it in a vice. Once the PVC has cooled, it is an effective spray nozzle. Salt spray is a lot more apparent in this case, but gas exchange will be improved.

Dissolved oxygen levels in an isolated broodstock tank fitted with an external power filter can be maintained by keeping the water level one inch below the water return. In this way gas exchange and oxygen saturation are increased by the action of falling water breaking the surface. A canister filter attached to a spray bar is another fine al-

ternative. Rearing aquariums have a similar demand for high levels of dissolved oxygen. The method for maintaining dissolved oxygen depends greatly on the juveniles' size and stage of development. Multiple airstones are the best choice for rearing aquariums with juveniles less than an inch or so long. (Powerheads create a strong current that wears out young fish and limits the swimming space available to them.)

Testing dissolved oxygen levels can be difficult and expensive. The most reliable method for testing oxygen levels is to provide good circulation and observe your fish. Healthy fish with good appetites, good color, fully erect fins, and a feisty attitude, without increased respiratory rates are swimming in an oxygen-rich environment.

Lined Seahorse (*Hippocampus erectus*) snapping food from the fingers of its owner, reef aquarium authority Julian Sprung. Hand-feeding of broodstock is advocated by some marine fish breeders.

CHAPTER 5

CONDITIONING BROODSTOCK

Nutrition & Foods to Trigger Spawning

In becoming a breeder of marine fishes, you may need to leave your old feeding habits behind along with those stale cans of flake and cheap frozen brine shrimp. Getting broodstock fit and in the mood to reproduce requires much more attention to foods and feeding than simply maintaining a community marine aquarium.

Not only do broodstock need surplus energy to produce healthy eggs and sperm, they may be reluctant to spawn unless they are given a diet that manages to replicate or nutritionally replace the things they favor back on the coral reef. For the purpose of spawning marine fishes, think fresh and of their wild environment.

The natural diet of a marine fish in nature may be highly specialized or quite broad. The choice of food organisms it consumes in the wild reflects the life habits of its species and the niche it fills in the reef ecosystem. These specific food organisms supply all nutritional requirements necessary for proper physical health and reproductive success.

All-purpose fish food preparations do not always meet the needs of our broodstock. To allow hobbyists to keep a diverse group of fish in the same aquarium, many aquarium food manufacturers have added a variety of ingredients, vitamins and minerals to their foods to suit the requirements of many species instead of targeting the diet of just one. (The cheaper brands also use cereal fillers that have no place in the diet of a marine fish.)

For the marine fish breeder, it is essential that the minimum dietary requirements be met for each species maintained. As your spawning and rearing successes grow, many hungry mouths will follow with the same dietary demands as the broodstock. It is, therefore, important to know what kind and the correct amounts of foods and supplements will produce a healthy fish that is eager to breed and produce quality offspring exhibiting vigor and brilliant coloration.

If broodstock is supplied with poor quality food, spawning often becomes irregular and the resulting eggs often fail to develop. Offspring typically suffer high mortality, and those that survive are of poor quality. When fed the appropriate foods in the proper amounts, broodstock remain healthy and willing to spawn on a reliable cycle, producing viable eggs with superior survival rates. The young will also exhibit the desirable traits that make the species marketable.

Fish with very broad feeding habits are much more apt to eat anything offered in captivity and their dietary requirements are easier to meet. It is a bit trickier to elicit a feeding reaction in specialized feeders and also to supply them with the proper nutrition. In fact, most species of marine fish bred in captivity thus far have been broad feeders. Their daily nutritional needs are easily met and these bold feeders greedily devour all food placed in the aquarium, fueling their metabolism and aiding in egg production.

In the wild, fishes have evolved myriad feeding schemes. Predators such as groupers, barracudas, lizardfish, and scorpionfish are used to eating one large meal every so often. They are opportunistic feeders ingesting large amounts of food when available, with the time of their next meal not guaranteed. Most fish, however, are adapted to a slow, continuous feeding pattern. Herbivores, omnivores, and planktivores eat continuously throughout the daylight hours. Surgeonfish rasp the algae off rocks, while basslets and anthias pick tiny zooplankton prey from the water column.

In the wild, these fishes usually have no shortage of food, and as spawning season approaches they are able to cope with the increased energy demands required for egg production and spawning by eating more. In captivity, the fish rely on their keeper to fulfill their dietary requirements by giving them the proper amounts and types of food at the right time of day.

One or two large meals a day is generally not a good feeding regimen to breed marine fish. Instead, several smaller feedings spread out throughout the day are better, as this will allow the fish to digest the food slowly and allow more energy to remain within their bodies.

Few species of fish on the reef can be categorized as strict carnivores or herbivores. Furthermore, the foods chosen may vary with the season. When available in high densities, single target organisms or food items may make up the bulk of their diet. When this food source is no longer available, the fish will resort to feeding on various substitute fare including algae.

As fish mature, feeding habits change. During the pelagic larval stage virtually all species are carnivores, feeding on plankton. After metamorphosis, when juveniles settle to the benthic reef structure, their diets shift and they start exhibiting the feeding habits of their particular species.

The more at home we can make captive broodstock feel, the more apt they will be to spawn.

A varied diet is essential. There are many choices of seafoods and other appropriate food items available in fresh, live and frozen forms from your local seafood or supermarket. These can be chopped and fed as is or mixed in a blender with other seafoods and enrichments. In this chapter we will examine some of these foods and the benefits of each.

PROTEINS & CARBOHYDRATES

The natural diet of marine fishes provides them with the essential nutrients, vitamins, minerals and trace elements needed for daily metabolic and reproductive activity. Although it is difficult to provide natural prey to fish living in captivity, it is possible to mirror the nutritional constituents of natural prey.

Perhaps the most important of these nutrients is protein. Unlike carbohydrates and fats, protein cannot be stored in any appreciable amounts within a fish's body; it must be ingested continuously. Protein contains essential amino acids required to build cells. While plants are able to synthesize amino acids from available raw material, fish cannot. A deficiency in protein leads to many symptoms,

 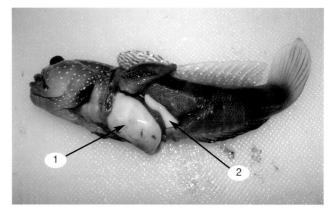

Overfeeding of fatty foods such as squid can lead to serious broodstock problems, as seen in this female Yellow Shrimp Goby (*Cryptocentrus cinctus*). Its swollen abdomen was not an indication of ripening ovaries, but rather a fatally swollen liver (right, arrow 1). Dissection also revealed that the fish's ovaries (arrow 2) were not developing on its rich but unbalanced diet.

eventually ending in death. High-quality protein appropriate for our purposes is found in marine fish flesh. Fish meals and crustacean meals are also good sources of protein, as are polychaete worms. Adult fishes typically require 25 to 50 percent protein in their diets. (Too much protein in the diet is wasted, as protein cannot be stored and excess is secreted.)

Carbohydrates and fats, while not required in high amounts to sustain physiological activity, are associated with foods high in vitamins and minerals and thus find their way into a fish's diet. When ingested to excess, these elements are stored as deposited fat. Too much deposited fat, however, can lead to severe disorders that stress the fish, reducing reproductive capabilities and over time causing degeneration of internal organs such as the liver. Fat deposits can build up in unhealthy proportions and eventually fill the body cavity putting much pressure on internal organs.

Considerable differences exist between the species and age classes as to how much fat can be assimilated without harm. Juvenile fishes utilize most excess carbohydrates and fats during the increased growth period. Very little is deposited as fat. Adult fish grow very little and instead store excess energy as fat. No literature exists to pinpoint the exact amount of carbohydrates and fats essential to the diet of marine ornamentals. In captivity, a varied diet eliminates worries of overfeeding fats. White worms, if used, should be limited and fed sparingly as a conditioning diet only.

FATTY ACIDS

Lipids are fatty substances, some of which are absolutely essential to the health of marine fishes and their progeny. Fatty acids, in particular, are of great interest to marine breeders. Omega-3 fatty acids, commonly known as *highly unsaturated fatty acids (HUFA)*, are essential in the diet of marine fishes. Of special importance to marine aquarists are two of these omega-3 fatty acids, EPA (eicosapentaenoic acid) and DHA (docosahexaenoic acid), with DHA proving to be more essential.

Lipid requirements have been analyzed for many marine species raised for human consumption. Generalized lipid requirements range from 10 to 20 percent of the total diet for larval marine fishes, while adults require roughly half the amount of larvae and juveniles. Together with protein, lipid intake represents a highly essential component of the conditioning diet. However, the balance of proteins and lipids must not be ignored. A diet containing too much lipid material will dampen the appetite of the fish as their caloric re-

Newly hatched brine shrimp are known as *Artemia* nauplii and are a nutritious food for occasional feeding to small species.

quirements are too quickly met. If this occurs, the fish will not ingest adequate protein for proper growth.

It is not essential to cater a breeding menu containing an exact percentage of lipids and proteins, but we must be aware of the importance of balance in the diet. Very little data exists as to the dietary requirements of any representative of the Pseudochromidae, Gobiidae, Pomacentridae or other commercially important ornamental families, and it will probably be some time before such data is available. Cod liver oil and other marine fish oils contain high fatty acid levels and are often used as supplements in gelatin mixes. So-called HUFA supplements are also available to pre-soak fresh or frozen foods before feeding. Frozen squid and krill both contain high levels of EPA and DHA. When shaved from a frozen block by means of a cheese grater, they offer an excellent supplement to the diet.

Lipids are short-lived compounds that are prone to ox-

idation. (Think of the bottle of rancid cooking oil in the back of the cupboard. Not only are spoiled fats unpalatable, but rancid foods can be harmful to fish that eat them.) The shelf life of such supplements is no more than a few months. Diets high in lipids are difficult to prepare and store, as the lipids are oxidized within a short time. For this reason, commercial dry fish foods often contain low levels of lipids. Fish oils and HUFA supplements are the ideal way to provide lipids in the diet of captive marine fishes.

VITAMINS, MINERALS & TRACE ELEMENTS

We will not attempt to discuss every vitamin, mineral and trace element required in the diet of marine aquarium fish. Studies targeting such dietary requirements have focused primarily on commercially important freshwater species such as salmon and trout. Marine aquarium fish breeders will certainly experiment with nutritional supplements, and some may prove very useful in the coming years.

Vitamins act as catalysts to initiate nutritional processes within the digestive tract. Manufacturers of prepared dry fish foods regularly incorporate vitamins and trace elements into their feeds, but live foods and fresh and frozen seafoods all contain these essential elements in the proportions found in nature. No single food will offer a complete set of these elements, but a well-balanced diet will provide sufficient quantities.

For the home-based fish breeder, I think it is best to rely on a varied diet of quality natural foods rather than supplementing with pure forms of vitamins and trace elements. It is far too easy to overdose a given dietary element, often with negative results. Too much of the fat-soluble vitamins A and D, for example, can retard growth and cause spine abnormalities. We will discuss more of the nutritional requirements of young fish in the chapters on larval rearing and grow-out of juveniles.

The efficacy of vitamins, minerals and trace elements in dry rations decreases rapidly after the packaging has been opened and the food exposed to air. Once opened, any dry foods you are using should be closed tightly after each use and preferably stored in a refrigerator. Whenever possible, buy in smaller quantities that will be used quickly, before oxidation takes its toll. Avoid fish foods sold in open bulk containers.

ROUGHAGE

Roughage has very little, if any, nutritional value to fish; however, like the fiber in human diets, it is vital to proper digestion. Roughage in the diet of marine aquarium fish is provided by the chitinous exoskeleton of crabs, shrimp and zooplankton. Cellulose is another important source of roughage provided indirectly through the ingestion and digestion of prey organisms. Cellulose is found in plant matter such as micro and macroalgae, which is consumed by grazing fishes as well as by their zooplankton and crustacean prey. A lack of roughage in the diet can lead to digestive disorders and malnutrition. Chiton and cellulose in the gut help grind food mechanically, preparing it for absorption in the intestine.

LIVE FOODS

Living organisms are the ideal food source for captive fishes. Fish are well adapted for life in water and have evolved elaborate systems of survival. Live food triggers a more vigorous feeding response in most fish. Add a netful of squirming, live adult brine shrimp to a tank of marine fish and watch the results.

Olfactory senses may contribute to the instinctive behaviors elicited by live foods, as may the fish's exquisitely sensitive lateral line and other vibration-sensing organs. Live foods, with their tempting odors and movements, seem to arouse a fish's senses much more than prepared, lifeless foods. As a result, the fish is likely to consume more, a precondition to reproductive success as it builds needed energy reserves.

The most appropriate foods for many marine fishes— live shrimp, crabs, polychaete worms and the like—may be difficult for most of us to supply on a daily basis, but there are many forms of living organisms that may prove useful in the diet of marine aquarium fishes.

Bloodworms (midge larvae, *Chironomus* sp.), black worms (*Tubifex* sp.), glassworms (phantom midge larvae, *Chaoboris* sp.), white worms (*Enchytraeus* sp.) and mosquito larvae are all available sources of nutrition used by freshwater aquarists but rarely thought of for marine species. These live foods do not originate from marine sources and will not survive in saline environments for long. If not consumed within several minutes they will perish and must be removed.

BLACK WORMS

There are two species of worms available in the fish trade and commonly referred to as black worms. For the purpose of feeding marine fish, I will refer to both species as one. Black worms are perhaps the one organism responsible for so much bad publicity about live foods for aquarium feeding. These worms originate from slow-moving freshwater environments rich in organic matter, usually found in high densities in the mud bottom. Pathogens and bacteria can be found in great numbers in the stomach and intestine of these worms that are often found in very polluted environments. For this reason, few aquarists rely on them as food items and some curse them. In the past I attributed much of my success to these worms. When the proper precautions are taken, black worms offer much nutritional value to spawning fish.

Although not fully studied, black worms seem to contain many enzymes and hormones that seem beneficial to spawning fish. In many freshwater fish species, black worms are widely credited with helping trigger the fish to spawn. The enzymes and other bio-chemicals in these worms are broken down soon after the worms die, and frozen and freeze-dried forms will not contain appreciable amounts.

The best approach to feeding black worms is to use them as a conditioning food to induce a first spawn. In the past I relied on these worms to build up the metabolism required to create eggs and induce a first spawn in reluctant species such as grammas and some dottybacks. Male dottybacks are often extremely aggressive towards females that are not receptive. By feeding live black worms several times a day for a few weeks, you can help the females build up eggs rather quickly and they will usually begin spawning in less than a month. If the female shows no sign of spawning or has not spawned before, the male may eventually kill her. The sooner the female fills with ripe eggs and spawns, the better off she will be. Once a first spawn has taken place, aggression is generally lessened and the pair's reproductive cycle becomes reliable. I would discontinue the feeding of black worms after a first spawn is observed.

Since these worms can carry pathogens and bacteria that have been known to cause systemic bacterial infections in fishes, extreme care must be taken to ensure that the worms are clean before they are fed. When they are stored in the aquarium shop, they are often exposed to poor water quality and poor handling. The worms should be properly cleaned for a week prior to using them as food. Black worms are best stored in a shallow dish of water in the refrigerator. The worms must be kept cold or they will perish.

The worms must be rinsed in fresh running water at least once a day and preferably more often. The more times the worms are rinsed, the less chance they will have of transmitting pathogens to fish. The water in which the worms are stored will turn brown and murky in no time if the worms are of poor quality. After a week of cold conditions and daily rinses, the water around them should be clear. At least one manufacturer has made a container to both store and clean the black worms. (*See Sources.*) The contraption is quite simple. A plastic box with the bottom removed is covered with a screen that will not allow the worms to pass through. This box then fits neatly into another plastic box that is waterproof. The inner box containing the worms is lifted out and rinsed under cool running water. The old water in the lower box is replaced with freshwater and the worms again put into the refrigerator. A black worm unit can be built quite simply with PVC pipe and some fine-mesh screening. Four-inch PVC pipe is cut in half and then glued together with a piece of micron mesh or silkscreen inserted between the pieces of pipe. This is then placed in a plastic dish and stored in the same manner as the previous container. This cuts down on maintenance time considerably. There is no need to feed the worms and more problems will be encountered if feeding is attempted.

Black worms should be fed sparingly and slowly introduced to the tank. Let the fish eat them up and then add a few more. Because the worms originate in fresh water, they make a lot of commotion when they enter the saltwater. This triggers the feeding response of the fish. It may take some time, however, for the fish to get used to the worms and some may never accept them. Many fish will not eat the worms once they have reached the bottom. If any worms are left uneaten on the bottom, they should be removed as they will soon die and contribute to the bio-load.

WHITE WORMS

White worms, a commonly available live food for fresh water aquarium fishes, can also contribute to the conditioning of non-performing broodstock. They contain unusually high levels of fat and must be fed sparingly. I recommend that their use be limited to that of a conditioning diet for reluctant spawners. Long-term or regular use is not advised. White worms and white worm cultures are available from many good local aquarium stores.

BRINE SHRIMP

Live brine shrimp (*Artemia salina*) is a popular and readily available live food sold by most full-service retail aquarium shops. However, if fed too often *Artemia* can lead to deficiencies. As much as fish love them, adult *Artemia* alone are a poor food, offering little more than roughage. To boost the nutritional value of this food, the shrimp must be fed with microalgae or soaked in an appropriate vitamin mix or an enrichment supplement such as Culture Selco, popular in commercial aquaculture. (*See Sources.*) Newly hatched *Artemia* (baby brine shrimp or *Artemia* nauplii)

Feeding adult brine shrimp to a female Mimic Blenny. Close interaction between keeper and broodstock is important.

are a rich source of protein, fats, vitamins and minerals, although few adult fishes will consume such small prey. The smaller species of clownfish, gobies and some dottybacks benefit greatly from this occasional offering.

LIVE FEEDER FISHES

The feeder fish available at local aquarium shops are usually either goldfish, guppies or rosy reds (bait minnows). The problem with these freshwater offerings is that the amino acids differ significantly from those of marine prey and if fed continuously for any length of time will result in

ill effects for marine fish. Goldfish flesh, for example, contains an enzyme (thiaminase) that causes the breakdown of thiamin.

Thiamin deficiencies and fatty degeneration are avoided by feeding a varied diet of foods originating from marine environments. Lionfish are especially prone to problems, and a steady diet of live freshwater fish will eventually kill them. If large predatory fish are your intended spawning subjects, live fishes of marine origin such as killifish or frozen marine baitfish such as silversides and shrimp are the best choices. Freshwater fishes can be used on occasion to elicit spawning behavior, but their use should be restricted. Fry from livebearers and other small fishes are a valuable food for some fishes such as comets, grammas and large dottybacks.

Marine fish that are accustomed to eating live fishes are best trained to eat frozen feeder fish such as silversides or shreds from fresh fillets of ocean fish bought at a local market. When this feeding regimen is undertaken, the table fish flesh is easily enriched with vitamins and minerals that will give the spawning fish all the essential nutrition they need.

ZOOPLANKTON

This is another live food available to hobbyists living near the seashore. Plankton nets are available in numerous sizes, varying in the size of the net as well as the fineness of the mesh. For feeding adult fish that feed on plankton in the wild, a net fashioned with 500-micron mesh is ideal. The organisms that make up the zooplankton are tremendously diverse and vary with the season. Copepods are always present, although the species may differ. Mollusk, crustacean, and fish larvae are present at various times of the year, and all make fine fish foods. It would be impossible to list all the organisms that may be caught in plankton nets. I have come across some truly unique organisms and some food items I would have never thought of offering before. During the winter in Long Island, I caught small jellyfish that were no larger than $1/4$-inch. A few of these jellyfish accidentally made it into a tank with the copepods I was feeding to a pair

Plankton towing from shore in the Indian River Lagoon in Florida: coastal residents can tap local resources of wild live foods.

of Clark's Clownfish (*Amphiprion clarkii*). To my amazement, the jellyfish were the first organisms eaten. I caught some more and fed the pair of clownfish the jellyfish for a couple of months until the organism was no longer present in the plankton. I've learned that clownfish and dottybacks are extremely active in hunting these organisms in the water column. I have spawned clownfish using nothing but wild plankton as food and find that, by offering them this food, egg quality was increased.

A series of plankton sieves should be made to size-sort the plankton. One made from fiberglass window screen removes the large debris such as macroalgae and sea grass as well as jellyfish and mysid shrimp. The rest of the water can be poured through a 500-micron mesh to get rid of organisms that are too small. Small organisms not suited to feeding adult fish may be acceptable as food for larval fish.

Wild plankton bring inherent risks. Along with beneficial and highly nutritious food organisms such as copepods, there are undesirable organisms found in plankton samples. Parasitic isopods and copepods are often present, as are ciliates and other pathogens. Caution should be used whenever dealing with live foods of marine origin. You may end up breeding things you never dreamed of.

OTHER LIVE FOODS

Live clams, mussels and oysters are readily available at most supermarkets. When these bivalves are broken apart they make an ideal food for larger species, and are particularly favored by large dottybacks. These soft-fleshed foods can be frozen and shaved into smaller morsels to make them acceptable to smaller species.

Live earthworms make a good supplement, being high in protein and vitamin D. Small red garden worms are the best choice as they can easily be cut into smaller morsels. Killifish are often sold in bait shops near coastlines and can easily be caught in plastic minnow traps in estuaries and bays along the coast. These live foods are limited in their application to larger species. They are acceptable to smaller members of the group when shaved into smaller pieces.

For the hobbyist living near the seaboard, mysid shrimp offer a great conditioning food that usually are only available live seasonally but can be frozen and fed throughout the year. Mysid shrimp can be found elsewhere along the coast, but are usually scattered around deep structures. Off Long Island, for instance, mysid shrimp begin to appear in massive breeding congregations beginning in mid-December. They reach their highest densities in January and February and remain in the water column until early April. Large swarms of these shrimp can be seen a couple of feet below the surface of the water. If a large dip net with a long handle is used, a 5-gallon bucket can be filled with them rather quickly. The shrimp should be maintained alive as long as possible by separating them rather sparsely into 5-gallon buckets with an airstone for circulation and aeration. They should be placed in the basement or in the garage where the temperature remains cold. These shrimp are available in a frozen form, but live mysids far surpass the frozen form.

Fresh & Frozen Seafood

Perhaps the most convenient and acceptable foods available are those found in local seafood markets or supermarkets. Frozen foods are easily prepared and stored and have the advantage of being perfect for mixing with a flavorless gelatin binding agent and vitamin supplements and frozen for later use. Fresh seafoods can be used as isolated feeds or mixed with other seafoods to create a regular diet.

Different and acceptable seafoods abound in local markets. Fresh or frozen table shrimp are available in virtually all markets. Most of the species offered are aquacultured in shrimp farms throughout the world. The most common shrimp found in local seafood markets are genera *Panneaus* and *Pandalus*. While panneaid shrimp are generally raised in aquaculture facilities, pandalus are smaller and usually caught off the coast of Maine and other northern states. Both

make excellent foods. Mollusks such as clams, mussels and oysters are acceptable. Squid, marine fish flesh, crab and shellfish are choices more readily available. Squid is an excellent addition to the diet as it contains high levels of lipids. When squid is fed in excess, however, fish develop fatty livers and appear swollen, ruining any potential to spawn.

Preparation is usually facilitated by freezing. Once frozen these foods can be shaved into appropriately sized morsels with a cheese grater and stored in plastic bags. Some aquarists shave the seafoods into appropriate sizes and freeze them separately. Others mix the shaved portions of several types of seafood together; add a multivitamin supplement, crumbled seaweed or spirulina and unflavored gelatin to bind it together. When perusing local markets in search of seafood ingredients, be sure they are fresh. Fresh or frozen foods should be chosen over thawed foods, and freshwater species such as catfish, trout and tilapia should be avoided. Rancid ingredients must be avoided. Be sure live clams and other bivalves are closed tightly. In short, take the same precautions you would when shopping for a family meal. A diet containing only raw seafoods has been linked to thiamin deficiencies in marine fishes. It is important to offer a diversity of foods to ensure proper nutrition.

Commercial Dry Diets

Pellets, flake and freeze-dried foods are readily available on the shelves of most aquarium shops. While the best of these diets do contain a good balance of nutrients, the sole use of dry food is unlikely to produce the necessary metabolic reserves needed for spawning and will adversely effect larval survival. Their use should be limited to rare occasions. Occasional additions of *Spirulina* (a genus of nutritious green cyanobacteria grown in freshwater) to the broodstock diet are welcomed.

It is important to keep all dry foods refrigerated to prevent rancidity. Vitamins and nutrients present in the mix quickly oxidize and break down when kept near the temperatures and humidity of a fish room. Vitamin C is especially important for growth, but its efficacy is limited when stored at high temperatures and humidity.

CAROTENOIDS

Marine fishes found on the reef exhibit some of the most astounding colors imaginable, often in truly intricate patterns. In captivity, these vibrant colors often fade into dull shades that do not catch the eye. A lack of color-enhancing pigments called carotenoids in the diet is often the cause of captive color loss.

Carotenoids are manufactured at the base of the oceans food web in microalgae. This food web continually becomes more intricate with copepods and other fauna ingesting the microalgae and thus accumulating carotenoids. Fishes found on the reef therefore have ready access to these color pigments and their colors are all the brighter for it. In captivity, the food chain is typically initiated in a manufacturing plant and lacks many color-enhancing pigments necessary for many species to retain their full color potential. An ideal example is the Diadem Dottyback (*Pictichromis diadema).* This species is normally brilliant yellow with an eyecatching magenta stripe along the dorsal region. In captivity, the colors of this fish often fade to dullness. The Yellow Tang (*Zebrasoma flavescens*) is another common example of a fish that can lose its beautiful color on an nonenriched aquarium diet.

Foods naturally rich in carotenoids include krill, young *Artemia*, fish and crustacean roe, *Spirulina* and nori (seaweed used in sushi making) although the pigments found in each are generally limited in the spectrum they enhance. Many specialty flakes and pellets have been developed with added carotenoid pigments to enhance the color of adult fish.

The vast majority of fishes are supplied enough carotenoid pigments in the conditioning diet they are offered. Pink, red and orange are common pigments in most food items. Yellow pigments can be difficult to find in any real quantities. Seaweeds are the best counter measure to keep yellow coloration bright.

It has been demonstrated that the red carotenoid pig-ment astaxanthin protects fish eggs from UV radiation, improves growth rates, aids in respiration and vision and acts as a precursor for vitamin A. It is probable that other carotenoid pigments play crucial roles in the overall physiology of fishes. Broodstock pairs are easily satisfied, while post-metamorphosis juveniles are more noticeably affected by a lack of carotenoids in the diet.

SUMMARY OF BROODSTOCK FEEDING

Any discussion of nutrition can be confusing to newcomers (and fraught with controversy among aquaculture veterans). HUFAs, DHA and EPA are terms few aquarists are comfortable with and for some they are just as mysterious as scientific names.

To keep things simple, the conditioning diet of marine species has two important considerations, quantity and quality. Broodstock should be fed several times per day with a varied diet. By offering several different foods throughout the day, chances are good that their dietary requirements will be met. Using a mix of live, fresh, frozen, and enriched commercially prepared offerings provides assurance that the fish are receiving all their essential dietary needs. Without knowing all the dietary science, it is still very possible to maintain and raise marine ornamentals in captivity, just vary the diet as much as you can.

FRESH SEAFOOD RECIPE

Perhaps the easiest of all foods to feed, is one that is made from a variety of highly nutritious ingredients and vitamins in a ready-to-use form kept in the freezer. This eliminates the need for cleaning the guts of earthworms or cutting off the armored rostrum of shrimp heads before each feeding. Local seafood markets and supermarkets offer many forms of seafood that should make up the bulk of a broodstock diet. When mixed together in a blender with vitamins and finally bound together with gelatin, this food offers an easy-to-feed highly nutritious mainstay ration. It is a balanced, highly nutritious diet that I have used for some years, and

Marine fish and seafoods are a mainstay of conditioning diets and have the right balance of nutrients needed by saltwater fishes. Items from a seafood counter can be frozen and grated to bite-size pieces for feeding or mixing.

This recipe can be used to maintain, condition and spawn marine fish in captivity. Measurements can be varied, and there is always room for experimentation and improvement.

I prefer to shave each frozen ingredient separately into appropriate-size morsels with a cheese grater (if frozen) or food processor if fresh or thawed. The bite-size ingredients are then added together in a large bowl and mixed evenly. The gelatin should be dissolved as recommended on the package and added to the mash. I place the mash into sealable plastic bags and freeze them flat. In this way small pieces are easily broken off for individual feedings.

4 ounces fresh frozen shrimp	1 ounce marine fish flesh
1 ounce squid	½ ounce nori or other seaweed
1 ounce clam	1 gelatin packet (unflavored)
1 ounce crab meat	1 teaspoon liquid fish vitamin supplement

it is sure to get the fish to spawn. The benefit to this food is that it is economical and can be manipulated to meet the needs of different species of fish by adding different ingredients. Also, when you are breeding marine fish, much food will be required if you end up with many pairs and many offspring. Large quantities are easily stored for months.

A trip to the supermarket will reveal many possible ingredients. It is best to add at least three choices of seafood and preferably more. This will offer the spawning fish a variety of nutrients in a small portion. Fresh-frozen shrimp, squid, clam, scallop, lobster, crab, and fish are all choices. Every hobbyist that prepares this food mixes it differently, and there is no concrete rule of how much of one thing to add.

For me, shrimp makes up the bulk of the mixture with clam, scallop, squid, and crab all added in varying amounts along with fresh sea lettuce (*Ulva lactuca*) or pulverized nori, *Spirulina* and a dry powder or liquid vitamin supplement. Many aquarists often add cod liver oil as a source of lipids. If squid is added to the diet, cod liver oil should not be used. Squid should never account for more than 25 percent of the total weight, as an excess of squid often leads to dietary dysfunctions.

Follow the directions on a package of clear, unflavored gelatin. Each ingredient should be finely grated and kept separate until mixing and preparation commences. A blender or mixer should be used to evenly mix all ingredients. It is best to dedicate a cheap or used blender for this purpose so fights among family members do not arise.

The basic process of making gelatin is simple. Heat water to 150 or 200°F, stir in the gelatin until it dissolves in a glass container. When the temperature falls to below 150°F, or according to specific instructions on the gelatin package, the liquid should be poured over the seafood paste and stirred until the seafood is evenly distributed throughout the mixture.

While stirring the seafood into the liquid gelatin, vitamins can be added. A multivitamin tablet can be ground up with a mortar and pestle and stirred into the mixture. Better yet, a liquid vitamin supplement formulated for ma-

Broodstock pair of Banggai Cardinals, larger male at right. Constant production of healthy eggs demands good nutrition.

rine fishes such as Selcon, Vita-Chem or Kent's Zoe Marine can be be used. The choice of vitamin supplements marketed to aquarists is growing, and you might also choose to experiment with adding individual vitamins to your rations. Vitamin E is a lipid that has been correlated to aid in hatching success. Vitamin C should be added in higher concentrations when a ration is being used to grow juvenile fishes. When the juveniles are fed foods fortified with vitamin C, they grow much faster. Bone meal can be added as a source of calcium and phosphorous. Color-enhancing supplements can also be mixed in. A little food coloring at this point will help the fish locate the mixture and also help the hobbyist find any uneaten morsels.

The mix should then be poured into a shallow tray and allowed to chill until set. The mixture is then cut into small blocks and separated into the refrigerator and freezer. The bulk of the mixture should be stored in the freezer with a few blocks stored in the refrigerator to be used in the next couple of days. The gelatin blocks can be cut with a sharp knife or razor blade or grated into bite-sized morsels and fed to the fish.

Often, I mix gelatin diets in a large bowl or bucket. After the gelatin mix is added and all ingredients incorporated, the mix is separated into sealable plastic bags and pressed thin, then stored in the freezer for later use. A chunk is broken off at each feeding and grated or allowed to thaw and broken into small pieces by rolling the mash by hand.

This recipe is infinitely adaptable. Some breeders create gel rations using just one seafood at a time and make only small batches. On alternating days, fresh shrimp, scallop, squid and clams along with live foods and flakes can be fed as a conditioning food. This is a little more work, but has the advantage of offering fresher offerings by purchasing smaller quantities of fresh seafood more often. The foods I have mentioned are my favorites, but many other choices of broodstock foods and ingredients abound. (You might even try using vegetarian gelatin, made of agar and available at health food stores.)

The next consideration is the amount to feed. The answer put simply: lots. Spawning fish in the wild require large amounts of food, and the natural feeding mode should be duplicated in captivity. All the fish I have ever maintained for the purpose of breeding have received no less than three meals a day. The size of the portion may vary, but they always get food several times daily. Broodstock should be fed as much as they will eat in several minutes. I know of many successful marine fish breeders who feed their fish only once or twice daily with good results, but I have found that broodstock fed three or four times daily spawn much sooner and more regularly.

Since there will be a greater output of waste, water quality must be maintained through vigorous filtration and frequent water changes. Any uneaten foods should be siphoned out before the next feeding..

GOOD DIET - HEALTHY SPAWNS

There is a direct correlation between the foods eaten by broodstock fish and the quality of their resulting spawns. Often poor larval growth, abnormalities and mortality can be attributed to poor broodstock diet. Over the past many years, I have witnessed the effects of various diets on both broodstock fish and their progeny. A varied diet is absolutely pivotal to successful spawning and rearing.

If broodstock fishes are not supplied with adequate rations of quality foods, receiving vital marine-source protein, lipids, minerals, and other nutritional elements, eggs fail to develop, develop with undersized yolks, do not hatch, and experience high percentages of deformities. The effect of poor diet varies widely between families and species, but the effects are very obvious within same-species spawns.

When fed a diet consisting exclusively of frozen, vitamin-enriched *Artemia*, pseudochromids produce eggs that fail to develop. This is, in essence, sterility. During an experimental trial, several pairs of Neon Dottybacks (*P. aldabraensis*), Orchid Dottybacks (*P. fridmani*) and Springer's Dottybacks (*P. springeri*) were fed a varied diet consisting mainly of freshly grated shrimp and squid with occasional fish roe and blackworms added to the diet. Spawns were robust, development was good, and the resulting larval survival was excellent.

The same broodstock pairs were then switched to one of two diets; exclusively vitamin-enriched adult brine shrimp or 50 percent vitamin-enriched *Artemia* and 50 percent grated table shrimp. Spawns from broodstock fed the *Artemia*-only diet produced sterile egg masses, greatly undersized and of ill form. Adhesive threads were underdeveloped and egg masses fell apart. Those fish fed *Artemia* and grated shrimp in equal amounts produced egg masses that were slightly better, but far inferior to those fed a varied diet. Egg development was poor and hatching was greatly reduced. Survival in these spawns was very low (less than 10 percent) with most larvae expiring before day six.

Spawning cycles are also interrupted by poor dietary conditions. The average spawning cycle of dottybacks is seven days but increases to nine and often 14 when fed poor quality foods. Clownfish and gobies suffer similarly, although usually not as noticeably, due to the advanced state of hatching larvae.

With the advent of new culture protocols for species being bred in captivity for the first time, dietary needs will require serious study and experimentation. Food, as we humans say, is life. For marine broodstock this simple fact cannot be forgotten.

Female of a pair of Blackbarred Convict Gobies (*Priolepsis nocturna*), a rare, beautiful species that the author found to be a ready spawner in captivity.

CHAPTER 6

SPAWNING

Courtship & Egg Production

Coral reef fishes have evolved many different and often fascinating survival behaviors to help them breed successfully in a very competitive, predator-filled ecosystem. Some of the tactics they use in courtship are quite rudimentary while others are more elaborate, but is has proved effective over many millenia. Since a majority of marine aquarium fish are small and reef-associated, promiscuous spawning is especially common. Exaggerated courtship rituals take place near the male's home territory. A simple game of "follow-the-leader" is all that many species exhibit.

For example, Red Sea pseudochromids such as the Orchid Dottyback (*Pseudochromis fridmani)* and Sankey's or the Striped Dottyback (*P. sankeyi)* are well known for their distinctive and comical courtship rituals. An adult male takes residence in a spawning cave, usually a tight hole in the rocky substrate, and darts out towards any passing female. He abruptly stops, facing her and hovering for a few short seconds, turns away and then slinks seductively back into his cave. He droops the rear portion of his body and quivers and shakes the whole way back to the dark spawning chamber. He repeats this ritual, often numerous times and with increasing urgency, until the female follows or moves away.

The Neon Dottyback (*Pseudochromis aldabraensis*) and Springer's Dottyback (*P. springeri*) shorten this version of courtship. Males approach ready females at a perpendicular angle. Typically, the male rests his body on the bottom and spreads his fins and mouth wide, remaining motionless for a few seconds. Males do not droop their body and shimmy; they swim back to the spawning cave in a normal posture. The female often makes up her mind slowly, watching the male repeat his

Male South Seas Devil Damselfish (*Chrysiptera taupou*) enters a flowerpot cave to tend a mass of eggs (arrows).

act over and over until she decides to cooperate with his advances.

The Shorthead Fang Blenny (*Petroscirtes breviceps*) exhibits a similar dance, but it is the female who initiates courtship, swimming back and forth parallel to the entrance of the male's cave. The male rarely leaves the protection of the spawning shelter, and signals his attention by bobbing his head in and out of the shelter in rapid succession. Male gobies whose pelvic fins are fused often use this anatomical adaptation to grasp solid structures. From a stationary platform above the entrance to the spawning cave, the male exhibits exaggerated swimming motions, often violently waving his body from side to side to signal his intentions to a passing female.

The rituals of most demersal spawners are centered around a spawning site. In the case of clownfishes, where both partners occupy the same territory, courtship may be a lengthy display lasting several days before actual egg laying begins. In the wild, this is typically close to the base of the host sea anemone with its protective stinging tentacles.

Pelagic spawners often follow a much more elaborate courtship ritual. Eggs are often shed high in the water col-umn, as the breeding fish often ascend in a spiraling dance toward the surface, consummating the courtship by simul-taneously releasing eggs and sperm to mix in a fertile haze as the fish recover and swim down to the shelter of the reef. Simultaneous hermaphrodites such as hamlets (*Hypoplectrus* spp.) are well known for their ritualistic open-water displays. These fish often act as both sexes during a single spawning bout and thus must distinguish which sex each will act during successive sequences.

In captive broodstock tanks, any behavior that deviates from the day-to-day norm should be noted and carefully observed. Heightened activity is a sure bet that spawning will occur. Cleaning of a spawning shelter, exaggerated swimming, swollen abdomen and protruding genital papilla (a small bumplike tube located just behind the anus in many fish species) usually indicate that spawning is imminent.

SPAWNING ACTS

Actual spawning events of demersal spawners are rarely witnessed by field researchers, as they generally occur deep within the confines of a spawning cave or within crevices created by the reef structure. Species such as damselfishes and many blennies and gobies that deposit eggs on solid surfaces near the top of reef structures are routinely observed courting and spawning in the wild, as are pelagic spawners that dart high above the reef.

Captivity offers a fantastic advantage to observe courtship and spawning activity. Spawning shelters can be situated to allow observation of the behaviors occurring within. Often this means angling a section of PVC pipe or ceramic tile so that the opening or artificial cave is pointed toward the front glass. After a male dottyback has success-fully lured the female into his chamber, the pair position their bodies so their genital pores are in close alignment.

Some hours before the female enters the cave, her abdomen swells as her egg mass is internally pushed rearward. The genital vent pushes down and becomes swollen in preparation for ovoposition. The female begins extruding the egg mass from her ovaries and readies herself for the actual release of eggs. Once inside the cave the female begins extruding the egg mass. This process may take several to many minutes. Males can often be seen waving their bodies against females in what looks like an attempt to quicken the process. Males may leave the spawning site several times during the release of eggs. This is done mainly to drive predators from the territory. If an observer is watching outside the aquarium, males will often charge the glass, hover in mid-water and twitch their bodies in annoyance before darting back to the cave. The male will fertilize the egg mass as it is being extruded. Once the egg mass has been released, the male chases the female away and undertakes his brood-care duties.

Clownfish are easily observed spawning. Once the protrusion of the genital vent is observed, spawning will generally commence within 24 hours. Spawning in many members of the damselfish family (clown or anemonefishes, chromis and damsels or demoiselles) resembles that of freshwater cichlids.

The female slowly pushes the sticky eggs onto a clean hard substrate in a delicate manner and each egg adheres individually. Slowly swimming in circles, the female deposits her eggs in tight, often very neat clusters. After a number of eggs are spawned, the male passes over and fertilizes the eggs. This ritual generally lasts nearly an hour and occurs in early morning or late afternoon.

On a number of occasions, I have seen larger species of dottybacks such as *P. steenei*, *L. cyclophthalmus* and *L. lineatus* pairs opt to spawn on the aquarium floor rather than in a spawning cave. Opting to spawn in the open may be caused by a lack of appropriate spawning shelters in the tank. The egg mass can be clearly observed being extruded from the female's vent, while the male hovers nearby, occasionally nudging the female with his open mouth, almost pushing her. Males of these species often sway their bodies side-to-side, slapping the spawning female. When spawning occurs in the open, the male immediately grabs the extruded egg mass in his mouth and carries it off to be incubated within a cave. During the entire episode, the males seem extremely nervous.

SPAWNING CYCLES

Once a heterosexual pair of reproductive age fish has been established and provided with an adequate diet and some privacy, spawning presents few problems. After a first spawn has taken place, it will become a cyclic event, typically occurring at 6- to 14-day intervals. Most species of pseudochromids are thought to spawn year-round where tropical conditions limit seasonal fluctuations. Those species outside of equatorial latitudes have distinct spawning seasons. Species such as *Pseudochromis fuscus* and *Labracinus lineatus* have wide distributions that extend to slightly subtropical regions where water temperatures seasonally drop to 68°F or below. Spawning in these populations is limited to the warmer water temperatures of summer months. In captivity, the vast majority of marine aquarium fish species require few alterations to environmental factors to initiate spawning. A constant photoperiod simulating long summer days and a warm water temperature are all it takes for some species and pairs.

TRIGGERING SPAWNING ACTIVITY

Captivity can create barricades to normal breeding patterns for any organism caught in the wild and transferred to artificial conditions. For whatever reason—lack of appropriate environmental conditions, poor diet or captive stresses—some fish will fail to initiate final oocyte maturation leading to successful natural spawning. The home marine breeder may have to cope with fish that prove reluctant to spawn in captivity.

In the wild, spawning is often triggered by a variety of environmental cues that usually occur cyclically. In the broodstock aquarium, lights need to be on a 12- to 14-hour cycle every day to mimic bright tropical days in the wild. Similarly, the water must be kept at a constant 78 to 80°F to replicate tropical shallow-water temperatures.

These environmental parameters are, of course, subject to change with individual species. They can, however, be the first environmental factors you might want to manipulate to induce spawning. An increase in the photoperiod from 14 to 16 hours and an increase in water temperature by a few degrees is often all that is needed to trigger spawning. Adjusting light and temperature cycles is easily done by changing the light timer and dialing up the heater thermostat, perhaps doing so over a period of several days or even weeks. As noted elsewhere, live foods may also help provoke spawning instincts.

If these changes fail to work and no spawning takes place, you may need to adjust other parameters after several weeks. Also, if none of the above suggestions has worked individually, you might try several methods simultaneously.

Longer days, higher temperatures and more live food meals can be a powerful combination, as fish often experience all of these changes in the wild simultaneously. Provided that good water quality is always maintained and a heterosexual pair of mature fish is present, these suggestions should work.

A slight increase or decrease in specific gravity has also been known to trigger the spawning of some species. If a starting value of 1.022 is maintained, it can be decreased to 1.020 over the course of a day or two by dripping freshwater into the aquarium. The specific gravity can be dropped to as low as 1.017 if no increased activity is noticed. On shallow coral reefs in the tropics, heavy rainfalls often lower the specific gravity and cause an increase in runoff from the land, which in turn triggers a plankton bloom and increased availability of live food items on the reef. An increase in specific gravity may occur in some coastal waters during the summer months, which may or may not trigger spawning. If you want to try a fluctuation of specific gravity with the intent of triggering spawning, it is best to lower the specific gravity rather than increase it.

Often, however, the problem is not the fish but rather the impatient aquarist. Above all else, marine aquarium species need time to adjust to their new environment before any attempt at spawning is made. The time required by each species seems to vary dramatically. Sexually mature dottybacks and gobies simply require the proper meta-

A tiny Many-host Cling Goby (*Pleurosicya mossambica*) perched on its clutch of eggs (arrows) on a live tunicate.

bolic intake to produce eggs. This can take a few days to a few weeks. Clownfishes and angelfishes, to name but two, seem to require much more time to acclimate to their surroundings, perhaps many, many months.

It is best to maintain a stable environment with as few fluctuations as possible. In my opinion, providing good feeding and constant good water, lighting and temperature conditions are more important than trying to mimic natural fluctuations. Only after several months in a stable environment should a fluctuation in specific gravity occur if the broodstock has showed no signs of spawning.

FAUX PLANKTON BLOOM

One trick that can work before resorting to extreme measures with a particularly stubborn pair is to replicate a plankton bloom. Environmental factors that contribute to the survival of the larvae send powerful signals to broodstock. A plankton bloom offers larval fish a more abundant food source, so pairs will often spawn at the onset of such an event. Heavy rainfalls often trigger plankton blooms, so a slight decrease in specific gravity along with a plankton bloom simulation may trigger spawning.

Recreating a plankton bloom in a broodstock aquarium is an easy task. A couple of scoops of newly hatched *Artemia* or wild zooplankton will do the job. This should be done daily until the fish spawn. It is important that external filters be cleaned more regularly if this technique is employed, as the uneaten plankton or brine shrimp will become trapped in mechanical filters. If a central water system is used, do not place a tight screen over the overflow since the screen will quickly clog and the tank may overflow. Instead, place a foam block, mesh pad or similar mechanical trap at the end of the pipe draining water into the sump. This can easily be removed and squeezed out with little fear of causing an overflow. Faux plankton blooms sometimes work for Comets or Marine Bettas (*Calloplesiops altivelis*), stubborn clownfish and dottybacks.

A similar technique involves adding turbidity to the water. Instead of newly hatched *Artemia* or other similar live organisms, a foam block from an established filter can be squeezed out into the aquarium. This seems a bit much, as the water often turns very dark with suspended particulates, but it has proved useful to stimulate many clownfish and gramma pairs to spawn. Once the muck trapped within the foam is added to the broodstock tank, the filter medium is placed in the filter where it will again trap particulate matter and the process can be repeated.

To summarize, live foods are often linked to successful spawning in many marine fish species. For instance, the Blackcap Basslet (*Gramma melacara*) often proves reluctant to spawn unless some live foods are added to its diet. Black worms, my favorite, are perhaps the best live food to inspire listless spawners. If any species of marine fish is reluctant to spawn, feed them live black worms several times a day until they begin spawning. Although not as nutritious, adult brine shrimp have also worked for some breeders to induce cardinalfishes and clownfish to spawn.

Lunar cycles also appear to be a great spawning influence. A waxing moon, leading to a full moon, can be a nat-

ural trigger. This moonlight can be simulated during the nighttime hours by adding a small nightlight outside the aquarium. Small, blue Christmas lights work well as they do not produce a large amount of light. (Lunar cycle lighting timers and LED moonlight fixtures are available for those with a less restricted budget.)

Finally, a large water change (20 to 50 percent) will sometimes bring on a spawning event. An increase in water movement or aeration (using a small powerhead or air stone) may induce others to spawn.

However, if the fish are not well fed and well acclimated to their surroundings, none of these attempts will work. Fish must feel completely comfortable in their environment if they are to spawn.

HORMONE-INDUCED SPAWNING

The use of reproductive hormones to induce captive spawning has been well documented in commercially important food-fish species since the 1930's. Captivity-induced stress and a lack of appropriate environmental spawning cues are blamed as the foremost reasons causing reproductive dysfunctions in many species (Zohar 2000).

The wild, external environmental factors work collectively to trigger internal mechanisms responsible for successful spawning. The brain receives and translates environmental stimuli (including change of seasons, lunar cycle, etc.), triggering the hypothalamus to those cues of reproductive significance.

Gonadotropin-releasing hormones (GnRH) are produced by the hypothalamus, which is thought to then stimulate the pituitary gland. The pituitary gland then produces and releases gonadotropin hormones (GtH). Successful ovulation in females is dependent upon the release of GtH from the pituitary. Gonadotropin hormones released to the gonads trigger a further progression. Steroids and prostaglandins within the gonads are the local controlling factors of ovarian development. The cascade of hormones beginning in the brain is a complicated prerequisite for eggs to mature within the ovaries and spawning to occur.

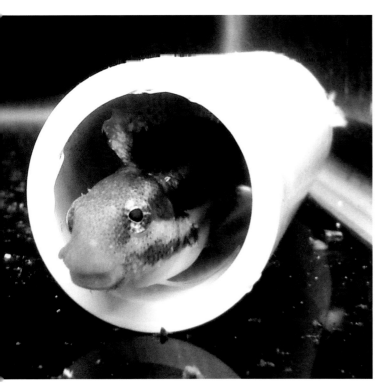

Male Mimic Blenny (*Petroscirtes breviceps*) in his PVC tunnel, courting a female to enter and spawn with him. Such spawning rituals are common to many families of reef fishes.

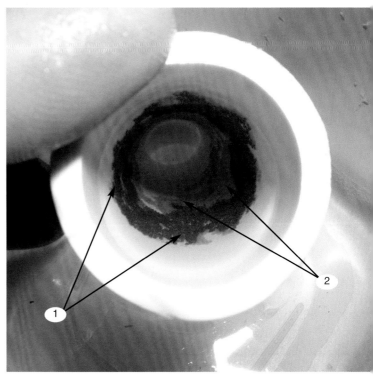

Two spawns of Mimic Blenny eggs, laid on different days create an interesting mosaic. Older eggs are darker and more developed (arrow 1), newer eggs are still a light pink (arrow 2).

Many hormones, extracts, and analogs have been used in past years within various families of freshwater and marine fish species to initiate spawning at different levels. The most successful results are obtained when the fishes are manipulated at a high level. Simulating a proper series of environmental conditions creates a natural surge of hormones resulting in successful spawning. Ideally, the aquaculturist can trigger a surge of the fish's own hormones and limit the use of synthetic material toward final oocyte maturation.

Pituitary extracts are common in developing countries in the breeding of food fishes for aquaculture, as they are the least expensive injectable hormone. Pituitary extracts cause a surge in the amount of gonadotropin hormones circulating in the blood, bypassing the brain-pituitary link. Dosage recommendations are the subject of confusion. In less sci-

entific breeding operations, the regimen of using pituitary extracts is highly variable.

Human Chorionic Gonadotropin (HCG) is the most widespread hormone in commercial aquaculture. When injected, this hormone mimics the fish's natural gonadotropin hormones produced by the pituitary. It acts directly on the gonad-triggering hormones to initiate final oocyte maturation. This hormone works in essentially the same manner as pituitary extracts by bypassing the brain-pituitary link, but is more effective due to the purified form of the hormone. HCG is produced in standardized units allowing for effective quantification of content and dosage rate.

The use of reproductive hormones to induce captive spawning in marine ornamentals has been limited to experimentation with no real guidelines available. Hormonal manipulation has real potential for several groups, including the Plesiopidae and many more. These species readily adapt to captive conditions, but have proven difficult to spawn with any regularity. The Marine Betta (*Calloplesiops altivelis*) has been spawned and reared several times. This species, however, seems to lack any cyclic behavior in its reproductive scheme. Vitellogenesis (yolking of eggs within the ovaries) has been observed many times, but the eggs are not released into the ovarian lumen leading to successful natural spawning.

Before any attempt can be made at hormone-induced spawning, the correct environmental stimuli must be present. Fish must be in excellent health and provided with a sufficient conditioning diet, photoperiod, temperature and, most importantly, a suitable social environment that brings together heterosexuals of reproductive age. Environmental and physical conditioning should precede hormone induction by at least 4 to 6 weeks to allow the fish adequate time to build metabolic reserves in preparation for spawning and also to acclimate to present environmental conditions.

Human Chorionic Gonadotropin (HCG) has been used experimentally to induce several species of clownfish to spawn and has worked with at least three species of dottybacks and several species of angelfish. It must be stressed that little if any scientific literature exists on the use of hormones for marine ornamentals, and investigators must pioneer the technique for different species.

Tremendous difficulties are encountered when using hormone injections to trigger spawning in small, ornamental species. HCG is available in standardized international units and dosage rates are based on the weight of the broodstock. The dosages required by males are typically much less than for females, as the process of spermiation is simpler and requires little manipulation.

The freshwater ornamental industry is largely dependent on hormones for the continued long-term production of several species. The common Redtail (*Labeo bicolor*) and Rainbow Sharks (*Epalzeorhynchos munense*), several species of loaches, and many species of catfishes and cyprinids must be induced to spawn with hormones to control reproduction. The size of these freshwater species is not much different from the average dottyback, for example, suggesting good potential for hormonal manipulation of reproduction.

CAUTIONARY NOTES

Blind attempts at hormone injections on broodstock fish would be ill-advised, especially by home breeders.

Protocols exist for commercially important species such as groupers and rabbitfish. Taking known, published dosage rates and protocols and shrinking them for use with marine ornamentals is the best approach. At least 31 species of Serranidae (primarily groupers for food production) have been induced to ovulate using hormones, many of these with HCG.

Average dosage rates for female serranids are 500 to 1,000 IU HCG/kg body weight. Ovulation typically occurs within 24 to 72 hours after the first injection. Groupers are generally strip-spawned. Biopsies of the gonads are taken periodically to determine ripeness and the fish are stripped when oocyte diameter reaches a predetermined size. If natural spawning does not occur, the oocytes will overripen and undergo atresia or resorption by the female's reproductive system.

The goal with marine ornamentals is usually to spur oocyte maturation and ovulation resulting in natural spawning. Hormones should be considered as a last resort only for species displaying extreme hesitation to initiate or complete natural spawning in captivity. Every attempt should be made to trigger spawning by providing the proper physical, social and environmental factors necessary for successful spawning.

For most home-based marine breeders, the use of hormones is neither necessary nor recommended. These are tools available to commercial, experimental and very advanced amateur aquaculturists, but for most small-scale breeders the rewards of getting our fishes to spawn naturally override the hypothetical returns from resorting to chemical intervention.

CHAPTER 7

EGGS & INCUBATION

Hatching Methods—Natural & Assisted

Getting marine aquarium fishes to spawn, in many cases, is the easy part. The challenges and real vexations tend to mount rather quickly after the fish have produced their first eggs.

For pelagic spawners or those species that do not practice brood care, the eggs and parents must be separated immediately, and the methods for accomplishing this are detailed separately in the species descriptions, beginning on page 164.

In demersal spawners, the role of the male during incubation and brood care is generally quite complex and very important to the developing embryos. The first major decision facing the home breeder is whether to leave the eggs in the care of the brooding male or move them to a hatching container for artificial incubation.

The male is the primary guardian in most species that tend their spawns: protecting and caring for the eggs, aerating, and agitating them until hatching. In several species, the male also physically assists the larvae in freeing themselves from their egg shells. Whenever possible, the eggs should be left in the care of the male until the day of hatching. I have found that the condition of the eggs during incubation and the eventual hatch rates (the percentage of spawned eggs that actually yield live larvae) are generally highest when the male is allowed to care for the eggs.

Unfortunately, males in captivity often prove unreliable as brooders. Many factors may be responsible for a male's seeming disinterest in his egg-tending role. Whenever possible it is best to determine the cause behind failed brood care and try to correct the problem. More often than not, bad behavior can be corrected with seemingly simple solutions.

Moving clownfish eggs (arrow) laid on a tile into a rearing tub with an airstone to keep fungus from developing.

Coral reef fish must be maintained and conditioned on many steady cycles. Constant environmental parameters are necessary to foster natural behaviors. Temperature, photoperiod and feeding times should be steady and predictable. Fishes will become conditioned to feeding at certain times throughout the day and will await the coming of their keeper, rather than feeling threatened or stressed from their approach. Everything in and near the broodstock tank should occur as part of a rhythm. If all activity near the aquarium or in the breeding room occurs at the same time each day, it will become an environmental normality rather than a disruption to natural habits.

Before giving up and resorting to artificial incubation, try these tactics that have proved successful for others

- Add more structure to the tank such as PVC sections or flowerpots
- Place daily feedings on schedule
- Feed more fresh and high-quality frozen foods such as shrimp and squid
- Limit outside disturbances near the broodstock tank
- Add live brine shrimp to the diet
- Place the broodstock aquarium at eye level or move to different, more private location

7 REASONS BROODING MALES PROVE UNRELIABLE

In order for captive males to successfully incubate clutches of eggs to term they must feel secure in their environment. Often due to a variety of factors males prove unreliable and either abandon their broods or consume them.

1. Broodstock tank too small or too little shelter areas present
2. Inadequate light cycle
3. Inadequate feeding cycle/diet
4. Poor tank positioning
5. Outside disturbance
6. Poor broodstock
7. Inexperience—first spawns

The male can be more than negligent; he—sometimes joined by his mate—will often eat the entire spawn. The number one reason eggs are consumed is an unsuitable brooding environment. When a pair is housed in a high-traffic area or seems skittish toward multiple human keepers, they will often consume their brood at some point during development.

Often, pairs will eat their first few clutches but eventually settle into their roles as reproductive partners. I think it's unwise to give up on a male or pair too soon. If the eggs are pulled prematurely from skittish broodstock, there is often a chance of their ceasing reproductive behavior. I believe it is best to sacrifice the first few spawns and determine if the fish will settle and brood them to full term or determine the cause. Only as a last resort should eggs be pulled.

If broodstock pairs repeatedly fail to incubate eggs to full term, keep records and determine at which stage the eggs are being consumed. Then, only pull them on this day or a day before so that they are left in the care of the parents as long as is feasible.

Masses of *Pseudochromis* eggs from four separate spawnings (arrows—note size differences) in an artificial hatching chamber. Constant, gentle flow of water keeps eggs moving.

ARTIFICIAL INCUBATION

Taking on the responsibilities of the male fish and artificially incubating marine fish eggs is not an easy task and should be relied upon only when all attempts have been made to offer the brooding male ideal care and a sense of security in the broodstock tank. Have some patience: males often eat their first few broods, being new to the duties that have been bestowed upon them. Only in special cases should the eggs be prematurely removed from the tending parents. There is no substitute for Mother Nature, and the eggs should be left in the presence of the parental fish as long as possible. Hatch rates are usually sacrificed during artificial incubation, but the whole clutch will not be lost. However, if the male continues to consume or ignore spawns after several attempts, changes must be made.

A surrogate human brooder has clearcut tasks: Eggs must be dealt with in such a way that will allow them to develop properly without the ill effects of fungus, bacteria and parasites such as copepods and ciliates. Then, the larvae

must be freed from their eggshells successfully; all by artificial means.

It can be very labor intensive to siphon newly hatched larvae from a broodstock aquarium. This can also cause harm to the tiny, delicate larvae. Typically, only clownfish should be allowed to hatch in the broodstock tank and transferred to the rearing tank via shallow bowls or mechanical means.

The larvae of other species are just too delicate to endure this process. Transfer losses are generally extremely high in dottybacks, gobies, and the like and alternative means of hatching must be employed. Their eggs need to be moved to a larval tank and some form of short-term artificial incubation must provided to tend the eggs until hatching.

Ideally, the hatching tank will have new, aged saltwater and will have UV filtration and protein skimming to keep water quality high and pathogens and parasites at bay.

The means by which the eggs were deposited influences the techniques that you can use to incubate them. Demersal spawning fish deposit their eggs in a variety of different ways. The ceramic tile or flower pot in which a clutch of clownfish, gobies or blenny eggs were deposited in or on should be removed to the rearing tank and placed at a roughly 45° angle using some form of holder. Use a measuring tape to measure the distance from the bottom to the top on opposite sides of the rearing tank. An alternative when using a central system is to measure from the top of the stand pipe to the bottom of the outside wall. Then, cut a length of Plexiglas or acrylic roughly 4 inches wide to fit this space. This sheet of acrylic will rest at roughly a 45° angle and can be used to mount ceramic tiles containing spawns. One-inch PVC pipe can be cut in thin, $1/4$ to $1/2$-inch, cross sections and then spliced to create clamps that will secure the ceramic tile to the plexi support. On the bottom edge of the acrylic sheet, an airstone should be mounted so the air will travel the length of the board following the angle over the eggs. Alternative incubation holders include shelves constructed by heating and bending thin sheets of acrylic. Holders can be made to fit any spawning shelter at a 45° angle to the flow of air bubbles and water current.

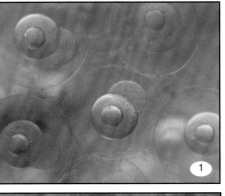

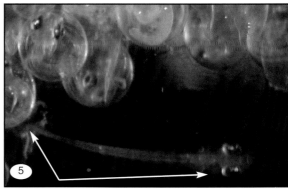

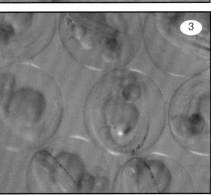

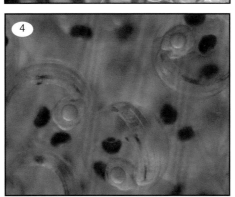

Diadema Dottyback Eggs,Spawning to Hatching:
1. *Pictchromis diadema* eggs soon after fertilization. **2.** Same dottyback eggs 2 days after spawning. **3.** Eggs 3 days post-spawning.
4. Eggs 4 days after fertilization, showing developing, curled larvae with eye spots. **5.** Hatching eggs with bright metallic eyespots. Note unfurled dottyback larva moments after hatching (arrows), head at right with prominent eyes.

A WORLD OF EGGS

It's hard to believe that the diversity of life on a coral reef stems from a tiny and simplified, almost undistinguishable single cell: an egg. Eggs of marine fishes vary tremendously in size and shape, color and texture as well as their mode of dispersal.

The Dwarf Goby (*Trimmatom nanus*)—currently documented as the smallest fish in the world—grows to a mere 8 to 10 mm in length and probably produces some of the smallest eggs in the marine fish world. Angelfishes, surgeonfishes and most pelagic spawning coral reef fishes produce tiny, transparent eggs that are nearly perfect spheres measuring less than 1 mm in diameter. On the other side of the spectrum lie such species as the Oyster Toadfish (*Opsanus tau*) that produce eggs rivaling the size of a pencil-tip eraser. At nearly 5 to 6 mm in diameter, toadfish hatch as benthic fry with an enormous yolk sac. This species lacks a pelagic larval phase and its yolk reserves last until the juvenile form is attained. Most freshwater cichlids produce eggs in the neighborhood of 2.5 mm in length. This can be likened to the eggs of benthic spawning reef fishes such as clownfishes, Neon Gobies (*Elacatinus oceanops*) and jawfishes whose eggs measure over 2 mm in length.

Fishes such as the bluefin tunas (*Thunnus* spp.) produce millions of eggs in a single spawning event, whereas the Royal Gramma (*Gramma loreto*) may shed no more than a dozen. Commonly, the size of the egg and the mode of dispersal are directly proportional to the numbers produced.

Historically, in the absence of human threats, marine fish populations have remained stable. For every million fish eggs and larvae cast into the sea, a surprisingly small percentage survive to the juvenile stage. Reproductive strategies, although wildly diverse have a common goal: perpetuate the species. The number of eggs produced, their size, color, and texture all work to ensure the reproductive success of a species.

Pseudochromid eggs and those of the roundheads (Plesiopidae) are shed in gelatinous masses. Egg size and quantity varies between the species, but the general structure remains constant. *Pseudochromis steenei* and similarly large species such as *Ogilbyina* sp. and *Labracinus* sp. lay a mass of eggs comparable in size to a golf ball containing nearly 2,500 eggs. Smaller pseudochromids lay a much smaller egg mass containing 600 or so eggs. First time spawners always shed small egg masses containing far fewer eggs than is typical for the species.

It is often reported that the egg mass of pseudochromids is adhesive, being attached to cave walls and ceilings. This is especially noted for the Plesiopidae. Individual eggs lack a true adhesive gland present on many other demersal spawning families such as clownfish (Pomacentridae) and gobies (Gobiidae). In these families, individual eggs are attached to solid surfaces by means of adhesive glands. Pseudochromid eggs are shed in a mass with each egg exhibiting characteristic threads that effectively hold the egg mass together. These threads are similar to Velcro and support the egg mass only on rough surfaces that can act as anchoring points for the threads. Egg masses shed in PVC tubes do not exhibit an adhesive nature, whereas those shed in rock caves often do. The main attribute of the strands protruding from the eggs is to keep the egg mass together so as it can be effectively incubated and agitated by the guarding male.

Eggs of gobies, blennies, damselfishes and clownfishes are very different from pseudochromids and roundheads. Eggs are deposited individually on solid surfaces by means of adhesive filaments on the proximal end of each egg. Females are very diligent in preparing the spawn and eggs are kept close together in a well-defined nest site.

The male usually guards the eggs and often rubs his belly against and fans them with his pectoral, pelvic and caudal fins. Males typically remove fungused or dead eggs. Blenny eggs are unusual in that they often possess a large, brightly colored yolk that is thought to aid in oxygen metabolism through the egg membrane. Males of such species often leave the nest for variable lengths of time and oxygen levels are often very low in the deep crevices in which the eggs are placed.

Different characteristics of eggs, such as size, shape, position and method of deposition will ultimately affect the means in which they are incubated and hatched. Ideally, most eggs are left in the care of the brooding male until shortly before they are due to hatch. At this point the eggs are removed from the care of the male and reared by some form of artificial means.

Airflow should be adjusted directly over the eggs at roughly 500 to 1,000 mL/min. This is not something easily measured, but eggs should sway back and forth continuously with the direct flow over the entire spawn. The resulting stream of bubbles should keep the eggs in constant motion, but not be so strong as to rip the eggs from the substrate. Without adequate aeration the eggs will fungus. It seems to go against common sense to allow a vigorous current of air bubbles to come in direct contact with the eggs, but if the airflow is simply placed nearby, the majority of the spawn will succumb to fungus. Proper agitation may appear lethal to the eggs, but in fact is essential. Many spawns are lost to hobbyists thinking the airflow is too strong. Once the eggs have hatched, the spawning substrate is removed and the larvae raised as described below.

Eggs of cavity spawners such as damsels, gobies and blennies are more easily satisfied. The PVC pipe section containing the spawn should be removed to the rearing tank and fastened in a vertical position, ideally clamped to the center standpipe by means of rubber bands or cable ties. If a standpipe is not available, a suspended pipe can be rigged. An airstone is fastened to below the pipe and the exhaust from the airstone allowed to rise through the pipe and over the eggs. Again, air flow should be adjusted to roughly 500 to 1,000 mL/min. After hatching, the pipe is removed and the air flow reduced.

Eggs that are not attached to a substrate are usually clinging to each other with threads or sticky substances. The male usually guards this ball of eggs until the larvae hatch, whereupon he boosts the hatching larvae into the water column with the beating of his tail. Hatching eggs such as these requires a little more care.

Ideally, the eggs are taken from the male's care on the day they are to hatch, or perhaps the day before. A hatching container is prepared in any number of ways to facilitate artificial hatching. The top half of a 2-liter soda bottle makes a simple and effective hatchery. With the cap in place, the container is inverted, filled with water from the broodstock tank and suspended in the rearing aquarium with an airstone. The eggs are placed in this sheltered container until hatching occurs; the larvae are then released into the rearing aquarium. It is important to keep the eggs confined to the hatching container in order to aerate and agitate them. The males of many species usually help free the larvae from the egg cases with their mouths. It is thus important to have an airstone nearby, creating some motion to aid the hatching larvae. The eggs held in the soda-bottle hatchery sit in the cap at the bottom of the container. If the eggs have some days before hatching, the airstone is placed directly above the eggs and the airflow turned up as high as possible without the eggs rising out of the cap and being destroyed by the rushing bubbles.

If, however, the eggs have been collected a few hours prior to their estimated hatching time, the airstone should be adjusted to provide a slow, gentle flow. Downwellers and other techniques listed below are also suited to species with entangled egg masses.

Eggs shed by different marine fish groups can be very different in size and physical characteristics, and artificial incubation may need to be customized for the species you are attempting to breed. The one absolute key to proper incubation is water circulation. It must force fresh, oxygenated water over and through the egg mass so that each egg is effectively kept clean and incubated. Many methods exist to incubate a spawn. Ideally, an incubator should mimic the role of the male fish.

Ocellaris Clownfish (*Amphiprion ocellaris*) pair spawning on a vertical ceramic tile. Larger species, such as the Tomato Clown (*A. frenatus*), often opt for a diagonally oriented tile.

Water vs. Air for Incubation

Incubating marine fish eggs is often a difficult task, but with creativity and a wealth of products available, creating a simple incubation device can be uncomplicated. Air pumps are ubiquitous and it seems every aquarist has a few lying around. Incubating demersal eggs from groups such as the clownfish, gobies, blennies and damsels poses few difficulties if they are moved as close to hatching as possible. They can be incubated with a moderate flow of bubbles rising across the eggs.

For most demersal spawning fishes, air movement offers a random motion of bubbles and water currents over the eggs. The size of bubbles rising from an airstone is generally not uniform and each bubble is highly influenced by the flow of water created by others rising nearby. In this way, rising air bubbles tend to wander side to side as they move up the water column. As they crisscross the eggs, dead spots (with poor water movement) are eliminated and agitation is more successful.

However, air is limited in its applications as it will only travel in one direction—up. In many instances, eggs are

Transferring a spawn of damselfish eggs, deposited in the short section of PVC pipe, to a rearing tub. The nesting pipe will be fastened vertically to the standpipe for hatching.

Egg Tumblers

Egg tumblers for species that produce a ball or mass of eggs (rather than attaching them to hard substrate) can be created in a number of different ways, but all have the same goal. The idea is to keep the egg mass in constant slow motion, rolling around in a small area.

A length of thin-wall clear plastic undergravel lift tubing (approximately 3/4-inch in diameter) can be cut into two separate sections. One section is heated with a cigarette lighter and molded over the other section so a tight coupling is created. A small section of mesh (a piece of mesh from a fish net works well) is inserted between the two pieces of clear pipe. On the bottom end of this tumbler, a diaphragm from an air pump, a soda bottle cap or similar PVC fitting is used to cover the bottom-end section of pipe, making it leak-proof. A short length of rigid airline tubing is inserted into a hole drilled in the cap or in the case of the rubber diaphragm the existing hole. The rigid airline tubing is connected to a gang valve and subsequently to a powerhead or small water pump. Aquarium heater suction cups fit the diameter of the undergravel lift tube and work well to hold the tumbler vertical and stationary. The egg mass sits on the screen on the top part of the tumbler, and water is forced up through the bottom. In this way, the water flow is adjusted so the eggs tumble slowly. Water must not be pumped at too high a level to cause the egg mass to exit the top of the tumbler.

Ideally, the tumbler would be situated in a rearing tank connected to a central filtration system. Water entering the tumbler would come directly from the sump or another tank located nearby. The water overflowing the tumbler would fall into the rearing tank and down through a standpipe into the sump. In this way the powerhead is not located in the rearing tank to create a threat to newly hatched larvae. The top of the tumbler is best located only a centimeter or two above the surface of the water. The egg mass can be left incubating like this until the larvae have hatched. At hatching the larvae will be forced up and out into the rearing tank. A fine micron mesh screen is required to cover the standpipe. Although the flow from the tumbler is not great, a risk

spawned in a flower pot, on a standpipe or on a heater tube. Eggs spawned on the inside roof of a flower pot, for instance, are difficult to incubate with air. Air can be forced to rise in an angled direction as on a ceramic tile, but it proves very difficult to harness in a sharp corner without creating air pockets and uneven flow patterns.

For these and other odd situations, moving water can be equally or more effective for short-term incubation. The water flow from a powerhead can be diverted to a plastic airline gang valve or similar valve system to regulate the flow of water through a piece of airline tubing. Several of these water jets can be aimed to provide a continuous flow of water over a mass of eggs. Randomly moving the waterflow several times daily will increase the efficacy of incubation and prevent dead spots from developing within the egg mass.

The use of water is often necessary to incubate eggs. Eggs placed in difficult-to-access corners of flowerpots are one example. Dottyback eggs similarly must be incubated with water, as small air bubbles quickly become lodged within the sticky egg mass.

Artificial incubation of damselfish eggs in a short section of pipe. Note gentle flow of air bubbles that keep eggs healthy.

of larvae being sucked out by the standpipe is still present. This method proves ideal for Banggi Cardinal eggs stripped prematurely and disinfected dottyback eggs.

Glassware

A small, round-bottom flask can also be used to incubate egg masses. The flask is filled with broodstock tank water and sunk in the rearing tank. A suction cup used for aquarium heaters is fitted to the neck of the flask and fastened to the rearing tank wall so as the mouth of the flask is only a centimeter above the surface. Water is pumped down into

the flask by means of rigid airline tubing. Larvae hatched in such an incubator are effortlessly delivered to the rearing tank.

Downwellers

Moving water is preferred over moving air to artificially incubate the eggs of dottybacks. In a round-bottom flask or similar glassware, the water is forced to the bottom of the flask and must exit at the same entrance point. Often times this results in the egg mass exiting the flask if the flow is not properly adjusted. Downwellers are constructed of PVC pipe and force the water out through a bottom screen. The top of the incubator or downweller is above the surface of the water and allows no exit points for the egg mass to escape. A length of 3- or 4-inch PVC pipe is cut to roughly 12 inches. Then, the section is halved and a micron screen placed in between them before being glued back together. The downweller then stands vertically in the rearing chamber. Water is forced down from the top and exits through the screen and out the of the pipe. A vigorous water flow will agitate the egg mass and keep the interior aerated.

Any combination or modification of these methods should yield satisfactory results. Many more problems will be encountered when the eggs are removed shortly after spawning as compared to those removed a day or two before hatching. The eggs should remain in the care of the male for as long as possible to prevent bacterial and fungal invasions as well as dead spots from developing within the egg mass. The methods of artificial incubation mentioned above work well in some instances but can also yield very poor results in others. Many of the failed attempts using these methods probably stem from poor water circulation within the egg mass itself. Bacterial and fungal infections are the most commonly encountered problems during egg incubation.

Mesh Baskets

Often times, the most foolproof approach to solving a problem proves the simplest. Perhaps the easiest means of both incubating and hatching a mass of sticky eggs (as from the dottybacks) uses nothing more than mesh baskets and aeration. Flexible plastic mesh sheets used for needlepoint and other arts and crafts projects are available with perforations of roughly 1/8- to 1/4-inch. Cable ties can be used to construct a conical with an inside dimension of 4 or 5 inches and a height of maybe 5 or 6 inches. The basket is then attached to a standpipe or fixed in a vertical position within the rearing tank. The top of the basket should extend above the surface of the water. An airstone is placed within the basket along with the egg mass and allowed to flow at a strong rate. It is a good idea to secure a few cable ties to the inside so as the loose strands protrude to the center of the basket. In this way the egg mass will become trapped on the tie and will be effectively agitated by the airflow. Near 100-percent hatch rates can be achieved with this method. If hatch rates are low, increasing the flow from the airstone will usually help. At hatching, the larvae are freed from their egg shells by the aeration and escape further mechanical harm caused by the bubbles by exiting the basket through the perforations. The water motion created by the rising bubbles causes water to rise from the bottom and spread as it reaches the surface. It is this action that spreads the larvae throughout the whole of the rearing chamber.

INCUBATION TROUBLESHOOTING

Many problems, both predictable and unique, can rise during the incubation and hatching of marine fish eggs. Stumbling blocks surrounding the propagation of marine fishes are frequent and most often attributed to the early larval stages and the developmental stages near metamorphosis. When artificial incubation must be employed it adds a whole new challenge. Many of the hindrances associated with incubation and hatching are due to inadequate water circulation through the egg mass, but other problems do exist.

Problem 1: Bright Light

Inexperienced breeders commonly use small flashlights to observe new spawns within the dark confines of spawning caves. When the beam of light is concentrated on newly

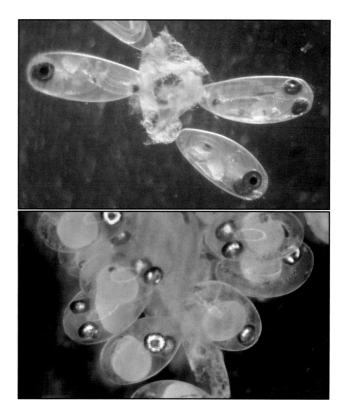

Healthy Neon Goby eggs (top) display an elongate shape typical of the species, while abnormal eggs (lower) have a round shape and cramped larvae due to high-nitrogen tank water.

spawned egg masses, little harm is done to the developing embryos. At a later stage of development, after the eyes have pigmented, beams of light can do great harm to unhatched larvae.

Many years ago I took great joy in witnessing the hatching of dottybacks. After the lights had gone out, I would use a small blue incandescent light to provide dim, diffuse illumination in the room. In this lighting, I could see silver streaks of newly hatched larvae darting from the hatching container. Other times I used a small flashlight to check the progress of the egg mass. After coming under a strong beam of concentrated light, very few eggs would hatch for me. I observed that a bright light shined on the egg mass before hatching can prevent any larvae from hatching out. If I shined no direct or strong light on the egg mass, most or

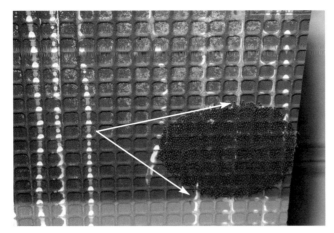

Mass of freshly laid Clark's Clownfish (*Amphiprion clarkii*) eggs (between arrows) on the botton of a ceramic floor tile.

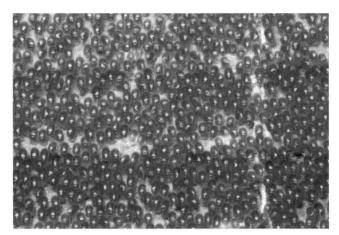

Detail of just-laid, bright red and featureless Clark's Clownfish eggs at C-Quest hatchery. Note uniformity of placement.

all hatched out. Rules of elimination suggested the beam of light as the culprit.

Problem 2: Parasites

Invasions of parasites and pests are common problems during artificial incubation. Bacteria and fungus often attack eggs quickly and without warning. These are not large predators visible to the naked eye. Unfertile eggs quickly turn white. The fouled eggs of substrate spawners that deposit single rows of eggs are easily removed with a small syringe or tweezers.

The tangled egg mass of dottybacks makes the extraction of a few fungused eggs extremely difficult. It is best to dip the egg mass in a fungus-preventative solution prior to artificial incubation. Malachite green in low dosages, acriflavine, hydrogen peroxide (2 mL for every 1 L) or formalin (2 mL of 37-percent solution for every 1 L of treated water) work well for this purpose. The eggs go into short-term baths of 15 minutes using rearing tank water kept at the same temperature. Antibiotics should not be used routinely in tank water during incubation.

A far less common problem affecting eggs are larger pests such as copepods and ciliates. Within most conventional incubators with slow-moving water driving the rotation of the eggs or egg mass, these organisms can gain a

foothold and consume many eggs, leaving very few larvae to hatch out. The best strategy against such intrusion is the use of formalin dips prior to incubation and an effective artificial incubation device designed to strongly agitate eggs.

Problem 3: Water Quality

Under artificial conditions, water quality plays a crucial role in the success of incubation. Without the male actively partaking in brood-care duties, the eggs are vulnerable to many maladies and foes.

High levels of organic and nitrogenous wastes restrict the development of the larvae within the egg membrane and they often perish before hatching. Incubation should take place in clean water. The most effective method of artificial incubation involves the use of newly mixed synthetic seawater that has been aged. Chlorinated natural seawater filtered down to several microns also works effectively. The water must be kept as clean as possible with minimal amounts of decaying matter. Artificial incubation taking place in a broodstock tank or central filtration system is rarely successful due to the high waste levels.

The Disinfectant Solution

Any attempt to hatch marine fish eggs by artificial means will be greatly improved if the eggs are disinfected prior to

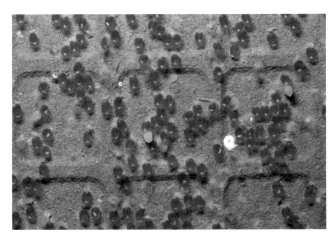

Four-day-old Maroon Clownfish (*Premnas biaculeatus*) eggs. The brooding male removes any infertile or fungused eggs.

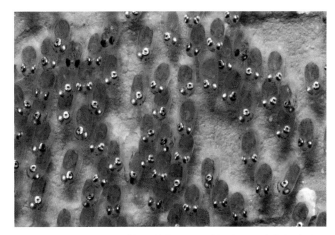

Eight-day-old Ocellaris Clownfish eggs with cleary visible dark eyespots that are telltale sign of the approach of hatching.

placing them in the hatching chamber.

Ciliates, protozoa, bacteria, fungus, and a myriad of other microscopic organisms threaten the viability of eggs under artificial incubation. Disinfect the surface of all eggs before placing them in clean, new water to increase developmental and hatching rates of embryos.

I recommend a simple bath in formalin or hydrogen peroxide. Isolated egg masses from dottybacks and round-heads and those eggs deposited in or on small sections of PVC can be bathed in small pitchers containing approximately 1 quart (1 L) of tank water. Larger spawns on ceramic tiles or flowerpots can be bathed in buckets containing 2.5 to 4 gallons (10 to 15 L) of tank water mixed with a disinfectant.

If using 37 percent formaldehyde as the disinfectant, it is added at a dosage of 1 to 2 mL per liter (quart) of water. (One liter equals 1.05 quarts so these measures can be considered equivalent in this sort of treatment.) Eggs should be slowly stirred or the water slowly agitated with an airstone for 15 minutes.

Next, the treatment water containing the formaldehyde should be drained and replaced with clean tank water for a rinse before placing the eggs in the rearing system for artificial incubation. Hydrogen peroxide can also be used, at dosages ranging from 1 to 5 mL per liter or quart of water.

I prefer the stronger dosage for 15 minutes, accompanied by slow agitation of the eggs. Again, rinse the eggs in clean saltwater before placing them in the rearing system.

There are many other commercial anti-fungus and similar incubation chemicals that can be used to deter fouling. Directions should be followed as per the manufacturer. If eggs are pulled the day hatching is expected, surface disinfection is generally not required. Eggs pulled shortly after spawning, however, should be disinfected.

Again, in an ideal situation, eggs should be placed in very clean, even sterile, incubation systems with heavy UV sterilization and protein skimming to avoid fouling. Eggs can be removed from artificial incubation and disinfected daily if water conditions continue to cause losses. Eggs pulled for the immediate purpose of hatching should not be disinfected. Eggs due to hatch within a 24-hour period should also not be disinfected, as formalin may induce premature hatching or inhibit hatching by coating the egg surface.

Finally, for the home-based breeder, having functional breeding pairs that allow natural hatching of spawns is the ideal and fraught with far fewer headaches. I would do everything possible to encourage parental brooding, even if it means losing a few spawns as things get sorted out, before resorting to artificial incubation schemes.

CHAPTER 8

LARVAL REARING

Housing Your Newly Hatched Larvae

R earing marine fishes past metamorphosis is no longer the mysterious challenge it once was. For many species, the task of raising larvae has turned more towards a number of well-accepted routines or protocols rather than the uncertainty and experimentation of the not-so-distant past.

How you choose to raise larvae will be up to you, your budget, and your goals, whether ambitious and bottomline oriented or relaxed with the intention of raising a few fishes successfully. Many guidelines now exist for raising various families of marine fishes, and protocols differ from species to species. What follows is a brief overview of rearing tank options with considerations and information on the most ideal rearing environments to match the scale of most marine breeding hobbyists.

Upon hatching, larval fishes take on a drastically different lifestyle than that of their parents. Instead of swimming over and around the coral heads and grottos of the reef, they float with the ocean currents near the surface, often drifting many miles away from the home reef where they were spawned. This is a treacherous existence for a larval fish, floating amongst the plankton with little physical development to aid in escape from predation and no shelter whatsoever. The larvae are at the mercy of the open ocean. Of the hundreds or thousands of eggs in a single spawning, perhaps less than 10 will reach sexual maturity.

Before numerous species of marine fish were spawned and reared in captivity, many skeptics claimed marine fishes would be impossible to raise in captivity due to the pelagic stage of the larvae. While this has been proven false, the pelagic stage of the larvae does pose a challenge to captive rearing efforts. An ideal rearing tank must be set up as a pseudo pelagic environment.

The larvae cannot be raised in the broodstock tank. The parents will devour the eggs or larvae shortly after they have hatched, and filters, skimmers and water pumps will similarly trap or kill delicate larvae. Everything from 10-gallon glass aquariums and 30-gallon rubber trash cans to 400-gallon round fiberglass aquaculture vats have been used to successfully raise marine fish larvae.

Rearing Tank Size

Two main factors limit the size of suitable larval rearing vessels, water quality and food densities. Larval marine fish need to be swimming amongst their prey items, allowing them to feed easily and frequently, lest they starve. While a 300-gallon fiberglass tub will maintain water quality at optimal levels, it is impractical, by hobbyist standards, to provide an adequate density of prey organisms as well as having them remain high in nutritional content in such a large volume of water. On the other hand, small glass aquariums are easily provided with adequate densities of food, but water quality can quickly fall below tolerable limits and the boxy shape is ill-suited to larval rearing.

Larvae are extremely vulnerable to deterioration of water quality prior to metamorphosis. For this reason, a vessel should be chosen that contains no less than 10 gallons (38 L) of water. A water volume of between 10 and 50 gallons (38 L to 190 L) is not difficult to stock with an appropriate density of rotifers, and tanks of this size are capable of buffering some water quality problems.

Shape

I tend to avoid the word aquarium when discussing larval rearing since, in my experience, glass aquariums are not the best vessels for raising marine fish larvae because they are rectangular with corners that prevent a smooth, homogenous flow of water distribution. Because larval fishes need dark, preferably black, side walls to help spot food items in the water, glass tanks also need painted outside panes.

Newly hatched larvae are small and delicate and seem to exhibit much stress when raised in aquariums. The average survival rate of most marine fish larvae is low to begin with, and when exposed to inappropriate physical conditions, their mortality rates only increase. I do know of many successful hobbyists who raise larvae in 10-gallon aquariums, and if this is the only option available, by all means try it. In general, however, only large robust larvae that hatch in a somewhat advanced stage such as those of the clownfishes should be considered for rearing in rectangular tanks.

One better approach to standard glass "display" aquariums lies in the so called "breeder" aquariums that are wider and shallower than show tanks and offer a larger surface-to-volume ratio. Forty or 50-gallon breeder tanks work well for the larval rearing of many species. Twenty-gallon "high" aquariums work well for many species of clownfish.

However, I firmly believe that the ideal vessel for the larval rearing of marine aquarium fish is one with round walls. I have experimented with such containers over the years and found many that work extremely well and are very affordable. Round containers—or at least those with rounded corners—seem to distribute early-stage larvae in the water column more evenly rather than having them stack in the corners. The increased water flow also keeps food more evenly distributed.

Depth is an important consideration as well, and most successful larval rearing culturists advocate a cylindrical tank with a depth of at least 24 inches (61 cm). Most demersal spawning species can be successfully raised in significantly shallower depths, but this depth should be kept in mind for more delicate species of larvae. Increased depth aids in creating good circulation patterns and allows larvae considerable more room to initiate prey capture.

Plastic trash cans with a volume of 30 gallons (114 L) or more can be used as is or cut to roughly 24 inches (61 cm) in height and successfully used to raise larvae. Ideally the trash can should be fitted with a bulkhead and standpipe for maintenance of water quality. One method is to place two bulkheads through the side walls of the container; one near the top and one towards the bottom. Early-stage larvae can then be reared in a low water volume and as the larvae grow or more food becomes available, the water level can be increased to the top bulkhead. The opaque walls of the con-

Simple sump serving a small larval rearing system at the author's Florida Institute of Technology laboratory. Note black 20-gallon barrel-liner tubs—ideal for larval rearing.

There are many available materials and containers that can prove workable for the purpose of larval rearing. Even small-scale hobbyists usually end up needing a battery of larval rearing tanks, so it is advised to think ahead and obtain several of the intended vessels and plumb them together in a central system. Black plastic inserts for decorative whiskey barrels are round and black so they are perfect for this situation.

Dark Walls

The sides or walls of the chosen larval rearing vessel must be dark in color or covered from the outside. Light should be allowed to penetrate the vessel from the top only. Any illumination that penetrates the sides of the vessel will cause disorientation, resulting in stressed larvae that fail to feed and develop normally. This glare is automatically prevented in utility sinks and other similar containers. Aquariums must be painted or covered with an appropriate material to keep light from penetrating.

Ideally glass aquariums should be painted on three sides and the bottom outside panels. For visual observation of the larvae, the front glass is not painted, but covered with black plastic from a garbage bag, construction paper, dark towel or the like. Take care to ensure that all light is blocked from the sides. Small holes allowing light to penetrate will cause early-stage larvae to congregate at these points.

The choice of color for the sides is very important. In addition to blocking side illumination, dark walls also provide a background of contrast behind prey organisms to aid in feeding efficiency. Ultimately, the best choice of color is black. If the sides are left clear, as in the case of aquariums, or white or light blue as in utility sinks and fiberglass tubs, feeding efficiency will be dramatically reduced.

tainer provide an ideal contrast against prey organisms and eliminate unwanted side illumination.

Plastic utility sinks, available at most hardware stores at a relatively inexpensive price, are another choice for ideal larval rearing vessels. These sinks are square but have rounded corners providing ideal conditions for early-stage larvae. A hole is present in the bottom of the sink and easily accommodates a standpipe and associated plumbing. In more elaborate set ups, many of these sinks can be placed in a row to create a larval rearing system connected to a low-maintenance central filtration system. The only downfall to these sinks is the white color universal to all makes. A light sanding and application of marine epoxy paint will quickly transform them to excellent rearing vessels. It is best to place a strip of masking tape along both axis of the bottom before paint is applied. When the paint dries, the tape is removed and two white lines are present on the bottom to aid in visual observations of food densities.

The sides of the aquarium or rearing chamber should be permanently dark or covered until the larvae have completed metamorphosis. Although the larvae are tolerant of side illumination after a period of roughly 15 days, they can be stressed by external activities near a tank with transparent walls. At this point the larvae have typically developed enough visual acuity to find prey organisms and strike at them efficiently, but there is still a considerable growth differential observed and not all larvae will be at this advanced stage. If the larval vessel has a viewing panel, a removable cover such as painted cardboard or black plastic can be employed for the early stages and removed to monitor the progress of the larvae then re-installed after observations are complete.

Because larvae do not generally look down when searching for food, the bottom can be painted a light color to aid the aquarist in visual observations of accumulating debris and prey densities. White or light blue is fine for this purpose, but I suggest keeping the bottom dark with a few strips of white to provide a sufficient view when the keeper looks down into the vessel.

Top Tactics

Conventional tops are not needed or recommended for larval tanks. The amount of maintenance required to keep the larval tank clean makes a top impractical. It is best to leave the top open for full light penetration. If a top is required as a shelf to support feeding or drip containers, plastic egg crate is the ideal choice. Available at hardware stores, egg crate is used in overhead lighting fixtures. It is easily cut with a saw or just by ripping a blunt metal tool, such as a screwdriver, through the small square boxes.

Light the Larvae

Light is an important consideration in larval rearing tanks. A delicate balance of light must be provided to assure larvae can visibly locate and capture prey organisms without being blinded by it and driven to the bottom. If light levels are too strong, larvae have a natural reaction to swim away. In the course of their escape, they inevitably slam into the tank sides, become disoriented and do not feed properly. Ideal lighting for larval rearing systems can be nothing more than the existing overhead room illumination. Lights should not be placed directly above the rearing tank as they are in display tanks. If a single rearing tank is all you have in the rearing space, a single fluorescent light strip can be used, but keep it at least 18 inches (46 cm) above the surface of the water—better yet, on the ceiling.

LARVAL REARING WATER

It's hard to overstate the fact that larvae are delicate creatures susceptible to most every change within the environment around them. For this reason it is important to use water that has been properly aged. Simply using newly mixed synthetic seawater aged in a sterile garbage can for about a week is not enough. It will be devoid of proper microbial populations present in mature seawater and in synthetic seawater allowed to age in an aquarium containing live organisms.

Mature water contains free-floating bacteria capable of rendering larval waste products less active. Heterotrophic and nitrifying bacteria are seeded in the rearing tank in this way. For the first few weeks in an isolated larval tank, source water should consist of water siphoned from the broodstock system or aquarium. This minimizes transfer shock and limits changes to water chemistry in the rearing tank.

Eggs should be removed from the spawning tank on the day of hatching. Transferring larvae from the broodstock tank after hatching is often detrimental to survival. While still contained within the egg membrane, unhatched larvae are tolerant of slight environmental changes such as specific gravity and pH. The water they are moved to does not have to be an exact match.

Ideally, 100 percent of larval rearing water should originate from the broodstock tank. In practice, however, this is difficult to accomplish as broodstock pairs are usually maintained in small aquariums, while the larvae demand a large water volume to be successful. An entire water change in the broodstock tank spells doom and is not an option.

Larval rearing tubs with central standpipes are used for hatching and getting larvae past the critical first 4-5 weeks of life.

With this in mind there are two ways a successful larval system can be created.

The first option is to maintain a small water volume consisting entirely of broodstock water by filling the rearing tank only half the way up. This small water volume can be increased over the course of days by dripping water into the system. This water must originate from the broodstock tank while new synthetic replacement water is added to the broodstock aquarium.

Another method is to mix mature water from the broodstock tank with new synthetic seawater (with the salt fully dissolved and the temperature brought to 78 to 80°F) and then age the mixture for a few days at a ratio of 1:1 or 2:1, new:mature. As long as this mixing is carried out before the eggs are added to the system for hatching, few problems should arise. I have successfully transferred eggs to completely different systems with no significant losses. The major consideration is the addition of a beneficial microbial population to begin the task of waste removal.

Once the eggs have hatched, the larvae are highly sensitive to environmental changes. In large rearing systems, water changes are not carried out for the first week after hatching. In small glass aquariums, water changes may have to occur daily to rid fouling matter in the small water volume. A good rule of thumb is to perform no water changes for the first six days. Then, the bottom muck should be siphoned out. This should take 5 or 10 percent of the total volume, but no more. This schedule should be repeated every two to three days. After a few trials while fine tuning your skills, you will learn how best to do these water changes in your own vessels. Water changes are important during the remaining course of the larval phase and so is the water added to replace that siphoned off.

Because it is so critical, all water being introduced into the larval rearing system must originate from the broodstock tank or similarly seeded marine aquariums until after metamorphosis. When adding water to the rearing tank after cleaning, it should be dripped in to avoid drastic changes. Providing an aquarium or bucket located above the rearing tank equipped with a gravity-fed drip line is all that is needed. One drip per second should be the fastest rate new water is allowed to enter the system.

DEDICATED LARVAL-REARING SYSTEM

The concept of a dedicated larval rearing system is similar to that of a broodstock system or other central water system. Maintenance time is greatly reduced and water quality is more efficiently managed within desired limits while reducing stress affiliated with the addition of newly mixed seawater or water of a different chemical make up.

To build such a system makes sense, even if only a single pair of broodstock is maintained. Due to the frequency of spawning cycles of many demersal spawners, it is possible to fill several rearing tubs in a month's time. Isolated rearing tanks are difficult to maintain and when several of them are active at the same time, it becomes increasingly difficult to keep up with all of them adequately. Furthermore, when maintained on a central system the effective overall volume of each rearing tub is increased by virtue of being connected to a central sump and numerous other rearing tubs. This increase in total volume yields great stability to the system.

Fiberglass tubs, plastic bins, laundry tubs, glass aquariums and virtually any other vessel deemed adequate for larval rearing can be plumbed to a central system. The basic rule of central systems is to include a standpipe or overflow box that allows water pumped in from a main sump, an exit point to maintain a stable water level. As the water overflows the rearing tub, it skims off protein deposits, amino acids and other flocculants that would otherwise cover the water's surface, impeding gas exchange and trapping small larvae. The water overflows into a main drainpipe, where it runs through a series of filtration media and devices.

To insure good water quality in a dedicated larval rearing system, filtration should consist of a UV sterilizer, hefty biological filtration and a protein skimmer. Water is either delivered through these filters in series by gravity or is pumped through the filters in series from the sump. Since flow rates will vary, as different larval stages require different flow rates, it is best to use a separate pump to run the filters. Water is pumped from the sump and again delivered back to this common source. Another pump supplies water to the larval vessels, each with an adjustable water flow valve.

The return pump must be fitted with a pressure-release valve to prevent back pressure when water flow to the rear-

Inexpensive laundry tubs with rounded corners for egg hatching and larval rearing. Insides are coated with black marine epoxy paint and each has its own sump tank.

ing tubs is limited. If a release valve is not present and the individual valves on the rearing tanks are turned off, the life of the pump will be greatly shortened. A PVC T-fitting is placed between the pump and the main return line and fitted with a ball valve or gate valve. When no water or a limited amount of water is being pumped to the rearing tanks, the valve is opened to allow a release of water pressure, with the water simply pumped back into the sump.

One sure way to avoid back pressure on the pump, as well as avoiding a high-pressure spray into the rearing tanks, is to pump the water from the sump into a reservoir located above the rearing tanks. The rearing tanks are then supplied with gravity-fed water. An overflow pipe or box positioned in the reservoir (and running back to the sump) will eliminate the need for pressure-release valves and prevent the reservoir from overfilling onto the floor.

Transferring eggs from an existing broodstock system or isolated spawning aquarium to a larval rearing system poses few if any of the problems associated with operating an isolated larval rearing vessel. Transfer losses and hatch rates are controlled by monitoring extremes in water chemistry. Specific gravity and temperature levels in both the broodstock system and rearing system should mirror one another to limit difficulties.

During the early life stages of marine larvae, the rearing tub on the main system is run like an isolated rearing tank. Each tank is fitted with its own heater and air supply for the first 5 or 6 days. Rotifer densities are extremely important early on, but the addition of HUFA-enriched rotifers often brings an accumulation of fatty surface films when the rotifers are not properly rinsed. Since surface film is potentially deadly, water is dripped in from the main system and allowed to overflow the standpipe through a 240-micron screen. The screen prevents larvae from being sucked down, but does not prevent them from being pinned against it. Careful attention to water flow is a must. One drip per second is all that should be allowed until the larvae are roughly one week old. Dripping water into the system helps eliminate surface films and has a slow but steady diluting effect to remove waste and maintain water quality.

Replacement water should be similar in chemistry and temperature so that any stress caused by the addition of new water is limited. Water should be dripped into the rearing tub at night at a rate of one drop per second for the first five days. At night, larvae are less active and tend to move lower in the water column, although this varies with species, age and rearing tub. Prey densities will be adversely affected by water dilutions. Larvae do not feed during the night, so prey densities during this time are of no consequence. Rotifer density must be brought back up to the desired levels at first light. It is a good idea to place the airstone at the base of the standpipe to create a safety zone, so that larvae are gently pushed away and not pinned against the mesh screen.

As larvae grow, the flow rate of incoming water must be increased. Water quality before and during metamorphosis is critical as high nitrogen levels and weak currents are associated with increased development of deformities.

After metamorphosis, the young fish can be moved to rearing tubs for grow-out. Be sure to monitor water qual-ity and filtration devices carefully so that the wastes from one batch of larvae do not impact those that follow.

Replacing Evaporation

Evaporation in larval rearing tanks is often quite high, due to the lack of cover. In a dedicated fish room or closed area, humidity levels are kept high and evaporation is diminished. To replace evaporated water, drip fresh water from a reservoir placed above the rearing tank at a rate of less than one drop per second. Monitor specific gravity regularly so that large shifts and disruptive additions of large volumes of fresh water are avoided.

The specific gravity of larval rearing tubs fitted to central systems is corrected in the common sump. Fresh water is safely added to the sump and dripped into the rearing tubs during the night. In this way, stress is reduced and large shifts in specific gravity are avoided.

Heating Elements

A submersible heater should be positioned inside each isolated rearing tank above an airstone. The airstone will distribute the heat evenly throughout the aquarium and the risk of larvae getting burned by hanging around too close for too long is reduced. Also, the pilot light of the heater should be covered with black electrical tape. Larvae are attracted toward light during their initial days, and the heat from the heater can damage young larvae that get too close. If a light-emitting heater is positioned above an airstone, the larvae will exhaust themselves trying to get closer to the light. In larval tanks plumbed to a central system, the heater is kept in the individual tanks until the exchange rate of water passing through the tank is adequate to maintain proper temperature. The temperature should be set at 80°F, as this seems to be the optimal temperature for fast, healthy growth rates.

Aeration

Oxygen demand is high in a rearing tank, so aeration must be provided, but too much aeration can damage the larvae. When the larvae are small and delicate, lacking both fins and muscles to power them, the airflow should be very gentle.

One air pump should be attached to a gang valve feeding two outlets per larval rearing tank. When airstones are choked down to provide gentle, minimal aeration, they have a tendency to slow or stop. Utilizing two airstones lessens the chances that both will stop at one time. It also allows for better water flow throughout the tank.

Each airstone should be attached to a control valve that allows just enough air flow to agitate the surface and cause movement. During the first couple of days, adjust the air flow so the larvae can swim around but aren't fighting currents that cause exhaustion. Watch the larvae to determine the amount of aeration to provide. As the larvae grow the aeration can be increased.

Early-stage larvae should be supplied with gentle aeration of about 10 to 100 mL/min dependent on the species of larvae and the food being fed. Trial and error is the usual approach for most larval rearing husbandry.

Feeding efficiency on such prey types as copepods is generally increased in high-flow tanks. Circulation in the rearing tank is important to keep prey organisms moving around. Many larval prey are attracted to light and will become concentrated around the tank walls near the surface if circulation patterns are weak. Once the live prey clusters out of the water column, they have effectively been removed from the visual field of small larvae.

LARVAL REARING OPTIONS

Conventional larval rearing techniques must be rethought when more delicate larvae are being raised. Most serious breeders rearing marine fishes do so in round tanks with airstones to provide circulation. Alternatives are available for those aquarists willing to be creative.

Early-stage larvae are sensitive to physical damage caused by contact with tank walls and air bubbles created by passing compressed air through a diffuser. In the ocean, larvae seldom have contact with solid structures such as those that surround them in captivity. Contact with hard walls and vigorous bubble flows can be reduced or eliminated by using proper circulation techniques.

Traditional rearing tanks have one or more airstones fitted to the standpipe in the middle of the circular rearing tank. If one were to add dye to the rearing tank to trace the circulation pattern, a simple flow regime would be observed. As the bubbles rise in the center of the tank, water is brought to the surface and pushed equally outward from this single point. Surface tension keeps the water traveling out until it reaches the tank walls. Water then descends along the wall and is brought to the center of the tank floor and again back to the surface by the rising air.

A seldom used but worthwhile technique is to move water instead of air to achieve water circulation. By locating a water inlet near the center of the tank floor, a reversed-flow regime can be established in the absence of air bubbles. A flow of water is directed down at the center of the bottom of the tank. Minimizing the gap between the water inlet and the tank floor will maximize flow. Water hits the tank floor and spreads out evenly. Once the water reaches the tank wall it travels up to the surface and, again using surface tension, flows to the center of the tank where it descends, following the pull of water being injected to the tank. Flow rates can easily be adjusted to achieve the desired effect.

UNCONVENTIONAL TANKS: *KRIESEL*

Many home-based hobbyists and several scientific larval culturists are experimenting with plankton *kriesels* for use in larval culture. *Kriesel* or carousel in German refers to the slowly rotating, circular motion of water created within the tank. Originally designed to keep delicate pelagic jellyfish alive in captivity and their associated larval forms from settling to the tank floor, this design has since been refined for use in larval culture. In a kriesel, the water circulation keeps the jellyfish suspended in the middle of the tank or slowly rotating on the outside of the tank.

These systems need to be properly planned and constructed. Simple designs force water downward along a straight vertical wall. Water is forced in a circular motion

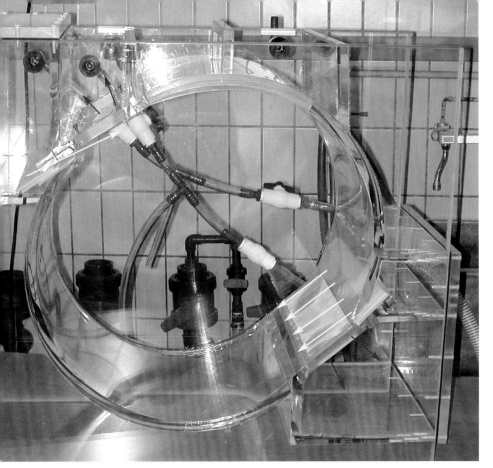

Plankton kriesel developed by Dr. Howard I. Browman at the Austevol Research Station in Norway is designed to keep pelagic larvae suspended in a body of water with gentle currents and no sharp corners or other obstructions. Pressurized water enters through narrow slots (yellow arrows) and exits through micron-mesh screens (red arrows). Constant currents keep the larvae from being drawn against the water outlet screens.

The jellyfish tanks were originally designed as display tanks and as such are typically narrow and quite tall to prevent settling. Larval *kriesel* designs benefit from being slightly wider. Commercial designs are available, although the price of such units would be prohibitively high for most hobbyists.

Still, the concept of these tanks is very simple and their construction is easily achieved with a bit of skill. Acrylic or polycarbonate materials are the most aesthetically pleasing when the seams are joined cleanly, but construction is often difficult due to the bending involved. Plywood is a simple to use material that can be formed to just about any configuration. A plywood box can be created from $\frac{3}{4}$-inch sheets to frame the outside dimensions. The circular pattern is then created by use of $\frac{1}{4}$-inch or lighter sheets of plywood or $\frac{5}{8}$-inch thick sheet PVC. Sheet PVC is easily worked with and provides a waterproof, smooth surface.

Larval fish and prey organisms are confined by the water flow in the middle of the tank, reducing potential for contact with tank walls and maximizing predator-prey interactions to aid in feeding efficiency. I have run many trials in homemade *kriesels* to observe their potential as larval rearing tanks and have been pleasantly surprised with the results. Pelagic seahorse juveniles feed efficiently in the moving water and do not get hung up in corners or surface films. Survival is generally increased with commonly raised marine species such as dottybacks and gobies, and even larval ornamental shrimps have been raised in *kriesels*.

Because of the life cycle of the fishes involved, the ma-

by bent walls, the acrylic or polycarbonate tank walls are bent to form a near circle or oblong oval. Following the bottom contour, water flows up the walls and uses surface tension to maintain momentum in a circular motion. A large intake screen is usually placed below the water inlet to continuously wash it to prevent larval fish from becoming trapped, pinned, or otherwise entangled in the mesh. The large size of such screens diffuses the strength of outgoing water. More complex models are completely closed with no access to the surface layer. Usually completely circular in nature, these units have an acrylic top fitted below the surface forcing water more uniformly in a circular flow.

rine breeder has a whole set of challenges not faced by the freshwater breeder. In order to be successful, an open and creative mind must be used to solve challenges. The potential of *kriesel*s as rearing tanks is real and, in my view, should be explored and exploited.

THE GREENWATER METHOD

Adding microalgae (phytoplankton) to turn rearing tank water green (or light brown) is a common practice in the rearing of many marine species. Water cultured to have a high concentration of microscopic, single-celled microalgae is commonly called *greenwater*.

Greenwater serves a variety of important functions. Perhaps foremost, greenwater is added to rearing systems to offer a food source to food organisms that fish larvae eat, such as rotifers, allowing prey populations to reproduce and maintain high nutritional quality. For this reason cultured phytoplankton species are typically limited to those containing high levels of omega-3 fatty acids such as *Nannochloropsis* and *Isochrysis*. *Chlorella* is often used in the Far East, although this species of microalgae lacks essential marine lipids.

Another important reason the greenwater technique is thought to work so well is the addition of contrast between prey organisms and the background. Visual acuity of fish larvae in early life stages is limited to just a few millimeters. When the water is crystal clear with no background color (in the case of clear aquariums) or a light background color, larval fish often have difficulty seeking out and hunting prey. Black backgrounds aid visual acuity, as does the greenwater. Feeding is more successful so that larvae grow faster and healthier. (The live microalgae population also helps maintain water quality by consuming dissolved wastes

Basic larval rearing tub: note slow drip of incoming greenwater from central filtration system, gentle bubble flow, and micron mesh protecting the standpipe.

and keeping them from building up in the rearing tank.)

When greenwater is employed under indoor culture protocols, as in the case of small-scale hobbyist production, prey organisms are usually limited to rotifers.

In contrast, commercial-scale outdoor systems use large concrete or earthen ponds. These ponds are typically fertilized, filled and then stocked with rotifers and often copepods after an algae bloom has occurred. In this way, prey organisms are allowed to multiply and the addition of copepods and mature water supports a plethora of microscopic organisms that contribute to the food web. Larval fish are stocked in such ponds and allowed to prey on whatever organisms may be available. Little control can be exerted by the culturist, but substantial numbers of fish are raised in such ponds.

Greenwater management in contained vessels is generally regarded as an art rather than a science. Aquaculturists in countries such as Taiwan and Tahiti who most often use this technique, add greenwater by sight to obtain the desired shade or consistency of color. The color used, that is the species of microalgae, seems unimportant. For providing omega-3 fatty acids, the golden-brown *Isochrysis* is better. Add only enough algae to the rearing tub so that a white disc submerged in the water will sink roughly 6 inches (15 cm) under the surface before disappearing from view. These discs are commonly sold as *sechi discs* and are a way to estimate the density of microalgae present. A precise density is not important here, only that not too much algae is added.

Preserved microalgae are readily available and will tint the water color boosting the visual acuity of larval fish, but this algae is not living and will not aid in the breakdown of ammonia. Preserved forms of microalgae will not alter pH levels, which is a benefit. The trade offs are simple: using preserved algae drastically reduces labor time and offers equal rations of fatty acids and background contrast to aid in larval fish feeding. Live algae feed on nitrogenous wastes. If water quality can be maintained within desirable limits without the use of live microalgae, pastes and bottled microalgae offer an ideal, labor-saving alternative.

POLYCULTURE

Polyculture is possible in larval rearing. Often the hatching rates of many species is quite poor. For various reasons, most often stemming from artificial incubation, what seem like full-term, developed embryos fail to hatch. If low numbers of larvae are raised in isolation, the nutritional value of prey organisms becomes a primary concern as the prey are eaten so slowly that they lose their nutrient value. (This is the so-called "clearing rate" in aquaculture, or the speed at which prey organisms are consumed.) It is possible to raise different species together to both conserve larval rearing space and increase clearing rates. As discussed in the next chapter, clearing rates and the addition of nutritionally adequate feeds is of utmost importance.

Larval polyculture is possible with different species as well as different spawns of the same species. The time each species requires to feed on rotifers and the transition to newly hatched *Artemia* are nearly identical, and mixing species or mixed broods of the same species should result in little harm being done.

Species chosen for polyculture should be chosen with a few considerations in mind. Metamorphosis brings on a real change in a fish's behavior. Switching from a pelagic existence to one of territorial nature is sure to bring on real consequences if species of obvious differences are raised together. Common species of dottybacks such as *Pseudochromis springeri, P. sankeyi, P. aldabraensis, P. fridmani* and *P. olivaceus* are well suited to polyculture, as their behavior patterns are similar near and after the onset of metamorphosis. Clownfish are well suited to polyculture. Species such as *Amphiprion ocellaris, A. percula, A. sandarcinos, A. perideraion,* and similar species are suited to culture together, while the larger clownfish species *A. melanopus, A. frenatus,* and *A. ephippium,* to name a few, can be raised together.

However, large, more aggressive species will impede the growth and increase mortality rates of slower growing species and they should not be mixed. The many species of cleaner gobies can be raised together in polyculture. Fishes of different families should not be raised together.

Polyculture is possible when numerous pairs are established on a spawning cycle. Spawns of up to three days difference may be raised together. Groups closer in age will exhibit better uniformity. If strict records are necessary to account for mortality, polyculture is difficult as early-stage larvae are very similar in appearance unless you have considerable experience in separating fish by small differences. Once the fish have reached metamorphosis, the differences between species becomes apparent and they can be removed to separate grow-out tanks.

INDIA

Plankton-rich currents in the Arabian Sea, as recorded from space by NASA. Concentrations of phytoplankton are seen as green swirls, and these sustain countless marine fish larvae.

CHAPTER 9

LARVAL NUTRITION

Foods & Feeding for Newly Hatched Fish

It comes a surprise to most people to learn that a great deal of the Earth's oxygen is produced in the ocean. Countless microscopic specks of single-cell algae congregate near the surface of the oceans and seas, being drawn here by sunlight. These plants give healthy ocean water a slight greenish cast and use photosynthesis to transform sunshine into nutrition for themselves and form life-giving oxygen that is expelled into the surrounding atmosphere. This rich community of microalgae is collectively known as phytoplankton and is found throughout the surface waters of the oceans. It is perhaps the backbone for all life here on earth.

Zooplankton, which consists of tiny crustaceans such as copepods, and the larvae of fishes, mollusks, gastropods and myriad others, is also found high in the water column, drifting with the currents and feeding on phytoplankton. The oceans' pelagic zone, or upper water column, is an extremely productive layer with a dynamic food chain. Phytoplankon is the primary producer. Small zooplanktonic organisms prey upon the phytoplankton. Larval fishes and larger plankton-feeding fishes then prey upon the smaller forms of zooplankton. The chain grows exponentially with small plankton and fishes being consumed by larger plankton and fishes, with apex animals such as the great whales and sharks and, if you care to think this way, humans as the end result.

Larval fishes spend the first days or weeks of their lives carried mercilessly by the oceans' currents. Plankton-rich waters supply a never-ending food source for these tiny fishes. They can pick and choose the size, color, shape, and behavior of organisms they wish to consume. The driving force behind prey selection is often complex and dependent on the morphological or anatomical attributes of the larvae.

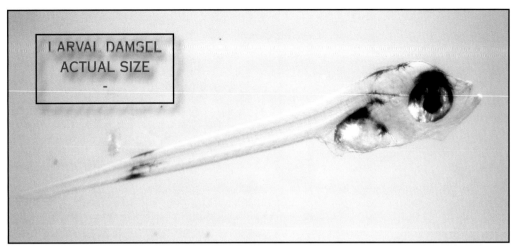

Much like a splinter of glass with blue eyes and a mouth: first-feeding-stage South Sea Devil Damsel larva greatly magnified. Its actual size is about 2 mm—the length of the tiny red line above [inset]. This specimen has been feeding on rotifers and has a full gut and healthy characteristics.

To raise marine fishes in captivity, the first requirement is to be a successful keeper of balanced, healthy aquarium environments. The second requirement is being a plankton culturist. It is possible to raise at least a small percentage of the spawns of some species using frozen or bottled plankton—even pulverized flake foods—but to be successful in raising large numbers of larvae past metamorphosis, you must culture both algae and plankton. Specifically, you will need to culture tiny unicellular algae that are fed to the slightly larger zooplankton which, in turn, will be fed to the larval fish which are bigger still. To put this microscopic food chain into perspective, more than 2 billion algal cells, perhaps three dozen rotifers and at least one fish larva could all fit comfortably in a single drop of water.

FEEDING PERFORMANCE OF LARVAE

The transition from *endogenous* to *exogenous* feeding, when larvae switch from living on their own internal yolk reserves to feeding on organisms they must capture, marks a critical period in the life history of marine fish larvae. This period is usually associated with massive and highly variable mortality rates. High mortality is well documented in both wild and cultured marine fish larvae.

In the wild, high mortality of marine fish larvae has been linked to predation from other fishes and pelagic invertebrates, but most often starvation due to insufficient zooplankton prey density of appropriate size. Many factors are known to influence the feeding success of both wild and cultured marine fish larvae, such as the development of the visual system and other sense organs, digestive system, swimming ability, feeding mechanism, and search behavior, as well as the size, color, density, and swimming behavior of zooplankton prey organisms.

It is known that the size of prey consumed increases with increasing body size of the larvae and that prey selection correlates with the mouth gape of larvae. This suggests that mouth gape limits the size of prey that could be effectively consumed by larvae and predicts that larvae might prey on organisms near the size of their mouth gape. It has been demonstrated, however, that most marine fish larvae consume prey that are only 20% of their mouth gape (Heath 1993), suggesting that other constraints besides mouth gape limit the size of prey that can be successfully consumed.

Recently, Turingan et al. (2005) concluded that the feeding performance of marine fish larvae is influenced by the development of their suction-feeding mechanism, the primary mechanism that fishes utilize to capture prey, sucking it into their mouths. The suction-feeding mechanism in fishes involves a complex suite of bones, muscles, ligaments and tendons in the head that develop through *ontogeny*, a genetically predetermined progression from simple to more

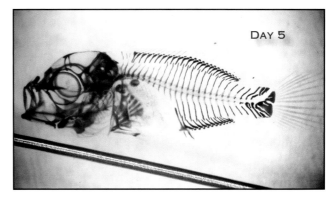
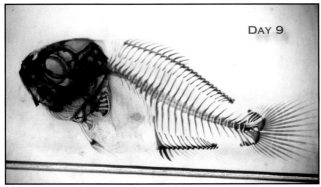
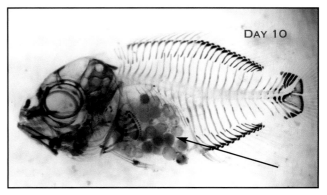

Development of the feeding apparatus and skeletal system in a larval Ocellaris Clownfish, illustrated by the author through the use of clearing and staining techniques. Soft cartilage appears as blue, bone as pink or purple. Increasing complexity and strength of the jaw allows the fish to catch and ingest progressively larger, faster prey. Note undigested *Artemia* cysts (arrow).

complex and larger anatomic structures.

For example, Stoecker and Govoni (1984) found that first-feeding larval Gulf Menhaden (*Brevoortia patronus*) selected only dinoflagellates and tintinnids that were small and less mobile before switching to copepod nauplii 10 days after hatching.

Many prey selectivity studies have relied on rotifers (*Brachionus* spp.) and *Artemia* as substitutes for wild plankton to determine the occurrence of shifts in the larval diet. Rotifers are typically viewed as small, less-mobile prey while *Artemia* as larger, more elusive prey (Beck and Turingan in press). Larval Weakfish (*Cynoscion regalis*) selected rotifers until 14 days after hatching, at which time they began consuming *Artemia* (Pryor and Epifano 1993). Similarly, Krebs and Turingan (1993) found that Red Drum (*Sciaenops ocel-*

latus) switch from feeding on rotifers to *Artemia* at 13 days after hatching. Prey selectivity is well documented in marine fish larvae, although the functional basis of prey choice is poorly understood. One theory is that the timing of dietary shifts occurs concurrently with the development of more advanced feeding mechanisms.

In my research at Florida Institute of Technology, we demonstrated that the pattern of prey selectivity is consistent with the pattern of development of the feeding mechanism in two marine aquarium fishes. The development of the head and its constituent mechanics are quite different among species of marine aquarium fishes at hatching. Large, robust larvae such as clownfish are well developed at hatching and have the ability to prey on relatively large, fast prey by day three after hatching. In contrast, dottybacks

BREEDING RELATIVITY: SIZES OF FOODS & FISH LARVAE

PHYTOPLANKTON	SIZE IN MICRONS (μM)
Nannochloropsis oculata	1 - 2
Pavlova	4 - 7
Isochrysis	5
Tetraselmis	12

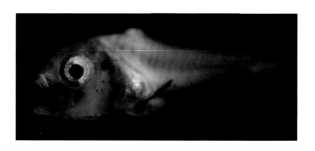

ZOOPLANKTON	NAUPLII	ADULTS
Copepods		
Typical Copepods	50 - 90	150 - 500
Tisbe spp.	55 - 80	180 - 250
Schizopera elatensis	50 - 75	500
Acartia tonsa	60 - 85	150 - 200

Rotifers
SS strain (*B. rotundiformis*) 80 - 100
S strain (Cayman strain of *B. plicatilis*)   180 - 220
L strain (Norwegian strain of *B. plicatilis*)   300 - 340

Artemia (Newly hatched)	
Argentemia (Grade 0, Platinum Label)	<450
Argentemia (Grade 1, Gold Label)	450 - 475
Argentemia (Grade 2, Silver Label)	500 - 525

Artemia	
24-hr-old *Artemia*	600 - 700
48-hr-old *Artemia*	720 - 850

FISH LARVAE	TOTAL LENGTH (MM)
DEMERSAL SPAWNERS	
Dottybacks	
Pseudochromis fridmani	3.35
Pictichromis diadema	3.27
Clownfishes	
Amphiprion ocellaris	4.06
Amphiprion frenatus	4.12
Gobies	
Gobiosoma oceanops	3.39
Gobiosoma multifasciatum	3.09
Gobiodon citrinus	2.61
Cryptocentrus cinctus	2.89
Blennies	
Petroscirtes breviceps	2.66
Meiacanthus grammistes	2.84
Grammas	
Gramma loreto	3.22
Gramma melacara	3.09
Jawfish	
Opistognathus aurifrons	3.87

FISH LARVAE	TOTAL LENGTH (MM)
Comets & Assessors	
Calloplesiops altivelis	2.98
Assessor macneilli	3.01
Cardinalfishes	
Apogon cyanosoma	2.69
Sphaeramia orbicularis	3.3
Damselfish	
Chrysiptera taupou	2.06
PELAGIC SPAWNERS	(Size at hatching)
Reef Basslets	
Liopropoma eukrines	1.89
Liopropoma rubre	1.69
Angelfishes	
Centropyge spp.	1.90
Pomacanthus spp.	2.35
Surgeonfish	
Acanthurus spp.	1.7
Dragonet	
Synchiropus splendens	1.19

PHOTO TOP RIGHT: SARGEANT MAJOR (*ABUDEFDUF SAXATILIS*) LARVA - **15 DAYS OLD** - MAGNIFIED APPROX. **14X.**

A NANO
FOOD CHAIN

RELATIVE SIZES OF
PREDATOR & PREY

ALGAL CELLS 1 MICRON

DAMSELFISH LARVA 4000 MICRONS

ROTIFER 200 MICRONS

In early-stage rearing of many species, the first food eaten by a fish larva is live rotifers, which in turn consume algal cells.

do not develop this ability until 10 days after hatching.

Without getting into great anatomical detail, we know that when a larval fish hatches there is no hard bone present. A fish is instead made up of flexible cartilage. Many of the key structures responsible for feeding are first observed as cartilage complexes that eventually give rise to bones that will allow the mechanics of adult feeding behaviors. Most first-feeding larvae have very few skeletal components.

Newly hatched larvae of dottybacks, damselfishes, blennies and even clownfishes are inefficient at capturing fast-moving prey probably due to the inherent simplicity of their feeding mechanism. As larvae grow and cartilage is replaced by bone that allows more complex feeding abilities, the feeding performance of larvae increases and they are better suited to capturing more elusive prey.

For aquaculturists it is extremely difficult to identify and successfully culture all the ideal food organisms for larval marine fish. Rotifers, while commercially important and necessary in many instances, offer relatively poor nutritional value to developing larvae. They are, however, small and slow moving, allowing most fishes to successfully capture them. Rotifers are still too large for many species of pelagic spawners to feed on as larvae.

Copepod nauplii are nutritionally superior to rotifers and in many cases much smaller; however, most advanced stages of these nauplii are too elusive for first-feeding larvae to capture. Nature's webs are seldom simple and not always possible (or desirable) to replicate in captivity. If one out of one million larvae survive in the wild, the population will most likely be sustained and reproduction deemed successful. In captivity, however, one larva making it through would seldom be called a success. We know that massive mortality due to starvation occurs during the early larval stages. We do not, however, fully understand why. There are no shortages of planktonic food organisms present in prolific wild plankton blooms. What a larva selects from this bloom and why are important questions, both ecologically and commercially.

Several possibilities exist. The first is that the larvae utilize a similar feeding behavior no matter what prey type is encountered and possibly exhaust their valuable energy reserves in failed capture attempts. If their feeding behavior is efficient at catching one type of prey, then those attacks will yield successful results, while strikes aimed at more elusive prey will not. In such cases, copepod nauplii or other nutritionally rich foods may be ingested by luck or happenstance and these larvae would, in theory, survive. Those whose actions come up empty each time will waste away.

Another possibility is that larvae are highly selective in choosing prey types based on the targets' color, shape, behavior and other cues. Captive observations suggest that larvae are highly selective and often turn down multiple prey organisms before initiating a strike. If this proves true, larvae in dense patches of suitable prey would survive while those cast adrift in less fertile ocean currents would starve. Additionally, some larvae may be primarily interested in the size of their target prey items. Gut contents of captive dottybacks, blennies and damsels reveal that multiple offerings are acceptable so long as they fit within the mouth gape and can be successfully captured. Dinoflagellates, ciliates, protozoa, and even diatoms have been found in the guts of larval fish. This gives us some clues about what to feed: get the size right and then it is simply a matter of nutritional value. If suitably nutritious foods have been ingested, larvae will survive, if not they will perish.

Though the development of the feeding mechanism and feeding ability are quite rudimentary at hatching, several factors play a very important role in feeding success. Feed-

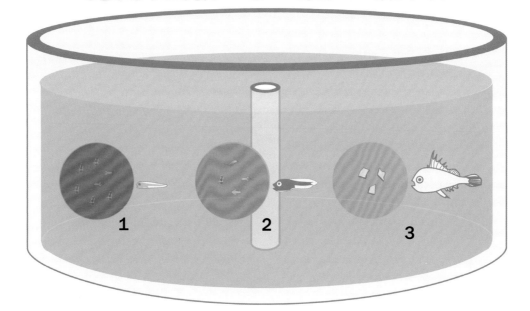

FEEDING REGIMEN: FIRST FOODS TO GROW-OUT

1

2

3

Stages of feeding in a larval rearing tub: 1. First-feeding larva is fed concentrated offerings of prey items such as rotifers or copepods with heavy additions of greenwater. Proper food density is crucial at this stage. **2.** Growing larva has moved up to larger prey, less densely stocked, such as *Artemia* nauplii; greenwater concentration is lowered. **3.** Metamorphosed fish is on a grow-out diet with flake foods that it finds and takes with ease; greenwater is phased out.

ing efficiency on such elusive prey as copepods is increased with water currents. Copepods have highly sensitive hairs similar to the nueromasts and lateral line of fish that pick up vibrations in the water column. In slow moving or stagnant water, copepods detect fish very quickly, making feeding difficult for larval fish. In faster moving water, however, larvae stand a much better chance of success. Larval rearing tanks benefit from a moderate water flow, usually provided by airstones. Visibility, contrast, illumination, and density of prey all play an important role in larval feeding.

Many food choices are available to hobbyists willing to put the time into their culture. Rotifers are no longer the only food available. Committed hobbyists should attempt to offer the most nutritious food possible and in appropriate densities. Even a small and random addition of prey types such as copepods will drastically improve survivorship. No matter what foods are available, a complex food web is needed to help make marine larvae thrive.

MICROALGAE OR PHYTOPLANKTON

Commercially prepared rotifer foods and preserved algae mixes allow small-scale marine breeders to culture rotifers without first culturing their own greenwater. Still, live microalgae offers several distinct advantages over the off-the-shelf products. First, live microalgae maintain water quality much more efficiently in rotifer cultures than do preserved foods. There are various species and cultured strains of phytoplankton available to aquarists as a food source for rotifers, each with its advantage as a culture organism.

Microalgae forms the base of captive food webs and each species available proves a suitable food for rotifers. The most common and, in my opinion, prolific are *Nannochloropsis oculata* and "Tahitian *Isochrysis*" (T-ISO). These species are easily cultured, provide good nutrition for the rotifers, and contain essential fatty acid and lipid content adequate for larval development. Other microalgae species available include *Chlorella, Tetraselmis, Nannochloris,* and *Pyramimonas. Nannochloropsis oculata* and T-ISO *Isochrysis* are microalgaes of choice, but local water conditions often force a different species into culture.

Culturing techniques are similar for each species mentioned here. It is best to set up a system of shelves for live food cultures. This will allow easy maintenance as well as preventing contamination. A top shelf should be dedicated to hold the greenwater cultures, another shelf or two below will hold rotifers and perhaps a third will be used for hatching *Artemia* . The idea here is to prevent contamination of your greenwater. Rotifers are notorious for getting

ESSENTIAL ELEMENTS REQUIRED FOR CULTURING MICROALGAE

Algae cultures for *Nannochloroposis, Isochrysis* and other recommended species are available from various aquaculture supply houses (see Sources).

Live starter culture of microalgae
Culture vessels (2 liter clear soda bottles)
48-inch double-bulb fluorescent light fixture
48-inch fluorescent light bulbs
Aquarium air pump
Gang valves (with 7 total outlets)
Lengths of rigid air line tubing
Flexible air-line tubing
Synthetic sea salt
Hydrometer
Small funnel
Phytoplankton fertilizer

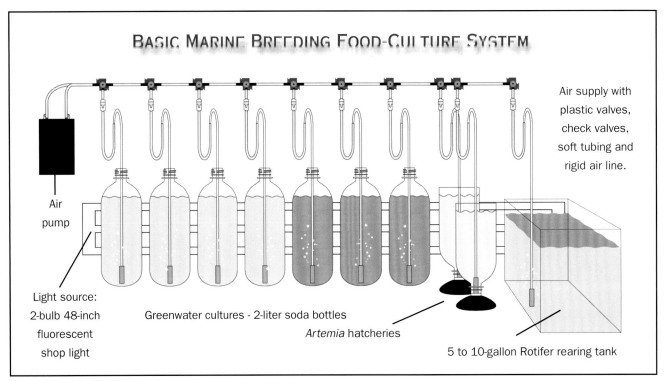

Air supply with plastic valves, check valves, soft tubing and rigid air line.

Air pump

Light source: 2-bulb 48-inch fluorescent shop light

Greenwater cultures - 2-liter soda bottles

Artemia hatcheries

5 to 10-gallon Rotifer rearing tank

A complete culture operation for the home marine breeder can fit on a small counter and will produce all the essentials for rearing many species of fish. A single air-supply line aerates greenwater cultures, brine shrimp hatcheries, and rotifer rearing tank.

into microalgae cultures, devouring every last algae cell as the rotifer population increases. This is not a problem if more than one algae culture is present, but can cause havoc otherwise. An ideal situation is to house rotifer cultures and algae cultures in separate rooms, although this is often impractical for small-scale systems.

Various methods exist for culturing and harvesting microalgae. The intended goal is to produce large quantities of a strain of microalgae that can be used as feed for rotifers and greenwater for larval rearing. Whatever methods offer the fewest headaches should be the ones you chose.

CULTURE REQUIREMENTS

As with any living organism, microalgae has certain requirements for it to survive and reproduce. These algae have chlorophyll in their cells, and the chlorophyll uses light to generate food for the algae cells during photosynthesis. Nitrogen and phosphorous are also required in a ratio of about 10:1. It also turns out that many other minor trace elements are needed, but for the sake of ease I will simply recommend that you buy and use a commercial microalgae feed—basically a specialty plant fertilizer. Bottled fertilizers sold by aquaculture supply houses (see Sources) have all major and minor elements required for algal growth, and directions for use are typically found on the bottle.

Light is needed by the algae cells to carry out photosynthesis. The most inexpensive means of supplying light with a fluorescent light fixture or shop light with two 48-inch fluorescent tubes available at most hardware stores. Generally, inexpensive bulbs (5,500 to 6,500 K) are sufficient for microalgae cultures, although full-spectrum or grow light-type bulbs are favored by some hobbyists.

The light fixture should be attached to the wall roughly

1 inch behind the culture bottles horizontally or vertically depending on the placement of the cultures. Direct the light toward the side of the culture bottles so the cells are exposed to more light to increase their growth rate. Lights should provide 24-hour illumination to the algae culture. For this reason, culturing is best done away from (or screened from) the fish room. A black plastic curtain can be used to prevent unwanted light pollution from the culture area.

Both microalgae and rotifers tolerate a wide range of salinity values. Rotifers, however, cannot tolerate drastic changes in salinity. It is important to keep both algae and rotifers near the same specific gravity as the larval rearing tanks to reduce osmotic shock and stress to food organisms upon their addition. If the change in specific gravity is too great between live feed culture tanks and larval feeding tanks prey organisms will perish and will not be added to the forage base.

Aeration should be provided to the microalgae culture bottles to facilitate gas exchange. Carbon dioxide is needed by the cells to drive photosynthesis. When aeration is not provided, the algae cells quickly utilize all carbon dioxide present and the culture will crash. Aeration also maintains pH and keeps the algae cells in constant motion to expose each cell to the light. Aeration also keeps the culture solution uniform in temperature and distribution of nutrients.

A large air pump should be set up with a series of gang valves to supply both the algae and rotifer cultures. Gang valves are available in many styles and differ in number of outlets. These valves can be joined together in series, making five, 10, 15, or more outlets available. A length of rigid airline tubing should be cut approximately an inch or two higher than the height of the culture bottle. There is no need for air stones and, in fact, when air stones are used they simply clog up. The rigid air line tubing is a no-fuss way of keeping the origin of the bubbles at the bottom of the culture bottle. The rigid air line tubing is attached to flexible airline tubing and finally attached to an inlet on the gang valve. Vigorous aeration is not essential. A slow stream of bubbles is enough to keep the mixture homogenous. The intended goal is to keep everything in the culture bottle moving. They don't have to go on a ride in an amusement park.

Household temperatures are fine for culturing microalgae. If you are culturing the microalgae and rotifers in a fish room, chances are good that the temperature will be above normal household temperatures, and this is good. The ideal culturing temperature for most species is around 75°F, although most species will tolerate temperatures down to the mid 60s. At one point I maintained a fish room in the basement of my upstate New York home where the temperature would drop to around 50°F during the winter. The microalgae growth rates subsided and productivity fell. I moved the culture bottles into 10-gallon tanks half filled with freshwater, equipped with a submersible heater set at 75°F, and a small powerhead for circulation. A rigid airline was added and the algae cells proved prolific.

The pH of microalgae cultures often increases as the algae densities increase. This is a result of the limited carbon dioxide available. An increase in aeration is usually enough to solve this problem. Adjusting the pH with commercial uppers and downers is not necessary for microalgae culture.

The easiest culture vessels to obtain and use are 2-liter soda bottles. Soda bottles are cheap, clear (to allow for light penetration), and easily replaceable should one become too messy to clean. The size of the bottles allows a series of them to be placed in a relatively small amount of space as well. Tinted soda bottles should be avoided as the color will cut down on light penetration.

Aside from soda bottles, there are numerous other choices that would qualify as good culture vessels. Inex-

TIP

Isochrysis (T-ISO) grows best at higher specific gravities. Saltwater of proximately 1.021 SG is ideal for rapid cell division. Many hobbyists do not have success with this species, reporting poor and often slow growth at lower specific gravities. The algae cells must divide as quickly as possible to suppress the growth of bacterial populations.

Jumbo-scale phytoplankton and rotifer culturing cylinders and tubs in a commercial aquaculture facility. In contrast, hobbyist-scale food culture systems can fit on a small counter.

cells held together with agar paste. These work well but are a bit time-consuming to use. The second choice is live starter cultures. These are shipped overnight and arrive at your doorstep in a bottle or a plastic bag. I prefer live innoculants as they are faster and easier to use.

Seven culture vessels should be obtained and cleaned before the microalgae starter culture is due to arrive. Assuming you are using 2L or 3L clear plastic soda bottles, labels should be removed and the bottles rinsed with hot water followed by a strong salt solution. After each bottle has been cleaned, the bottle cap should be placed back on to avoid contamination by any foreign matter. Although all seven bottles will be cleaned and capped, only one will be used to start the culture.

Artifical seawater should be mixed fresh to a specific gravity of 1.014 to 1.017 for most phytoplankton species and strains (1.021 for *Isochrysis*). It is a good idea to premix a batch of seawater and store it in a container such as a clean plastic garbage can with a tight fitting lid. This will save the trouble of mixing up seawater to match the salinity of the pre-existing water. Fill the first bottle about two-thirds full and insert rigid airline tubing to provide aeration. A ball of cotton or filter floss should be placed in the bottle's opening to prevent salt spray and evaporation and to exclude foreign contamination. The bottle should be placed on the shelf in front of the light fixture to await the arrival of the starter culture.

When the live microalgae starter culture arrives it should

pensive water jugs are available in both glass and plastic and work well as culturing vessels. Any clear jug that is cylindrical and tall will work. Commercial breeding facilities use huge columns made from Plexiglas or fiberglass to culture microalgae. Obviously, the home-based breeder is working in miniature, but the basic processes are the same.

The first thing needed to produce greenwater is an innoculant or starter culture of the microalgae you plan to grow (see Sources.) A friend who breeds marine fish and has cultures of microalgae is the easiest source. Another source for algae is a local college or university that offers courses in aquaculture. These schools usually maintain a culture of both rotifers and algae as part of their rearing projects and are usually generous in donating a small batch to a budding hobbyist.

Biological and aquaculture supply houses usually offer two forms of starter cultures. The first is a disc of dry algae

all be poured immediately into the warm saltwater in the prepared soda bottle. Use a small plastic funnel to transfer microalgae into the small opening of the soda bottle—this is messy stuff and you don't want to waste any. You may have to add saltwater so that the water level is near the top of the bottle, but before it begins to narrow. This will provide the most surface area for aeration and gas exchange. The light should then be left on at all times. The recommended dosage of fertilizer should also be added at this point.

In roughly seven days, but as few as four or five, the water will turn dark green with a dense population of microalgae. Congratulations! You have now cultured your own greenwater.

After the culture attains this dark green color (see accompanying photos) about a third of the culture is transferred to a new soda bottle. New seawater is added to replace the lost water in the first culture bottle. After 5 to 7 days, a portion of this culture can be used to start the third culture and so on until all seven bottles of microalgae are growing in front of the light.

This simple method for culturing microalgae is the easiest and is used by most small-scale breeders I know. Larger hatcheries and commercial facilities that produce tremendous amounts of microalgae (in excess of 100 gallons) or are concerned with contamination use a more rigorous approach. The procedure described next assures that the species of algae being cultured is not contaminated with another species of algae or more importantly bacteria that may out-compete the intended culture species. (The average home breeder does not have to follow this protocol, but it is good to know if you ever want to culture an absolutely pure strain of microalgae.)

Pure strains of microalgae are available from a biological supply houses, shipped and stored in sealed test tubes. Upon arrival, the algae cells are separated into four sterile test tubes with sterile seawater. These test tubes form the backbone of the microalgae culture. The unused tubes should be stored in the refrigerator until they are needed. The cells from one test tube are added to a larger culture vessel of sterile seawater, often one liter. When this vessel

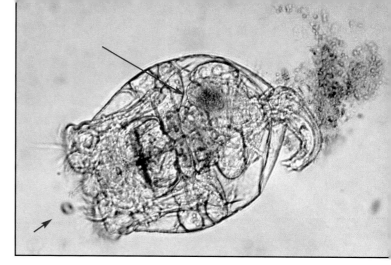

Rotifer (*Brachionus plicatilis*) greatly magnified, with mouth at left surrounded by hairlike cirri that allow it to capture and ingest green phytoplankton cells (arrows). Note algae in gut.

has bloomed, its contents are transferred to a larger culture vessel. This cycle continues until the largest culture vessel has bloomed and is harvested. New cultures are always started from the pure test tube samples. They are never started with algae cells from one of the larger culture vessels which may have become contaminated with different algae cells, ciliates or airborne organisms.

After each cycle, the culture vessels should be cleaned thoroughly with hot water, chlorine bleach or if glass, hydrochloric acid. Commercial facilities use autoclaves for the sterilization of all their culture vessels. For the average hobbyist such extreme steps to prevent contamination are not necessary, but are worth the extra effort if a problem arises during the production of the microalgae, namely if the green bottles suddenly turn clear.

ROTIFER CONTAMINATION

Every aquarist I know, myself included, who has ever cultured microalgae and rotifers has at least once run into a problem with rotifer contamination. At one point I was running two 5-gallon water jug microalgae cultures that became contaminated with rotifers. I first noticed several small dust size particles floating about in the microalgae. Assuming it was merely dust, I thought nothing of it. The

Instant microalgae paste products in many species allow the feeding of greenwater without having to culture live algae.

next day, more dust particles were observed and the dark green water seemed to lose intensity. Then the other culture lost color. Soon the beautiful green color faded into a color similar to tea and eventually became clear as the rotifer density increased and all the microalgae was lost. Many clownfish larvae also perished in this mishap.

There are many routes rotifers can travel to get into microalgae cultures and you must take precautions. Plug all culture vessels with clean floss to prevent airborne intrusions. Minimize aeration in rotifer cultures to reduce spray. The most important thing to keep in mind is to restrict all tools and materials used to microalgae cultures to microalgae cultures and rotifer tools to rotifer cultures. This includes funnels, airline tubing and anything else that may be found in the vicinity of the cultures. Keep your culture areas neat and tidy. Everything should have a place and should stay there. After working with rotifers, wash your hands. It is best to do any work that needs to be done on the microalgae first, before any work is done with the rotifers. Hitchhikers are the main threat.

INSTANT MICROALGAE

Reed Mariculture introduced Instant Algae® several years ago as an alternative to culturing live algae. Large microalgae cultures are essentially grown under sterile conditions and highly concentrated into a thick paste formula. (The algae cells are intact but not alive and cannot be used to start a live culture.) Algae paste is an excellent alternative for those unable to spend the time or resources to culture their own algae. Large amounts of algae can easily be stored, effectively eliminating problems associated with live culture crashes or small crops. Most strains have a long shelf life and can be frozen for over two years.

Like cultured greenwater, this Instant Algae® has two main roles in larviculture. The main goal is to feed and maintain rotifer cultures and the second is to create and sustain greenwater in the larval rearing tanks. Both can be successfully accomplished with algae paste. When proper water quality is maintained few differences can be observed between live and preserved algae. *Nannochloropsis oculata* should be the main algae species chosen in paste form to accomplish the desired goal of raising marine aquarium fish.

Care should be taken to ensure that algae is used before its expiration date and stored properly. Upon arrival, take the time to smell the paste and observe its color. If not properly stored, microalgae paste will foul turning brown in color with a distinct pungent smell. If it is added to rotifer cultures or larval rearing tanks, mortality will quickly ensue.

Care should be taken when feeding microalgae paste to rotifer cultures and larval rearing tanks. It is easy to add too much of this algae to a tank. It is highly concentrated and best mixed in a separate container before application to a culture tank.

ZOOPLANKTON & VOLUMETRICS

Securing an adequate supply of nutritionally acceptable prey organisms or zooplankton is still the largest bottleneck to larval rearing and often the biggest stumbling block to breeding a species for the first time. Since the commercial culture of many marine aquarium fishes—as well as food-fish species—became common practice, many advances have occurred in nutrition and the availability of appropriate first foods. The implications of diet on the survivorship, appearance and overall health of larvae and juveniles is becoming better understood.

After obtaining and culturing acceptable prey organisms, the breeder's next most-difficult task in larval feeding is maintaining adequate prey densities in the rearing tank.

Larval fishes are innately poor hunters in their early stages. It takes several attempts before newly hatched larvae are capable of actually catching and ingesting a prey organism. Larvae may encounter dozens of prey organisms, all visually inspected and ignored before finding one that is suitable. In order to get larvae to ingest sufficient nutrients, a proper density of prey organisms must be maintained.

Most larvae will require a prey density of 3 to 15 organisms per milliliter. During early developmental stages a high density of prey organisms is extremely important. As the larvae grow and hone their hunting skills, lower concentrations of live zooplankton are acceptable.

In order to estimate the number of prey organisms present in both the culture chamber and rearing tank, organisms are estimated volumetrically as the number of prey per mL of water. To estimate this number several methods are available.

The most foolproof technique makes use of a Sedgewick-Rafter counting slide. This is a graduated microscope slide, that when covered with a cover slide, contains exactly one mL of water. Under a compound light microscope or dissecting microscope, the total number of prey are counted and thus estimated as the number of prey occurring in one mL of rearing water. One mL depression slides work just as well and are available in glass or ceramic. Typically these depression slides are available as single units or arranged in a 12-well block. Perhaps 5 mL of water from the rearing tank is extracted and counted as five isolated mL's to get an accurate average reading.

It is useful to have liter marks etched in the side of the rearing tank walls similar to that of the rotifer cultures. In this way the volume of rearing tank water can be used to calculate the number of prey organisms present and the number needed to be added.

ROTIFERS

The microscopic or near-microscopic rotifer (*Brachionus plicatili*) is the most commonly cultured larval food in the aquaculture industry today. Its name (Latin for "wheel-bearer") comes from the crown-like cilia or tufts that encircle its oral opening and appear to spin as it sieves microscopic foods out of the water. Its use as a food organism for captive-bred fishes dates back to the 1950's when it was first developed as a larval food in Japan. The ease with which this organism is cultured allows incredible densities to be main-

ROTIFER SIZES & STRAINS

When people attempted to rear a species of marine fish in years past, they would simply culture "rotifers." Today this term is too vague to offer any real advice or direction toward success.

Many scientific studies now target the first feeding of commercially important species as especially crucial. Many of these reports stated that rotifers are an unacceptable diet for first feeding in many species. What these papers fail to report is the species or, more importantly, the strain of rotifer in use. Extensive culture protocols exist for rotifers and it is beyond the scope of this book to examine their culture in detail. It is, however, worth paraphrasing some important aspects of their culture and enrichment.

Rotifers are well suited to commercial aquaculture practices as they are extremely adaptable to varying levels of salinity and temperature. The Phylum Rotifera as a whole occurs in salinity levels of 1 to 97 ppt and temperature values from near freezing to well over 90°F. Optimal culture values for commercial species lie in the range of 1.014 to 1.020 S.G. and a temperature in of about 75 to 80°F. It is very important to identify the culture conditions such as temperature and salinity from which a newly acquired rotifer culture existed. Each strain has slightly different requirements that must be met in order to exploit the full reproductive potential.

Phytoplankton culture room at Florida Institute of Technology: pure culture flasks are on top shelf, growout vessels (glass carboys and large fiberglass cylinders) are below and left.

lionth of meter (μm). Some strains of *B. plicatilis* from Norway are as large as 350 micrometers in length, whereas other strains of *B. plicatilis* from the Caymans are just 150 micrometers in length.

To further add to this confusion, *Brachionus rotundiformis*, once thought quite common in the aquaculture industry and denoted as the *S-type* rotifer, is not as widespread as previously thought. While *B. rotundiformis* is a recognized species, it is not likely to be available outside private cultures. A strain of rotifer from Japan is reported at 80 μm in length. For anyone rearing marine fish and reporting techniques or methods for others to follow, it is now necessary to state what strain of rotifer was used (if known) or at the very least its source.

Fortunately, rearing most demersal spawners will be successful with all but the largest strains of rotifers. It is always advisable to choose the smallest strain possible for culture. The ideal length of rotifers suited to culture marine aquarium fish range from 150 to 250 μm in length. Small rotifers are always present within any given culture system and can be sieved to isolate small individuals and in essence create a smaller strain of rotifer. In common culture and harvest practices, larger strains usually dominate and must be periodically sieved if a small strain is desired.

Many distinct rotifer strains are available. In today's aquaculture industry there are strains suited to culture under most conditions. The generation time of these organisms is extremely short and adaptations are quickly observed. When transferred to different culture conditions, rotifers adapt at varying rates. If the change in conditions is drastic, a major percentage of the population may be killed, with few survivors left to reproduce. The progeny of these rotifers continually adapt through each generation to thrive under the given set of conditions. Evolution is marked by natural selection. While evolution may seem a strong word for such a short time lapse, it helps to understand the occurrences within a rotifer culture.

Stable rotifer cultures

Rotifer culture can be an intimidating and time-consuming

tained and harvested. An organism of swamps and polluted water holes, the rotifer can thrive in many different environments, including saltwater.

It is now obvious that a tremendous amount of confusion exists in literature pertaining to rotifers. In older literature an *L strain* and *S strain* of rotifers (large and small strains respectively) are mentioned. A few years ago it was demonstrated that these strains of rotifers represented two distinct species. It is probable that many strains or species are represented in the aquaculture industry, as extreme variability exists with both size and culture protocols. The unit of measure used for rotifers is the micrometer, or one mil-

process. It often takes some time for aquarists to become comfortable with its details and to maintain reliable cultures at high densities. Keeping a stable culture of rotifers that can be reliably harvested for food is paramount to larval rearing. Newcomers to rotifer culture should be aware of several facets of their care.

In order to maintain stable cultures of rotifers, their broad nutritional requirements must be met. As noted above, rotifers are filter feeders armed with a ring of cilia that constantly deliver water and suspended particulate matter to their mouthparts. As long as the particles are of acceptable size, rotifers will ingest a variety of feeds, including bacteria and unicellular algae as well as manufactured rotifer diets with or without the inclusion of yeast.

Optimal growth and reproduction are achieved when cultures are maintained on a diet of live microalgae or greenwater. This diet is, however, labor-intensive to supply. Satisfactory results can be obtained when rotifers are fed manufactured diets that drastically reduce the time involved in maintaining cultures. The main options available are rotifer foods containing yeast or those based on feeding microalgae or phytoplankton.

Caution should be used when feeding yeast-based diets to ensure rotifers remain the dominant organism. Rotifer cultures maintained on a yeast-based diet often become contaminated and overrun by ciliates.

Microalgae paste is a good alternative to live microalgae. *Nannochloropsis oculata* followed by the Tahitian strain of *Isochrysis galbana* (T-ISO) are the best choices for rotifer culture. There is no set standard for the amount of algae to add each day, as culture conditions constantly fluctuate along with the density of rotifers. A good tip is to tint the water light green and observe the time required for it to clear. Then, add more slowly to the culture tank each day until it takes roughly 12 to 14 hours to become clear. Each morning the rotifer culture should be clear, or more accurately, tea colored. Rotifers are ravenous feeders that consume food particles and pass them through their digestive tracts within 45 minutes. When the water is clear, the culture is not being overfed. Overfeeding is a quick and easy way to bring instability to a culture. It is advisable to underfeed until experience is gained. More frequent smaller feedings are preferred to a single large dose of algae.

Cultures must be started with an initial high density of at least 5 to 10 rotifers per mL of culture water—preferably more. If lower densities are stocked or maintained, ciliates and bacteria may gain a foothold and out-compete your rotifers. When a starter culture of rotifers arrives, usually by mail from a biological supply house, a small number of rotifers is present in a small volume of water. This density and volume of rotifers must be increased slowly to stock a large culture tank effectively. Small glass aquariums or plastic containers work well to increase densities.

The initial inoculation of rotifers should not be diluted by more than 100%. Water with the proper salinity and temperature should be pre-mixed and added to a small culture tank simultaneously with the rotifer stock. A single air line without an airstone should be fixed near the bottom of the tank and set to bubble slowly. Microalgae is then added to lightly tint the water. It may take several days for the initial rotifer stock to multiply sufficiently for dilution.

MICROALGAE COMPOSITION

Nannochloropsis oculata
- Lipid 28%
- EPA 37%
- DHA 0%
- Protein 52%
- Carbohydrates 12%
- Calories 49

Isochrysis galbana Tahitian strain
- Lipid 17%
- EPA 2.5%
- DHA 10.2%
- Protein 47%
- Carbohydrates 24%
- Calories 45

Source: Reed Mariculture

Once the culture is brimming with rotifers near a density of 200 to 400/mL, the culture can be stocked into a larger tank. The water volume of cultures should be increased slowly to keep up a sufficient density of rotifers. Cultures become unstable if insufficient densities are present.

Rotifer cultures should be maintained as continuous cultures and at least two separate cultures should be maintained in case one rotifer culture crashes. After the initial rotifer culture is operating at a total water volume and maintained in sufficient densities, a portion of this culture can be harvested and used as an innoculant for a second culture. Periodically, at roughly weekly or bi-weekly intervals, the rotifer culture should be completely harvested and re-started. Over time, detritus and bacteria begin to develop on tank walls and the tank floor quickly accumulates fecal material, dead rotifers and settled microalgae. This material becomes anoxic and has the potential to ruin a culture. If a high organic load builds up in the rotifer culture tank, ciliates and bacteria begin multiplying quickly. If the culture is not harvested, the rotifer culture will begin to crash, being replaced by ciliates and bacteria. By harvesting the rotifers through a 54-micron sieve and re-starting the culture in new, clean water this problem is resolved and the continued success of the culture maintained.

If you use large rotifer culture tanks, an alternative method can be used to maintain good water quality and prolong the life of the culture. Once a week the tank walls and bottom should be wiped clean with a foam pad or similar tool. After the aeration has been removed allow the culture to settle for about one hour. This stagnant environment will allow the suspended material to settle to the bottom while the oxygen-poor conditions will drive the live rotifers toward the top of the culture tank. Using a siphon, vacuum the bottom and replace the removed water with clean water of the same salinity and temperature. Regular partial water changes can greatly extend the life of sustainable rotifer cultures. It is important to note that although this method is useful for maintaining water quality in continuous cultures it promotes the selection of larger strain rotifers. Complete harvests and re-starts of the culture offer the advantage of selectively removing large rotifers from the population.

Rotifer cultures readily climb to extremely dense levels of near 500/mL and reports of experimental cultures maintaining near 2,000/mL are common. In the presence of pure oxygen, rather than simple aeration, and careful attention to food densities experimental labs have been successful at attaining densities of 10,000/mL. At high densities, rotifer cultures become unstable.

A healthy culture and the goal of aquarists should be in the range of 200 to 500/mL. Even if rotifers are not needed as food, a portion of the culture should be harvested daily in order to maintain a healthy and stable population. The status of rotifer cultures can be monitored by a visual inspection of egg-carrying rotifers. As all the rotifers in a healthy culture are haploid females, they are all capable of reproduction. The more rotifers carrying eggs, the healthier the population. A culture with approximately 50 percent of the observed rotifers carrying at least one egg is considered healthy. When the number of egg-carrying rotifers drops or as the number of eggs carried drops, the culture is becoming unstable and should be diluted.

Nutritional Values

The nutritional value rotifers offer early-stage larval marine fish is dependent on the food source ingested by the rotifers themselves. Highly unsaturated fatty acids (HUFAs) are essential for the survival of marine fish larvae and these must be a supplement in the diet of rotifers. The highly unsaturated fatty acids EPA and DHA are important in the culture of marine fish, with DHA being the more essential. These HUFAs are present in commercial microalgae feeds and it is possible to raise marine fish larvae on rotifers fed this diet exclusively. Different strains of microalgae have different levels of both EPA and DHA. Arguably, the most desirable microalgae feed is the previously mentioned Tahitian strain of *Isochyrsis galbana* (T-ISO), which has high levels of DHA. The most common microalgae feed, *Nannochloropsis oculta*, contains high levels of EPA, but no appreciable level of DHA.

20 liters of water and the density of rotifers in the culture is 100/mL the total number of rotifers in the 20-liter culture is 2,000,000. Thus, if the desired density of rotifers in the rearing vessel is 10/mL and the volume of this rearing vessel is 20 liters, 200,000 rotifers would be needed. Since the rotifer culture tank contains 100 rotifers per mL of water we multiply 100 by 1,000 as there are 1,000 mL in one liter. One hundred multiplied by 1,000 is 100,000. Using this, 2 liters of rotifer culture water need to be harvested to obtain the desired 200,000 rotifers.

Home-scale food culturing setup of a European clownfish breeder, with rotifer culture tanks, left, and *Artemia* hatching cylinders in the aquarium at right.

HARVESTING ROTIFERS

Rotifers are easily collected by means of a sieve constructed of tightly woven synthetic micron mesh screening. The grid-work of perforations is available in various sizes to trap the desired organism. For the purpose of marine fish larviculture, 35, 56 and 73 micron screens are ideal. Rotifers are siphoned or otherwise drained from the culture tank through a sieve of the desired size. All rotifers collected on the screen will act as a food source for larvae. Smaller size screens trap younger, smaller rotifers and provide a gradient of sizes for the larvae to prey upon.

It is helpful to scribe liter marks on the culture vessel walls. A dissecting microscope or other magnifying instrument can be used to get readings on culture densities in a single mL of water, and from this you can estimate the total number of rotifers in the culture as well as the number of rotifers per liter of culture of water. In this way the desired number of rotifers to be fed can be harvested by volume rather than estimating the number after they are added to the rearing tank.

Here's one example: If a rotifer culture tank contains

ENRICHING ROTIFERS

Depending on the food source offered to the rotifers, the need for enrichment may be quite small or very large. Rotifers cultured on a diet of *Isochrysis galbana* Tahitian strain and *Nannochloropsis oculata* in equal parts will need little further enrichment. When fed with these two microalgaes (either live or as Instant Algae), the harvested rotifers should contain high levels of EPA and DHA.

However, it is generally advisable to enrich rotifers prior to their use as food, because most strains of microalgae and commercial diets do not deliver the essential levels of nutrients and HUFAs. Although the survival rate of many

HUFA DEFICIENCY EFFECTS

Without proper HUFA enrichment in larval feeds, juvenile fishes can fail to develop proper adult characteristics. Snubbed noses, shortened bodies, and drab coloration are only a handful of defects caused by improper supplementaion in the diet of larval fish.

species of marine fish fed unenriched rotifers will appear unaffected, the effect of this malnourishment will appear later as metamorphosis sets in. Higher than average percentages of deformed juveniles with kinked spines and other morphological mutations often become apparent at this stage. Many species that normally attain their brilliant adult coloration at metamorphosis will, instead, appear drab and dingy if their rotifer diet has been deficient in marine lipids and HUFAs.

Enriching rotifers is now a simple task. Many products have entered the marketplace offering different levels of marine lipids and HUFAs. Enrichment recommendations for important food fish are available, but assimilation values for most marine ornamentals are not known. It is important therefore to enrich with a good quality HUFA supplement and follow instructions the manufacturer provides. Aquaculture supply houses and specialty suppliers (see Sources) carry both powdered and liquid enrichments. Powdered formulas have the advantage of a longer shelf life, but liquid formulas are easier to use. Culture Selco® and Selcon® are two common enrichment formulas in the aquarium hobby.

Once an enrichment formula is obtained, the rotifers should be allowed to soak for 8 to 12 hours depending on the manufacturer's instructions. Enrichment is most easily accomplished in conical vessels. A Plexiglas cone can be constructed with 3 or 4 panes siliconed together as an upside-down pyramid and fitted with a valve at the bottom.

ROTIFER COMPOSITION

NUTRITIONAL ANALYSIS

- 55% Protein
- 13% Fat
- 3.1% Omega-3 HUFAs

Values dependent upon foods and supplements provided to the rotifers.

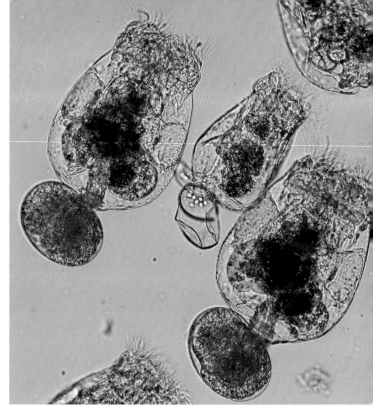

Live rotifers (greatly magnified) showing their digestive tracts well-filled with phytoplankton and displaying a range of sizes that will provide fish larvae a good menu of choices.

Artemia hatching vessels are ideal for enrichment. A concentrated portion of rotifers can be added to the cone with a minimal amount of water so less HUFA supplement is required. An airstone in the cone ensures even distribution of the supplement and keeps the rotifers alive and gorging themselves on the fatty acids during this period.

It is important that enriched rotifers be rinsed in clean seawater before being added to rearing tanks. If rotifers are not properly rinsed, an oily film may be deposited on the surface of the rearing tank water. Drastically reducing gas exchange and often trapping early stage larvae, oil films must be removed by slowly dripping water into the larval tank from the main system, raising the water level until the surface film exits down a standpipe fitted with a mesh screen.

An inexpensive production and enrichment method is to feed rotifers with manufactured or yeast-based diets and later enrich them with proper levels of HUFAs. In this way, microalgae feeds are eliminated and labor is drastically reduced. By enriching rotifers prior to their use as food, the breeder has more assurance that he or she is providing the nutrition larvae need.

Another commonplace method to limit the labor time involved in microalgae culture is to condense microalgae cultures to supply only enough as is necessary to boost rotifer quality directly prior to their use as food. Rotifers are cultured with manufactured diets, harvested, and placed in a container with live microalgae for roughly six hours prior to feeding the larvae. For the average aquarist this will translate into less than one liter of microalgae culture a day.

FEEDING FIRST FOODS

To repeat the vital basics: For feeding to be successful, the proper size and type of prey organisms must be offered in the proper numbers. Larval fish are not physically equipped to seek out and catch their prey. Visual acuity is often lacking in newly hatched larvae and their mouth parts are still rudimentary.

It is important to supply the larvae with enough prey organisms to make it nutritionally worthwhile in catching them. They must also attract larval attention and be a catchable target. If a larval fish exerts more energy in catching prey organisms than it gains from eating them, it is not worthwhile and the larvae will soon perish.

For home breeders, a small aquarium allows high densities of prey organisms to be stocked and maintained. Larvae must be swimming around in a swarm of prey organisms so they do not have to travel far to ingest their next meal. The larvae need to eat continuously throughout the day.

Even the best food organisms will not suffice if they are not present in the proper densities. If food is not available for even one day it could mean the loss of all the larvae. Each larva needs to consume between 500 and 1,000 rotifers or similar prey organisms per day. A rearing aquarium with 200 larval clownfish will require roughly 200,000 rotifers at any given time to ensure feeding success.

Although almost a quarter of a million live items, this quantity of rotifers will not suffice if the rearing aquarium is too large. If the 200,000 rotifers were deposited in a 300-gallon round tub, the survival of one larval fish would not be guaranteed, let alone 200. No matter what size rearing aquarium you are dealing with, the proper densities of prey organisms must be available to the larvae. A 10-gallon aquarium may only need 200,000 rotifers while anything larger may need double or triple this number to raise the same number of larvae. When the proper density of prey organisms has been reached the larvae will only have to swim roughly one and half body lengths to get their next meal. It takes larvae some time to become successful in capturing prey organisms and they often miss, another reason to maintain high densities.

Calculating the number of prey organisms in an aquarium can be quite tricky. Just to make things more challenging, if too many prey organisms are added to the aquarium they may utilize all available dissolved oxygen resulting in the suffocation of the larvae. As you gain experience at calculating the proper density of rotifers or similar prey organisms, you will develop an eye for such things. Experienced aquarists can simply look into a rearing aquarium and see whether or not the proper density is present.

FEED GENTLY

Larval feeding should be done with care. Once the desired number or volume of prey items have been harvested, they should be distributed evenly and gently throughout the rearing tank. Pouring the water containing the live food slowly over a loosely cupped hand is a rudimentary method to get it dispersed in the larval rearing tank. Some breeders use more advanced gadgets constructed in the manner of a multi-outlet spray-bar to do the job and keep their hands out of the water. Prey should not be simply dumped unceremoniously into the tank. Great care should be exercised so that the delicate larvae are not physically damaged or disturbed by rapid water additions.

A proper density of rotifers is roughly 3-15 per milliliter of water. An ounce of water with the proper rotifer densities will contain roughly 450 rotifers. As discussed in the section on culturing rotifers, there are several techniques to count the number present. One approach is to use a small cup or beaker to sample 200 mL or so of water from the rearing tank. Then, using a similar method as described for counting phytoplankton, place 1 mL of water on a Sedgwick-Rafter slide (see Sources) and count the number of prey. Similar methods are available and include squirting 1 mL of tank water in a thin bead on a piece of white paper. With the aid of a magnifying glass, count the rotifers or similar organisms. This gives a rough estimate.

The larvae bend their body in an S shape and then snap forward, pouncing on their prey. Their stomachs are another good indicator of feeding success. A well-fed larva will have well-rounded color with a silver sheen. The larvae should be fed with rotifers three to 12 times daily to maintain the proper density of rotifers within the rearing aquarium. If you cannot supply enough rotifers to the hungry larvae for any reason, cover the rearing aquarium to make it dark. This will lower activity and thus the metabolism of the larvae until you can resupply the rotifer cultures. The tank should only remain covered, dark and without new rotifers for a day or two.

The number of days that rotifers (or other first foods) are fed to the larvae varies from species to species. On average, however, newly hatched brine shrimp can be added to the diet when the larvae are eight days old. Rotifers also must continue to be fed until all the larvae are noticeably feeding on the *Artemia* .

Larval growth rates always vary within a single spawn. Smaller larvae need smaller foods for a longer period, but larger ones should be offered larger, more nutritious foods as soon as they are big enough to accept them. There is a point when rotifers are no longer beneficial to the larvae; that is, they gain no more energy from their food than they exert in catching it. Feeding schedules are established as guidelines for many species, using the standard progression from rotifers to *Artemia* nauplii to flake foods (See chart.)

ROTIFER TACTICS

The speed at which a quantity of food organisms is ingested and reduced in numbers in the larval rearing tank is known as the *clearing rate*. It is dependent on the number of larvae present and conditions in the rearing vessel.

If a larval tank contains a high number of larvae, the clearing rate will be high and rotifers must be replenished more frequently. When the density of larvae is low the frequency of rotifer feedings will be lessened. Clearing rates pose a significant impact on the nutritional value of prey organisms. A rotifer is, in essence, simply a package to deliver essential nutrients and lipids. The nutritional value of rotifers is highest just after they have been given microalgal feeds and HUFA supplements. With slow clearing rates in larval vessels, their nutritional value diminishes over time.

In larval tanks containing hundreds of larvae the task of supplying prey organisms of adequate nutritional value is made easy as clearing rates are high. Rotifers must be added frequently as they are being consumed at higher rates than in those tanks containing fewer larvae. Thus, as long as rotifers are supplemented with proper microalgae feeds or HUFA supplements prior to their use they are ensured to be nutritionally adequate. Nutritional supplements should be offered to the rotifers for a minimum of six hours to ensure that their systems are packed with nutrients.

The density of rotifers in larval tanks containing low numbers of fish larvae rarely seems to fall. The larvae are, in fact, consuming rotifers, but the rotifers themselves may be multiplying at a rate as high as or even higher than the rate of consumption by the larvae. The nutritional value of these rotifers is dropping, but it is impractical to add fresh rotifers that have been nutritionally supplemented. Two methods exist to solve this problem.

The most logical approach calls for the addition of live microalgae to the rearing tank. Two significant problems are solved by the use of greenwater in the rearing tanks, the most important being boosting the nutritional quality of the rotifers. By mixing *Isochrysis* and *Nannochloropsis* (either from your own live cultures or as a mix of Instant Algae),

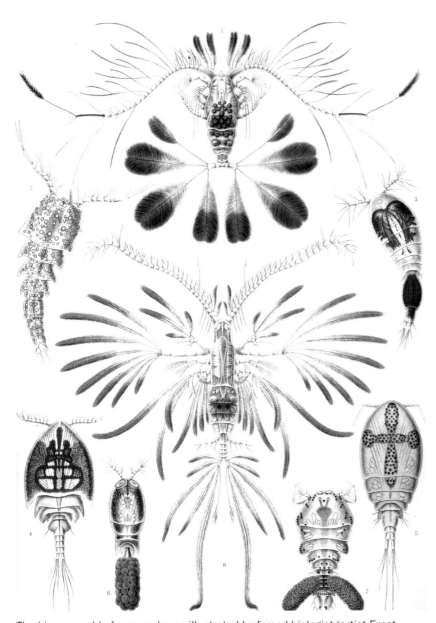

The bizarre world of copepods, as illustrated by famed biologist/artist Ernst Haeckel in his Kunstformen der Natur (1904). Copepods are some of the most prevalent crustaceans found in collections of wild marine plankton and of great interest to advanced marine fish breeders today. Key to Species above:
1. *Calanus pavo* (Dana); **2.** *Clytemnestra scutellata* (Dana); **3.** *Oncaea venusta* (Philippi); **4.** *Cryptopontius thorelli* (Giesbrecht); **5.** *Acontiophorus scutatus* (Brady); **6.** *Corycaeus cenustus* (Dana); **7.** *Sapphirina darwinii* (Haeckel); **8.** *Augaptilus filigerus* (Giesbrecht).

you are ensuring high levels of the two important fatty acids, EPA and DHA. The microalgae will allow the rotifer population to thrive and stay packed with the right nutrients, which are in turn ingested by the larval fish.

If you are using live greenwater, rather than the preserved cells in a product such as Instant Algae, the microalgae also utilize ammonia and nitrogenous waste secreted by the larvae and decomposing organic matter created by heterotrophic bacteria. In essense we try to create a miniature food web in the larval rearing vessel. Live microalgae helps ensure adequate water quality during early life stages of the fish, as well as adding color contrast between prey organisms and the background.

ROTIFER SHORTAGES

Most every aquarist at one point or another will be faced with a shortage of rotifers. Whether this happens as a result of over-harvesting or, more commonly, population crashes in the rotifer culture tanks, action should be taken promptly to avoid losses. The metabolism of larval fish is influenced by many chemical and environmental cues, most notably water temperature and illumination. At high temperatures, the larval fish's metabolism is quite high and effectively makes use of all nutrition ingested. Metabolism is linked to activity levels, which are always highest during daylight hours when the larvae are actively seeking out and ingesting prey organisms. During the night or periods when the rearing vessel is only

Aquaculturist Martin Moe collecting plankton from shore in the Florida Keys for his experiments with breeding dottybacks, pygmy angelfishes and threatened *Diadema* sea urchins.

dimly illuminated, larvae remain relatively still in the water column, not burning much energy. Clearly this is their natural pattern in the wild, where they would be drifting in the plankton and conserving energy during the night.

The aquarist can use this ability of larvae to go into slow

metabolism mode to his or her advantage during rotifer shortages. By turning the lights off and darkening the rearing tank, we can trick the larvae so they will not expend energy in hunting. This is a short-term solution. Rotifer cultures must be brought up to healthy densities as quickly as possible, as the larvae can withstand not eating for only a limited period of time. Depending on the age and developmental state of the larvae, two days seems to be the maximum time we can keep them dark and unfed. After that mortality rates begin to increase as a result of malnourishment.

WILD PLANKTON

Aquarists living near the coastline have access to an incredible food source that may prove beneficial for those trying to achieve a breakthrough with a new species of marine fish. Plankton can be found near the shoreline, and aquarists with a plankton net can take full advantage of this diverse group of food organisms. Wild plankton can be taken in handheld nets dipped around piers and jetties or in a larger net towed behind a boat. For dedicated hobbyists, this food source is inexpensive, highly nutritious, and more acceptable as a first food to a wider diversity of fish species because it usually combines many organisms of different sizes.

Wild plankton is the natural food source of larval fishes. If it can be provided, higher survival rates and vigorous, healthy larvae are sure to follow. The species of organisms found in the plankton varies with every location and latitude. I have used plankton collected off Long Island, New York to successfully rear several species of tropical marine fish. Breeders in Florida and Hawaii have also reported good results with wild plankton.

Wild plankton is not usually considered cost effective in commercial propagation of marine ornamental fish. For home-based hobbyists, however, using wild plankton to feed species is possible. A dissecting microscope (20X to 100X) comes in handy to identify and isolate potential food organisms for use in isolated monocultures. An assortment of wild plankton can be added to the rearing aquarium. A few larvae can be dissected, if the proper equipment is available, and inspected for gut content to see what organisms are being preyed upon. Those organisms are then sorted out and a homogeneous culture started.

Plankton nets can be obtained from marine supply stores and biological warehouses. The sizes of the nets vary dramatically from over four feet in diameter with a bag length of over 10 feet to an opening of 4 inches and a bag length of only about one foot. A large net can be a great advantage if you can afford it and if you have a small boat to tow it. The most convenient size plankton net for most aquarists is one with an open-end diameter of 12 to 16 inches and a bag length of 2 or 3 feet. A plankton net this size can be walked along a dock, suspended from a fishing bridge in a tidal flow, or slowly towed behind a small boat. A net much larger than this will prove to be inconvenient in all conditions. Smaller nets are easier to handle when walked along a dock and will still work in a tidal flow.

Once a plankton net has been obtained, a bucket, some rope and an assortment of plankton sieves will be required. There are a number of methods for collecting plankton. As long as the plankton net is moving through the water—or water is flowing through the net—some plankton will be caught. A long dock is a good collecting site. Simply toss the net in the water with about 10 feet of rope attached and walk the net back and forth. In about 20 minutes, enough plankton will be collected for a day or two of feeding. If you have access to a bridge built over a body of water that experiences a tidal flux, suspend the net from the bridge during an incoming or outgoing tide. Enjoy the scenery and in half an hour or so pull up the net and dump the plankton in a bucket. If you are towing the plankton net from a small boat, use 20 feet of rope and slowly drag the net through the water.

The bottom of the net is supplied with a collection jar. The water that enters the net exits through the micron screen. The plankton that is too large to squeeze through the micron screen is pushed back into the collection jar. When the net is pulled up, the water escapes through the screen and any leftover plankton follows the falling water

CONSTRUCTING A PLANKTON SIEVE

Collecting wild plankton requires the use of several sieves in assorted sizes. From the same source where your plankton net and possibly rotifers were obtained, micron mesh screen should also be available. The screen comes in sheets and rolls in different lengths and sizes. All that is needed for one plankton sieve is a square roughly 1 inch larger than the diameter of pipe. Scrap pieces may be available through a local university or aquarium society.

Four-inch PVC pipe is my preference. Cut a 6 to 8-inch length into two pieces; one roughly 1-inch tall and the other 5 to 7 inches. Use a felt-tip marker to draw a line along the length of pipe before the cut is made, so that the two pieces can be lined up again after the cut has been made. Cut a square piece of micron mesh about 1 inch larger than the diameter of the pipe. Apply PVC pipe cement to both sections of pipe and place the micron screen over one section of pipe. Using the marker line, rejoin the two pieces of pipe. An assistant is helpful at this point, as the micron screen should be pulled tight while the sections are joined and the glue dries. Place a heavy weight on top of the sieve for a few minutes while the glue dries. When the glue has cured, use a razor blade to trim the excess screen from the outside of the sieve. If the inside of the sieve has gouges in it, a thin layer of silicon can be applied to make the inside of the sieve, around the screen, smooth so plankton will become trapped. Rinse in hot water and it's ready to use.

The next consideration is the size of the micron mesh screen used to make the plankton net. A plankton net that will catch organisms roughly the size of a rotifer is ideal. It will also help if the net catches organisms slightly smaller and larger than the size of rotifers to offer the larvae a variety of prey organisms. 53 or 73-micron mesh is a good size. If you are spawning fish with small larvae, plankton nets with mesh sizes larger than this will prove ineffective. If only two choices of nets are available, choose the smaller since small organisms that are of no use as food can later be sorted out with plankton sieves.

Harpatacoid copepod from an aquarium maintained by Norwegian author Alf Jacob Nilsen. These copepods are common in established tanks.

level into the collection jar. The collection jar is then unscrewed and dumped into your bucket.

Depending on the water, many interesting by-catches may be present. These include large organisms such as jellyfish and larval fishes and algae, silt, and perhaps litter. You now use assorted plankton sieves to screen out the inappropriate items. It is usually easier to bring the collected plankton home and do the sorting there but the sieves can be used to sort through the plankton as it is hauled in. This makes it easier to throw back larger, unwanted catches.

Sorting Plankton

Making a multi-level plankton sieve is quite easy. First, a simple sieve should be constructed using fiberglass window screen. This will catch all large undesirable organisms. Next, if you have various sizes of larvae and post-metamorphosed juveniles, the plankton can be size-sorted to feed larger juveniles while saving smaller organisms to feed young larvae. A 240-micron sieve will remove average-size plankton such as copepods and the larvae of mollusks and gastropods; this usually makes up the bulk of the catch. This plankton is then fed to juvenile fish and adult fish. The re-

mainder of the plankton is then passed through various sizes of sieves to harvest proper-sized organisms for feeding larval fish. If newly hatched larvae are to be fed, a 100-micron or 73-micron sieve should be used to screen out organisms too large to be accepted by the larvae. The final step is to strain the plankton through a 35 or 53-micron sieve that will separate out the organisms too small to be useful. The sieve is then rinsed in the rearing tank water and the planktonic organisms enter the water volume to be preyed upon by the larvae. As the larvae grow in size, larger micron screens are used as the final sieve. Organisms too small to be used as food fall through the sieve.

Along with the beneficial food organisms obtained in the tow, many undesirables will be caught as well. In the open ocean, larval fish have an enormous supply of food. They also have an amazing array of predators that can be transferred into the rearing aquarium unintentionally. A closed system such as a rearing aquarium offers such organisms a chance to thrive and compete for food. Rotifers do not stand a chance, as they are eaten by the larval fish. When wild plankton is introduced, however, it may contain various organisms that will grow larger than the average rotifer and perhaps even the larval fish.

Jellyfish are a common pest found in the plankton. These can easily be sieved out if they are large enough. Often small ones will pass through the sieve and mature in the algae- and plankton-rich environment. They are easily spotted and consequently removed. Parasitic copepods may find their way into the aquarium as well. They look similar to the pelagic copepods that larval fish prey on, but differ significantly in life style. Isopods and other organisms may prey upon larval fish. Normally these predatory organisms are not highly represented in the plankton and are easily spotted and removed in a small rearing aquarium. Only when large aquariums or tubs are used do these organisms normally pose a significant problem.

CILIATES FOR SMALLER LARVAE

The larvae of many species of marine fish are too small to accept rotifers as their initial meal and rely on smaller planktonic organisms. Ciliates—usually single-celled organisms covered with fine hairlike cilia—are a good choice for many of these larvae, but will prove inadequate for others.

Ciliates are still rather an experimental first food for marine larvae, but there are innumerable species of ciliates available as culture subjects and one or more may well provide a solution to feeding small-mouthed larvae. Ciliate cultures are not readily available commercially.

The easiest way to start a culture of ciliates, however, is to let a rotifer culture crash. When the rotifer population increases to unsupportably high numbers, the population will suddenly die off. After some time with no water changes and allowing much bottom debris to accumulate, ciliates will appear, as if by magic. In fact, they are found in most rotifer cultures.

Microalgae should be fed in the same manner as rotifers. Yeast and Selcon® should also be added to stimulate the growth of ciliates. Although ciliates will show up in other situations, it is important to feed them microalgae and other foods to make them nutritionally acceptable. If the ciliates are malnourished or fed inadequately the larvae will perish. The ciliate population will then increase to a dense population and can be harvested. Water should be changed periodically to prevent the ciliate from crashing although this is a rare occurrence. Often times, ciliates will contaminate and take over a rotifer culture. A 25 or 35-micron plankton sieve will trap the ciliates intended for feeding smaller larvae. Sieves up to 80-micron are useful to screen out a variety of sizes. It is usually not clear what size the larvae are feeding on. Ciliate densities should be maintained at about 5 to 10 per ml in the rearing aquarium.

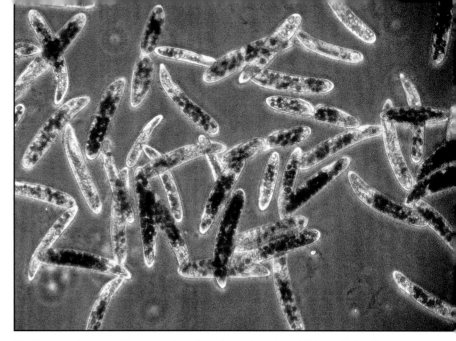

Ciliates may be possible future first food for certain larval fishes. This ciliate *(Helicostoma nonatum)* has been implicated in stony coral deaths.

COPEPODS

Copepods are a class of small crustaceans occurring in oceans and estuaries and actually may represent the greatest biomass of any living animal group on earth. Given their widespread presence and infinitely high populations, they play a major role in the diets of most larval fish in the wild.

The nutritional value of copepods is far superior to rotifers, containing more dense nutrition including vital lipids by weight than rotifers. Experimental studies clearly demonstrate that having copepods in the diet drastically improves survival rates and decreases physiological dysfunction such as swim bladder inflation in captive larvae.

With this in mind it seems odd that more marine fish culturists do not use these organisms as captive prey. A creative, problem-solving mind is important when it comes to rearing difficult marine species, but creativity should not override observations in the wild. Mother Nature was generous in creating a readily available food source for larval fish. As aquarists, we should strive to model nature, and in so doing will drastically improve survival in captivity.

Copepod Culture

Copepods have long been viewed as too challenging to maintain reliably in large quantities. The life cycle of copepods is much longer than rotifers and they reproduce sexually. The high densities observed in rotifer cultures are not obtainable in copepod cultures. Although copepod nauplii production is low compared to rotifers, it is well within the means of dedicated aquarists to produce a reliable culture yielding 50 to 2,000 nauplii per liter per day of culture water.

As a simple illustration, let us assume a larval tank with a total operating volume of 75 liters (roughly 20 gallons). If copepod nauplii are introduced at a density of 2/mL, then 15,000 copepod nauplii will be required to stock the rearing tank initially. Let us assume, too, that nauplii production in the copepod culture tank is low at around 100 nauplii per liter per day. Under this production schedule, a 150 liter (40-gallon) culture would be necessary to stock the larval rearing tank with 15,000 copepod nauplii per day.

Copepods offer far more energy than rotifers (even though raised on a similar diet of greenwater) and can thus be maintained in lower densities in the larval rearing tank. Copepods dramatically improve survivorship, form, color and growth rates of larvae. Even when fed sparingly or occasionally, significant improvement in larval development can be observed. In most species that exhibit high mortalities near metamorphosis, copepods offer a real advantage. The addition of copepods to the diet a few days prior to metamorphosis and then scattered throughout can decrease mortality by as much as 50 percent. When copepods are integrated into a conventional feeding routine of only rotifers, high numbers of copepods are not necessary and they may give your larvae an important nutritional boost.

Copepods have long been viewed as the food source capable of alleviating the stresses involved in first-feeding larvae, but most species of marine aquarium fish larvae are poorly suited to capturing copepod nauplii in the first few days of feeding. The benefits of a copepod diet are typically observed later in the larval stage, when they drastically reduce mortality during metamorphosis. While the nauplii of some species may prove pivitol in raising small larvae, copepod nauplii are generally only acceptable after 2 to 6 days of initial mouth opening.

Culture methods vary slightly depending on species and reproductive mode. For use in larval rearing, it is important to choose a copepod whose naupliar stages are pelagic or free-floating. Many harpacticoid copepods in commercial culture are bottom dwellers, associating with benthic substrates as adults. Nauplii are generally pelagic, but tend to settle from the water column quickly. Calanoid copepods are entirely pelagic throughout their life cycle and are probably most suited to feeding larval fish. Most calanoid copepods carry their eggs on their abdomen until hatching and are generally more suited to closed culture. Naupliar stages of commercially grown copepods vary in size from about 80 μm to over 150 μm in length. This size is ideal for most larval fishes.

Various culture methods have been developed for copepods and differences can be observed in nauplii collection, feeding, maintenance of water quality, and stocking. Many publications are available for the specifics of culture, but I suggest Rippingale and Payne (2001) for a detailed synopsis of copepod culture. In short, inoculant copepods are stocked in intensive culture tanks connected to a slow recirculating system. A tank of 175 liters (roughly a 50 gallon water drum) is not too large for the average aquarist to maintain in the corner of a room. This tank is connected to a smaller filtration tank consisting of a bio-filter and protein skimmer. Water exchange is slow, around five gallons per hour or less and water intake in the culture tank is covered with a 50 μm screen to prevent nauplii from escaping to the filter. The culture is fed daily with live *Isochrysis galbana* (Tahitian strain). Often times, these culture systems are fully automated with dosing pumps supplying algae continuously throughout the day.

Harvesting nauplii from such a system can be simple. With the room lights turned out, a small light is used to concentrate the copepods. Then, the nauplii are siphoned

Red Tide off the coast of New Zealand: these colorful swirls seen from the air are swarms of toxic dinoflagellates, but fair game for many fish larvae that can eat them without harm.

toxic dinoflagellates are consumed in great abundance by various aquarium fishes. (*G. splendens* is associated with Red Tides.) Culture methods have been well established in toxicology labs and typically call for slightly cooler water temperatures (72 to 75°F) and feeding with the common microalgae fertilizer known as *Guillard's F/2*. Most labs culture dinoflagellates in sterile glass flasks against a light bank without aeration. Turbulence caused from heavy aeration has been implicated in slowing cell division.

The use of dinoflagellates as a first food for larval fishes has been poorly studied, but their small size and attractiveness to both wild and cultured larvae warrant further investigation. Dinoflagellates are best obtained from stock sources found at various universities or through biological supply houses. They can also be isolated from local coastal waters, but the difficulty in identification and the number of toxic species present makes this challenging. Small larvae such as those of pelagic spawning species may benefit most from such a diet when included in the first few days.

out through a 150 μm screen. This ensures only the naupliar stages are removed leaving the reproductive population in the culture tank. Water exiting the siphon is poured through a 50 μm screen to concentrate the nauplii for feeding.

DINOFLAGELLATES

Feeding selectivity trials have demonstrated a strong attraction to dinoflagellates by first-feeding larvae of various families of marine fish. The unarmored dinoflagellae *Gymnodinium splendens* has been used to successfully culture larvae of anchovy and selectivity studies show that even

OTHER FOOD ORGANISMS

Currently, ciliates, rotifers, copepods and newly hatched *Artemia* are the main food organisms used by commercial facilities and home-based hobbyists. If enough time and

Newly hatched *Artemia* nauplii greatly magnified, a rich live-food item. Note round, white, unhatched brine shrimp eggs.

dedication were put into discovering other food sources and methods for their culture, it is very likely that more species of marine fish could be raised in captivity.

Several criteria must be met to qualify as an ideal food source for larval fish. First, the organism must be small enough to be ingested by the larval fish without too much difficulty. Second, the organism must offer movement that is interesting to the larvae, but not too fast to avoid predation by the struggling young larvae. Third, in order to be used successfully as a food organism, it must practice a reproductive mode that will allow dense cultures of the organisms to be maintained in captive production conditions. Enough food organisms must be culturable to stock the rearing tank with sufficient numbers of prey items to make feeding successful.

Some interesting live foods have become available for the small-scale marine breeder who is willing to invest some time in obtaining them. Clam and oyster larvae make an ideal food source for larger fish larvae. Obtaining the larvae is somewhat of a hobby in itself. Clams or oysters can be

obtained from a variety of sources. The first place to look is the ocean. Oyster and clam species can be found in virtually any shallow saltwater environment. Secondly, try the supermarket. Fresh seafoods are often available and clams and oysters are capable of surviving over long periods of time with their shells held closed. Place the clams or oysters in a bare aquarium on the basement floor to keep them cool. Keep the tank filled with microalgae at all times. These are filter feeders that strain the algae from the water column. After a few months of this conditioning, raise the water temperature a few degrees with the aid of a heater and spawning should take place. This is, of course, a quick overview on spawning clams and oysters. If this simple technique proves unsuccessful, the gonads from one specimen can be pulverized and spread throughout the aquarium water containing the clams or oysters. This should trigger them to spawn. The eggs are then collected and allowed to develop into a trochophore stage (which look like tiny, spiny shrimp) and fed to the fish larvae.

Sea urchins can be induced to spawn with an injection of potassium chloride. Millions of eggs result and the larval stages are very nutritious. As an experiment, I have used sea urchin larvae to feed the larvae of clownfish. Clownfish larvae did consume early life stage sea urchins, but this did not constitute their sole diet. The eggs and early larval stages of other organisms, although difficult to obtain, can be extremely nutritious delivering the rich contents of yolk sacs. More experimentation needs to be done to discover further uses of these foods.

THE NEXT STEP: *ARTEMIA* NAUPLII

Newly hatched brine shrimp are known as *Artemia* nauplii and they are the worldwide staple food for raising larval marine fishes after they have graduated from their first larval foods. *Artemia* are small crustaceans found in high salinity areas, such as San Francisco Bay, and they produce masses of encysted eggs that can be collected and stored dry for long periods of time—up to several years if packed without oxygen. When reintroduced to water, they rapidly hatch (remember the Sea Monkeys?), producing tiny nauplii that are rich in lipids and fatty acids. Marine breeders buy the dry cysts and hatch them in batches as needed.

As with rotifers, several strains of *Artemia* are available to aquarists, and these exhibit differences in both size at hatching and nutritional quality. Average *Artemia* strains hatch at 430 to 500 microns in length. *Artemia* referred to as "very small" hatch at less than 430 microns in length. By contrast, we usually feed rotifers in the 150-250 micron range; *Artemia* nauplii are roughly twice as big.

Marine fish larvae develop the ability to prey on *Artemia* nauplii in as few as three days in some species but as long as 32 in others. At first, only freshly hatched *Artemia* less than 12 hours old should be offered to the larvae and should be introduced slowly. *Artemia* grow extremely quickly, and within a day transform into unacceptable prey organisms for most small larvae. The appendages developed by the *Artemia* (remember, this is a crustacean) and the fast-vibrating motion the nauplii exhibit makes them a threat to small larvae. They can become trapped within the mouthparts, throat and digestive tract of the larvae.

Also, unhatched *Artemia* cysts or shells from hatched eggs remain a constant threat as these, too, have the potential of becoming lodged within the digestive tract of young larvae. *Artemia* cysts must be decapsulated before hatching. (See box, next page.)

Just as with the rotifers, *Artemia* nauplii should be enriched with protein and essential fatty acids prior to their use as food. Easy Selco® is one brand of supplement intended for enriching newly hatched brine shrimp, but there are other choices. Hatching cones or inverted soda bottles make ideal enrichment chambers. Light aeration will allow the *Artemia* to mix within the enrichment chamber while supplying oxygen to the water.

Enrichment should commence 6 to 12 hours prior to feeding. Newly hatched *Artemia* do not begin feeding for 12 hours after hatching. It is thus difficult to enrich *Artemia* less than 12 hours old. Since small fish larvae require small *Artemia,* collect the *Artemia* soon after hatching and feed them to the larvae without enrichment. A day or several

Artemia hatching cones in a small marine breeding operation. Aquaculture supply houses sell such units in a range of sizes.

days later, when larvae have grown significantly larger and are able to accept *Artemia* that is 18+ hours old, enriched *Artemia* can be added to the diet.

Artemia is generally stocked at much lower densities than rotifers, as the larvae preying on them are typically larger, more developed and capable of hunting prey more successfully. Typical prey densities for *Artemia* are 1 to 2/mL. For the first week of feeding, this number should be less than the average as it will take some time before all larvae are preying on this food source.

Because *Artemia* grow so quickly they may become unacceptable as an early food for many species within a matter of hours. If too many *Artemia* are added to the rearing vessel, it may become choked with an inadequate food source that must be removed. Removing *Artemia* from the rearing vessel is a considerable challenge. The best tactic is to place a 500 to 750 micron screen over the standpipe and slowly drip water into the rearing vessel at night. The nauplii should float out, while the larvae are prevented from exiting. Another method is to shut off the air supply after

To avoid difficulties arising from indigestible, unhatched eggs and egg shells, *Artemia* cysts must be decapsulated. You can buy decapsulated cysts, but doing it yourself can save money. Prior to the actual removal of the cysts' outer membrane, the cysts must be hydrated. Soaking the cysts in freshwater for roughly 30 minutes smoothes out the miniature wrinkles and pits found on the surface of the tough little cysts and aids in the decapsulation process.

One tablespoon of cysts can be hydrated in 2 ounces of water. Household bleach is the decapsulating agent of choice. Equal amounts of unscented chlorine and fresh water are combined to decapsulate the cysts. Once the bleach has been added to the hydrated cysts, the mixture must be stirred as heat is emitted during the reaction. Depending on the strength of the bleach, the process can be very quick or quite lengthy. The mixture will become quite frothy after the addition of bleach. The cysts soon turn from their origi-

Professional-grade *Artemia* cysts yield different size nauplii depending on strain.

nal brown color to a dull gray and finally to a bright orange. When a uniform orange color is attained throughout the whole of the decapsulating chamber, the mixture of bleach and cysts should be drained through a 125-micron screen or similar sieve, rinsed under running fresh water and then de-chlorinated with sodium thiosulfate or a commercial dechlorinator.

The cysts are now decapsulated and ready for hatching. Placing the wet, decapsulated cysts in a hatching cone will result in a significantly shortened incubation period—from 8 to 14 hours dependant upon temperature. If the cysts are not to be used immediately, they can be stored for short durations in a cold hyper-saline solution. To do this, add about 50 mL of freshwater to a small fingerbowl. Then, stir in small increments of salt. Once the salt no longer dissolves, a small amount is allowed to rest on the bottom. The cysts are placed in this mixture and stored in the refrigerator for up to 14 days.

the lights have been turned out and, using a small flashlight, concentrate the *Artemia* (which are strongly attracted by light) at the surface where they can be netted out.

It is best to add *Artemia* via a small syringe for the first few feedings to get an idea of how many are consumed and how many larvae are preying on the food source, characterized by their bright orange bellies. (A handheld magnifying glass can be a useful tool.)

As the number of *Artemia* being consumed increases, you can ramp up the number being fed. Again, because it is so important: enriched rotifers must be co-fed until all larvae are visibly eating the *Artemia*.

ARTEMIA SHOCK

Newly hatched *Artemia* can pose a significant threat to larval fish. If fed as a sole diet for too long, the larval fish can become very prone to shock. Any sudden movement or unnatural experience is likely to cause the larvae to perish. When fiberglass tubs or similar rearing chambers are used with the only viewing field at the top, shock is not likely to occur unless the larvae are removed. In glass aquariums, shock is more evident. Frank Hoff (1996) describes a method used to see if any given group of clownfish larvae is vulnerable to shock. A few larvae are netted from the rearing tank, placed in the palm of a hand and then dropped back into the rearing tank. If *Artemia* are fed too heavily and this rather baffling tendency to go into shock is evident, the larvae will spiral around on the surface in a sudden burst before sinking motionless to the bottom. These larvae may revive, but more times than not it is deadly. To prevent this problem, flake food or other small morsels should be offered. A few days after flake food has been added to the diet, the larvae will be free of the dangers of shock.

WEANING DIET

After the larvae have begun to accept newly hatched *Artemia,* supplemental feedings of flake food or similar weaning diet should be added. Weaning diets offer another food source to make more balanced nutrition and begin the transition from live foods to prepared foods. High-quality flake or frozen, finely grated seafoods should be used for the most benefit to the growing fish. *Spirulina* flake food mixed with a high-quality marine flake food works well for this purpose as does finely minced table shrimp. Many acceptable weaning diets are available, with the common goal of moving juvenile fish to convenient, nourishing adult diet.

When first offered, flake foods and other non-living foods are likely to be snubbed by the larvae. Weaning the larvae onto non-living foods is often frustrating, offer these foods when the larvae are most hungry. Using a mortar and pestle, flake foods can be finely ground to appropriate size for the larvae. In the morning, add flake foods as their first meal. It may take several days for the larvae to accept these new foods, but it is extremely important that they do.

Recently, flake foods have been developed that include special ingredients that aid in intensifying the colors of marine fishes. These foods are especially effective with young clownfish to increase the red, orange and yellow colors. In my experience, previously pale or faded specimens will start to show bright coloration within a matter of days after the start of feeding with color-enhancing foods. In addition to natural pigment enhancers such as carotenoids, Vitamin C is also important to growing fish.

Tank-raised adult brine shrimp (enlarged): a nutritious live food for juveniles if properly enriched before feeding.

As they grow, large fish will graduate from pulverized dry foods to flakes crushed between your fingers. Sprinkle the food over the surface of the rearing aquarium or juvenile grow-out aquarium. Newly hatched *Artemia* fed along with flake foods offer the best results to growing fish.

FEEDING SUCCESS FACTORS

1. Prey organism density. Larvae can only perceive prey organisms less than 1.5 body lengths away. It is important for the larvae to be in frequent contact with prey.
2. A dark background and water tinted with microalgae (greenwater) help establish contrast between prey organisms and the surrounding environment, making it easier for the larvae to capture prey.
3. The prey organisms must be of the appropriate size and type for the species of fish being fed. They must be easy to capture, but also demonstrate swimming behaviors that will elicit a response from the larvae.
4. Darkness—as well as bright light—will inhibit feeding.

CHAPTER 10

JUVENILE GROW OUT

Metamorphsis & Rearing Young Fishes

At first, after hatching, larvae are streamlined missles that glide effortlessly through the water in search of food. It doesn't take long, however, for the larvae to put on some weight, grow fins and begin to look like real fish. The whole body structure along with the internal organs, including the stomach, change drastically to accommodate the different lifestyle of living on the reef rather than drifting in the ocean currents.

Metamorphosis is a complicated and fascinating process. In general terms, metamorphosis is the transformation of life stages with a marked difference from one form to another. The most familiar examples of metamorphosis are found in the insect realm. Caterpillars transform themselves into butterflies and aquatic stone-flies become dragonflies. These are abrupt and discrete changes that are easily observed. Metamorphosis as it applies to marine fish is rather a slow process requiring several days or weeks to complete.

At hatching, marine fish larvae are typically poorly developed and resemble a tadpole more than a reef fish. Generally, body pigmentation is lacking at first, as transparent, hard-to-see larvae have a definite survival advantage over those with pigmentation in the predator-filled upper water column of the ocean. The mouth is initially poorly developed and the digestive tract quite rudimentary. A single finfold (see illustration) outlines the body of the larvae where future fins will emerge, and rudimentary pectoral fins are in place. As the larvae grow, their body length and depth increases, they take on diffuse body pigmentation and their pectoral fins often become exaggerated. The mouth becomes more developed and the abdominal cavity expands with increasing complexity of the digestive system.

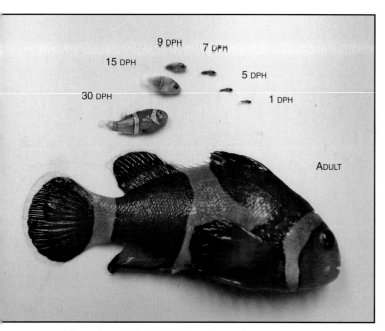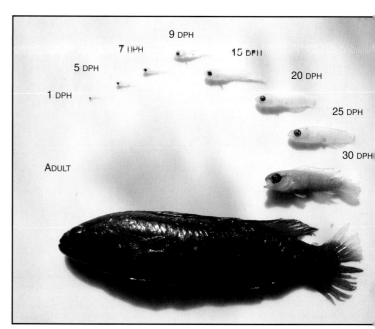

Life cycles of Ocellaris Clownfish, left, and Orchid Dottyback, right, showing development marked in days post-hatch (DPH).

Flexion or bending of the tail fin, in which fin rays begin to develop, occurs and the finfold eventually separates to form the dorsal, anal and caudal fins. Morphological, behavioral and dietary shifts are all important components of metamorphosis. In the early stages of metamorphosis the fish are still very larvae-like, but by completion they have begun to resemble adults of their species.

Metamorphosis is a sensitive period during the development of the young fish. This transformation requires tremendous energy output and is stressful. Mortality is typically highest in the days surrounding this process and often surpasses the toll seen in the initial days of first feeding.

If water quality has deteriorated or the larvae have been poorly fed or subjected to stress conditions, many mortalities are sure to occur. Keep in mind that it takes an average of more than one week for larvae to complete metamorphosis and any deterioration in water quality will lead to adverse effects in post-larvae. Mutations such as bent backs, shortened gill covers, stunted growth, and similar deformities are more often due to an inappropriate environment during metamorphosis than genetics. It is extremely im-

portant to supply a constant drip of water from the central filtration system or perform small partial water changes to assure proper water quality during this time. Entire batches can be lost if larvae were improperly fed or exposed to poor water quality during metamorphosis.

In virtually every batch of larvae there are always those that are slow to reach metamorphosis. When it seems that all the larvae have completed metamorphosis, careful scrutiny of the aquarium will usually reveal a few stragglers that exhibit no signs of metamorphosis. Some species may experience a lag in completing metamorphosis. The time required to complete metamorphosis may differ by as much as 30 days or more in the same batch of larvae. Some larvae grow fast and complete metamorphosis quickly, while others appear as if just-hatched even weeks into the rearing process.

GROW-OUT AQUARIUMS

Upon completion of metamorphosis, the larvae have become juveniles with the normal swimming behaviors and appearances of adult fish. They settle to the bottom and begin acting like representatives of their species. The diet of post-metamorphosis juveniles should contain more protein than larval diets. Crushed flake food and finely minced seafoods should constitute the bulk of the diet at this point.

These post-larvae are still too vulnerable to becoming overstressed and they should not be moved into the grow-out tank for at least a week after completing metamorphosis (or until the juveniles have been successfully weaned off *Artemia* nauplii). Soon after metamorphosis, a seasoned sponge filter can be added to their larval rearing tank. This will maintain good water quality for a while, but the young must be moved soon as they grow larger and water quality begins to deteriorate.

Because food densities are no longer a problem and the fish are growing rapidly in cramped quarters, a larger aquarium will be necessary to keep the young fish healthy. Fifty-five gallon aquariums make good grow-out vessels, but just about any size aquarium can work. If a large aquarium is not at your disposal, the juveniles will have to be divided into a group of smaller tanks. Any aquarium with adequate filtration will do. Properly maintained external power filters, fluidized beds, wet-dry filters and protein skimmers can all provide adequate filtration for grow-out aquariums. Biological filtration and regular partial water changes are essential to maintain good water quality in a crowded aquarium. An extra airstone is recommended to keep saturated oxygen levels high. As many as 200 young fish can be grown out in a 30-gallon aquarium if good maintenance is practiced. Often times, however, one fish will establish itself as dominant and will claim half the aquarium as its own. The other half is shared between the other 199 young fish. Any dominant fish that exhibits these aggressive tendencies should be removed.

Transfer to grow-out is a critical period in the rearing process. Young fishes are very sensitive to mechanical damage caused by nets or other means of capture and stress is a leading cause of mortality during this stage.

Once the young are weaned and the grow-out tank (or tank is ready), it is wise to transfer only a few juveniles and

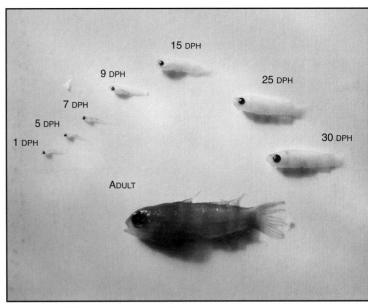

Life cycle of Diadem Dottyback, day one to metamorphosis.

closely observe their reactions. If the juveniles quickly succumb to the stress of the move, do not attempt to move the rest of the batch. Wait a week and try again. Nets should only be used to corral the juveniles. Two nets used simultaneously can quickly and efficiently corral most juveniles in the tank. Once the young fish are inside one net, submerge a small plastic container into the tank. Invert the net and gently push it toward the container, transferring fish from net to container. Lift the container carefully from the tank, never lifting the fish out in a net or removing them from the water. Capturing and transporting juvenile fishes in plastic containers greatly reduces stress caused by transfer.

The water in the grow-out tank should be similar in chemistry to that of the larval tank. If central filtration is being used, water can be exchanged between the systems (larval rearing and grow out) several days in advance and virtually no acclimation will be required. The preferred method when a central system is employed is to use water from the larval rearing system to fill a tank in the grow-out system. All juveniles are transferred to the grow-out tank containing larval system water and simply placed in the tank with no acclimation. Once all the fish are moved,

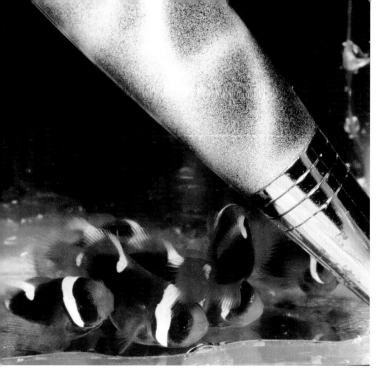

Post-metamorphosis Saddleback Clowns (with tip of pen for scale) in a grow-out tank at C-Quest Hatchery in Puerto Rico.

a slow drip of water from the grow-out system is started and the fish are slowly acclimated to the new system water.

Without central filtration, water can be manually exchanged between the larval tank and the grow-out tank over a period of days or a week before the day of first transfer.

TROUBLESHOOTING & DISEASE

It often requires several attempts and many sacrificed larvae for a new breeder to become proficient at raising any percentage of a spawn to maturity. (Experienced breeders can have the same challenges when starting with a new species or new breeding pair.)

The developmental stages of larvae are very complex and many difficult moments are sure to be encountered. (If it's any consolation, the survival rate of eggs and larvae in the wild is extremely low. You will lose many fishes, but so does Mother Nature.) It pays to be ready for the most predictable of these troubles before they occur so that you can take a positive route of attack in trying to avert disaster.

In addition to the expected challenges, there will be perplexing and unique problems that occur from time to time. This is especially true for species with little or no history of being spawned in captivity. Even for the many commonly spawned species, countless unknowns still exist. There is always room for improvement, better survival rates and lower mortality. In my view, different food sources and improved water quality can solve many of the usual problems that can beset a small-scale operation.

Inferior Eggs & Weak Larvae

Difficulties associated with larval rearing often stem from the eggs. Many times eggs will be shrunken or undersized, resulting in thin larvae with undersized yolk sacs. The larvae are weaker and suffer from malnourishment. This problem is directly traced to the broodstock diet and can be corrected with better foods. Feed the broodstock more fresh seafoods along with some live foods—squid is especially helpful in situations such as this.

Undersize larvae from such spawns must learn to be successful in hunting and capturing food very quickly as their yolk sacs are depleted. Rotifer densities in the rearing aquarium should be increased to 15 or 20 per milliliter, and the photoperiod should be increased to at least 16 hours per day to allow these undersized larvae more time to feed and gain nourishment.

Falling Eggs

Demersal spawning fishes such as clownfishes adhere their eggs to solid objects. If chitin is not available in sufficient quantities within the broodstock diet, the eggs may fall off the substrate on which they were deposited or the eggshells may be weak and easily damaged by air bubbles and the like. Fresh shrimp, with their shells, should be finely chopped in a blender. This can then be added to the broodstock food. Future spawns should not exhibit this quality.

Fungus Attack on Eggs

Bacteria and fungus will attack any eggs that are not fertile. A brood-tending male fish will remove any infertile or fungused eggs left in his care. At times, when the eggs are removed for artificial incubation, fungus may attack an entire clutch. If eggs are turning white, remove all such eggs with a pair of tweezers and increase the aeration passing over the eggs. Typically, the best solution to avoid such fouling is to treat the eggs with formalin or hydrogen peroxide before they are placed into artificial incubation. If after treatment the eggs are still prone to fungus, the eggs can be treated daily until hatching is imminent.

Hatching Problems

The hatching of the larvae usually occurs without problems. However, if the broodstock have received too much chitin (from crustacean shells) in their diet, the egg cases may be too hard and hatching made difficult for larvae. This is generally non-problematic, but has been observed in certain gobies and damselfish when removed from the care of the male for hatching. (Enzymes secreted by the mouth of the larva in the midst of hatching aid in dissolving the shell and allowing an exit for the larva.) Sometimes the larvae hatch, but the remnants of an eggshell may be stuck to their heads. Increased water movement and aeration will remove this eggshell fragment. If clinging bits of eggshell are not dislodged, the larvae will perish in a short time. Less chitin-based food should be fed to the broodstock. Peeled shrimp should be used in such instances.

Transfer Losses

Any larvae that hatch out in the broodstock aquarium must be transferred to the proper rearing facilities. Much stress will be placed on the larvae even when this is carried out in a careful and delicate manner. Siphoning the larvae out (or using a turkey baster to suck them out) will generally result in some mortality. Wafting them into a shallow bowl or container, while generally less stressful than a siphon, can still result in mortality. The larvae are very delicate at this point—they look like mere glass slivers. Any young fish that perish within two days after being transferred can be recorded as victims of transfer damage. Collecting larvae in the broodstock tank should be limited to only the most

robust of marine fish larvae. In fact, clownfish larvae should be the only candidates for this method of transfer. While some species of gobies and blennies may be able to handle such transfer, high mortalities are the general rule. Be careful—move the eggs, not the larvae.

Upside-Down Larvae

Larvae that seem to be cowering in the corners of the tank in an upside-down position are being driven there by intense illumination. These larvae will die in a few hours if the light is not reduced or moved farther away from the tank.

Listless Larvae

Larvae that seem listless are either experiencing oxygen deprivation or are weak from inadequate food intake. These two problems have similar symptoms but are easy to differentiate. Malnourished larvae will appear thin, whereas oxygen-starved larvae will have well-rounded bellies assuming food intake was high prior to this condition.

If lack of oxygen is suspected, aeration should be increased if the larvae are old enough to withstand the increased water movement. Oxygen depletion can occur if there are too many food organisms present or aerobic nitrifying bacteria is gaining a foothold and, of course, if the aquarium is poorly aerated. Using algae paste (rather than live greenwater) to tint the rearing water can also contribute to oxygen depletion.

Dying Larvae

Poor water quality is the leading cause of larvae dying at any given point. All too often, there are just too many larvae and too many food organisms in the larval rearing vessel to maintain the pristine water conditions found in the ocean. The best we can do this is to perform regular partial water changes and add live microalgae to combat the wastes. Daily ammonia tests are a good idea. Sometimes water changes may be necessary more often or in larger amounts. Having a central filtration system can be a big help in maintaining good water quality. A slow drip can be increased to a steady stream should water conditions turn bad.

Starving Larvae

Larvae that are provided with inadequate food organisms or the food organisms of improper size have very poor prospects. Larvae will survive on the energy-packed yolk sac for some time after they have hatched.

For some species such as pygmy angelfish, lionfish, wrasse bass, damselfish and many more, the yolk sac may keep them strong for as long as 8 days. Hobbyists spawning these species think they are in the clear when the larvae are still alive after 8 days. After this point, however, the larvae often die within the next day or two. When the yolk sac has been absorbed, food organisms are required. If the larvae die a day or two after their yolk sacs have been used up and appear thin, we must assume that they died of malnourishment. If it is a species listed in this book, the food organisms each larvae feeds on is listed. For others, you are on a trial-and-error basis.

Juvenile Shock

Shock is a possible cause of death among juvenile fish. This usually occurs around the time of metamorphosis when the fish are fed a high-fat diet consisting of newly hatched

SIX RULES TO LIVE BY

1. Use an appropriately sized (not too large) rearing chamber that will allow a proper density of rotifers to be maintained, but big enough to maintain proper water quality until the larvae can be moved into grow out aquariums.
2. Cover all sides of the rearing tank for the first week to exclude light.
3. To increase feeding success, keep rotifer densities high, at a minimum of 6 to 10/mL.
4. Keep aeration low but slowly increase the bubble flow as larvae grow.
5. Add microalgae to the rearing chamber to achieve a light green or brown color.
6. Make daily water changes while siphoning bottom debris or allow a slow drip from the central system.

Artemia. It is important to begin weaning the young fish off *Artemia* early. Feed flake food more often and do not feed newly hatched *Artemia* more than a day or two per week. When you approach the tank, if the fish frantically dart around in nervous circles and suddenly drop dead, you can be bet it was shock caused from tissue laden with fat—a consequence of overfeeding with *Artemia*.

CULLING JUVENILES

A portion of any given batch of larvae will contain juveniles with undesirable characteristics. These may be a small percentage of the spawn or a dismayingly large percentage. Any juvenile that is not a good representative of the species should be discarded. Missing eyes, shortened gill covers, missing vertebrae, and similar deformities should be cause for immediate culling. If marine fish propagation is to have a future, it is important that we all weed out deformed fishes. The recommended method of disposal is anesthesia in MS-222 (tricaine methanosulfate) or clove oil (*see page 163ß*) followed by freezing or formalin. If this seems harsh, consider that life in the wild is even more ruthless, and these are the same fish that nature would also eliminate.

Dealing with juveniles that turn up with color anomolies, on the other hand, is the breeder's decision. Some breeders are purists and rogue out any fish that are not typical of the species. On the other hand, fish with unusual stripes or markings or even enhanced finnage may be chosen as future broodstock. Aberrations such as these can be useful in catching the attention of buyers and may be very valuable if sufficiently attractive or interesting.

DISEASE

Outbreaks of disease occur most often in grow-out aquariums where juveniles are reared in high densities. Instances of disease can be directly linked to deteriorating water quality due to an increasing bioload. As the larvae grow into juveniles, they demand more food intake which in turn puts more strain on biological filtration—and an onus on

Ready-to-market Canary Fang Blennies (*Meiacanthus oualaunensis*) being inspected and sorted at Oceans, Reefs and Aquari-

the aquarist to perform regular partial water changes. Larval fishes, fortunately, are resistant to most diseases and so we primarily need to pay attention to juvenile grow-out tanks in watching for parasites and other afflictions.

Disease-causing organisms are ever-present within most aquarium systems. It is important for larvae to establish a functioning immune system to ward off such invasions. Severe or long-term exposure to internal or external stress is a leading cause of disease outbreaks. Most commonly, overcrowding and overfeeding cause deterioration in water quality and slowly lower a fish's immune system, rendering it vulnerable to parasite attack and disease.

To successfully eradicate a disease, look first to ensuring that the environment is clean and properly maintained before any attempt is made to cure the disease itself. Most diseases can be subdued by performing a large water change and cleaning the filter media. When environmental factors are back on track and in good standing, the fish's inherent

immune system will usually combat the disease.

Most drugs and medications will impede the performance of biological filtration (indiscriminately killing the beneficial bacterial along with any foes), causing further water quality deterioration. Regular water changes and good aquarium management is essential to the well-being of juveniles. The juveniles should be observed several times daily for signs of stress and disease. If any juveniles are behaving unusually or have white spots or a hazy white slime, make a water change. I would resort to medications only if the outbreak is severe. Disease-causing organisms often go through many different stages, and the obvious external signs of disease such as white spots and slime signal an advanced stage. Signs of stress should be obvious hours or days before these external signs occur.

The following is a listing of the most-common diseases likely to be encountered in a home breeding operation. It is important to identify with certainty which disease is af-

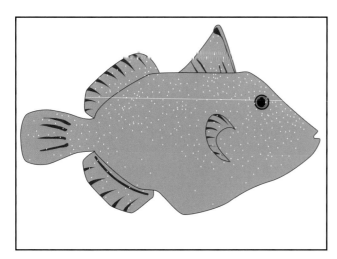

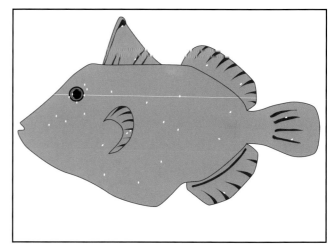

Amyloodinium occellatum: early detection and large daily water changes can stop this potentially deadly parasitic disease.

Cryptocaryon irritans: note large, distinct white spots. Treat with formalin, copper sulphate or lowered specific gravity.

fecting the fish before any successful treatment is employed. It is a safe bet to perform a large water change before taking additional steps. If the infected aquarium is connected to a main system, isolate the aquarium for treatment and perform a large water change on the other aquariums within the system while observing them for signs of similar disease.

Amyloodinium ocellatum

Amyloodinium, commonly referred to as velvet disease is perhaps the most common parasite that attacks young fish. *Amyloodinium* is a single-celled flagellated protozoan, and its presence is characterized by a very large number of tiny white spots that seem to fuse together forming a white haze covering the fish's body.

This disease is easily distinguished from *Cryptocaryon* by the telltale appearance of the white dots. The spots of *Amyloodinium* are smaller, not well defined, and appear cloudy. Affected fish can be seen swimming in fast, short bursts, while scratching themselves on objects in the aquarium. They may stop feeding. Later stages of infection include small white dots, a white haze, clamped fins. Listlessness and death soon follow.

As soon as the first symptoms are noted, large daily water changes of up to 50 percent should be performed.

Most often this is enough to reverse the effects. If, however, the disease progresses to the point where most of the juveniles are visibly infected, more involved measures will need to be taken. If the aquarium is crowded, it may help to separate the juveniles into several aquariums and simply maintain good water quality. Chances are good that the fish will become symptom-free within a few weeks with the help of clean water and a lower stocking density.

Place heavily infected fish in a formalin bath for 45 minutes with brisk aeration. One milliliter of 37-percent formaldehyde per gallon of treatment water is the general rule. This treatment should be performed three separate times every other day. Fish should be netted out of the bath and never add the treatment water to the grow-out tank.

Copper sulfate is another common aquarium treatment for *Amyloodinium* and ich. Care should be taken when using copper sulfate, which will kill the parasites but also impact the beneficial bacteria populations in your biological filtration. If possible, disconnect the biological filtration system and place it on another aquarium until the copper treatment is finished. Then, perform a large water change and reconnect the filter to the original aquarium. Aeration should be kept high in the treatment tank and water changes should be performed daily while adding more copper to make up for that lost. Successful treatments should take 10 to 14 days.

Crytocaryon irritans

Also called Saltwater ich or white spot is caused by a ciliated protozoan with a very complex life cycle. The white spots that characterize this disease are larger than those of *Amyloodinium* and appear shiny and well defined. They are also more sparsely located, most heavily concentrated on the fins and head region.

Early symptoms include scratching against aquarium objects and rapid respiration. Many treatments are available, but the best remedy of all relies simply on prevention. Certain life stages of *Cryptocaryon* are vulnerable to drops in specific gravity and higher temperatures. It is advisable to lower the specific gravity to roughly 1.015 before any medication is added. (Over a period of hours, remove saltwater from the aquarium and replace it with dechlorinated freshwater at the same temperature. Measure the specific gravity until it drops to the desired level.) For hardy species such as clownfish and dottybacks, the temperature can also be raised to 85°F. Formalin can be added to a bare aquarium at a dosage of 2 drops per gallon for two days. After the two-day treatment, a large (30 to 50 percent) water change should be performed. Copper sulfate in a liquid form is another common remedy (*see above*).

Brooklynella hostilis

Brooklynella is a serious disease but is, fortunately, relatively rare among cultured fishes that are not exposed to high stress levels such as capture and shipping. It is commonly known as *anemonefish disease* as its most common hosts are wild-caught clownfishes, especially maroon clowns, although all marine fish are susceptible. This is a ciliated protozoan that attacks and irritates the body of the fish, causing heavy mucus production in isolated clumps along the fish's body. Appearing as a white haze on the body of the infected fish, this disease will cause the victim to exhibit clamped fins and elevated respiratory rates. The fish's skin may actually slough off. Before any

Brooklynella hostilis: note heavy patches of mucus. Treatment calls for improving water quality and dosing with formalin.

treatment is given, the cause of the disease must be found and corrected. This means checking water quality and performing water changes, as high levels of nitrogen waste and dissolved organic matter may be at the root of the problem. Even if only a few juveniles show signs of the disease, the entire aquarium should be treated with formalin at a dosage of 2 drops per gallon. Another method, perhaps better suited to small operations, would be to bathe all juveniles in formalin for 45 minutes at a dosage of one mL per gallon. Three separate treatments, every other day, should eliminate symptoms.

Uronema marinum

This disease is characterized by open lesions, ulcerations and sores usually surrounded by a ring of mucus. Again, this disease is caused by a single-celled protozoan and usually appears as a consequence of poor water quality. Perform a large water change, clean filter media and treat with formalin or malachite green.

Bacterial Infections

Bacterial infections are a secondary response to stress, open sores from mechanical injury or disease. Frayed fins, and open sores are the symptoms. Bacterial populations can also be a consequence of heavy feeding and deteriorataing water conditions in the rearing vessel.

As fish larvae begin feeding on *Artemia* nauplii, they become susceptible to mycobacterium infestations as the tissue within the larvae becomes enriched with fatty acids. Larval culture vessels are also a breeding ground for bacteria. The conditions in a larval culture vessel are not unlike those found in a Petri dish designed to culture bacteria: the water is kept warm, food is constantly available, with larval densities typically quite high and organic matter added daily.

Many species of bacteria can be responsible for mass mortality among larvae. *Vibrio* sp. are notorious for causing massive fish kills in larval culture systems with deteriorating water quality and crowded conditions. It is often difficult to know if bacteria are the culprit of mass mortality—and if they are, determining the species responsible is challenging. There are laboratories and fish veterinary services to help identify these pathogens, but they primarily cater to larger-scale aquaculture facilities.

There are many antibiotics available to treat such infections, but I strongly advise against resorting to these remedies unless you have professional advice and know what you are doing. If water quality and tank conditions are below standard levels (with an overload of waste, poor circulation and lowered oxygen content), treatment with any available medication or antibiotic will prove unsuccessful. Having ample biological filtration, doing water changes and keeping the tank bottoms clean are the keys to maintaining good water quality and limiting disease causing organisms in your breeding and rearing tanks.

Aiptasia & Other Nuisance Anemones

Fast-spreading nuisance anemones such as *Aiptasia*—also known as glass or rock anemones—can wreck havoc on larval tanks. Generally, problems with these pests begin around the time newly hatched *Artemia* is added to the diet. *Aiptasia* thrive on this particular food item and can quickly reproduce into plague proportions. If not controlled *Aiptasia* and other anemones will quickly cover all solid surfaces within the rearing vessel and broaden their dietary preferences to more than *Artemia*. They can sting and even consume your larval fish.

Although not the least labor-intensive method of eradication, extraction by hand may be the most effective approach in a larval rearing tank. A length of rigid airline tubing can be attached to flexible airline tubing and used as a mouth pipette. Rigid airline tubing is used to scrape the base of the anemone in an attempt to free it from the substrate. This is an easy task on the smooth, solid surface of an aquarium or utility sink used as a grow-out tank. Next they are sucked into the flexible tubing and discarded. Daily observations may be necessary to rid a tank of these unwanted intruders. After metamorphosis they are rarely a problem.

CLEANLINESS COUNTS

Cleanliness is a very important consideration in breeding marine fishes and nurturing delicate larvae. We need to be mindful of keeping our various cultures separate and to avoid cross-contamination. For example, rotifers should stay in the rotifer tanks and the *Nannochloropsis* used to feed the rotifers should not be allowed to get into other algae cultures.

Disease pathogens and parasites from one aquarium should not be passed to another, and if wild plankton or other food sources are used, they too should be isolated. Outbreaks of disease can be prevented when careful attention is paid to cleanliness. It is important to maintain an orderly working environment where everything has its place. Every breeder needs a daily scheme to get the essential tasks done and this routine should be worked out to help you reduce the risk of contamination.

For example, it makes sense to work with the microalgae before the rotifers, as it doesn't matter if microalgae gets into the rotifer culture tanks, but you really need to keep the rotifers out of the phytoplankton.

Always wash your hands and arms with a disinfectant soap, being sure to rinse well, after working with possible contaminants.

Beautiful batch of Tomato Clowns in a large grow-out tank at Proaquatix. Responsible breeders cull out all defective fish.

The notion of culling physically deformed or undesirable offspring is often viewed with great apprehension among hobbyists, but it is essential to prevent unwanted traits from being perpetuated. Offspring with missing tails, vertebrae or gill covers, poorly developed or misaligned mouths, bent backs or any other physical deformities must be destroyed.

Many long-standing practices for disposing of aquarium fishes are not acceptable by today's standards. Freezing, asphyxiation in soda water, pithing (destroying the central nervous system by severing the spinal cord and "scrambling" the brain tissue), and electrical stunning should be avoided. Contrary to popular belief, few marine aquarium fishes survive flushing and this is certainly not a humane method of euthanasia. Never release aquarium fishes into local waters.

The most widely used anesthetics to cull undesirable aquarium fishes humanely are MS-222 (tricaine methanosulfate) and clove oil (eugenol). MS-222 is available through commercial aquaculture supply houses, but is often prohibitively expensive and a known carcinogenic. Clove oil is commonly used in home brewing recipes and aromatherapy and can be found in many home brewing supply houses, specialty outlets and most drug stores. When used for anesthesia, roughly 10 drops per gallon will immobilize most aquarium fishes. A lethal dose is roughly 50 drops per gallon. The fish to be destroyed should be placed in a small known volume of water. In a separate jar mix the appropriate dosage of clove oil with tank water and shake vigorously to form an emulsion (e.g., add 30 drops of clove oil to three gallons of water; 50 drops to five gallons of water). Slowly add this emulsion to the bucket with the fish to be culled and watch the behavior of the fish. Once the fish have fallen on their sides and have no visible voluntary muscle control, they should be frozen or placed in vodka, ethyl, or isopropyl alcohol. Overdosing with clove oil is lethal, but there is a chance the fish will revive if placed in water. Humanely freezing or preserving in alcohol will ensure specimens are dead before disposal.

Banggai Cardinalfish (*Pterapogon kauderni*) are mouthbrooders and among the easiest of marine aquarium fishes to breed.

CHAPTER 11

SPECIES GUIDES

Breeding Marine Aquarium Fishes

The coral reefs of the world are home to well over 3,000 species of marine fishes. Of these, several hundred commonly enter the aquarium market, and many, many more make rare, sporadic appearances. For a newcomer to marine breeding, picking the right first species to breed out of the myriads available can pose a perplexing challenge. The tried-and-true approach is to learn the basics with a relatively easy species, have some success and then perhaps move on to other, more challenging fishes. So how does one choose the ideal candidate to start?

Often, this occurs by chance or the fish find us. Most marine aquarists become interested in rearing reef fishes when they witness mating behaviors and spawning events in their display aquariums. For me, it was clownfish that sparked my interest. For many others, it is gobies, blennies, damselfish or nearly 100 other species that can rather readily be coaxed into spawning.

In captivity, getting marine fishes to spawn is often an uncomplicated task. When conspecifics are placed together, kept in healthy conditions and fed properly, there is a high potential to observe reproductive behavior. Rearing the larvae, however, can be the catch. Some larvae are large and relatively forgiving of a beginner's mistakes, while others are so small and demanding they defy the best efforts of the experts.

I think it is important for novice aquarists to wet their fingers with easier species before tackling the more difficult ones. Only after gaining some initial experience with live food cultures and fundamental rearing protocols should aquarists move on to more challenging species. Just as the freshwater hobbyist begins raising guppies and mollies and danios before attempting to breed discus, a marine enthusiast should familiarize him or herself with marine fish larvae and the concepts of rearing before taking on the more difficult species.

Rearing marine fishes is a hobby of passion, often of obsession. If you insist on tackling a difficult group such as angelfish or surgeonfish as your first breeding candidate, failure is virtually guaranteed. Failed attempts often leave hobbyists frustrated and confused. Confidence should be built with easy species such as certain clownfish, Banggai Cardinals or Neon Gobies.

Several aspects of a fish's early life history determine the difficulty of captive rearing. Clownfishes are the most widely raised marine fish, due their particularly large larvae and reduced pelagic phase. Clownfish larvae are ravenous feeders that metamorphose and look like miniature clownfish in as little as 7 days after hatching. The average pelagic larval phase of most marine fishes is around 25 days. Species with longer pelagic phases are invariably more difficult to rear. Mortality is a continuous process during the larval stage, and surviving numbers will always be greater in those species exhibiting a shorter pelagic larval duration.

The size of newly hatched larvae has a direct relationship to survival rates, both in nature and in the aquarium. Small larvae are delicate and prone to stress from light, water movement, rearing tank design, physical handling, and most importantly, improper nutrition. Small larvae are difficult to feed and many times will refuse commonly available fare such as rotifers. In general, larvae that hatch near 3 mm in total length or larger are not too difficult to rear. Some larvae, such as those of fang blennies and various cardinalfish are slightly smaller than 3 mm at hatching, but are relatively easy to raise.

For the most part, all demersal or benthic spawners (those that make nests and offer some degree of parental care) are within the grasp of hobbyists and small-scale marine breeders.

Pelagic spawners that cast their eggs to the seas are, in general, more difficult to rear. Dream species like large angels, butterflies, tangs and triggers require extraordinary equipment and resources that are—at least at this writing—usually out of the range of all but skilled, well-funded professionals.

The following species accounts move from the easier groups to the ones that demand more skills, more experience and more investment in specialized systems.

CLOWNFISHES

SUBFAMILY AMPHIPRIONINAE

Clownfishes have long aroused keen curiosity and admiration among divers, underwater naturalists and aquarium keepers alike. With their bright colors, startling white bands and their unusual symbiotic relationship with sea anemones, clownfish have become the icons of coral reefs and marine aquariums. Virtually every saltwater hobbyist in the world has kept at least one clownfish in his or her home aquarium.

Like the damselfishes that share the family Pomacentridae, the clownfishes are blessed with many qualities that make them ideal candidates for life in captivity. Perhaps the best quality for our purposes is that they are strongly site-attached. In the wild, clownfishes rarely venture far from the protection of a sea anemone. They are not strong swimmers and are not stressed by the limited quarters of a home aquarium. Life in a glass box suits them just fine, and they spawn quite readily.

Clownfishes have been spawning in captivity since the early 1900s. They have been raised commercially since the early 1950s, and today it is easy for novice marine fish breeders to raise the larvae with relatively few problems.

In my opinion, these are the fish that novice marine fish breeders should work with first. There is a vast pool of knowledge surrounding this subfamily and most of the initial hang-ups have been solved. It would be difficult to spawn these fish with any consistency if an anemone was re-

Clark's Clownfish (*Amphiprion clarkii*): male tending newly laid eggs. Male Clark's Clownfish are often as large as their mates.

quired for the fish's well being. Many species of sea anemones are hard to keep alive in captivity and require powerful lighting and expert care. Fortunately, an anemone is not needed.

The Ocellaris or Common Clownfish and Percula Clownfish (*Amphiprion ocellaris* and *A. percula*) commonly spawn in 10-gallon aquariums; a large broodstock aquarium is not essential. A small-scale clownfish breeding program could easily start with just three aquariums. A 10-gallon aquarium for breeding, a 10-gallon tank for larval rearing and a larger aquarium or tub of some sort to act as a grow-out tank. These fish are easy to spawn and easy to raise, making them the ideal choice for novices. Some are easier to spawn and raise than others. Chances are good that any

clownfish you run into at your local aquarium shop will prove to be one of the easier species. Good first choices are: the Ocellaris, Common or False Percula Clown (*A. ocellaris*), Percula (*A. percula*), Clark's Clownfish (*A. clarkii*), the Tomato Clownfish (*A. frenatus*), the Red and Black Clown (*A. melanopus*) and the Maroon Clown (*Premnas biaculeatus*).

There are many species of clownfish that rarely show up in the trade and are often expensive. *Amphiprion* species such as *A. latezonatus*, *A. nigripes*, *A. bicintus*, *A. tricintus*, *A. akindynos*, *A. allardi*, *A. leucokranus*, *A. mccullochi* and *A. akallopisos* are all examples of clownfishes that require a bit more effort to spawn and raise. If these species are available and seem to be in good condition, you may want to

Percula Clownfish (*Amphiprion percula*): a desirable species, but less hardy than the closely related *A. ocellaris*.

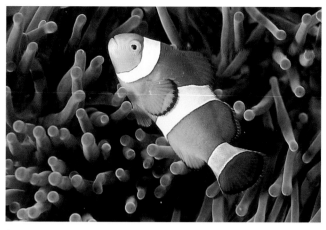

Ocellaris Clownfish (*A. ocellaris*): model for a clownfish named Nemo and among the most-popular of marine fish species.

Maroon Clownfish (*Premnas biaculeatus*): a big, rugged species sometimes seen with gold-tinged bars as in this fish.

Saddleback Clownfish (*A. polymnus*) guarding a nest of eggs showing bright eyespots, a sign of imminent hatching.

purchase a pair and place them in an aquarium all their own. Feed them well and give them privacy and good water quality and wait. In the meantime, I advise concentrating your efforts on easier species until you have gotten the hang of things. This second group of clownfish species can be difficult to maintain.

There are 28 species of clownfish limited in geographic distribution to the Indo-Pacific and Red Sea. Of the two genera, *Amphiprion* and *Premnas*, 27 species are found in the genus *Amphiprion*.

Breeding Aquarium: The size of the breeding aquarium required for each species varies. *A. ocellaris* and *A. percula* will readily spawn in 10-gallon aquariums. Most other species will spawn in 20-gallon "high" aquariums. A 29-gallon aquarium makes an ideal spawning aquarium for just about any species. Many successful hobbyists place broodstock pairs of all species including the bigger Tomatoes and Maroons into 10-gallon aquariums with great results. The determining factor seems to be time, not space, with all these species.

Black Percula Clownfish (*A. percula*): pair spawning in a community aquarium. Note dark or melanistic color form.

Clark's Clownfish (*A. clarkii*): a great aquarium species, but one requiring larger broodstock tanks of 40-gal. or more.

Tomato Clownfish (*A. frenatus*): a robust species, always popular with aquarists and relatively easy to breed and rear.

Pink Skunk Clowns (*A. perideraion*) clustering in a rearing tank at C-Quest Hatchery. This behavior is seen only in aquariums.

While these fish will readily spawn in community aquariums, it is best to give them an aquarium all their own. The aquarium can be fully furnished, brightly lit and supplied with a host anemone or the aquarium can be bare. It seems that clownfish will spawn more readily in a bare aquarium. Spawning sites are provided with ceramic tiles or flowerpots. Ceramic tiles have emerged as the best choice for a spawning substrate. The underside of the tile with the most texture is especially attractive to spawning clownfish. The tiles should be placed on an angle and leaned up against

the back glass. Clay flowerpots will work, but the eggs are difficult to aerate and artificially hatch when the eggs are placed on the interior. The bottom and three sides of the tank should be painted blue or black to provide privacy and give the pair a secure feeling.

Establishing Broodstock Pairs: Clownfish are protandrous hermaphrodites. The sex of any individual fish is determined by its social rank. In any group of clownfish restricted to one area (be it in an anemone on the reef or in an aquarium) the most dominant fish within the group de-

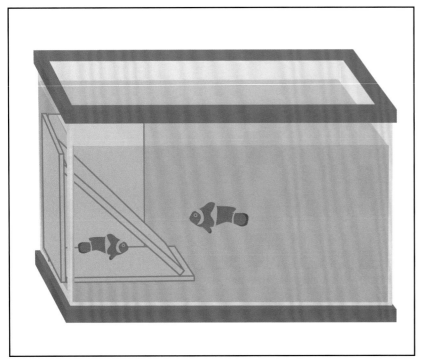

Ideal broodstock aquarium setup for a pair of clownfish, with a versatile spawning shelter constructed with four ceramic tiles in one corner.

pairs. Pairing often takes some time with small individuals, but the chance of obtaining a spawning pair is greatly increased. The conditions in which the pair is raised is also much better and good water quality and adequate feeding of high quality foods can be assured. (Wild-caught clowns do not always survive the stresses of capture and transport, and some reef conservationists oppose their collection. Captive-bred clowns are always to be preferred as your first broodstock.)

Once in an aquarium shop many possible pairs can be observed. A group of juveniles held in cramped quarters will develop a hierarchy and sex determination begins. Often two fish begin to spend much time together and form pair bonds. If two fish are observed defending a small territory while chasing off other approaching fish, chances are good that the pair will begin spawning in a few months' time.

Alternately, one large fish can be placed with a substantially smaller fish to establish a pair. The larger of the two will be in a female role. This female will harass the smaller one and put it in a submissive role. A functional male will be the outcome. This is the best method for pairing maroon clownfish. Females of this species often grow three times larger than males. A large female is more receptive to a tiny male than to one roughly half her size. It seems a smaller fish does not pose as much of a threat and is more readily accepted. When attempting this method it is best to give the smaller fish some sort of safe refuge to retreat to if the female's attentions become overwhelming. Placing a tank divider of egg crate in the aquarium with a small hole cut out to allow the male access to the female's domain will work. The male should initially be placed in the protected side of the divider. When he feels comfortable in venturing out, he will discover the entrance hole and swim through. By placing him in the protected compartment he knows where the entrance hole is

velops into a functional female. This will become the largest individual present. The next individual in the hierarchy becomes the functional male. Any other individuals present remain asexual. If the female dies, the functional male will change sex and assume the role of the female. The asexual fish have their own a pecking order as well. The most dominant of these asexual fish will transform into the functional male.

In captivity, all that is needed to establish a pair is two small clownfish. As the two grow to maturity, they will quarrel and compete to establish who is stronger. The stronger fish will develop into the female. The weaker of the two will assume a submissive role and become the male. This is an easy process to orchestrate. Most species of clownfish are available at small sizes. With the now commonly available captive-raised clownfish comes an increased size range availability. Clownfish can now be bought in very small sizes. These should be the choices for broodstock

Average incubation time of representative species of clownfish. Eggs are highly temperature dependant, hatching faster at higher water temperatures. Lower water temperatures may result in larger sizes of larvae at hatching.

Species	Incubation Time
Amphiprion ocellaris Ocellaris Clownfish	7 - 8 days
Amphiprion percula Percula Clownfish	7 - 8 days
Amphiprion clarkii Clark's Clownfish	6 - 8 days
Amphiprion ephippium Red Saddleback Clownfish	8 - 9 days
Amphiprion frenatus Tomato Clownfish	8 - 10 days
Amphiprion melanopus Red and Black Clownfish	8 - 10 days
Amphiprion polymnus Saddleback Clownfish	7 - 8 days
Amphiprion nigripes Maldives Clownfish	7 - 8 days
Premnas biaculeatus Maroon Clownfish	6 - 8 days

So-called Black Ocellaris Clownfish, a melanistic color morph from Darwin, Australia, bred and marketed by ORA.

and can retreat when threatened. Given time, the two will bond and the divider can be removed. (Always be sure that the aquarium is covered. The female may pursue the male to the point of causing him to leap from the tank.)

Conditioning Foods: A variety of fresh seafoods, including grated shrimp and squid, should make up the bulk of the conditioning diet and should be offered to the pair several times daily. Vegetable matter should also be supplied. *Spirulina* flake foods are eagerly accepted.

Spawning: Spawning is initiated by the female. Smaller species such as Ocellaris and Percula lay small batches of eggs, up to 200, while larger species such as Clark's and

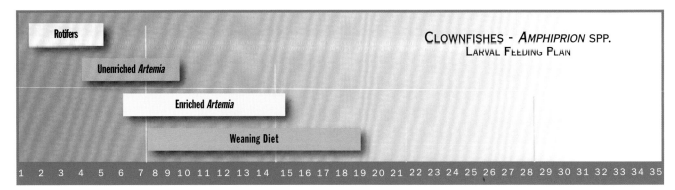

Clownfishes - *Amphiprion* spp.
Larval Feeding Plan

Rotifers

Unenriched *Artemia*

Enriched *Artemia*

Weaning Diet

| 1 | 2 | 3 | 4 | 5 | 6 | 7 | 8 | 9 | 10 | 11 | 12 | 13 | 14 | 15 | 16 | 17 | 18 | 19 | 20 | 21 | 22 | 23 | 24 | 25 | 26 | 27 | 28 | 29 | 30 | 31 | 32 | 33 | 34 | 35 |

Guidelines: Feed rotifers at 10/ml; unenriched *Artemia* nauplii less than 12 hrs. old; enriched *Artemia* less than 24 hrs. old.

Maroons may lay 1,500 or more eggs. It is the male's duty to aerate and guard the eggs until they hatch. He agitates them to keep them viable and actively removes fungused eggs. The eggs hatch an hour or two after darkness on days 7 to 11.

Incubation times are generally species-specific and dependant on water temperature; the warmer the water, the faster the eggs develop. The eggs should be removed on the day they are predicted to hatch. The eggs are orange in color when first deposited and a silver color eventually develops as the eyes of the larvae begin to pigment within the egg case. The entire tile should be lifted out of the broodstock aquarium and placed in the rearing aquarium, propped diagonally against the glass or on a hanger with an airstone placed directly under the eggs to aerate and agitate the eggs to aid in hatching. As long as the eggs are not allowed to dry out there is no need to keep them submerged in water during transfer. When the larvae hatch, the tile should be removed and the airflow reduced. Feeding should begin on the first day with rotifers. Newly hatched *Artemia* can be added to the diet at roughly day 4. Metamorphosis is complete in most species by day 9. Larval rearing is generally non-problematic as long as live feeds are enriched properly and good water quality is maintained through metamorphosis. High initial mortality is generally attributed to transfer stresses. Often, if eggs are exposed to artificial incubation methods, hatching, is delayed by one or more days, which increases early mortality rates.

DAMSELFISHES

FAMILY POMACENTRIDAE

Marine aquarists are intimately familiar with members of the damselfish family. These are the species most heavily relied on to break in or seed a new aquarium and those commonly chosen by aquarists setting up their first saltwater system. They are inexpensive, highly-disease resistant, mostly small and often beautifully colored.

These traits and the fact that most are site-attached, some being downright territorial, gives this family another positive benefit: they are easily spawned in the confines of home aquariums. Unlike the clownfishes that are also part of the family Pomacentridae, the damsels and *Chromis* produce larvae that are considerably more challenging to rear.

Many damselfish species are exceedingly common in the aquarium trade and thus the challenge of acquiring broodstock is eliminated. The most common species spawned in captive facilities are the smaller blue damsels. "Blue damsel" is a rather vague common name and is used to denote several to many species in the genus *Chrysiptera*. Three species are routinely available and commonly spawned in home aquariums, the Blue Devil (*C. cyanea)*, the Yellowtail Damsel or Demoiselle (*C. paresema)* and the South Sea Devil (*C. taupou)*. Starck's Damsel (*C. starki)* enters the

A pair of Green Chromis in typical spawning behavior often witnessed in home aquariums. Raising larvae past metamorphosis is still a challenge.

almost 15 cm (5.9 in.) in length, these fish require a bit more space in the aquarium to successfully spawn and will almost certainly eliminate other fishes present. The coloration of adult fish fades somewhat from the distinct black and white of juveniles. Adult pairs exhibit both size and color dimorphism.

The popular green *Chromis* species, actually a group of very similar and often-mislabelled species, are another set of frequently spawned marine fishes. When small, a large group is easily maintained with little aggression observed between members of the school. Reproductive adults in the confines of an aquarium, however, can prove quite belligerent during the spawning season. Males are always larger than females and develop heightened coloration.

The Green Chromis (*Chromis caerulea*) may develop black dorsal fins or pectoral fins near spawning accompanied by a yellow anal fin or yellow margins along the caudal fin. Male Blackaxil Chromis (*C. atripectoralis*) exhibit yellow margins on the dorsal, anal and caudal fins as spawning approaches, accompanied by heightened spotting in the head and a general darkening of body pigmentation. The Blue-green Chromis (*C. viridis*) usually darken in color to almost an olive-green shade.

Most *Chromis* species live in large aggregations over coral heads, rocky outcroppings, over turtle grass, or near oyster beds. Generally females outnumber males by as much as 6:1. Living in such aggregations, males are typically quite quarrelsome in their attempts to attract and keep spawning partners.

Many damselfish species exhibit protogynous hermaphroditism. Juveniles are virtually always female and change to males later in life should the need of the social unit require. One to several males dominates a social unit of females that also establish a hierarchy. Should a male be lost or

trade on an infrequent basis. A stunning species, *C. starki* would surely be welcomed as captive-bred stock.

Many damselfish exhibit permanent sexual dimorphism. Most often this is observed in the size of the fish, but occasionally sexual dichromatism is seen. Both *C. taupou* and *C. cyanea* exhibit drastic sexual dichromatism. Males of *C. cyanea* display a bright red to orange tail whereas females remain solid blue with a clear outline of the tail. Both male and female *C. taupou* display a bright yellow belly, but only the female has yellow displayed on the caudal peduncle. Male *Chrysiptera* are almost universally larger than females.

Members of the *Dascyllus* are equally common throughout the trade. Perhaps the most common of these is the Domino or Trimac Damsel (*D. trimaculatus*). Growing to

killed, the dominant female changes sex and each female then jumps rank. In captivity this phenomena is easily used to our advantage. Two juvenile fish will ultimately become a reproductive pair of adult fish. Similarly, three young fish will yield a male and two females. This is, of course, highly generalized and each species in question has limitations and social and environmental cues that stimulate sex reversal.

Although spawning is commonplace in captivity, larval rearing continues to be problematic with very few successful reports existing in published literature.

Eggs are demersal and guarded by the male until hatching. Most species are promiscuous spawners and males will often mate with any receptive female present and may be guarding several clutches within the same nest site. These eggs create an intricate pattern in the nest site. The nest seems to change and move as developing embryos change color. Adhesive eggs are produced that vary in size from .5 mm to nearly 2 mm in length. The Spiny Chromis (*Acanthochromis polyacanthus),* a damselfish that lacks a pelagic phase produces eggs that measure just over 4 mm in length. Eggs of *Chromis* require an average of two to three days to hatch, *Dascyllus* three days, and *Chrysiptera* four days. Newly hatched larvae measure an average of 2 mm in length. The yolk is fully depleted and first feeding commences the morning after hatching.

Captive damselfish are easily spawned in bare aquariums with PVC or ceramic tile spawning shelters. Eggs are removed to a rearing tank the day hatching is expected and supplied with aeration directly over the egg mass. Hatching occurs two hours after the lights have been turned out. Larvae are small and congregate near the sides of the rearing tank until greenwater is added. To date it seems the largest bottleneck in the commercial culture of damselfish is the first feeding stage of larvae. Rotifers, while accepted by many species, prove an inadequate diet and mortalities are very high.

Competition with wild imports will remain a leading delay in the commercialization of these fishes as it is economically unfeasible to spend the needed monies for research and development on species that fetch such low prices. Hobbyists may stand the best chance at raising such species. I have included just a few representative species typifying reproduction and what is known of larval rearing for the family.

Blue Damsels

South Sea or Fiji Devil Damsel
Chrysiptera taupou (Jordan & Seale, 1906)
Yellowtail Damsel
Chrysiptera paresema (Fowler, 1918)
Azure Damsel
Chrysiptera hemicyanea (Weber, 1913)

Maximum Length: 8 cm (3.1 in).
Sex Allocation: Protogynous.

All three *Chrysiptera* species are gorgeous fish, wellsuited to the confines of home aquariums. Spawning is easily accomplished with little effort on the part of the aquarist. Once spawning is initiated, pairs become prolific spawners offering plenty of larvae to test new skills and techniques in larval rearing.

Habitat and Range: Found from near shore lagoons to offshore coral reefs in the Indo and West Pacific regions. *C. taupou* ranges from the Coral Sea and northern Great Barrier Reef to Samoa, *C. parasema* from the Solomon Islands, Philippines, and northern Papua New Guinea, and *C. hemicyanea* from the eastern Indian Ocean, most notably Ashmore and Scott Reef to Indonesia.

Sexual Dimorphism: Males are always larger than females; however, the overall small size of these species makes using size to tell them apart less than a sure thing. However, permanent sexual dichromatism exists in *C. taupou*. Both sexes are blue with yellow on the ventral portion of the body. The yellow color of females extends to the caudal peduncle and is usually observed higher in the midbody than males. Females also exhibit more yellow dorsally. Both the dorsal fin and the body below the dorsal fin exhibit yellow. The yellow color sported by males is generally limited to the fins, rarely extending to the body. Females of all species

Azure Damsel (*Chrysiptera hemicyanea*): a brilliant little reef fish that spawns best in small aggregations, not single pairs.

Yellowtail Damsel (*Chrysiptera parasema*): an electric-blue species and perpetual bestseller in the aquarium hobby.

become plump rather quickly in captivity and are less belligerent than males.

Spawning: Heterosexual pairs are best isolated in bare 15 gallon tanks supplied with cut lengths of 1-inch diameter PVC to act as spawning shelters. If pairs are not readily identifiable, it is best to place a small group in a 30-gallon aquarium and observe their interactions. Breeding attempts with *C. hemicyanea* are greatly increased when a group is present. This species is less aggressive than others and can successfully be maintained and spawned in small aggregations. Females deposit adhesive eggs to the ceiling of provided shelters. Flowerpots, ceramic tiles, clam shells and conch shells will be accepted as spawning shelters; however, the ease of removal and incubation is generally simplified by the use of PVC pipe. PVC spawning shelters can be cut in half and re-assembled by use of a rubber band if fecundity estimates are needed or a clear acrylic transparency sheet inserted into the pipe. Isolated pairs are not overly aggressive toward one another.

A simple conditioning diet of grated shrimp and squid supplemented with flake food is sufficient to induce spawning. Males become very excited when courting receptive females and often utilize the entire aquarium to perform elaborate swimming behaviors ultimately enticing the female back to the spawning shelter. Many false runs occur

before actual egg laying is observed. Spawning occurs in much the same fashion as the clownfishes and other substrate spawners. Females deposit a number of adhesive eggs to the ceiling of the provided shelter. She then backs away from the substrate allowing the male to fertilize them. Several egg laying passes are made over the nest site until 250 to over 500 eggs are deposited. The male guards the nest until hatching occurs 4 days later. Egg production is very reliable at intervals of roughly 10 days.

At first the eggs are a translucent cream color and measure just shy of 1 mm in length. As incubation progresses, the eggs darken with pigmentation on the yolk, body and eyes of developing embryos. On the fourth day after fertilization the PVC section containing the spawn should be removed to a rearing tank and fixed vertically to the center standpipe or similar structure. An airstone fixed below the pipe should supply roughly 500 to 1,000 mL/ min of aeration through the pipe. Hatching occurs a few hours after darkness. The following morning the aeration should be reduced to 50 to 100 mL/min and the PVC section removed. Larvae measure near 2 mm in length at hatching, have fully pigmented eyes, a functional mouth and exhausted yolk. The tiny larvae can be seen clustered around the sides of the rearing vessel and require the addition of greenwater to bring them away from the sides and initiate

Blue Devil Damsel (*Chrysiptera cyanea*): note male coloration.

Blue Devil Damsel (*Chrysiptera cyanea*): typical female.

Blackaxil Chromis (*Chromis atripectoralis*): sold as Green Chromis.

South Sea Devil Damsel (*Chrysiptera taupou*): aka Fiji Devil.

feeding. At the Fish Ecophysiology Research Lab at Florida Institute of Technology we have routinely raised *C. taupou* larvae to day 8 using small-strain rotifers. By day 5 the larvae have grown to 2.6 mm in length and 3.2 mm by day 7. Roughly half of the total number of larvae consume good numbers of rotifers and exhibit well-rounded green stomachs from the ingested rotifers. On day 8 however, mortality rates are predictably very high.

First feeding is a major bottleneck in this species. Size-sorted wild plankton gives inconsistent results to day 20. Gut content exams have revealed a wide assortment of prey organisms including dinoflagellates, copepod nauplii, diatoms, ciliates and many unidentified items. Larval growth rates observed are probably an artifact of poor nutrition. Ten-day-old larvae measure near 3.5 mm in length.

At least a single successful rearing report exists for each species of *Chrysiptera*. In each of these cases rotifers and *Artemia* were used as feed. These are affordable, interesting species that home breeders may find challenging and worthy of experiments in larval feeding tactics to get past the tricky stages.

DOTTYBACKS

FAMILY PSEUDOCHROMIDAE

No other group of fish, with the possible exception of clownfishes, has caused such a surge of excitement in recent years than have the dottybacks. Until the turn of the century, the only members of the Pseudochromidae commonly encountered in aquarium shops were the Royal or Bicolor Dottyback (*Pictichromis paccagnallae*), the Diadem or Pinkstripe Dottyback (*Pictichromis diadema*), and the Magenta or Strawberry Dottyback (*Pictichromis poryphrea*). These species occur over a wide geographic distribution and are typically found in close association with others of the same species, often on vertical walls where their presence is quite conspicuous and their collection relatively easy.

Occasional imports of Red Sea species and other Indo-Pacific species showed up, although sporadically and always carrying high price tags. The related Royal Gramma (*Gramma loreto*) and the Comet (*Calloplesiops altivelis*) were the most common relatives available to the hobby.

It was not until pioneering fish breeder Bill Addison started shipping captive-bred specimens from his C-Quest hatchery in Puerto Rico that dottybacks became widespread throughout the aquarium hobby. More and more hobbyists became aware of their brilliant colors, reef-safe characteristics, and their inquisitive natures. The popularity that came with captive-raised stock was a welcome happening for both commercial breeders and collectors who have helped amplify the popularity and availability of these species. Today, roughly a dozen species of dottybacks are readily available either through the efforts of commercial breeders or keen-eyed collectors. Many more species turn up in the trade occasionally.

Due to their relatively small size, interesting behaviors and often striking color patterns, the dottybacks have become popular targets among commercial collectors and

Royal Dottyback (*Pictichromis paccagnellae*), typical of a family of alluring species with bold colors and brash personalities.

breeders for the aquarium industry. They offer home breeders many opportunities to augment the supply of wild-caught fishes, as well as the chance to experiment with species not commonly bred by commercial establishments.

Sexual Dimorphism

On the reef, pseudochromids are difficult to observe because of their cryptic lifestyle, and it is only those species displaying drastic differences between the sexes that can be readily identified as male or female. Subtle differences between the sexes are more common than drastic ones and these differences are best observed in captive specimens in excellent health.

Depending on the type of hermaphroditism displayed by a particular species, the dominant fish will develop into

Allen's Dottyback (*Manonichthys alleni*): male with characteristic dark red dot on its pectoral fin. Possible female at right.

Allen's Dottyback (*Manonichthys alleni*): possible female, color variant or a new species. Note red pectoral dot.

a male (protogyny) or a female (protandry) when two juveniles are placed together. Aquarium observations are fascinating since many individuals of a given species can be observed closely and repeatedly to note physical and behavioral changes and variations from fish to fish.

Subtle differences between sexes have been reported for many species of pseudochromids. Many of these differences are not universal and must not be overstated. In *P. fridmani* and *P. sankeyi* the lower lobe of the caudal fin is reported to grow longer in males. While this may be true of many isolated pairs, the caudal fin of females can also grow quite long, making this an unreliable indicator. Mature males of both *P. fridmani* and *P. sankeyi*, in my experience, grow slightly darker than females. The dark purple slash running through the eye of *P. fridmani* is darker in mature males as well. Males of this species often develop dark edges on the body scales giving them a fishnet pattern overall. Difficulties arise when dealing with such subtle differences as they are not universal and are subject to interpretation. A trained eye is the best tool.

In most species of dottybacks, large size differences are apparent between the sexes. In protogynous species, males virtually are always larger sizes than females. In protandrous species, it is the female that grows larger. The degree to which males and females differ in size is often species-dependant. Male Australian Dottybacks (*Ogilbyina novaehollunidae*), a protandrous species, are roughly half the size of females. In Springer's Dottybacks (*Pseudochromis springeri)*, a protogynous species, males and females differ only slightly in size.

Sexual dichromatism in some pseudochromids is spectacular and positively identifies an individual's sexual function. In early years males and females of sexually dichromatic species were often identified as separate species, an indication of just how different the colors of the sexes can be in dottyback pairs.

Dottyback Sex Allocation

It has long been assumed that members of the subfamily Pseudochrominae were simply protogynous hermaphrodites. Although little scientific analysis was available to support claims of hermaphroditism, aquarists spawning these fish knew sex changes were occurring. In all cases, when two juveniles were placed in the same aquarium a male and female would result. Statistical analysis eliminates coincidence in such occurrences. Protogyny was suggested, since in all aquarium observations males were the larger individuals of spawning pairs.

Today it is clear that dottyback hermaphroditism is not the simple process of female-to-male sex allocation we once believed. Protogyny, while still observed as the dominant mode of sex change, is no longer a concrete rule. In fact, all known forms of sequential hermaphroditism have been observed within the group. It will surely take some time before the sexual strategies of all species is understood, but for the time being it is apparent that the rules once set for them have been broken. Sex change appears a very elastic process in the Pseudochrominae.

Protogynous Hermaphroditism

Sex change from female to male or protogyny is the most common form of hermaphroditism in both the dottybacks and in marine fishes in general. When two females are isolated, social dominance will determine which assumes the reproductive function of a male. Experimental trials have determined the length of time required for a female to change sex and become a functional male. Philip Munday of James Cook University and I performed a series of replicates using 13 female pairs of Sunrise Dottybacks (*Pseudochromis flavivertex*) to how long it took for a female to allocate sexual function completely and yield fertile eggs. Of the 13 female pairs isolated, 6 females had completely changed sex and functioned as males in producing spawns of fertile eggs within 36 days of their isolation.

Still, I have often observed isolated female pairs of known protogynous hermaphrodites to be extremely hesitant to change sex in the male direction. This unusual circumstance is typically witnessed during the reproductive season. Both females repeatedly produce egg masses, but seem uninterested in assuming the male role. Obvious hierarchies are established in such female groups. It seems likely that sex change is inhibited during reproductive seasons when the females are actively producing eggs. When females of such pairs are separated and provided a diminished diet and a water temperature a few degrees cooler, breeding ceases and sex change quickly ensues. It has been reported in wild populations of some coral reef fishes that sex change occurs after the reproductive season.

This situation is rare among psuedochromids, but should it occur, environmental stimuli can be relied upon to provide essential cues responsible for sex change.

SPECIES KNOWN TO BE SEXUALLY DICHROMATIC

Pseudochromis dilectus
Pseudochromis steenei
Pseudochromis cyanotaenia (P. tapeinosoma)
Pseudochromis coccinicauda
Pseudochromis wilsoni (P. xanthicolor)
Pseudochromis jamesi
Pseudochromis moorei
Pseudochromis tonozukai

Cypho purpurascens

Ogilbyina queenslandiae (P. longipinnis)
Ogilbyina novaehollundiae
Ogilbyina velifera

Labracinus lineatus
Labracinus cyclopthalmus

* Species in parentheses indicate the former identification of females.

Protandrous Genera

Protandrous hermaphrodite are in a minority among the dottybacks, but present nonetheless. To date, male-to-female sex change has only been recorded from members of the *Ogilbyina* and *Cypho* genera, with all members practicing this strategy of hermaphroditism. It is difficult to understand why fishes from similar environmental niches practice opposite forms of sex allocations. Protandrous sex change is believed to have evolved independently of protogynous hermaphroditism.

Bi-directional Species

Rare dottybacks occur in the aquarium trade with some degree of frequency, but acquiring a successful heterosexual pair is often the most elusive challenge facing breeders. Observations described by Ferrell (1987) suggest bi-directional sex allocation may occur in *O. queenslandiae,* and many aquarium observations suggest that *P. steenei* may be capable of multiple sex reversals. To date, at least three species of dottybacks are known to change sex in either direction and it is probable that many more species of pseudochromids are capable of bi-directional sex change. The ability to change sex in either direction makes pair formation a slightly simpler process.

Collaborating with Dr. Philip Munday of James Cook University, we tested the potential for bi-directional sex change in three species of dottybacks, *Pseudochromis flavivertex, P. aldabraensis* and *P. cyanotaenia* (Wittenrich and Munday 2005). The species were first isolated as female-female pairs to determine if female to male (protogynous) sex change would occur. As pairs began spawning, males were removed and paired with other sex-changed males in isolated 10-gallon tanks to determine the potential for bi-directional sex change. In all three species, sex change from male-to-female (protandrous) took longer than sex change from female-to-male (protogynous). Most *Pseudochromis, Manonichthys* and *Pictichromis* species are primarily protogynous, changing sex from female to male in 18 to 56 days. Sex change in the reverse direction takes 52 to 93 days.

Spawning Sites

In the wild, pseudochromids spawn in caves created by rocks or dug in the sand. If such an arrangement were used in captivity it would be virtually impossible to remove the egg mass for the purpose of artificial hatching. The goal when setting up a spawning aquarium and supplying spawning sites is ease of maintenance. PVC pipe is easily worked, configured and cleaned, making it an ideal choice for artificial spawning caves.

Most species require little more than cut lengths of ³/₄-inch diameter PVC to successfully spawn, up to 1.5-inches

for the larger species. While spawning may be successful in such configurations, the male's brood care duties may be influenced by having two open ends. Many times in captivity males prove unreliable brooders due to the environment in which the eggs were laid. Adding a PVC end cap to one end of each cut length of pipe seems to provide a heightened sense of security to brooding males. It is the sense of security that proves important. If both ends of the pipe are open males often move the egg mass around to different sites in a sort of nervous frenzy until the mass is eventually discarded. Larger diameter PVC sections (1 to 2-inches) can be capped on both ends and an entrance hole roughly ¹/₂- to ³/₄-inch drilled in the center of one of the end caps. This gives the male a snug, easily defended retreat.

Males of some species prefer the entire shelter to be located away from the bottom. PVC shelters can be hung near the surface by means of string, plastic cable ties or other means. It is best to use a method that is not permanent so the cave can be lifted out to inspect and remove the egg mass. One method of hanging a shelter is to use a T-fitting with the leg of the the T pointing straight up. The bottom of the T, the horizontal plane, is capped on one end. Then, a length of pipe inserted into the perpendicular opening and fitted with two 90° elbows create an upside-down J-shaped bracket that can be hung on the rim of the aquarium. Spawning sites such as this work very well with species such as the Spendid Dottyback (*M. splendens).*

For ease of maintenance, it is best to point the opening of spawning shelters toward the front of the tank. Positioned this way you will be able to see new spawns more easily.

However, first-time males will often eat or discard their first few spawns. Nature should be allowed to take its course in these situations while the aquarist hopes that the male will settle into his brood care duties. Directing the opening to the cave away from the front glass of the aquarium often helps in these situations. Larger-diameter PVC pipe sections can be placed in a vertical position with the aquarium bottom acting as the bottom of the cave. Some male specimens regularly choose this arrangement, probably for security reasons, with all horizontal planes blocked from

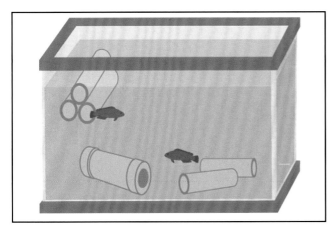

Broodstock tank for many dottybacks with PVC spawning caves on the bottom and female shelter tubes near surface.

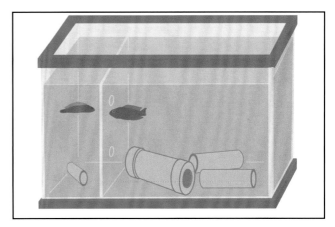

Divided pairing tank with a refuge chamber for the female (left) who will eventually emerge to spawn with her mate.

view. This gives a sense of security to brooding males, but makes observation difficult.

Large clam shell halves resting on their "lip" work equally well as dottyback spawning sites. A small chip is removed to act as an entrance. It's difficult to view new spawns in such a cave, but the security offered to the male is a good trade off. Caves can be created from numerous objects. Try broken pieces of flowerpots with low ceilings or masonry bricks.

It is not necessary to visually observe egg masses in the care of the male. It is often better to prevent such occurrences. Males can become extremely edgy and nervous when tending eggs. The more privacy allowed, the better his chances of successfully caring for the brood. Spawning is imminent when the female becomes quite round with hydrated eggs. It is easy to distinguish patterns in spawning fish and to predict when spawning will occur. When the female is at the surface begging for food with a slim new profile, you can be sure that spawning has occurred. From this date hatching can be predicted and there is no need to view the egg mass until removed for hatching.

When supplying a spawning tank with spawning sites, provide myriad of choices. Once the fish have spawned, they generally use the same or similar spawning sites. If the tank seems cluttered, unused sites can be removed once a favorite cave is known. It's important to remember that although the main purpose of PVC and shelters is spawning, an impor-

tant second function is shelter for females, who often end up battered in the mating process. The more configurations present the better. This gives females a variety of retreats when pursued by belligerent males and also limits visual contact between the sexes to prevent undue aggression.

Lined Dottyback, Dampiera Grouper

Labracinus lineatus (Castelnau, 1875)
Maximum Length: To 25 cm (9.8 in.); usually under 20 cm (7.8 in.).
Sexual Allocation: Protogynous; possible potential for bi-directional sex change.

I first began studying this species in its native waters off Western Australia several years ago. Before poking my head under a rock in the shallow, murky waters and seeing a large male Lined Dottyback staring me in the face only inches away, I was not particularly aware of this species. Since that time the Lined Dottyback has become one of my favorites. It is large, fiesty and has many admirable traits.

Habitat & Range: The Lined Dottyback occurs in Western Australia from Jurien Bay to Broome, sometimes in water that would be regarded as cold by most hobbyist standards. This species is quite tolerant of water temperatures below 68°F. They occur on shallow rocky reefs found near the shoreline as well as coral reefs found well offshore. This is one of the few species of dottybacks that regularly swims in the open, approaching divers rather than darting to the back of a cave. Large overhangs provided by plate corals or boulders are preferred lairs.

The largest concentrations of this species that I have seen were in relatively shallow water (less than 3 m [10 ft.]). In an area about 10 m long by 5 m wide, I collected over 100 of these dottybacks. After these initial collections, it was apparent that I had sampled only a fraction of the population. I estimated that more than 300 Lined Dottybacks lived within this small area. The water was generally heavily silted with little coral growth and rarely showed visibility more than 1.5 m (5 ft.). Instead, large boulders were strewn along the coastline, creating large caves and labyrinths coinhabited by myriad fish and invertebrate species.

Sexual Dimorphism: *Labracinus lineatus* is sexually dimorphic, although the so-called Firetail Devil (*L. cyclophthalmus*) is often confused with *L. lineatus* females. *Labracinus cyclophthalmus* females display bands on the gill cover that are absent in *L. lineatus,* being replaced by irregular dots and small lines . The bands present on *L. cyclophthalmus* may appear dull on light-colored fish. Further distinguishing characteristics of female *L. lineatus* include a fluorescent blue border on the dorsal and anal fins, and a comparatively dull-colored dorsal fin. The dorsal fin of *L. cyclophthalmus* is bright orange-red while that of female *L. lineatus* is generally brown with irregular dark markings.

Female Lined Dottybacks are generally smaller than males. With an overall body color of brown to tan, their horizontal body bars blend, making them inconspicuous. The most obvious characteristic of females is the presence of a large red oval on the side starting below and behind the pectoral fin base and extending slightly past the beginning of the anal fin. Males are large and characteristic of the species.

Social Structure & Reproductive Biology: Large dottybacks often do not practice a simple reproductive mode of promiscuity as once thought. In the case of the Lined Dottyback, social structures and reproductive modes are often complex and rarely promiscuous.

Several approaches to reproduction are taken by this species. Promiscuous spawning does occur among solitary

Lined Dottyback (*Labracinus lineatus*): a favorite of the author, but a large, fiesty species best-suited to a species aquarium.

individuals, although this was rare among the populations I observed. The majority of Lined Dottybacks found in the field occurred in pairs. A large male was usually found with a female roughly 2 inches smaller. Shallow water along with snorkeling rather than SCUBA gear allowed me to watch these fish for extended periods of time, and the proximity to shore allowed frequent, often daily visits, to assure that they were in fact pairs. Over a three-month period, I observed many pairs that appeared to have long-term bonds. I hesitate to use the word monogamous with this group. The territory a pair maintained was always centered around a main haunt which both fish occupied. Although the pair separated several yards apart in feeding forays, they always returned to the cave and their mate. Feeding generally occurred early in the mornings and toward the evenings with each member of the pair going its own way in search of food. In midday two fish could be seen side-by-side at the entrance to the lair. Day after day the pairs remained, with no aggressive displays between the sexes. They seemed quite content. Eventually I caught one of these pairs and transferred them to an aquarium of roughly 5 gallons. An aquarium of such small size is usually enough to make any dottyback erupt in bursts of aggression, but after a week the male and female Lined Dottybacks were settled in the small tank in a peaceful manner and rarely left one another's side.

Another common reproductive mode I saw in this species was the formation of harems. One male, usually quite large, maintained a territory in which several females established their own smaller domains. Harems are interesting in that it often takes some time to locate the resident male. While the territories of the females seem to be fixed, the male wanders the perimeter, ranging around all the female territories. Spawning among harems takes place in the male's lair, which is usually in-between the territories of several females. The entrance to the male's burrow seems to be the only well-guarded area and only when a spawn is being brooded.

Diet: Prey items in the wild include a broad range of vertebrates and invertebrates. Preferred prey includes small crabs and shrimp, although everything from limpets and chitons to clams and polychaetes are eaten. In captivity they are voracious—you get the feeling that if a shoe fell into the aquarium, it would be eaten. Table shrimp cut to appropriate size, clam, scallop, marine fish, mysid shrimp and crab all prove excellent fare in captivity. Spawning requires several feedings to satiation per day. Heavy feedings will give the female the nutrition needed to mature eggs on a regular schedule.

Spawning: Little is required to initiate spawning once a pair has formed. Establishing a pair in captivity, however, is often challenging. The availability of breeding stock in the aquarium trade seems very uneven. When available, Lined Dottybacks are usually quite large and in male coloration. It is unclear whether this species is capable of bi-directional sex change, but the social structure and spawning modes suggest it is possible.

Males of marked size difference will often cohabitate with few problems. In my experience, large males will display at smaller males that show a submissive posture. This is usually as far it goes, although care should be taken to avoid serious injury to the smaller fish. I have successfully housed two males in small tanks (about 10 gallons) with no serious

problems. Partitions can be made with entry holes only large enough for the smaller individual to fit through. Should the large male's attention prove too much, the smaller individual can retreat to the safety of the partition.

Courtship is much more elaborate and gentle than seen in the smaller, promiscuous dottyback species. A 50-gallon aquarium is the minimum size for Lined Dottybacks, although I have successfully kept and spawned this species in smaller aquariums. A larger space will help facilitate pair formation. The aquarium can be set up in any number of ways. Live rock and decorations can be added in an aesthetically pleasing manner, as this species is large and the worry of broods being lost among the network of holes and crevices in the live rock is diminished. Two-inch diameter PVC pipe is an ideal spawning shelter, as are caves created by tiles and rock. Keeping the setup simple, however, will limit the amount of time needed to search for the spawn and make cleaning easier.

Maintenance and conditioning should proceed in much the same manner as other pseudochromids species. This species spawns on 14-day to one-month cycles, creating a large egg mass roughly 3 to 4 cm in diameter containing 1,500 to 3,000 eggs. Hatching occurs on the fourth night at 79°F, taking progressively longer at cooler temperatures.

In captivity, new pairs are often unstable with the male exhibiting extreme nervousness around his first few broods often carrying the egg mass from shelter to shelter in his mouth. Females of such pairs are often the target of extreme aggression during this time. Males of compatible pairs will often rest inside the PVC spawning site guarding the eggs. While the female is not allowed to enter the pipe, she is not the target of aggression. Males will often leave their incubation duties for short periods of time to court the female.

Larval Rearing: *Labracinus lineatus* larvae are well-formed at hatching, which occurs approximately one hour after the lights have been turned out on the fourth night. Feeding on rotifers begins the following morning. Large vessels are needed to rear this species as the sizes of the spawns are much larger than most species. Metamorphosis occurs 28 to 35 days after hatching.

Red Dottyback, Dampiera Grouper

Labracinus cyclophthalmus (Müller & Troschel, 1849)
Maximum Length: To 25 cm (9.8 in.); normally to 18 cm (7 in.).
Sexual Allocation: Protogynous.

The Red Dottyback is the most common of the large dottybacks to be imported to the aquarium trade. Occupying a wide geographic distribution and possessing an inquisitive disposition, they are relatively easy to catch and subsequently a common offering on dealers' lists.

Red Dottybacks are good candidates for a community aquarium containing larger, more aggressive fish. They remain quite peaceful to most bigger fish, but will target and eat smaller tank mates. They readily seize prey that are not quite small enough to swallow whole and thrash them against the substrate to break the victim into edible-sized chunks.

Habitat & Range: Red Dottybacks occur on near-shore rocky reefs, in lagoons, on coral reefs and virtually anywhere rocks create structure in relatively shallow water from southern Japan to the Philippines and Indonesia to New Guinea and northern Australia.

Sexual Dimorphism: This species is probably a characteristic protogynous species. Males are virtually always larger than females; this size dimorphism is often quite drastic. Males sport a bright red body color with fluorescent blue edges on the unpaired fins. The head of males is typically dark brown, although I have seen many large males completely red in color. Females are smaller, usually with a drab cream to tan color with horizontal bands of from spotting on the body. The dorsal and anal fins are red and a light yellow cast is often seen midbody. Females often turn pure white when stressed.

Spawning & Rearing: See *L. lineatus* (*page 181*).

Flamehead or Steene's Dottyback

Pseudochromis steenei (Gill & Randall, 1993)
Maximum Length: To 12 cm (4.7 in.).

Red Dottyback (*Labracinus cyclopthalmus*) a gorgeous fish for enthusiasts who like aggressively territorial species.

Sexual Allocation: Protogynous; aquarium observations indicate bi-directional sex change.

Although just described in 1993, this spectacular species has made an impressive debut among aquarists. *P. steenei* is a perfect dottyback for those uninterested in smaller, mild-mannered marine fish. Steene's Dottyback is surely a species capable of terrorizing an entire marine aquarium community. Never place this species in a tank with smaller fish. This species is best suited to aquariums containing larger species such as *Pomacanthus* angels, triggers, groupers and others that can defend themselves. Even so, I have seen a male *P. steenei* battle a large Picasso trigger and win the fight. Truly a beautiful and intriguing species, it is often worth the effort to establish a species aquarium dedicated to a pair of these dottybacks.

Both males and females reach a respectable size and neither sex is prone to hiding. Full-grown males are truly an impressive sight with their bright orange bodies and canine teeth. Wild importations have become regular and adult specimens are available.

Female *P. steenei* are subject to misidentification, with

Steene's Dottyback (*Pseudochromis steenei*): male is unmistakable when seen side-by-side its mate, right.

Steene's Dottyback (*Pseudochromis steenei*): female of a species with extreme sexual dimorphism, see male left.

most simply labeled "black" or "dusky" dottybacks. Since females are much less spectacular than males they were often less expensive. Captive-raised specimens are sporadically available. Large dottybacks such as these are raised in batches and offered on occasion to keep the market interested.

Habitat & Range: Found around Indonesia from Bali to Flores, they are said to inhabit deeper water around isolated reefs or rock outcroppings located on sandy slopes, and prefer locations near crinoids. According to both photographs and personal reports by divers who have observed them, this species is almost always found in pairs hovering near a common cave.

Sexual Dimorphism: *Pseudochromis steenei* exhibits one of the most extreme examples of sexual dimorphism within its subfamily—so extreme, in fact, that they are often labeled as different species. Males are unmistakable with their bright orange heads. Females are available in two forms. The most common import is entirely black, sometimes fading to a dusky gray in captivity, with a fluorescent blue line below the eye and a bright yellow tail. I assume this is the more common color form imported, because it is more at-

tractive than the alternative. Females not displaying an entirely yellow tail have two bars on their tail, one on the upper lobe of the tail and one on the lower. These bars are orange on the male.

Social Structure & Reproductive Biology: Aquarium observations suggest that this species exhibits a unique social structure. It seems that pair formation is a common social structure among *P. steenei* in the wild, and established pairs peacefully cohabitate in as small as 20 gallons.

I emphasize the term "established" since during pair formation or first introduction, a male and female can be brutal to one another. Newly formed pairs seem to keep their distance from one another and aggressive displays are few and far between. They generally do not occupy the same cave or reside in the same area. Instead, the male usually takes over a PVC pipe or similar shelter on the aquarium floor while the female remains near the surface. In a larger aquarium, each will have a separate territory. It is probable that it takes some time and trial and error to find two fish to form a close bond. Of the many pairs I have formed, only two became tight pairs occupying the same den. When the male was guarding the spawn, the female was not allowed to enter. The aggression displayed by smaller promiscuous species during pair formation and spawning is not common in this species. A calm, elaborate display precedes any actual aggression.

Diet: *Pseudochromis steenei*, like other large dottybacks, dines on a diet of crustacea, polychaetes, small fish and plankton in the wild. In captivity most meaty morsels are accepted with relish. Preferring large chunks of table shrimp, squid, clam, scallop and crab, they will also accept flake and pelleted food. The conditioning diet should consist of several feedings of fresh frozen seafoods daily.

Spawning: Captive reproduction of Steene's Dottyback, despite its recent introduction, is well documented. Obtaining a spawning pair is a simple proposition, although it may take a few weeks to obtain both sexes. The easiest approach is to purchase a male and female, based on coloration. When this method of pairing is used it rarely takes more than two weeks for the fish to begin spawning.

Another method involves the potential for bi-directional sex change. A large male is placed in the same aquarium as a smaller male, preferably with a noticeable size difference, and time allowed for the smaller male to revert to its original sex. This method often proves risky to the smaller male, but allowances can be made for his safety. A barrier is best provided with a hole only large enough to permit the smaller male's entrance. Breeder baskets or hanging conglomerates of PVC pipe sections also work—anything to act as a refuge should the dominant male's attention become overbearing. This method of sex reversal may take several weeks to end up with a female.

If two male Steene Dottybacks of roughly the same size are placed together, aggressive displays will quickly lead to battles resulting in one fish severely wounded or dead. There should be no question as to which will become the dominant and submissive fish. The size difference makes it so.

An ideal spawning aquarium is 30 gallons or more. I have kept pairs in 20-gallon high aquariums continuously without harm to the female but a larger aquarium would is for newly formed pairs. Bare aquariums are ideal as they are easily cleaned. Several PVC sections roughly 2 inches

Orchid Dottyback in broodstock tank with PVC shelters, one with a drilled endcap to create a secure spawning cave.

in diameter are all the aquascaping needed.

Spawning & Rearing: Egg masses rival a golf ball in size and contain nearly 2,000 eggs. Larval *P. steenei* are freed from their egg shells on the fifth night after spawning. Larval rearing is similar to others mentioned here although the sheer number of larvae puts constraints on water quality and feeding demands. Metamorphosis occurs on roughly day 23 and extends to day 35. Juveniles first develop a diffuse yellow coloration before obtaining a juvenile coloration similar to that of the male.

Orchid Dottyback

Pseudochromis fridmani (Klausewitz, 1968)
Maximum Length: 7 cm (2.8 in.).
Sexual Allocation: Protogynous.

Orchid Dottybacks are one of the most beautiful and sought-after members of the family. Older marine aquarists remember when they were only available as rare imports from the Red Sea, always selling for very steep prices.

Their aquarium debut for most aquarists came with the introduction of captive-raised specimens from C-Quest, which made them widespread and affordable. With their beauty and more peaaceful nature, they have become a favorite species for reef aquariums, and *P. fridmani* is easily the most popular dottyback in the marine aquarium hobby. Wild importations are available from time to time, but the refinement of rearing techniques has rendered them inferior to captive stock.

Habitat & Range: *Pseudochromis fridmani* is found in the Red Sea on shallow reefs, under plate corals or similar rock ledges and caves. Orchids are often seen in small groups or at least in close association with other members of the species.

Sexual Dimorphism: Any two sexually immature juveniles will ultimately form a male-female pair through female-to-male sex change. Males are larger and develop a longer lower lobe of the caudal fin, although older females will also develop this trait. Females in good condition become almost square in the abdominal region as their ovaries swell with developing eggs. Their abdomens often take on a yellow cast from the eggs swollen inside.

Spawning: Spawning this species is a rather simple task once a heterosexual pair is established. Once started, spawning occurs roughly every 7 to 10 days. Hatching occurs the fourth night after spawning and larvae begin to settle at days 24 to 38. See page 186 for a detailed protocol of breeding *P. fridmani*.

Larval Rearing: Rotifers are the first food added and at day 9, newly hatched *Artemia*. A diffuse magenta color develops at roughly 15 mm when the fish settle out of the water column. At this point numerous PVC pipe sections or fittings should be supplied to quell aggression.

High HUFA enrichment is essential to bring out strong coloration of post metamorphosis juveniles. Most larvae are lost near metamorphosis due to inadequate nutrition. When available, plankton or copepods should be added to the diet near day 15 to reduce mortality.

Neon Dottyback, Arabian or Aldabra Dottyback

Pseudochromis aldabraensis (Bouchot & Boutin, 1958)
Maximum Length: 8.5 cm (3.3 in.).

Neon Dottyback (*Pseudochromis aldabraensis*): a beauty that aquaculture has made widely available to reef enthusiasts.

Sexual Allocation: Protogynous; bi-directional hermaphroditism has been observed under captive conditions.

Pseudochromis aldabraensis is one of the most popular dottybacks in the aquarium trade. Adorned with fluorescent blue streaks against a bright orange body, this species is a spectacular sight in virtually any aquarium. Admired among reef aquarists for its dietary attraction to bristle worms, this species has proven a mainstay.

Habitat & Range: Most Neon Dottybacks collected in the wild are exported from the Persian Gulf. The entire range of this species includes the Gulf of Arabia, Gulf of Oman, Pakistan and the Aldabra Islands.

Sexual Dimorphism: It has been said that virtually no external characteristics differentiate the sexes of this species. Males grow larger and are more aggressive than females; however, this is only apparent when a pair has been established. Females become quite rotund near the time of spawning, and the developing egg mass can be seen well before actual spawning. One trait only in larger, mature males is the development of a slightly forked tail. I have observed very large males with quite elongated upper and lower lobes

Olive Dottyback (*Pseudochromis olivaceus*) a fish often seen with colors but potentially quite attractive if properly cared for.

of the tail fin giving it a forked appearance. Females of these pairs were the same age, but never developed forked tails.

Social Structure & Reproductive Biology: Neon Dottybacks are promiscuous spawners with no pair bond ever being established. In their native waters, males and females maintain distinct boundaries that are well-guarded outside of reproductive periods. It is possible in captivity to maintain a pair in aquariums as small as 10 gallons with little threat to the female. Neons are among the more aggressive members of the group when it comes to pair formation and spawning, but individuality limits generalizations. Some pairs coexist in confined quarters while others will not tolerate conspecifics in anything but very large aquariums.

Spawning: Spawning is similar to other species mentioned here. Eggs hatch on the 4th or 5th night after spawning and feeding begins the following morning. Large adult females are capable of producing large spawns. Spawning and larval rearing is best accomplished at slightly cooler water temperatures, near 76 to 78°F.

Larval Rearing: See protocol for the Orchid Dottyback, page 186. Metamorphosis and settlement occurs at roughly 15 mm in length, at day 28 to 30, when they de-

velop the first hints of adult coloration. As with most dottybacks, losses are greatest near metamorphosis and can be attributed to poor nutrition. High initial mortality is generally attributed to artificial incubation and hatching methods as well as first feeding.

Olive Dottyback

Pseudochromis olivaceus (Rüppell, 1835)
Maximum Length: 8 cm (3.1 in.).
Sexual Allocation: Protogynous.

Olive Dottybacks have never achieved great popularity among aquarists. Captive-raised stock originating from C-Quest were the only specimens offered in the trade with any regularity. Now, captive-raised fish are difficult to find due to their reputation for dull coloration. However, when maintained under ideal conditions, this fish can be quite attractive. Males develop a yellow belly with bright fluorescent blue spots against an olive body. This species tends to be bolder than most dottybacks and will spend a considerable amount of time in the open, and they are not as scrappy as many other dottybacks.

Habitat & Range: Olive Dottybacks are found from the Red Sea to the Gulf of Arabia and the Arabian Sea.

Sexual Dimorphism: Sexes can be manipulated in young fish. Two fish, especially of different sizes, should develop into a male-female pair. Females are smaller, more rotund and typically exhibit more solemn coloration. The blue spots of most males become brighter near the onset of spawning. Specimens from some localities and many captive-raised fish remain dark and drab. Feeding enriched, color-enhancing foods may bring out the best pigmentation.

Spawning & Rearing: As per Pseudochromis fridmani. (See page 186.)

Striped Dottyback, Sankey's Dottyback

Pseudochromis sankeyi (Lubbock, 1975)
Maximum Length: 8.5 cm (3.3 in.).
Sexual Allocation: Protogynous.

Striped or Sankey's Dottyback (*Pseudochromis sankeyi*): closely related to the Orchid Dottyback. See hybrid, right.

Indigo Dottyback (*Pseudochromis sankeyi* x *P. fridmani*): a new hybrid propagated by Oceans, Reefs & Aquariums.

The Striped Dottyback is another Red Sea species and a gorgeous representative of the group. The body, like *P. fridmani*, almost appears to slither like a small eel when it swims. The lower lobe of the tail grows to great lengths adding to its anguilliform appearance. If the color and patterns were stripped from both *P. sankeyi* and *P. fridmani* they would appear almost identical. An accidental hybrid of these two species has been reported by Oceans, Reefs & Aquariums in Ft. Pierce, Florida. ORA is marketing the new fish as the Indigo Dottyback, and Vince Rado of ORA reports that the F_1 generation is proving to be fertile, raising interesting questions about the relationship of *P. sankeyi* and *P. fridmani*.

Habitat & Range: *Pseudochromis sankeyi* occurs in the southern reaches of the Red Sea into the Gulf of Aden on shallow coral reefs.

Sexual Dimorphism: Sexes can be manipulated when young to form heterosexual pairs; any two young fish raised together and well-fed should form a pair. Similar to *P. fridmani*, male Striped Dottybacks become larger than females and often develop an exaggerated lower lobe of the caudal fin. The overall coloration of males darkens with increas-ing age, and the abdomen of older males also appears sunken as if the fish were emaciated. Females remain smaller and become well-rounded when carrying eggs.

Spawning & Rearing: Spawning occurs in similar fashion to *P. fridmani* and occurs roughly every 7 to 10 days. Hatching occurs on the 4th night after spawning and larvae spend an average of 25 days in the water column.

Use the same protocols as for the Orchid Dottyback, page 186.

Bigfinned Dottybacks

Longfin Dottyback
*Manonichthys polynemus (*Fowler, 1931)
Allen's or Red-dot Dottyback
Manonichthys alleni (Gill, 2003)

Maximum Length: 12 cm (4.9 in.).
Sexual Allocation: Protogynous.

I have grouped these two so-called Bigfinned Dotty-backs together, as they are very similar and easily confused when found in the aquarium trade. (See also the Splendid

Longfin Dottyback (*Manonichthys polynemus*) males such as this tend to be thinner than their mates.

Dottyback, below.) Early reports for spawning and rearing *M. polynemus* probably can be traced to the actual species and to a color form of *M. alleni* resembling *M. polynemus*.

Both species are relatively new to the aquarium trade and are seen only sporadically. In my experience *M.* cf. *alleni* is more common in the aquarium trade than *M. polynemus*. The bright white pelvic fins of this species are quite long, giving the fish a graceful appearance and its common name. A red (*M.* cf. *alleni)* or yellow-orange (*M. polynemus)* splotch appears at the base of the pelvic fins and seems a variation useful for species identification rather than any clue to sexual dimorphism. Both *Manonichthys polynemus* and *M.* cf. *alleni* are rather peaceful species that can be maintained in community aquariums or as pairs in isolated spawning aquariums with little difficulty. Both are beautiful species worthy of attention, and both have been successfully reared in captivity a number of times.

Habitat & Range: *Manonichthys polynemus* occurs from Indonesia around the Lesser Sunda Islands to Micronesia. In contrast, *Manonichthys* cf. *alleni* occurs around Sabah and Borneo.

Sexual Dimorphism: Longfin Dottybacks are easily sexed when a group is at hand. Females are slightly smaller and quite plump. Males appear rather thin. Males are quite aggressive toward one another while they cautiously and excitedly react toward females. When two conspecifics are present and not quarrelling, a pair is had.

Spawning & Rearing: Spawning occurs in typical dottyback fashion with the absence of extreme aggression. (See *P. steenei, page 184.)* The male incubates the clutch until they hatch on the 4th or 5th night after spawning. Rotifers are taken the following morning and metamorphosis begins roughly 26 days later. Pairs spawn every 10 to 12 days. Rearing is non-problematic and most mortalities occur during the first feeding stage and near metamorphosis.

Splendid Dottyback

Manonichthys splendens (Fowler, 1931)
Maximum Length: 10 cm (3.9 in.).
Sexual Allocation: Protogynous; aquarium observations indicate bi-directional sex change.

With its bold attitude, striking color pattern and bright yellow and purple colors, this is perhaps the most sought-after of the dottybacks. Long known only by photographs taken in the wild, Splendid Dottybacks were until recently unavailable in the aquarium world. Then, in 1998, ORA's larval culturist Paul Schlitt raised the first Splendid Dottybacks past metamorphosis. *Manonichthys splendens* present distribution in the aquarium hobby is primarily an artifact of this successful propagation. Since that time wild imports have become more common and the Splendid Dottyback is no longer the elusive and rare gem it once was. Full-grown Splendid Dottybacks look unlike any other. Everything about this fish from the body shape, to behavior and color pattern makes it a standout. Easily fed, it thrives in reef aquariums and community fish-only aquariums alike. With good feeding, its purple color intensifies against a bright yellow background.

Habitat & Range: Splendid Dottybacks are found in a limited geographic area in Indonesia from the Lesser Sunda Islands to the Banda Sea, often living around the base of bright yellow barrel sponges. They can be found as shallow

Splendid Dottyback (*Manonichthys splendens*): captive-bred young adult. Males are very aggressive with thin abdomens.

as few meters to about 40 m (131 ft.) deep.

Sexual Dimorphism: Little differences exist between the sexes of this species. Males are reportedly more colorful than females and grow larger. In my experience, males and females are often of comparable size. This is especially true of captive-raised broodstock. Also, the coloration of wild-collected fish is often faded. The differences between the sexes are subtle, and it is often difficult to interpret the sexual function of isolated individuals. In captivity, large, isolated fish are generally males. Males are best distinguished by size, aggressiveness toward conspecies, and a slim profile. Mature males often appear emaciated with a thinning of the abdominal region. Females are typically smaller and quite robust. They are capable of sex change, but based on two isolated male pairs, I found that roughly 69 days is required for the submissive individual to revert to female reproductive function. I have often observed isolated female pairs being extremely hesitant to change sex. Both females produce egg masses on a cyclic basis and it may be that sex change is inhibited at certain times during the reproductive cycle.

Spawning: Spawning can be dangerous for females, as the large canine teeth of males often leave torn fins and missing scales and a badly bruised mate. At least a 20-gallon aquarium should be used for broodstock pairs. If offered a spawning shelter off the bottom, the male will usually choose to spawn there. This is generally a length of ³/₄-inch PVC suspended off the bottom. Females must be offered frequent feedings to recuperate from spawning. If extreme aggression persists after spawning, a barrier must be supplied or the female removed. Divided pairing is often best in extreme cases of aggression. Spawning occurs every 8 to 10 days. Eggs hatch on the 4th or 5th night after spawning.

Larval Rearing: Enriched rotifers should be maintained in the rearing tank at concentrations of 10 to 15/mL. Larvae reach metamorphosis 28 to 30 days after hatching. High initial mortality is typical, and attributed to current hatching methods and first feedings. Metamorphosis is also a major critical period whenß nearly entire broods can be lost due to nutritional deficiencies. Proper enrichment of rotifers and *Artermis* nauplii is critical to reduce mortality. This is a species worthy of dedicated home breeders.

Blue or Yellowfin Dottyback

Pseudochromis wilsoni (Whitley, 1929)
Maximum Length: 8 cm (3.1 in.).
Sexual Allocation: Protogynous.

While still extremely rare in the American aquarium trade, in its native waters of Australia the Yellowfin Dottyback is quite common and occasionally makes an appearance in fish shops. A truly beautiful species, it is similar to most common dottybacks available in the trade. It is hardy, colorful and easily spawned under captive conditions. They will surely become widespread throughout the trade if dedicated breeders can supply captive-raised stock. Female *P. wilsoni* were once thought to be a separate species—in older literature they are represented as *P. xanthicolor*.

Habitat & Range: *Pseudochromis wilsoni* is found from Port Denison in Western Australia to Bargara, Queensland. While in Australia I observed this species extensively in the wild as well as in aquariums. In my experience this species is more common on near-shore shallow rocky reefs.

Habitats such as this are nutrient-rich and typically high in sediments. This species was found alongside *Labracinus lineatus* in Western Australia. They typically occupy small nooks between boulders and crevices deep within corals. Like most smaller dottybacks, they are very cryptic and rarely stray from the protection of corals and rocks.

Sexual Dimorphism: Sexes are sexually dichromatic. It is difficult to say if one sex is more colorful than the other as both are equally brilliant. Every male specimen of this species I have observed has been a brilliant powder blue color. The color throughout the body is uniform. The iris is often bright red. Under stressful conditions, however, the body coloration of the male fades into a dusky gray. Photographs of this color variation do the species no justice.

Females look markedly different. The body varies from a dusky tan to brilliant turquoise color. The most obvious characteristic of female *P. wilsoni* are two horizontal yellow bands on the caudal fin and a horizontal yellow streak at the base of the dorsal fin. Often times the entire dorsal fin is yellow. Spawning is similar to others species.

Springer's Dottyback

Pseudochromis springeri (Lubbock, 1975)
Maximum Length: To 6.5 cm (2.6 in.).
Sexual Allocation: Protogynous.

With fluorescent blue streaks laid against a jet black body, this fish is truly remarkable and a gorgeous example of the striking color contrasts present in this group. *P. springeri* has been raised in captivity many times, although commercial propagation has not made them as common as *P. fridmani* or other Red Sea species. Today, wild-caught fish are more common. They seem to be more peaceful than the average dottyback and remain small. This is an excellent choice for reef aquariums as they consume small bristle worms. In my experience, this species is much more bolder than most dottybacks and remains in the open rather than hiding at the slightest hint of a threat.

Habitat & Range: *Pseudochromis springeri* is endemic to the Red Sea, where it associates with stony corals in la-goons and shallow reefs.

Sexual Dimorphism: Obvious differences between the sexes are not apparent in this species. *Pseudochromis springeri* is a small species; size differences are difficult to judge until sometime after a pair has been established. On average, males grow larger than females. Females in good condition become quite rotund. The sexes can only be reliably judged under captive conditions. Males of this protogynous species are always more aggressive than females. A pair or trio housed together from the juvenile stage will result in one male and one or two females, respectively. (Females often prove stubborn to change sex in the male direction if maintained under ideal conditions which keep ovaries ripe.) The majority of females turn gray in the presence of a male, which is usually jet black. Older specimens, however, may fade to gray making color an unreliable indication of sex.

Spawning & Rearing: Similar to the Orchid Dottyback (*P. fridmani*), page 186.

Yellowhead Dottyback, Yellow Flame Dottyback

Pseudochromis cyanotaenia (Bleeker, 1857)
Maximum Length: 6 cm. (2.3 in.).
Sexual Allocation: Primarily protogynous; capable of bi-directional sex change.

This is one of the lesser-known dottybacks and one that is only available from time to time as wild importations. They have been successfully propagated a number of times, but wide distribution has yet to occur, probably due to the species' rather inconspicuous appearance. In times past males and females were reported as separate species—females mistakenly assigned the name *P. tapeinosoma*. Although sometime a bit drab when in dealers' tanks, male Yellowhead Dottybacks can be quite striking in both color and pattern. The yellow stripe running the course of the body can become bright yellow to orange and the body fluorescent in green and blue. However, when stressed by poor feeding, rowdy tank mates or constant movement outside the aquarium, they tend to exhibit subdued coloration and are not easy to identify. *P. cyanotaenia* is usually timid, tend-

Springer's Dottyback (*Pseudochromis springeri*): an excellent reef-tank species that is still mostly harvested from the wild.

Yellowhead Dottyback (*Pseudochromis cyanotaenia*): marked differences are seen in this pair, with male at top.

ing to find shelter in caves and holes and flitting from one hiding place to another in the aquascape.

Habitat & Range: *Pseudochromis cyanotaenia* occurs over a broad geographic distribution from Northwest Australia to the Great Barrier Reef, throughout South East Asia, the East Indian Ocean and the West Pacific occupying virtually every habitat from inshore silt laden rock reefs to offshore coral reefs, isolated patch reefs and rock outcroppings on sandy bottoms. In its natural habitat they are very secretive, living under plate corals and within the branches of large corals and rarely straying more than a few inches away from a protective retreat. In Fiji I observed pairs separated by a meter or so, each residing in its own respective territory with obvious invisible boundaries.

Sexual Dimorphism: The coloration of males varies dramatically. Most often, the body is blue to turquoise with fluorescent scales of green and blue making up vertical bands. A yellow flame runs from the head toward the tail. This flame varies from a brilliant yellow to orange but is completely absent in some specimens. Old or captive males fed a diet devoid of proper pigments fade into a dusky gray with a faded yellow flame. Color variations within this species are a rule not an exception. Females are usually tan to slightly red throughout the body with either a yellow or red tail and are easily distinguished from the males.

Spawning & Rearing: Spawning and rearing are similar to other pseudochromids. This is an interesting species for the breeder who wants to work with a less common species that presents few problems in establishing a pair and rearing the larvae. (*See page 186.*)

Dusky Dottyback, Yellow Dottyback

Pseudochromis fuscus (Müller & Troschel, 1849)
Maximum Length: 8 cm (3.1 in.).
Sexual Allocation: Protogynous; bi-directional.

In nature, this is a widespread species and quite polymorphic with several distinct color forms. The Dusky or Yellow Dottyback, while presenting some confusion about its identify, is also an extremely aggressive fish, making pair formation and juvenile growout a challenge.

Habitat & Range: *Pseudochromis fuscus* occurs throughout the Indian Ocean and western Pacific in near-shore lagoons as well as coastal and outer reefs. Although a larger dottyback species, they are very secretive, darting into the depths of coral cover at the slightest sign of danger, only to

Dusky Dottyback (*Pseudochromis fuscus*): highly territorial and not the most flamboyant of dottybacks but easily spawned.

reemerge a few moments later.

Sexual Dimorphism: Colors once thought to separate the sexes are now known to be simply an artifact of where the fish were collected. Given time, any two individuals are capable of forming a spawning pair. It is best to isolate two specimens with a significant size difference to avoid confrontation and dominance disputes. Females are typically smaller and become well-rounded at the onset of spawning. Well-fed males become plump with distended stomachs directly behind the pectoral fin, while the female's egg mass swells more toward the rear of the abdominal cavity.

Spawning & Rearing: Spawning is an easy task if a pair is offered plenty of food and cave-like shelters. Pairs should be given a 20-gallon aquarium as minimum and plenty of PVC pipe segments. Spawning occurs on a 7 to 12 day cycle. Hatching occurs on the 4th or 5th night and metamorphosis begins on day 25. See protocols for the Orchid Dottyback, page 186.

Royal Dottyback, Bicolor Dottyback

Pictichromis paccagnellae (Axelrod, 1973)
Maximum Length: 7 cm (2.7 in.).
Sexual Allocation: Protogynous.

Perhaps the most common member of the Pseudochrominae appearing in aquarium shops, the Royal Dottyback is a bold, attractive species with contrasting magenta and yellow body colors distinctly separated. It is notoriously belligerent, especially toward other small, substrate-hugging species. This dottyback should not, for example, be kept with the similarly colored Royal Gramma from the Caribbean, as aggressive displays will quickly turn to tattered fins and a severely beaten or killed gramma. In a nano-reef, the Royal Dottyback could make a nice centerpiece species and be allowed to rule over its own tiny domain.

Habitat & Range: *Pictichromis paccagnellae* are found over a broad range: Indonesia, the Philippines, the Great Barrier Reef, New Caledonia, and the Solomon Islands in relatively shallow water where they have a particular affinity to walls and elevated coral outcroppings. On one wall in the Solomon Islands I found a remarkable concentration of them in a surprisingly small area. Individual territories were created along the vertical axis of the wall and each fish was separated by only 46 cm (18 in.) of horizontal distance. I counted 30 fish living in close association of conspecifics and a far smaller territory than normally seen in flat terrain. These fish showed aggressive displays—a slightly bent body posture with outstretched fins—as a warning to the intruding fish whenever their invisible boundaries were approached. A few body slaps along the lateral line and the intruder left without bodily harm.

Sexual Dimorphism: Obvious differences between the sexes are absent in this species, the only exception being the round shape of gravid females near the onset of spawning.

Social Structure & Reproductive Biology: Like most smaller dottybacks, Royal or Bicolor Dottybacks are promiscuous spawners. Males and females maintain individual territories near one another for the purpose of spawning. These territories are defended vigorously in non-spawning periods.

Diet: Although small, these dottybacks are ravenous feeders, conditioning them is seldom a challenge. Shaved table shrimp, vitamin-enriched *Artemia*, scallop and similar seafoods should make up the bulk of the conditioning diet. Spirulina flakes can be added several times per week to add additional vitamins and roughage to the diet.

Spawning: Commercial breeders have shunned this species, probably due to their great abundance in the wild and low price. For the home breeder, however, this offers an advantage if you want to try your hand at captive propagation without investing a small fortune in obtaining broodstock.

Pair formation in this species is sometimes hindered by their aggressive nature. The best route to pairing involves the use of a bare aquarium and many PVC shelters strewn about, replicating a reef site with many hiding holes. Several lengths of pipe should also be hung near the surface of the aquarium as submissive fish are virtually always driven there. Sometimes the smaller fish will have to be isolated in a protective breeder basket. Some weeks later, once the submissive fish is well-fattened, the box should be submerged a few centimeters below the surface. This will allow the female to interact with the male but flee to a safe retreat whenever necessary. If the breeder box method is used, it is best to add only a couple cut lengths of PVC or similar spawning shelters in the aquarium.

Courtship seems limited in these dottybacks. The male approaches the egg-heavy female slowly, stopping to flare his fins as well as his mouth, often slapping the female in exaggerated sideways swimming motions. The male will then turn and swim back to the den. If the female does not follow the male often become aggressive and attacks the female. Eventually the female will follow.

While within the confines of the spawning cave, males seem extremely impatient and slap females with the posterior portion of their bodies. Behavioral postures by both

Royal Dottyback (*Pictichromis paccagnellae*): the abundance of wild-caught specimens makes broodstock easy and inexpensive to procure.

sexes, mostly involving opened mouths, are frequently seen inside the cave. With the release of the egg mass the female is quickly pushed from the cave and the male begins his brood care duties. Spawning in this species seems to be a period of high tension.

Larval Rearing: Eggs hatch in 5 days and larvae spend 23 to 28 days in the water column. Larvae are in the same manner as other smaller dottybacks. See page 186.

Diadem Dottyback

Pictichromis diadema (Lubbock & Randall, 1978)
Maximum Length: 6.5 cm (2.5 in.).
Sexual Allocation: Protogynous.

Like the Royal Dottyback, this is a popular fish in the aquarium trade due to its flaming colors and affordability. However, *P. diadema* can become very aggressive in community aquariums containing small species, especially bottom-dwelling fishes and damsels. This should be one of the last additions made to a community tank, as it quickly establishes a territory and defends it vigorously.

Habitat & Range: *Pictichromis diadema* occurs throughout the western Pacific from the Malayan Peninsula to the

Diadem Dottyback (*Pictichromis diadema*): a staple species in the marine aquarium trade and not as aggressive as the Royal Dottyback.

Philippines on shallow reefs.

Sexual Dimorphism: Only subtle differences exist to differentiate the sexes and are subject to interpretation. Males are slightly larger than females with a more stream-lined body. Females exhibit a wider girth and become well-rounded near spawning.

Social Structure & Reproductive Biology: The inherent aggressive nature of this fish limits any pair formation and spreads territorial boundaries far. Promiscuous spawning seems to be the rule. See previous species.

Spawning & Rearing: See the Royal Dottyback (*P. paccagnellae*), previous account, and the Orchid Dottyback for hatching and rearing methods, pages 186.

Magenta Dottyback, Purple Pseudo

Pictichromis porphyrea (Lubbock & Goldmann, 1974)
Maximum Length: 6 cm (2.3 in.).
Sexual Allocation: Protogynous.

Pictichromis porphyrea, joins *P. pacagnellae* and *P. diadema*, as the most popular and widespread dottybacks available to the aquarium trade. The Magenta Dottyback and the previous two species (*P. paccagnellae* and *P. diadem*) were described in the 1970s and all imports to the aquarium trade are wild-caught. This is another feisty species, but one that deserves its share of attention from enthusiasts who can cope with its territorial nature. *Pictichromis porphyrea* exhibits a brilliant magenta color when fed quality foods, and it is often confused with the much more expensive Orchid Dottyback (*P. fridmani*). Clear differences exist, and the Orchid is a much less aggressive species. Although commonly available at low prices, spawning and raising this species is a challenge.

Habitat & Range: Magenta Dottybacks occur in the central west Pacific from the Philippines to Samoa, Japan and the Moluccas. Preferring shallow reefs, this species leads a solitary existence with well-guarded territorial boundaries.

Social Structure & Reproductive Biology: See *P. paccagnellae*

Spawning: See P. fridmani and P. paccagnellae, pages 186 and 194.

Sailfin Dottyback, Speartail Dottyback

Oxycercichthys velifera (Lubbock, 1980)
Maximum Length: 9 cm (3.5 in.).
Sexual Allocation: Protandrous; probably capable of bidirectional sex change.

An uncommon but beautiful species, *O. velifera* is the only member of the Pseudochrominae to exhibit a spade-shaped tail. Two distinct color forms exist in this species, probably owing to collection in different geographic areas. The body of both color forms is a light cream to tan, fading to yellow or blue posteriorly. One form is significantly lighter in color than the other, including both males and females. One color form is bright red with dark brown to black above. Both males and females of the lighter color form are pastel blue and yellow.

Sailfin Dottybacks are aggressive additions to commu-

Magenta Dottyback (*Pictichromis porphyrea*): the poor man's Orchid Dottyback, a colorful but belligerent little fish.

Sailfin Dottyback (*Ogilbyina velifera*): an example of the lighter of two color forms, both with the characteristic spadelike tail.

nity aquariums. They are pugnacious toward smaller fishes and bottom-dwelling fishes of all sizes. Sailfins are best suited to community aquariums containing larger fishes or a species tank of their own.

Habitat & Range: *Ogilbyina velifera* occurs mostly in reef areas along the Great Barrier Reef system in Australia, along with some scattered islands in the Coral Sea.

Sexual Dimorphism: In this protandrous species it is the female that grows larger. Males are typically darker, with a blue color that shadows the head and dorsal area extending into the dorsal fin. The tail is generally yellow. Females display a soft yellow color about the head region fading to pink toward the rear. The tail may be yellow or pastel blue. In the darker color form, females are orange to red dorsally becoming brightest near the head.

Spawning & Rearing: Once the sexes have been sussed out and a compatible pair obtained, spawning comes naturally but it may take some patience. This species often proves reluctant to spawn and should be offered live foods and plenty of fresh-frozen shrimp and squid. Once spawning occurs, it will continue on a 10 to 14-day cycle. Hatching occurs on the fifth night, and larvae are raised in a fashion similar to others in the family.

Flame or Oblique-lined Dottyback

Cypho purpurascens (De Vis, 1884)
Maximum Length: 6 cm (2.3 in.).
Sexual Allocation: Protandrous; probably with the potential for bi-directional sex change.

The Flame or Oblique-lined Dottyback is simply a stunning fish. Photographs hardly ever do it justice—when viewed in the aquarium, the fish seems to glow. It is rare in the aquarium trade and specimens that do appear command a hefty price—an open invitation to enterprising home breeders. Taxonomic confusion surrounds this species—as it does so many of the pseudochromids, especially those with sexual dichromatism. It is sometimes mislabeled as *Pseudochromis mccullochi*.

Habitat & Range: This species is found from the Great Barrier Reef system to the Fiji Islands on shallow coastal and outer reefs.

Sexual Dimorphism: Being protandrous, the usual dottyback rules have changed and females are larger. Males of this species are stunning red-orange with purple-blue outlines on the unpaired fins. Females, depending on origin and state of reproductive maturity, are purple anteriorly

Flame or Oblique-lined Dottyback (*Cypho purpurascens*): a stunning species and golden opportunity for home breeders.

Female *Cypho purpurascens*: compare to brightly colored male at left. Sometimes known as McCulloch's Dottyback.

fading to pink-orange around the midbody and eventually yellow toward the tail. Both sexes have dark outlines on their scales giving them a black meshwork pattern.

Spawning & Rearing: The largest obstacle facing aquarists is pair formation. Starting with a group of juveniles is out of question. Divided pairing and spawning—starting with two fish and keeping them together but separated by a clear barrier until one is heavy with eggs—is the best approach to spawning this expensive and rare fish.

Larval rearing is similar that described above.

Other Dottybacks

For the breeder who happens upon a new or rare dottyback, or a species not covered specifically in this book, the general protocols should be similar to those for the Orchid Dottyback. Special attention to pair formation will be needed in the more belligerent species as per the Royal Dottyback. Divided pairing is often a necessity.

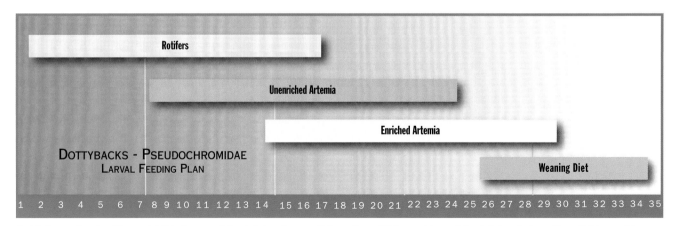

Guidelines: Feed rotifers at 10/ml; unenriched *Artemia* nauplii less than 12 hrs. old; enriched *Artemia* less than 24 hrs. old.

FAIRY BASSLETS

FAMILY GRAMMATIDAE

Royal Gramma (*Gramma loreto*): *Caulerpa* or other macroalgae in the broodstock tank will be used in nest-building.

Brilliantly colored, disease resistant and always in demand by marine aquarists, members of the Family Grammatidae make ideal subjects for home-scale breeding. Because they produce relatively few eggs per spawning, these fishes have not been bred on a large commercial scale and captive-grown fishes are readily marketable. The Royal Gramma (*Gramma loreto*) was, in fact, one of the pioneer marine fish experimentally propagated in the 1960s.

The fairy basslets or grammas are closely related to the dottybacks but are geographically isolated in the tropical West Atlantic Ocean and the Caribbean Sea. They readily adapt to aquarium conditions and spawning is quite simple, assuming a heterosexual pair of fish is housed in a suitable broodstock aquarium and are well fed. The larvae are large enough to accept rotifers as a first food. Fungal infections of the eggs and collection of the larvae seem to be the largest obstacles in rearing the common basslets. Male basslets guard the nest of eggs, but do not give the constant attention given by brooding male dottybacks.

Breeding information on this family is generally limited to the Royal Gramma and Blackcap Basslet but several less common species are available from time to time. These include *Gramma linki*, *G. brasiliensis*, and the much rarer *Lipogramma regia*, *L. klayi* and *L. trilineata*. Little information exists for these species as they hail from deep water and their aquarium appearances are few and far between.

Gramma linki has been raised in captivity with limited success. Widespread distribution never occurred and this account seems to be isolated. It is plausible to assume that *G. brasiliensis* spawns in much the same manner as the Royal Gramma and the Blackcap Basslet, but details are sketchy.

The species of *Lipogramma* imported occasionally should be considered ideal captive breeding candidates if healthy individuals can be found. Again, there appears to be no published information regarding their captive culture or reproductive modes in the wild. Dim light and slightly cooler water temperatures should be provided.

Sexual Dimorphism: The Family Grammatidae exhibits little sexual dimorphism and without knowing the age of a particular fish it is quite difficult to determine its sex. As a rule, males grow larger than females and remain lean. Females in good condition become very rotund compared to their male counterparts, who often appear emaciated in the abdomenal region, especially with increasing age. When a group of fish is housed together these subtle traits become more easily visible. Social interaction is also a good indicator of sex in these groups and is often the best method upon which to base decisions.

Once thought to be capable of sex reversal, the grammids are now known not to change sex. The Royal Gramma does, however, exhibit a very unique trait while still sexually immature. This species typically lives in a harem-type social structure with many females controlled by one to several males. Although not able to change sex, the Royal Gramma is able to differentiate its sex while immature, and young fish can either mature into male or female based on the need of the group. If the dominant male has been killed or is lost, an immature fish can mature to fill the reproductive role of the male. Similarly, if a juvenile recruits to a male-dominated group, it will mature with female reproductive function if male pressure is severe enough. The anatomical feature that allows this is known as a bi-directional juvenile gonad. This trait can be used with juvenile grammas raised in captivity and while still young to form additional pairs quite easily. Any grammids purchased at a local aquarium store are past the age of sex determination and therefore the sexes cannot be manipulated to form spawning pairs. Shortly after metamorphosis and settlement isolated pairs typically mature as heterosexuals.

Conditioning: Maintaining captive grammids with commonly available aquarium fare is seldom a challenge. Initiating a first spawn while feeding commercial fish food will, however, generally end in disappointment. Grammids have a large mouth used to swallow large crustaceans found in both the open water and also clinging to the rocky reef structure. This diet of copepods, mysids and similar crustaceans provides spawning fish a diet rich in proteins, marine lipids and other nutrients. Grammids seem to require copious amounts of fresh-frozen table shrimp and squid to initiate spawning. The oils present in squid are particularly useful in triggering a first spawn. Live foods such as black worms, enriched adult *Artemia,* and even livebearer fry are useful in helping initiate a first spawn. Once you have them spawning, most of the live feeds can be cut from the diet and replaced with on a fresh-frozen seafood diet.

Royal Gramma (*Gramma loreto*): long a favorite of marine aquarists and an ideal species for small-scale breeders.

Royal Gramma

Gramma loreto (Poey, 1868)
Maximum Length: 10 cm (3.9 in.), usually to 8 cm (3.1 in.).
Sexual Allocation: Gonochorist.

With vibrant colors of yellow and magenta, these fish are appreciated by most marine aquarists and will always enjoy a popular market. Being small and hardy, the Royal Gramma is well-suited even to novice marine-fish breeders. This species is rather site attached and adapts well to aquarium conditions. They readily adapt to common aquarium foods and will readily spawn if provided with the proper conditions.

Habitat & Range: In the West Atlantic Ocean, Caribbean Sea and the Bahamas, Royal Grammas are found on shallow coral reefs from 2 to 100 feet, amongst coral rubble, and on the underside of ledges and upside down in caves with their bellies hugging the roof.

Sexual Dimorphism: Royal Grammas cannot be reliably sexed by external differences, that is, they are sexually monomorphic. Well-fed females in good condition will exhibit a swollen abdomen as ovaries fill with developing eggs. When viewed from above or below she may take on a "squarish" look. Males remain slim bodied. When pairs form they are comprised of one large and one smaller fish. At first, if all the fish are of the same size or age, pairs will form and one will grow larger while the others remain the same size. It is the male that grows larger. It has been observed on several occasions that the pink portion of the body in males is less than that of females. The pink portion of males extends only to the pectoral fin whereas it may extend to the midbody or beyond in females. This is not a reliable indicator of the sexes, but merely an observation I have made. If several specimens are housed in the same aquarium in the fish shop, it is worthwhile to watch how the fish react toward one another. Heterosexual pairs can usually be chosen based on their interactions with conspecies. Males will be aggressive toward other males while carefully, cautiously courting females.

Social Structure & Reproductive Biology: Occurring at a wide range of depth, the social unit maintained by Royal Grammas is quite variable. Those in shallow water are generally found singly or living in close association with other single individuals. Small to large aggregations are found in deeper water. These groups typically consist of one to several males and multiple females. Spawning sites are usually found to be in caves, where this species is commonly seen swimming upside down near the ceiling.

Diet: Although this species is not fussy in regards to foods and will readily accept flake foods, a more balanced diet will be required if a spawning attempt is to be successful. Fresh frozen shrimp as part of a gelatin mixture with other seafoods is the common conditioning food. Live black worms are often used to induce spawning. Live mysid shrimp and *Artemia* are a welcomed addition and help with spawning. Fish fed with live foods are more likely to spawn than those fed a diet solely of fresh or frozen foods—this can be the sole dictating factor as to whether the fish will spawn or not. Algae is also important in the diet. This is most easily supplied by spirulina flake foods along with the *Caulerpa* added as a spawning substrate.

Spawning: Twenty-gallon or even ten-gallon aquariums are suitable for single pairs. Larger aquariums should be used if multiples of each sex are obtained. A single male and up to three females can be successfully maintained in 30-gallon tanks. Since it is difficult to discern between the sexes, the best approach is to place a group in a 40-gallon aquarium and allow them to pair off naturally. Once the sexes have been identified the individual pairs can be moved into smaller aquariums.

The aquarium should be bare and supplied with PVC pipe spawning caves and a bunch of *Caulerpa*. The bottom and three sides of the broodstock aquarium are best painted with black paint to make the fish feel more secure. Lighting should be kept dim, direct illumination is not recommended. If gravel or live rock is added to the aquarium the fish will dig burrows or occupy a crevice in the live rock making it extremely difficult to observe spawning or to remove the eggs that result. The *Caulerpa* is used along with other algaes to line the inside of the spawning cave as a mat for the eggs to rest upon. Many captive pairs choose to incorporate tremendous amounts of debris and algae to the spawning shelter, while others seem reluctant to add a single filament.

Long filamentous hair algae, an unwelcome occurrence in display aquariums, is an excellent addition to a Royal Gramma breeding aquarium. If none is present, rocks or PVC pipe from an infested aquarium can be placed into the breeding aquarium. One or two inch diameter PVC pipe should be cut in lengths of roughly 5-7 inches and capped on both ends. On one end the cap should be drilled with a one-inch bit to act as an entrance to the spawning cave. The end caps are slipped onto the ends of the pipe, not glued, so they are easily removed to transport the eggs that are laid should this be necessary. C-Quest hatcheries uses small masonry bricks drilled with a one inch drill bit to create a spawning cave. Ten or 20-gallon breeding aquariums suited to a single pair of fish should be supplied with at least two of these caves. Larger aquariums with more Royal Grammas will require caves for every fish to prevent quarrels.

The most reliable way of pairing this species is to purchase a group of juveniles and allow them to grow to maturity in the presence of one another. In this fashion the fish will be allowed to form their own pairs. It is important to feed the fish a well-varied diet of fresh seafoods and live foods to allow the fish to reach sexual maturity fast and in good condition. When the fish are kept isolated in groups, courtship will soon take place. Males can be seen actively courting females and quarreling amongst themselves. In the meantime, females will begin to fill with eggs. As long as the aquarium is large enough and all the occupants peaceful they can be allowed to remain in this aquarium to breed. Otherwise, individual pairs should be isolated in 20-gallon aquariums. In the wild this species can be found living in social aggregations of over one hundred individuals. In the limited space of an aquarium, however, males often become intolerant of one another and must be separated.

Spawning is accomplished when the male persuades the female into his spawning cave, which has been prepared ahead of time. Pre-spawning activity can be observed with the male carrying mouthfuls of *Caulerpa* into the cave while courting the female intermittently. The male courts the female by arching his body and displaying all his erect fins in front of the female while quivering. The female enters the cave and is followed by the male. The pair may remain in the cave for up to half an hour. The female may deposit anywhere from 20 to 200 eggs at a time.

Unlike most species, Royal Gramma pairs spawn on a nightly basis for a prolonged period of time, usually a few weeks. All the eggs are not deposited at one time. The pair will spawn in the same cave and newly laid eggs will be deposited beside the older eggs. The male will guard the eggs until hatching, but because the eggs are bound within folds of algae, meticulous attention cannot be given to each egg. Since the eggs have been laid on different days, they will hatch on different nights. It then becomes difficult to capture and transport the larvae.

Incubation usually lasts 7 days depending on water temperature. A temperature of 80°F will result in a shorter incubation period, but larvae will hatch slightly smaller than those incubated near 78°F. The larvae can be collected on a nightly basis using a concentrated light source and a shallow dish. With the filter turned off, the diminutive larvae are transferred to a rearing tank by slowly submerging a shallow dish below the surface. The water that rushes into the dish will bring the larvae with it. Since spawning occurs every day, a nightly routine is the best approach to collecting the larvae. This method, however, typically results in high mortality associated with the physical stresses of transfer. An alternative method is to remove the eggs to an incubator on the day of hatching. Eggs removed from the care of the male earlier often yield lower hatching rates. The eggs are not adhesive and must be placed in an egg tumbler or downweller, as described for the dottybacks, pages 103-104. A length of airline tubing is fitted to a water line from the larval rearing system and a slow stream is pumped into the tumbler from above to agitate the eggs.

Larval Rearing: Automated larval collectors are another option. The newly hatched larvae can be collected easily, without the fuss of shallow bowls. Some sort of overflow chamber fastened to the top of the aquarium to draw the surface water in will aid in collecting the larvae. Since the larvae are attracted to light and immediately head to the surface they will be sucked into whatever trap you have set. A plastic specimen cup used for catching fish at pet shops can be hung on the side just below the surface. A hole should be drilled in the bottom of the specimen cup and supplied with an airlift. Half-inch PVC works fine for this. The vertical section of PVC is then drilled to fit a short length of rigid airline tubing. The PVC that is exposed on the inside of the collector should be supplied with a large piece of fine foam to prevent the larvae from being sucked back out. When set up and adjusted, an air pump will create bubbles that push up the airlift and spill back into the aquarium. As the water level increases in the aquarium, the water will then fall back into the collector bringing with it the newly hatched larvae. This is just one example of collecting larvae. Overflows commonly used on reef aquariums should be the model for any design. I prefer to use an overflow design that transfers larvae directly to a rearing tank. Water from the broodstock tank is siphoned by surface skimming to a rearing tank. The water flows to the rearing tank and through a standpipe fitted with a 250 μm screen before being temporarily diverted to the broodstock sump. After several nights of collecting larvae, the water flow is re-directed from the broodstock tank and the larval rearing tank is isolated.

If glass aquariums are used for larval rearing, the sides should be covered with dark paper until the 2nd week after hatching. Round, black tubs are the preferred rearing vessel; using them will provide a marked increase in larval survival. The larvae are quite large at hatching (3.5 mm) and can accept rotifers as their initial diet the following morning followed by newly hatched *Artemia* roughly 10 days later. Newly hatched larvae exhibit a faint black striped pattern before developing adult coloration near day 26. Metamorphosis begins around day 21, but many larvae require up to 35 days to reach metamorphosis.

Metamorphosis is coupled with an increase in aggressive tendencies. The post-metamorphosis juveniles should be supplied with cover in the form of cut lengths of PVC to limit aggression. Mortalities are highest during the first 3 days of life and during metamorphosis.

Blackcap Basslet

Gramma melacara (Böhlke & Randall, 1963)
Maximum Length: 10 cm (3.9 in.).
Sexual Allocation: Gonochorist.

This species is less available in the aquarium trade, as its deep water habits make it difficult to capture, decompress and transport. This is a beautiful and sought-after species offering many positive opportunities for captive

Blackcap Basslet (*Gramma melacara*): a prize aquarium fish with limited availability of broodstock and more of a challenge to spawn and rear than *Gramma loreto*.

breeding. The progeny are worth more than the average captive-bred marine fishes. As they are infrequently available, the most difficult aspect of breeding this species is obtaining broodstock pairs. Most fish shops will have only one specimen offered for sale if any. This species often proves difficult to induce to spawn, but the larvae are relatively easy to raise.

Habitat & Range: This deep-water species is most commonly found at depths greater than 30 m (100 ft.), in the West Atlantic and Caribbean Sea where it is supposedly common.

Sexual Dimorphism: No external differences are readily observed. Females are somewhat smaller and more rotund with developing eggs. Males are more aggressive and larger. During courtship the males can be seen decorating their nest sites with algae and other decorations found in the aquarium. Again, observing social interactions are the best way to deterine the sexes.

Social Structure and Reproductive Biology: Black cap basslets are limited to deeper water where they are most often found in caves and near ledges often in association with Royal Grammas. Blackcaps can be found singly or in small groups. Large aggregations are seldom observed.

Diet: Feed similar foods as the Royal Gramma, but increased rations of live foods may be needed to trigger spawning.

Spawning: Pairs can be successfully propagated in 20 gallon tanks although a 30 or 40-gallon would be better. The aquarium should be decorated as described for the Royal Gramma. Lighting should be rather dim to simulate deep-water environment. If a fish room is available, rely only on room lighting, not direct aquarium illumination.

Spawning is often difficult due to the difficulty of obtaining stock animals. A group of 4 individuals will usually result in at least one pair. Feed them well with live and frozen foods. Live enriched *Artemia* and black worms remain a favorite with these fish.

Spawning occurs in much the same manner as described for *Gramma loreto*. Spawning begins in midday and is accomplished when the male successfully lures the female into the cave where she deposits up to 250 eggs. Spawning occurs daily. Pairs are often reluctant to spawn without the inclusion of live food in the diet. Live adult *Artemia* enriched with microalgae feed is a good conditioning diet as are live mysid shrimp and wild collected, size sorted plankton.

The incubation period lasts 7 days with hatching occurring an hour or so after dark. Newly hatched larvae wiggle free from the *Caulerpa* inside the nest and make their way to the surface. Here they are concentrated with a small light source and transferred to a rearing tank with a shallow bowl or similar device meant to concentrate and thus transfer the larvae. High mortality is generally associated with transferring the larvae to a rearing tank. Whether mortality is due to physical stresses involved with transfer or the effect of high light levels, entire clutches are often lost by moving them this way. An alternative method is to use a larval collector fitted with a highly diffused light or use a collector with no light at all. I prefer to maintain broodstock pairs in a central water system. Spawning tanks are fitted so that water can be diverted to a rearing tank temporarily connected to the common sump. In this way all water from the broodstock tank flows through the rearing chamber before flowing to the sump. The standpipe within the rearing tank is fitted with a 250 μm screen to keep the larvae in the rearing tank. Hatching is staggered over several days and all larvae from that brood will concentrate in the same rearing tank without the mortality associated with physical transfer.

Larval Rearing: Larvae measure slightly over 3mm long at hatching and are capable of taking rotifers as their initial food the morning after hatching. Newly hatched Artemia are added to the diet on day 10. Metamorphosis occurs from days 19 to 32. At the completion of metamorphosis the juveniles become aggressive towards one another although there is rarely a time when juvenile densities are so high as to cause great losses due to aggression. Mortality is highest during the first 5 days after hatching and is probably attributed to stresses involved in transferring larvae rather than feeding. Metamorphosis also poses a bottleneck to rearing in this species. Proper enrichment is essential for larvae to successfully complete metamorphosis.

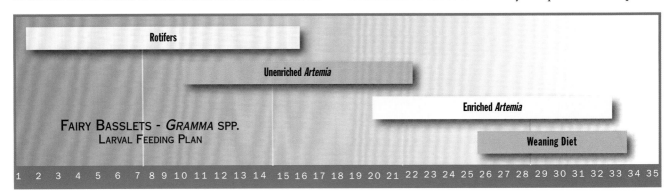

FAIRY BASSLETS - *GRAMMA* SPP.
LARVAL FEEDING PLAN

Rotifers

Unenriched *Artemia*

Enriched *Artemia*

Weaning Diet

1 2 3 4 5 6 7 8 9 10 11 12 13 14 15 16 17 18 19 20 21 22 23 24 25 26 27 28 29 30 31 32 33 34 35

Guidelines: Feed rotifers at 10/ml; unenriched *Artemia* nauplii less than 12 hrs. old; enriched *Artemia* less than 24 hrs. old.

ASSESSORS & COMETS

FAMILY PLESIOPIDAE

Yellow Assessor (Golden Mini-Grouper)

Assessor flavissimus (Allen & Kuiter, 1976)
Maximum Length: 5.5 cm (2.1 in.).
Sexual Allocation: Not known.

Blue Assessor (MacNeill's Mini-Grouper)

Assessor macneilli (Whitley, 1935)
Maximum Length: 6 cm (2.3 in.).
Sexual Allocation: Not known.

Assessors are often available in specialty marine fish stores, but obtaining more than one specimen is sometimes a challenge. Both species are most often found living in small aggregations in the wild and spawning attempts are greatly increased when multiple individuals are housed together. Assuming a group is assembled, kept under ideal conditions and well-fed, spawning should start easily once the group is acclimated to its surroundings. Many skilled aquarists have observed captive spawning, but successful larval rearing has been achieved by only a few breeders, including Oceans, Reefs and Aquariums in Florida.

Habitat & Range: Both species are found on the Great Barrier Reef system. *Assessor macneilli* has a wider range, extending to New Caledonia. These fish are shy and retiring, living in pairs or small aggregations in caves or under ledges during the day. They are seldom spotted in the open during the day in the wild.

Sexual Dimorphism: Assessors are for the most part sexually monomorphic with virtually no differences to separate the sexes. In groups containing mature fish, males are typically larger than females. Females appear swollen at the onset of spawning. Also, only the males of both species orally incubate the eggs. Behavior is sometimes a good indicator, as males are more quarrelsome and aggres-

Yellow Assessor (*Assessor flavissimus*): will spawn in promiscuous aggregations with males mouthbrooding the eggs.

sive and displays between males can readily be witnessed in captivity.

Social Structure & Reproductive Biology: Assessors are inhabitants of underwater caves and ledges where they occur in small to large aggregations. The ratio of sexes is not known in these groups, but observations seem to indicate a reasonable number of males is present. One of the most interesting traits of these species is the oral incubation undertaken by the male. The social structure maintained would bode well for protogynous hermaphroditism, however, in a population with a limited number of males, reproduction could occur only as fast as the incubation period would allow. Multiple to many males occurring per population alleviates this constraint as multiple spawns could be orally incubated.

Males engage in aggressive disputes, but are generally not as severe as in other groups. The group's close affinity to the serranids does suggest sex change, but the exact allocation is unknown. Spawning probably occurs promiscuously.

Diet: Provide fresh frozen shrimp, squid, marine fish flesh, clam and similar offerings several times daily. Live or frozen mysids are also a welcomed addition to the diet as is vitamin-enriched *Artemia* and live black worms.

Spawning: Assessors are mouthbrooders, so a bare tank is neither essential nor advised. A single pair can coexist and

Blue Assessor: a mouthbrooding male can be isolated in the rearing tank to avoid transfer losses of delicate larvae.

breed in tanks as small as 10 gallons. A small aggregation should be housed in 30-gallon or larger aquariums. These species are shy and retiring and do not appreciate strong illumination. A single fluorescent bulb of low wattage should be provided to replicate the dim light found in deep water and under ledges. Caves, ledges and other similar structural offerings should be provided in the form of PVC pipe sections, ceramic tiles or bricks.

Again, the best way to spawn this species is to establish a small aggregation and let them spawn naturally. They seem to be promiscuous, and the male orally incubates the eggs for 14 days before releasing the larvae into the water column. The male takes no food during incubation.

Larval Rearing: Two methods are available for transferring larvae to a rearing tank. The larvae can be concentrated with a light source and transferred to a rearing tank with a shallow bowl, or the male holding the brood in his mouth can be removed to the rearing tank and the hatching allowed normally. I prefer to move the male to a rearing tank, as transfer losses of larvae are typically quite high when they are removed from the broodstock tank by physical means. Central systems are useful in avoiding stress associated with different water chemistry. Care should be taken to capture

the male as gently as possible. The brooding male should not be transferred using an aquarium net. A plastic container should be submerged and the male gently transferred to it. Transferring a brooding male must be done with great care as he may spit the spawn if highly stressed.

In the rearing tank, the male can be placed in a basket made from plastic mesh such as that used for rain-gutter guards. When the larvae hatch they will be released in the tank and the male can be removed with ease. If the male is not placed in an isolated basket he may prey on the newly hatched larvae and become difficult to remove. One technique that works well is to build the mesh basket with a solid bottom and short sides. The entire container can then be lifted from the rearing tank with the male isolated in perhaps an inch of water as he is transferred back to the broodstock tank.

Larvae are large enough to accept rotifers as their initial meal. Greenwater and a rotifer density of 15/mL is advised. Larval rearing is similar to the Orchid Dottyback (page 186). Round, black tanks are best for larval rearing.

Comet (Marine Betta)

Calloplesiops altivelis (Steindachner, 1903)
Maximum Length: 16 cm (6.2 in.).
Sexual Allocation: Unknown.

The Comet (sometimes dubbed the Marine Betta) is a very beautiful species adorned with flowing fins and a spectacular spotted pattern against a contrasting dark brown background. (To some it suggests a streak of celestial sparkles in the tail of a streaking comet.) A false eyespot is present on the dorsal fin. When the anal, dorsal and tail fins are all together and the fish assumes a head-down position in a crevice it is thought that this offers protection by mimicking the head and eye of a moray eel. Virtually every specimen offered for sale is wild-caught so this is a species that always commands a respectable price. These fish are very peaceful, disease resistant, and beautiful, making them a good candidate for captive breeding. The young will surely be welcome by fellow aquarists. This species is difficult to induce to spawn, but the resulting larvae are not too difficult to raise.

Habitat & Range: Comets are found in the Indo-Pacific from the Red Sea to the southern tip of the Great Barrier Reef and north to Japan. Here they occupy caves and crevices on reef slopes.

Sexual Dimorphism: This species is reported to be sexually monomorphic exhibiting no external differences between the sexes. Jacqueline Baez in 1998 reported in an issue of *SeaScope*® that a broodstock culturist at the C-Quest hatchery in Puerto Rico observed that, in spawning pairs, the spots on male Comets were smaller than those on females. Furthermore, little information is available as to whether or not this species has the ability to change sex.

Social Structure & Reproductive Biology: Comets live a cryptic existence in the protection of deep ledges and crevices. They often occur under large plate corals and deep in the labyrinth of coral rubble caves. In the wild this species is rarely witnessed outside the shadows of ledges and caves. Primarily nocturnal, Comets slowly cruise the reef rubble bottom in search of shrimp, crabs, invertebrate eggs and small fish. They normally occur as solitary individuals, but can also be found in presumably heterosexual pairs. The related western Blue Devil, *Plesiops meleagris*, lives a solitary existence until it reaches sexual maturity whereupon it pairs up and lives out its days deep within the cavities of underwater caves.

It would be premature to assume the Comet lives a similar existence, but it does illustrate a possible close example. Males alone undertake the duty of brood care. In captivity the female may hover close by, but the male keeps her at bay.

Diet: In the wild, these fish are predators of small crustaceans and fishes. A good conditioning diet includes shrimp, squid, some algae and fish held together in a gelatin base. Marine crustacean prey should form the bulk of the diet, with occasional feedings of live guppies, black worms, killifish and enriched adult *Artemia*. Feeding should consist of at least three meals daily. Live foods are the best way to induce spawning.

Comet (*Calloplesiops altivelis*): a shy, handsome species that can be reluctant to spawn, but with easy-to-rear larvae.

Spawning: These fish grow larger than the average clownfish and are solitary in nature, so a larger aquarium is required. The minimum size I recommend for a single pair is a 40-gallon breeder. Although the fish may coexist peacefully in smaller quarters, they may not feel comfortable. The best breeding aquarium would be a 75-gallon aquarium or larger, depending on the number of fish. I have spawned this species in a bare 75-gallon aquarium with 4 specimens of unknown sex.

The tank should be bare and the bottom and three sides painted a dark color. PVC pipes are utilized as shelter and spawning sites. Four-inch T fittings and elbows work well. Many of these sites should be offered and not restricted or limited to one per fish. A single fluorescent tube to provide a dim effect is ideal. Again, if a fish room is available, rely only on room illumination.

Since there are few differences between the sexes, pairs cannot be formed on the basis of external characteristics. The best way to form spawning pairs is to obtain a group, place them in the same aquarium and offer good foods and good water quality. I recommend obtaining no less than 4 specimens to form spawning pairs. Better yet, if you are serious about this endeavor, start with 6 to 8 specimens. Chances are increased that you will obtain more than one

Comet juvenile home-bred by German aquarist. Full-color develops slowly over time following metamorphosis.

spawning pair. It often takes a while for these fish to feel comfortable enough in their captive environment to spawn, and little or nothing of their courtship rituals may be observed. At times the fish seem not even to recognize conspecies if they happen upon one, so do not assume the fish are all one sex; give them time. In my experience, this species is peaceful with conspecies and a tank containing many individuals should pose few problems.

Courtship and spawning seem to be accomplished either secretively or without much fanfare. Male Comets with mating on their minds tend to remain in the spawning cave and periodically leave the cave to display to a waiting fe-

male. This involves an arched body and fully erect fins while the mouth is held open. The male positions himself horizontally in front of the female and remains motionless before retreating to the cave. After some time, the female may follow and lay eggs.

There are no apparent cyclical patterns involved in the spawning season of this fish. They seem to spawn only when they are good and ready. A bloom of zooplankton can be used to induce spawning if the fish are in good condition and well-rounded. This can be done easily be dosing the tank with a large amount of wild-collected zooplankton or large numbers of newly hatched *Artemia*. These fish are extremely unpredictable in their spawning habits. Unlike their dottyback relatives, Comets have not been observed to spawn on a routine basis. The female leaves the cave soon after the eggs have been deposited and fertilized. The male will guard the eggs until they hatch.

Comets lay 300-500 demersal eggs held together in a gelatinous mass. Rich gold in color and attached to the wall of the spawning cave by sticky threads, this mass is vigorously guarded and cared for by the tending male.

On day 4 and 5 the egg mass begins to break apart and the eggs fall separately to the bottom of the spawning cave. The eggs will hatch on day 6 shortly after the lights have been turned off. Before this happens, however, the egg mass should be removed to a hatching container. More often than not, male Comets will eat the eggs shortly after they have been laid. The top half of an inverted soda bottle should

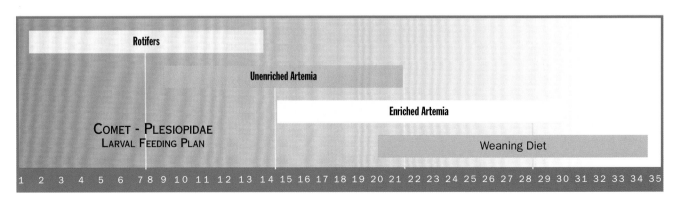

Guidelines: Feed rotifers at 10/ml; unenriched *Artemia* nauplii less than 12 hrs. old; enriched *Artemia* less than 24 hrs. old.

be submerged in the spawning tank and the ball of eggs gently transferred directly into it to avoid too much stress to the eggs. The eggs should not be removed from the water. The hatching vessel should be moved to a rearing tank and held at the surface with an airstone in the hatching container to keep the eggs viable. Some of the eggs may hatch on the 5th night but it may take longer than day 6 for all the eggs to hatch out.

Larval Rearing: Upon hatching, the larvae are near 4 mm long and strongly pigmented. There is no yolk sac present and the larvae are well-developed with a large mouth, black body and black eyes with a white dot on the tail and white mottled head. The dorsal, anal and tail fins are all fused as one, extending the length of the dorsal and ventral sides. Pectoral fins are also present. Since there is no yolk sac the larvae begin feeding soon after hatching. Unlike most marine larvae, these tiny Comets hatch out and sit on the bottom until comfortable with their new freedom. They then make short skips off the bottom and soon become accomplished swimmers, drawn to areas near water flow. At this stage, their favorite pasttime will be hanging around the airstones in the mild currents.

The larvae are accomplished swimmers and hunters that will take rotifers as their first food. Rotifer densities can be maintained lower than average, near 5/mL. It is important that, although larvae are capable of feeding successfully in low prey densities, prey must be constantly available. It may be necessary to feed up to three times daily to maintain sufficient densities of prey. Signs of metamorphosis are apparent by day 8. At day 9 the larvae begin feeding on newly hatched *Artemia*. At day 15 the larvae drastically change in both appearance and behavior. They disappear from the water column and take refuge in tank corners. It is at this time that lengths of PVC pipe and clay flowerpots should be added to the rearing tank. At day 20, a weaning diet consisting of crushed flake foods, minced seafoods or commercial feeds can be offered. By the end of the 5th month, the young have taken on the characteristic shape and fin development of the adults. Full adult coloration takes as long as 7 months to appear.

Yellowhead Jawfish (*Opistognathus aurifrons*) a burrowing species that needs a broodstock tank with deep substrate.

JAWFISHES

FAMILY OPISTOGNATHIDAE

Jawfishes are especially attractive to prospective marine fish breeders. Jawfishes are hardy, disease resistant and strongly site attached, so they are not stressed by captive conditions. They are easily spawned and the relatively large size of their larvae at hatching facilitates rearing. Closely related to fairy basslets and dottybacks, jawfish are interesting oddities that are within the grasp of dedicated marine hobbyists. Males mouthbrood the eggs, adding to the fascination of their mating and breeding behaviors.

Although the Yellowhead Jawfish is the most commonly available, many other interesting species have been spawned and reared in captivity. If adequate numbers of broodstock fish can be obtained, any member of the family will make a worthy investment. Most members of the family spawn

Dusky Jawfish (*Opistognathus whitehurstii*) male buried to the gills and holding a mass of ready-to-hatch eggs.

in roughly the same manner as Yellowhead Jawfish, with the most prominent difference being the level of aggression displayed between conspecies. Many species live in close association with others and may establish large colonies. Others, such as the Bluespotted Jawfish (*Opistognathus rosenblatti*) are quite aggressive toward conspecifics and compatibility is severely limited in the confines of a tank.

Jawfish are extremely site-attached. All members of the group are masters of architecture and construct vertical burrows in the sand, often adorning them with large shells and rubble near the entrances to reinforce the integrity of the tunnels. Jawfish presumably construct a terminal cavity or hollow at the burrow's end. Jawfish generally hover a few inches to a few feet above the substrate picking small crustaceans and larval organisms from the passing plankton.

Courtship varies between the many species, but mostly involves exaggerated swimming, fin flaring high above the burrow, hovering, and then dashing suddenly back to the protection of the tunnel. Some species display sexual dichromatism during the breeding season. Courting male *O. rosenblatti* turn white in the head region fading to black in the rear half of the body. Male Yellowhead Jawfish display a heightened color contrast, but with a radically different pattern as in *O. rosenblatti*.

Jawfish are not capable of sex reversal, so it is important to identify sexes prior to any attempt to induce reproduction. Sexual dimorphism varies throughout the group. The most reliable means of sex determination is to observe interactions with others of the same species. Females will generally be more solemnly colored than males and also be more rotund. These characteristics are, however, not readily apparent in newly imported specimens.

If several specimens can be viewed side by side, jaw structure is a good indicator. The maxilla (upper jaw bone) of male jawfish extends further posteriorly and is in general more pronounced. The entire head region of males are slightly enlarged compared to females. Choose only healthy individuals that appear alert and have a healthy appetite. If possible, choose several individuals that meet the characteristics of both sexes to increase the odds of obtaining a heterosexual pair. Species like the Yellowhead Jawfish can be maintained in large groups with little fear of harm to any individual in the group. Other jawfish are much more aggressive and difficult to maintain in groups. Trial-and-error based on morphological characteristics is the most reliable means of pairing in aggressive jawfishes. Isolated pairs are the rule of thumb for *O. rosenblatti*. Males and females are typically compatible. When placed together, males will approach females with curiosity rather than aggression.

Yellowhead Jawfish

Opistognathus aurifrons (Jordan & Thompson, 1905)
Maximum Length: 10 cm (3.9 in.).
Sexual Allocation: Gonochorist.

Habitat & Range: This species is found around southern Florida and the Caribbean in the West Atlantic Ocean. Narrow, vertical tunnels are constructed in sand flats. They often live in large colonies.

Sexual Dimorphism: Outside the spawning season, few sexual differences are apparent without a trained eye. A mouthbrooder, the adult male has developed a more massive jaw structure to support buccal incubation. The entire head seems slightly enlarged with the jaw being more de-

Yellowhead Jawfish (*Opistognathus aurifrons*) in a broodstock tank kept by Martin Moe. This species can be kept in groups provided enough bottom space is allocated to each specimen. As burrowers, these fish always require a deep bed of coral sand.

fined. These differences become more evident when a group of individuals is observed rather than trying to identify an isolated individual's sexual function. Females have subdued colors throughout the spawning season, but before spawning the female's abdominal region fills considerably. A sure sign of a male jawfish is the presence of eggs being carried within the buccal cavity. Only males brood the eggs.

Social Structure & Reproductive Biology: Aggregations of Yellowhead Jawfish concentrate on sand flats near adjacent patch reefs. For the most part they occur in open areas away from high outcroppings that impede peripheral vision. Yellowhead Jawfish often maintain long-term pair bonds with males and females often occupying the same burrow and working jointly to maintain the tunnel's integrity and guard the territorial boundary around the entrance. Promiscuous spawning also occurs.

Courtship is an elaborate spectacle. Males approach females in a horizontal position. Their fins are flared and the mouths stretched wide open. They circle hopeful females,

slowly, remaining motionless with a slight upward arch to their body, then slowly retreat to their burrows in hopes that a female will follow.

Diet: This species hovers above the entrance of its cave and awaits the passing of plankton. They will not venture far to take a meal, so foods must be offered accordingly. Crustaceans are their favored prey, and fresh frozen shrimp and other fresh seafoods are best. Uneaten food will not be picked up from the bottom by the fish so it is imperative that it be removed.

Spawning: The aquarium chosen to spawn this species is very important. Breeder aquariums are best as they offer more surface area for tunnel building than standard aquariums. This is important mostly to allow the sexes easy access to one another without having to travel over the territory of another. A bare aquarium will not do. Crushed coral sand or gravel should be added to a depth of six or more inches to allow adequate burrowing room. Large pieces of coral rubble should also be added as the jawfish incorporate this into the entrance of the cave to give it stability. No rocks or other decorations should be present, only gravel. A 40-gallon (150 L) breeder tank is best, although smaller aquaria can suffice for an isolated pair.

The best approach to spawning this species is to establish a colony in a fairly large tank. A 40-gallon breeder aquarium provides adequate room for 6 to 8 individuals. When such a colony is established the fish feel more comfortable and are more willing to breed than when kept as isolated pairs in smaller aquariums. Eggs will be had more often and the probability of obtaining both sexes is increased. The temperature should be maintained at 80°F with good water quality and regular partial water changes. Care should be taken with jawfish not to siphon the gravel bed anywhere near the burrow as it may collapse. With heavy feedings at least three or four times daily, and good water quality, the fish will breed with little coaxing needed. Yellowhead Jawfish often establish long-term pair bonds with a heterosexual pair occupying the same burrow and repeatedly spawning on a 14 to 22 day cycle.

Courtship and spawning takes place during dawn and dusk. The actual events that take place within the burrow are unclear, but the male emerges with a mouthful of eggs that he orally incubates until hatching. During brood-tending duties, the male can be seen spitting the eggs out and sucking them in again as he agitates and aerates the eggs within his mouth.

Hatching occurs at 7 to 9 days at 80°F. Larvae at hatching are slightly more than 3 mm in length and should be concentrated on the surface with a light source, while all filters are turned off, and transferred to a rearing tank with a shallow bowl. A dim light should be used as excessive light will increase mortality during transfer. Extreme care should be taken while transferring larvae to the rearing tank.

Larval Rearing: Larvae are best reared in a round, black rearing tank of 20 gallons or more. Enriched rotifers maintained at a density of 10/mL are an ideal first food.

Fins are fully formed by the end of the ninth day and newly hatched *Artemia* can be added to the diet a day or so before this. By day 15, metamorphosis begins and the young will shortly resemble adult jawfish ready to construct their first burrows. Care should be taken not to move juveniles until successfully adapted to a weaning diet to avoid losses associated with *Artemia* and shock. A small sample of juveniles should be moved before the entire clutch is transferred.

Upon completion of metamorphosis near day 20, the young should be transferred to a grow-out aquarium with hiding places provided. Rather than deep substrate, PVC caves are spread throughout the grow-out vessel. This way the juveniles are supplied with makeshift burrows to alleviate stress, but they are easily caught and transferred as needed. Juveniles in a bare tank will seek refuge by forming a swarming mass. Stress and disease quickly ensue in these situations. Leaping from uncovered tanks is also a side effect of not providing burrows.

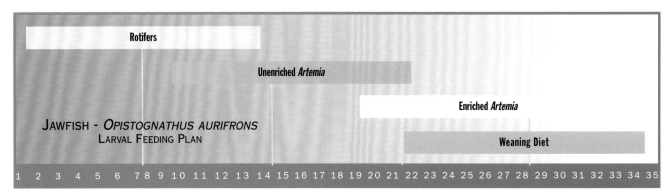

Guidelines: Feed rotifers at 10/ml; unenriched *Artemia* nauplii less than 12 hrs. old; enriched *Artemia* less than 24 hrs. old.

CARDINALFISHES

FAMILY APOGONIDAE

Although cardinalfishes are nearly ubiquitous in most marine environments, their exhibition in home aquariums is generally limited to a few iconic species.

Of the 250 or so representatives of the Apogonidae found worldwide, just a handful are commonly available to marine enthusiasts. Recent success in breeding the Banggai Cardinalfish (*Pterapogon kauderni*) has stimulated interest in propagating other apogonids. A handful of other cardinalfish species has since been successfully reared for the aquarium market, and there seems to be no bounds to the possibility of raising many more.

Cardinalfish have traditionally been viewed with little interest by aquarists or commercial breeding facilities, while scientific research laboratories have been successfully culturing many members of this important family for years. While many species of cardinalfish lack the instant, eye-catching appeal of the Banggai, many do possess subtle beauty and have ideal traits for captive propagation and adaptation to aquarium life. Most are generally small, hardy fish exhibiting interesting schooling behaviors and a peaceful demeanor that is ideally suited to marine community tanks and reef aquariums.

Captive propagation is easily initiated with little conditioning. The most difficult aspect of culturing apogonids is acquiring healthy broodstock animals. Members of this under appreciated family would surely be a welcome addition to retailers' tanks and provide hobbyists with a more diverse offering of hardy, captive-raised tankmates.

Cardinalfish play a pivotal role in marine ecosystems acting as both predator and prey. Their abundance on coral reefs can hardly be overlooked, as most species establish large schools surrounding and often engulfing stands of staghorn corals during the day. A single daytime school may

Schooling Banggai Cardinals (*Pterapogon kauderni*): the marine breeder's version of a guppy—easily kept and propagated.

exceed several thousand individuals. Mostly nocturnal, schools of cardinals break up at dusk to forage on passing zooplankton. Several species, mostly the *Cheilodipterus*, are predators of small fishes and invertebrates and of these a few are diurnal hunters. Cardinalfish are characterized by their primarily nocturnal habits, two separate dorsal fins and unique method of egg incubation. All known species of cardinalfish are mouthbrooders that orally incubate their eggs until hatching 7 to 8 days after fertilization. With the

Girdled Cardinalfish (*Archamia zosterophora*): not commonly seen in the aquarium trade, and a good target for breeders.

The reproductive biology of apogonids is highly diverse with courtship and spawning ranging from quite matter-of-fact and lasting only minutes to elaborate dances consuming hours or days prior to the spawning event. Most commonly, heterosexuals maintain long-term pair bonds. While many species are promiscuous, spawning with many individual partners throughout the reproductive season, the majority of cardinalfish species maintain at least temporary pair bonds during this period. These may or may not dissolve at the end of the spawning season. The fidelity of pair bonds in a few species is remarkable. During their nighttime forays, individuals scatter about the reef traveling to seagrass meadows and over sand barrens far from their protective daytime haunts. When dawn approaches and the fish regress to their coral shelters, pairs recognize their mates out of the hundreds or thousands of conspecifics present. A temporary spawning territory is established by many species with the female actively defending its borders and her mate.

Courtship: Courtship is usually initiated in the early afternoon with spawning taking place in the evening hours near the setting sun. After a courtship that is often elaborate, the female extrudes a mass of eggs held together with fine filaments extending from the surface of the individual eggs. Intertwined, these filaments hold the egg mass together forming a ball containing a few hundred to over 3,000 eggs. Most evidence suggests that the egg mass is either fertilized during release from the female's vent or immediately before the male takes them into his mouth. Fertilizing the eggs outside the mouth seems a less complicated method of fertilization and many reports indicate the male swims over the mass several times quivering with his genital pore near the mass before finally turning and inhaling it.

Most commonly, pairs of cardinalfish adopt a parallel posture near the bottom substrate while the female extrudes the egg mass. It is probable that this behavior aids in fertilization prior to oral incubation. Other reports suggest the male emits sperm into the water column and swims in circles while ventilating the buccal cavity to facilitate fertilization. The incubation period in most species lasts 7 - 10 days. Larvae typically hatch an hour or two after sun-

exception of the Banggai Cardinal that lacks a pelagic larval phase, the larvae of cardinalfish are released from the oral cavity after hatching and develop in the pelagic realm for approximately 25 days.

Sexual dimorphism is generally limited to the spawning season when temporary dichromatism is sometimes displayed during courtship. Males typically exhibit faded coloration, with some species appearing almost white near spawning, while the coloration of females intensifies to exaggerate the luminous shades already present. Few species are permanently sexually dimorphic, but the males of at least several species develop long filaments on the first or second dorsal fin. The males of many species are larger than females with an overall deeper body profile and larger head. The jaw structure of males is often more robust to facilitate paternal mouthbrooding.

Coincidentally, mouthbrooding is an excellent indicator of sex in most all species of apogonids, as this is solely the male's duty. Females may be larger and, in good condition, are almost always more rotund than males. As the spawning season commences, females often swell to enormous proportions making identification easy. Cardinalfish are gonochoristic; they are not capable of sex reversal.

Yellowstriped Cardinalfish (*Apogon cyanosoma*)

Australian Clownfish (*Apogon compressus*)

Flamefish (*Apogon maculatus*): a larger Caribbean species.

Seale's Cardinalfish (*A. seali*): one of many pretty cardinals.

set. Males fast during this period and often appear uncomfortable with large spawns. Males may cough or spit the egg mass out of the buccal cavity to rearrange and aerate the eggs. Some appear to chew on the egg mass as they slowly agitate them throughout the incubation period.

Reproduction in captivity is a simple matter once a group containing heterosexuals is established. Because sexual dimorphism is limited or non-existent, the best approach to spawning cardinalfish is to obtain a group of healthy individuals and place them in a large species aquar-

ium. With some species exhibiting size differences between the sexes, the chances of obtaining a heterosexual pair is significantly increased when fish of marked size differences are introduced to the same aquarium. Small groups of most commonly available species can be maintained in 20 or 30-gallon tanks.

Four to six cardinalfishes of the same species, housed alone and fed a conditioning diet, will reward their keeper with at least one successful spawning pair. Species such as the very pretty Bluestreak Cardinal (*A. leptacanthus*) seem to exhibit reproductive behavior more reliably in larger group settings. Aquariums are best kept bare with large-diameter PVC sections for shelter. Cardinalfish are seldom picky at feeding time and thrive on a diet of mysid shrimp, grated squid and shrimp and other common aquarium fare.

Cardinalfish larvae measure 2 to 4 mm at hatching and can be reared in a manner similar to that described for Orchid Dottybacks (see page 186). A major challenge in rearing cardinalfishes is the transfer of larvae to the rearing tank. Like most demersal spawning reef fishes, cardinalfish larvae are phototactic and can be concentrated to a light beam after hatching. Manual transfer by use of a shallow bowl or automated siphon systems can be used to transfer the larvae, however, these methods typically result in high transfer losses due to the physical damage or stress of transfer or damage to the visual system from the flashlight beam.

It is therefore best to move the brooding male to the rearing tank a day or two before the hatch is expected. Some risk is involved with this method, as stressed males may consume or spit the egg mass. This is generally limited to first-time spawners. Once adjusted to this cycle, seasoned males will rarely consume the egg mass during transfer. Prior to transfer, the rearing tank should be filled with water from the broodstock system to alleviate stress from shifts in water chemistry. A submerged specimen cup should be used to corral the male, slowly removing him to the rearing tank. A basket constructed of plastic mesh (or even a large livebearer breeder trap) should be used to house the brooding male in the rearing tank. Once the larvae are released from the male's mouth and freed from their membranes, they can pass through the plastic mesh into the rearing tank and the male can be removed back to the broodstock tank with minimal stress to the larvae.

Larval Feeding: First feeding is usually successful on small-strain rotifers. During the first feeding stage, proper HUFA enrichment is crucial and larvae benefit from added wild zooplankton (especially copepod nauplii). Metamorphosis and settlement to the bottom of the rearing tank is usually completed at 23 to 34 days after hatching.

There are many species of cardinalfish that appear spo-

radically in the aquarium market and keen-eyed breeders can take advantage of these chance imports. *Apogon compressus, A. cyanosoma, A. aureus, A. monospilus, Archamia zosterophora* and many other cardinals routinely spawn in home aquariums. Broodstock is easily maintained with little effort, and spawning is frequent under captive conditions. Rearing cardinal larvae is a bit more challenging than clownfish, but is well within the realm of possibility for beginning breeders. It is with captive propagation that rare and beautiful species could become commonplace in the hobby. One of my personal favorites, *Cheilodipterus nigrotaeniatus,* mimics the venomous Striped Fang Blenny (*Meiacanthus grammistes*). It is virtually never offered for sale unless confused as the fang blenny itself and imported under a misnomer. These are gorgeous fish that would be well-accepted if only they were available.

Pajama Cardinalfish

Sphaeramia nematoptera (Bleeker, 1856)
Maximum Length: 8 cm (3.1 in.).
Sexual Allocation: Gonochorist.

The classic colors and unique patterns of the Pajama Cardinalfish have earned them a permanent place in the marine aquarium hobby. This is an excellent species for beginners, as they are extremely durable animals in captivity. They are easily maintained with little effort, feed well on most any common aquarium fare, are not overly sensitive to water quality deteriorations and spawn quite readily.

Amazingly, captive-breds have not been available to the aquarium hobby and their introduction would surely be welcomed. While spawning is often a simple task, rearing the larvae is more challenging than the clownfish or jawfish. The ease and frequency in which larvae are obtained make this a perfect species to hone one's larval-rearing skills.

Habitat & Range: The Pajama Cardinalfish is found widely throughout the West Pacific from Java to the Fiji Islands, north to the Ryukyus, south to the Great Barrier Reef and New Caledonia. Adult *S. nematoptera* are found singly, in pairs or loose aggregations on shallow reefs, amongst mangrove roots and around manmade structures in shallow water. I have seen large aggregations consisting of several hundred individuals of the closely related Orbiculate Cardinalfish (*S. orbicularis*). Less than a dozen *S. nematoptera* were found in this mixed school. Pajama Cardinals rarely form large aggregations, preferring close association rather than schooling.

Sexual Dimorphism: Some reports suggest females are larger than males, but in my experience males are slightly larger than females and develop a deeper body profile and slightly more robust head structure. Females swell with eggs as spawning approaches. The most discerning characteristic of sexual function is the presence of eggs within the buccal cavity; only males perform this mouthbrooding behavior. Most specimens available at local aquarium stores are juveniles and will not display such dimorphism.

Spawning: The easy availability of broodstock animals is a wonderful benefit to potential breeders. Juveniles will require several to many months of conditioning and growout before sexual maturity is reached. It is best to place a small group of 4 to 8 specimens in a 20 or 30-gallon tank and grow them up without other tankmates. When properly fed with enriched mysids, grated squid and shrimp and other seafoods, the females become noticeably swollen and a hierarchy is formed among the group. Fin flicking and slow patrols of circular swimming around conspecifics are the usual route to asserting dominance. No harm is usually done. Spawning tanks should be 15 to 30 gallons depending on the number of fish present. Bare tanks with PVC sections are best to minimize stress during capture of brooding males.

Spawning is generally initiated in the twilight hours shortly before the lights turn off. In the wild this species is mostly crepuscular, being active during periods of low light around dawn and dusk. In captivity, fish become very active shortly before the lights are scheduled to turn off and before they come on. Chasing and biting are common hints of approaching spawning in this species. Bites are generally harmless and directed at the sides of the fish. Fin flicking is also common and involves the dorsal and pelvic fins.

Pajama Cardinal (*Spheramia nematoptera*): color-enhancing rations help bring out this species' psychedelic pigmentation.

A photoperiod of 14 hours of light is ideal to initiate spawning, and some hobbyists suggest a slight increase in water temperature will initiate spawning. When maintained under ideal conditions and well fed, the Pajama Cardinal will maintain a spawning cycle of roughly 2 to 3 weeks. Males commonly incubate large egg masses containing nearly 6,000 to 8,000 eggs. Hatching occurs on the 7th or 8th night at 80°F. Males should be removed to the rearing tanks the day prior to hatching.

Larval Rearing: Larvae measure roughly 3.4 to 3.9 mm at hatching and are routinely reared by scientific laboratories. Apparently, the addition of size-sorted wild plankton greatly increases overall survival as first feeding larvae need to consume small prey organisms. Small-strain rotifers can be used effectively, assuming they are properly enriched. Round rearing vessels treated with greenwater and supplied with water exchange from a central system should be employed when rearing this species.

Artemia nauplii can usually be added to the diet at around 10 to 12 days after hatching. By day 15 the larvae are remarkable in appearance with deep pectoral fins and hints of color. Metamorphosis is apparent around day 24 after

Bluestreak or Threadfin Cardinalfish (*Apogon leptacanthus*): young captive-reared specimens beginning to exhibit full adult coloration.

hatching and may extend to 34 or more days in slower growing individuals. By this time the larvae have grown to 12-18 mm in length and display hints of adult coloration. Swimming is limited after metamorphosis and individuals hover near the standpipe or accumulated debris.

Bluestreak or Threadfin Cardinalfish

Apogon leptacanthus (Bleeker, 1856)
Maximum Length: 6 cm (2.3 in.).
Sexual Allocation: Gonochorist.

This diminutive, beautiful species occasionally makes its way into retail outlets and is an ideal candidate for captive culture. Groups of *A. leptacanthus* create an impressive display in larger displays and are ideally suited to reef aquariums, where they are entirely safe with corals and most ornamental invertebrates other than small shrimps.

This species has been successfully reared in captivity, although larval rearing is a bit of a challenge. Broodstock is easily conditioned if healthy specimens are obtained.

Some specimens seem prone to shipping stress and often arrive at retail outlets in poor shape. Captive-cultured offspring would be welcomed by an enthusiastic market.

Habitat & Range: Found from the Red Sea to Samoa and Tonga, north to the Ryukyus, south to Micronesia and New Caledonia, *A. leptacanthus* often forms enormous daytime aggregations containing many thousands of individuals. Schools are often mixed with Orangelined Cardinals (*Archamia fucata)* and Girdled Cardinals (*A. zosterophora)*. They prefer branching corals and often congregate within the branches of fire coral. The entire mass can be seen hovering over the coral from a distance. On approach the fish slowly retreat within the protective reaches of the coral colonies. Towards dusk these schools can be seen becoming increasingly active. Courtship activity can usually be observed with individual pairs separating from the group to perform their mating activities.

Sexual Dimorphism: Subtle sexual dimorphism such as body size is common. Females are usually slightly larger than males. Some anecdotal information suggests the filament on the first dorsal fin is longer in males. Females in good condition become well-rounded with developing eggs. This species maintains pair bonds throughout the reproductive season and pairs are easily identifiable, keeping in close proximity to each other.

Spawning: Individual pairs or small groups consisting of five or six specimens can be maintained in 15 to 20-gallon aquariums. The bottom, back and side panels of the aquarium should be painted a dark color or covered to afford some isolation from outside traffic. Several cut lengths of 2 or 3-inch diameter PVC are all that is required in the breeding tank. A photoperiod of 14 hours of light and consistent feedings of high-quality feeds such as mysid shrimp and grated seafoods ought to result in cyclic reproductive behavior. Courtship is a near-continuous process among pairs. As reproduction nears, the pair exhibits heightened activity with parallel swimming and fin-flick-ing. As the female swells with eggs, courtship activity becomes frantic. Eventually, both male and female begin swimming parallel to each other, heads to the bottom, where the female spawns an egg mass nearly 2 cm in diameter. After release of the egg mass, the male immediately turns and takes them into his oral cavity.

Spawns contain from 300 to 1,000 eggs. Incubation lasts 7 to 8 days at 80°F. The male should be removed to the rearing tank the day prior to hatching. Larvae hatch 60 to 80 minutes after the lights have been turned off. Abnormal lighting during this period may delay hatching.

Larval Rearing: Larvae measure slightly over 3 mm in total length at hatching and begin feeding the following day. Small-strain rotifers are consumed by *A. leptacanthus* larvae and the bellies of examined larvae often take on a characteristic green glow from the ingested rotifers and phytoplankton. Mass mortality will ensue within the first two weeks of rearing if rotifers are not properly enriched. Wild zooplankton or copepod nauplii should be fed when available, as this greatly increases survival through the rearing phase.

Many scientific laboratories regularly culture this species using size-sorted wild plankton as the core first food for larval cardinals.

This species should not be reared in glass aquariums as the larvae are exceptionally prone to stacking up in sharp corners. Greenwater is an important addition to the rearing tank during the early larval stages to promote dispersion in the water column and aid in successful feeding. Newly hatched *Artemia* is accepted by the 10th day after hatching, at which time the larvae measure near 8-10 mm in length. Metamorphosis is a gradual process with juveniles settling to the bottom at 28 to 30 days after hatching. The most difficult aspect in culturing this species is supplying adequate nutrition during the first feeding stage.

Fivelined Cardinalfish (*Cheilodipterus quinquelineatus*): an interesting species and a good candidate for captive breeding.

Fivelined Cardinalfish

Cheilodipterus quinquelineatus (Cuvier, 1828)
Maximum Length: 12 cm (4.7 in.).
Sexual Allocation: Gonochorist.

The Fivelined Cardinal is a robust and common species throughout its range. It is occasionally imported and their menacing teeth are sure to thrill aquarium observers. This is a hardy species well-suited to captive propagation, but few aquarists have attempted to rear them. Fivelines have been successfully reared for many years at scientific institutions, proving an ideal research model for ecologists.

Habitat & Range: Most species exported to the aquarium hobby originate in Indonesia and the Philippines. The complete range of this species is reported from the Red Sea to Mozambique, extending eastward to the Pitcairn Group, east of Polynesia, north to southern Japan and south through the Great Barrier Reef to Lord Howe Island. Fivelined Cardinals can be found in virtually every marine habitat throughout this range. Mostly solitary, individuals of this species are commonly sighted in branching corals and under ledges created by the mosaic of reef structure. Heterosexual pairs are usually found close by, but rarely in the same haunt. Adults in some areas form loose aggregations under large ledges. Juveniles commonly find protection near the spines of sea urchins and tentacles of sea anemones.

Sexual Dimorphism: As with most cardinals, few external differences exist between the sexes. Males are often slightly larger than females and have more robust heads. On the reef, males are easily distinguished by their expanded buccal cavities while brooding eggs. In captivity, females become well rounded. Males often appear emaciated with pinched bellies even when well supplied with adequate intake of quality foods.

Spawning: Acquiring broodstock of this species is often challenging, as few local aquarium stores stock more than one or two at a time. Random pairing is the best route to obtaining a heterosexual pair of *C. quinquelineatus*. If a small

ARTIFICIAL INCUBATION OF CARDINALFISH EGGS

In rare cases, it may be necessary to incubate and hatch cardinalfish eggs artificially. Egg masses are often spit from the buccal cavity by inexperienced males in captivity. Generally, first-time spawners prove unreliable at brooding the eggs to full-term. This condition usually solves itself as males settle into their broodcare duties over the next several spawns. It is, therefore, best to leave first-time brooding males in the privacy of the broodstock tank for the first two or three spawns to let this problem sort itself out. Inevitably, larvae are sacrificed to filter intakes, but this technique often goes a long way in securing the male's cooperation in brooding future spawns.

In high-traffic areas, males often become nervous and spit the brood or swallow them before hatching. This is most common during transfer to the rearing tank. Every effort should be made to make this transition as stress-free as possible. Using water from the broodstock system and a specimen cup instead of a net to transfer the male alleviates much of this stress.

Still, there are times when males repeatedly spit their egg masses. A technique first introduced to me by Aaron Kaminski in the early 1990s has proven extremely successful in artificially incubating and hatching cardinalfish eggs. Originally, this artificial incubator design served to hatch eggs stripped from the mouths of freshwater anabantoids—wild mouthbrooding bettas. A 12-inch section of clear plastic tubing (undergravel lift tubing is ideal) is first cut in equal halves. Using a butane lighter, the cut edge of one half is slowly heated.

It is important to use a thin wall tube similar to aquarium lift tubing. Then, this section of tube is massaged over the other section to form a coupler, allowing the two halves to be fitted together. A small section of netting is then inserted between the two halves and they are slipped together. A rubber diaphragm from an air pump is fitted snuggly on one end of the tube. A small section of rigid airline tubing is then inserted into the existing hole in the diaphragm. Flexible tubing is then stretched to a gang valve to control water flow through the incubator. The gang valve is attached to a small powerhead, water pump or central filtration system instead of an air pump. Suction cups and holders from aquarium heaters are positioned around the incubator to hold it upright in a rearing tank.

With the egg mass positioned above the net divider in the top half of the incubator, the water flow should be adjusted to keep the mass in suspension. The flow of water should spin the egg mass freely without settling, but not strong enough to blow the mass out the top. The diameter of the tubing may have to be increased to facilitate the necessary water flow around the eggs depending on the size of the egg mass.

Initially the incubator can be set up so that the top of the incubator is above the surface of the rearing tank. Then, when hatching is expected, the incubator can be lowered below the surface of the rearing tank by about half an inch.

When hatching occurs the larvae will exit the top of the incubator into the rearing tank.

group of fish can be established in a 30 or 40-gallon aquarium, behavioral cues will quickly determine if a compatible pair is present. Once a male-female pair is established, they will generally not tolerate conspecifics. In the Philippines, I have observed pairs stationed in coral heads roughly five feet apart. Towards evening both members of the pair became increasingly active, moving nearer to the shared boundary. Members of these pairs approach one another head-on while quivering their tails, sometimes their whole bodies. These displays sometimes stopped and the pair would separate or they would continue with a ballet of circles and parallel swimming. Any conspecific was quickly chased away. Fivelined Cardinals are promiscuous spawners that do not seem to maintain a pair bond. When multiple specimens are placed in a large tank, spawning will occur with different partners.

Pairs should be maintained in 20-gallon or larger aquariums with cut lengths of 2 or 3-inch diameter PVC pipe. Fivelines are not fussy eaters in captivity and condition well on grated squid and shrimp, mysids and marine fish flesh. This species has a large mouth with noticeable teeth and benefits from the occasional treat of live feeder fish and ghost shrimp. Temperature should be maintained from 78-80°F and the photoperiod should be set to 14 or 15 hours. Successful spawning occurs after a lengthy courtship that starts near dusk. The pair assumes a parallel posture near the bottom, at times creating a curve with the two pressing their bodies against one another. The egg mass is fertilized during release and immediately taken into the male's buccal cavity. Incubation lasts 8 days. The male should be removed to a rearing tank on the day hatching is expected.

Larval Rearing: Larvae measure just over 3 mm at hatching and begin feeding on enriched rotifers the following morning. Proper enrichment of the rotifers is critical to successful rearing. Water exchange from the central

Banggai Cardinalfish (*Pterapogon kauderni*): obvious pair swimming in close proximity to each other and male, foreground, with more prominent jaw structure.

system should be initiated each evening to clear residual rotifers from the water column and maintain proper water chemistry. Prior to the first morning feeding, the water can be slowed to a drip or shut off until evening. Enriched rotifers should be added to the rearing tank at least twice daily to maximize the efficacy of enrichment products. When available, size-sorted wild plankton or copepod nauplii should be added to the diet of early-stage larvae. *Artemia* nauplii can be added by day 10 to 12. Metamorphosis is generally completed by day 25, when juveniles take on a cream color with faint horizontal banding.

Banggai Cardinal

Pterapogon kauderni (Koumans, 1933)
Maximum Length: 8 cm (3.1 in.).
Sexual Allocation: Gonochorist.

Tracked down and presented to the aquarium world only recently by Dr. Gerald Allen and underwater photographer Roger Steene in 1995, the Banggai Cardinalfish is now commonly spawned and reared in captivity. The first Banggai Cardinals sold for exorbitant amounts of money in some areas of the United States. Demand was over-

Wild Banggais as sheltering in a longspined sea urchin and, right, Martin Moe's surrogate urchin made of wood skewers.

whelming. Almost immediately, concerns arose about over-collection of this unique species, whose range is reportedly limited to the remote Banggai Islands of Indonesia.

Since that time the price of these fish has dropped dramatically and captive breeding has been compared to raising guppies, albeit on a marine aquarium level. Still, many reef-protection groups point to this fish as threatened with extinction by overcollection for the aquarium trade. Small-scale breeders can play an important role in preventing the demise of this species in the wild.

The Banggai Cardinal is one of a select few in this family that does not produce pelagic larvae. The male orally incubates the eggs until the young have developed into fully formed juvenile fish with the characteristics that resemble adult fish. Twenty-one days after spawning, the male releases tiny, miniature imitations of itself that readily feed on newly hatched *Artemia*. The young do not go through any form of metamorphosis and the trouble of feeding the larvae and transferring them to a rearing aquarium is diminished. The Banggai Cardinal is ill-suited to commercial aquaculture and the most common source of this fish in the future is apt to be dedicated marine fish enthusiasts. If this is, indeed, the guppy of the marine hobby, it can be

a triumph for sustainable fishkeeping.

Habitat & Range: This species has a very narrow geographic distribution. They are apparently only found in the shallow water surrounding the island of Banggai and a few neighboring islands in the Indo-Pacific. Since they do not produce pelagic larvae, the geographic distribution is limited. This species lives within the spines of longspined *Diadema setosum* sea urchin where they are difficult to see or reach. They are often found in large aggregations surrounding clusters of sea urchins as they disperse at night to feed.

Spawning: With a keen and trained eye, picking out male and female Banggai Cardinals from a group is an easy task. Within a large aggregation of cardinalfish found in the wild, many individual pairs can be found. If a group of Banggais is kept in a small tank, quarrels will ensue until only one dominant pair remains. Large public aquariums often display peaceful aggregations in 300-gallon tanks or larger.

Females are more rounded than males. It has been said that the dorsal rays of males are somewhat longer than females. It may or may not be true. The most reliable indicator of an individual's sex is the shape of the head and the jaw. When compared to a female, the male has a more massive head and more pronounced lower jaw befitting his mouthbrooding duties. Females have a more rounded-off look with a less prominent jaw. If a fish shop happens to be offering many larger individuals, look for two that seem to be hanging out together. These fish form pairs and rarely leave one another's side. Young specimens will school together and are difficult to sex. If only juveniles are available, a small group may have to be purchased. As soon as a pair seems to have formed, the others should be removed and conditioning accelerated.

It is almost a guarantee that a heterosexual pair will attempt to spawn if properly housed and well-fed. The fish will breed in just about any marine aquarium whether it is set up as a bare breeding tank or a decorative community tank in the living room. When the male releases the young, they must be recovered quickly so an aquarium with relatively few obstructions is best. A 20-gallon high aquarium with gravel and a few rocks would be best for housing a single pair of Banggai Cardinals.

It is the female of this species that initiates courtship and spawning. A well-rounded belly in the female and heightened activity between the pair signal spawning. Upon completion, the male holds up to 50 eggs within his buccal (mouth) cavity. The male does not feed at this time, but continues to display normal behavior and can be seen in the mid-water column hovering as if nothing significant has occurred. As the larvae grow, the male's gills swell outward.

An interesting note about brood care in this atypical species is that the female protects the male during this time—She will drive away fish several times her size. Males incubate the eggs for 21 days before releasing the fully developed young. The fry should be removed to the safety of a separate tank as soon as they are noticed.

In captivity, males often prove unreliable brood tenders, eating the eggs or larvae sometime after spawning. Even when disturbance levels outside the aquarium are low, the male may still eat the clutch. It is uncertain why this occurs, but it probably stems from stress. If the male eats the first spawn, no alarm should be raised. However, if this occurs continuously, the eggs or larvae should be stripped from the male's mouth a day or two before he normally eats them since he will predicably swallow the clutch on the same day of the cycle. The male should be caught with an aquarium net and held in one hand. The mouth can be pried open with a finger or a plastic spoon to serve as an exit for the young. With the mouth open, sway the male back and forth

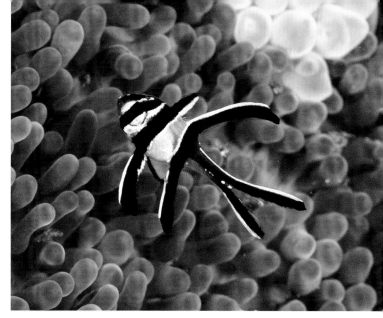

Baby Banggai is easily raised and is a perfect miniature of its parents the day it emerges from the male's mouth cavity.

in the water to push the eggs or larvae out. Depending on the stage of development, the eggs can be placed in an egg tumbler or can be placed in a small rearing tank. Alternately, the male can be kept in a breeding trap with a slotted or mesh bottom to allow the emerging fry to escape.

Larval Rearing: The young are tiny, perky miniatures of their parents (perhaps the cutest newly hatched fish known) when they emerge from the male's mouth, and they are able to take newly hatched *Artemia* and grow quite rapidly. Little difficulty is encountered with raising this species. The hardest part is getting the male to incubate the eggs for the full term, or artificially incubating the eggs.

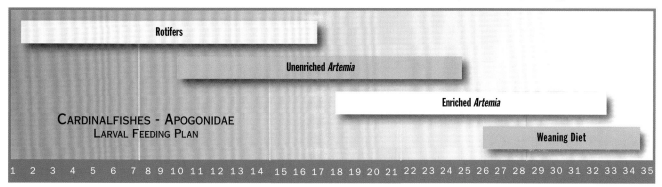

CARDINALFISHES - APOGONIDAE
LARVAL FEEDING PLAN

Rotifers

Unenriched *Artemia*

Enriched *Artemia*

Weaning Diet

1 2 3 4 5 6 7 8 9 10 11 12 13 14 15 16 17 18 19 20 21 22 23 24 25 26 27 28 29 30 31 32 33 34 35

Guidelines: Feed rotifers at 10/ml; unenriched *Artemia* nauplii less than 12 hrs. old; enriched *Artemia* less than 24 hrs. old.

GOBIES

FAMILY GOBIIDAE

Constituting one of the largest families of marine fishes, the gobies have representatives in virtually all aquatic environments, including freshwater, brackish water and saltwater. Some 2,000 species have been described, including some of the tiniest verbebrates on earth.

The peak abundance and variety of the 200 genera of gobies is, however, reached on tropical coral reefs. Gobies are typically small, elongated, benthic fish that offer a multitude of different appearances and interesting characteristics that make them one of the most popular groups of fishes kept in marine aquariums.

One distinguishing feature of most goby species is the presence of a fused pelvic fin that has evolved into a suction-cup-like disc that enables the fish to attach itself to solid surfaces. The so-called cleaner gobies are able to skip along the body of the host fish, sticking to the scales by using this fin while picking off external parasites. Other species use the fin to attach to solid substrates in turbulent waters or surge zones. Only true gobies exhibit this trait.

Most gobies are relatively-site attached and are thus not stressed by captive conditions. Most will readily spawn in captivity. Far more species of gobies have spawned in captivity than any other family of marine ornamentals. However, few of these species have been reared past metamorphosis, probably owing to the fact that few aquarists have tried—or known how to deal with the larvae. Some gobies have proven easier to spawn than others. The Neon Goby (*Elacatinus oceanops)* was a pioneer species in marine fish breeding in the late 1950s and has since been accompanied by many others, including several hybrids.

Gobies are perfect candidates to anyone wishing to propagate marine ornamentals and are surely a group offering the potential to expand the realm of species in captive propagation. Many species commonly available to the ma-rine trade regularly spawn in aquariums. The Yellow Watchman Goby (*Cryptocentrus cinctus*) is one such example. Isolated individuals seem quite territorial, and explosive battles often erupt if randon conspecifics are placed in the same tank. However, random pairing will ultimately result in a compatible male-female pair that will spawn regularly. This species has recently been raised in Europe. Similarly, the many species in the genus *Valencienna*, the Sleeper Gobies, routinely spawn in aquariums. The eggs of these species are quite large, as are the resulting larvae. Most species will prove to be easily raised. As many of these species are not as popular as dwarf angels or the dramatically colored damselfishes and clownfishes, commercial breeding establishments are unlikely to begin producing them in large numbers. This is a great opportunity for the home based hobbyist-breeder.

Sexual Dimorphism: The Gobiidae family exhibits varying degrees of sexual dimorphism with genital papilla morphology being universal to the family. External features for most species are limited to subtle differences in color and size. Comparably few offer drastic differences; however, extreme variation of these characteristics exists within the family and within same generas. Cleaner Gobies, Sand-sifting or Sleeper Gobies (*Valenciennea*), Coral Gobies (*Gobiodon*) and most Cleaner Goby species in the subgenus *Gobiosoma* or *Elacatinus* display sexual dimorphism to a limited degree. Females are typically more robust, displaying well-rounded abdomens close to the onset of spawning. Males are larger, often displaying sunken-in stomachs and appearing emaciated, and their cranial regions generally exhibit a heavier profile. Males of certain species display heightened coloration throughout the year, while others display this coloration only during courtship and spawning. Male Redheaded Gobies (*Gobiosoma puncticulatus),* among others, display temporary sexual dichromatism near spawning. The head region becomes dark, charcoal-gray fading to white near the caudal region. Male Sand Gobies (*Coryphopterus* spp.) often develop exaggerated dorsal and anal rays reaching past the caudal peduncle, and in extreme cases past the tip of the tail fin.

Citron or Yellow Coral Goby: member of a group of much-appreciated reef fishes that offer would-be breeders many species not previously bred in captivity.

As stated, the genital papilla structure easily identifies an individual's sexual function. Females exhibit short, blunt papilla, roughly equal in length and width. That of the male is elongated and tapered. When compared side-by-side, the two are unmistakable. In order to utilize this technique for sexing individual broodstock candidates, a microscope or magnifying glass is necessary. When the fish is restrained in an upside-down position, the genital area can be examined with the aid of a light-source magnification. In some species with light colored ventral scales, methylene blue can be swabbed on the area to offer contrast for better visual determination of sex.

Sex Allocation: As with so many aspects of fish biology, useful generalizations about sexual allocation patterns are difficult to make for the huge Gobiidae family. Protogynous hermaphroditism, bi-directional hermaphroditism, gonochorism, and bi-directional juvenile gonads are found among the various goby genera. Sex-change patterns have been examined many times within the family, although information on many species is lacking.

At one extreme, the Neon Goby complex (*Elacatinus* spp.) exhibit genetically determined sexes with no ability to change sex (gonochorism). These gobies are most often found in pairs or small schools throughout the year. On the other extreme, species of *Paragobiodon* and *Gobiodon* are reported to be bi-directional hermaphrodites. These fish typically live in small social units controlled by a dominant male. Females establish a hierarchy and only the dominant female is functional

Needlespine Coral Gobie (*Gobiodon aspicularis*): female depositing eggs on *Acropora* branch. Note genital papilla (arrow).

and spawns. In the absence of a dominant male, the dominant female will change sexual function and take on the role of the male, while one of the non-spawning females assumes the role of the spawning functional female. When two males are isolated within the confines of a coral head or aquarium, the submissive individual reverts to female sexual function.

One interesting trademark of many species of gobies is the presence of an AGS (accessory gonadal system) within the gonad. The exact function of this is unknown, but it is most probable that the AGS facilitates sex change. Testicular tissue has been found in functional ovaries and oocytes are regularly found within function testes. Typically the presence of opposing sex cells within gonads is thought to be a sign that sex change has occurred or is being undertaken.

In sum, the sex-change patterns of gobies are diverse, and it is possible that many more species are capable of bi-directional sex allocation. The following descriptions provide the known profiles of individual sex change and reproductive patterns for a number of species that are good candidates for captive breeding.

Citron Goby, Yellow Coral Goby

Gobiodon citrinus (Rüppell, 1838)
Maximum Length: 6 cm (2.3 in.).
Sexual Allocation: Probably similar to the Broadbanded Clown Goby (*G. histrio*); protogynous with the potential for bi-directional sex change.

The colorful *Gobiodon citrinus* is well-known in the aquarium hobby, but with available specimens coming almost exclusively from the wild. Because it is quiet sedentary, often remaining motionless resting on top of a coral head for hours on end, the Citron Goby has a relatively limited following. Reef aquarists should consider them a good candidate for small-polyp-stony-coral-dominated tanks, as they add a dimension of realism and may improve the health of the coral colonies they inhabit (providing water circulation and nutrients). Interestingly, all coral gobies secrete distasteful mucus from the epidermis to avoid predation. This species is easily spawned, but the diminutive size of the resulting larvae make rearing this fish a challenge.

Habitat & Range: This species is widely distributed throughout the Red Sea and Indo-Pacific region, living interstitially among the tightly clustered branches of *Acropora* and *Pocillopora* stony corals. The fish are usually found in monogamous pairs or small harems. They never leave the protection of the coral branches. Exhibiting a laterally compressed body, these gobies easily maneuver between the branches of coral heads in this well-defined micro habitat.

Sexual Dimorphism: Females of this species are skewhat pale in comparison to the more brightly colored males. The fluorescent lines present on the head region and base of the dorsal fin are more vibrant in males. Females fill with eggs as spawning approaches. The shape of the genital papilla is the best indicator of sex. A specimen should be placed in a small aquarium or clear specimen cup and viewed from below; a magnifying glass is useful.

Social Structure & Reproductive Biology: The most commonly studied species within this group is *Gobiodon histrio*. For the purpose of this short discussion, I refer only to this species, although other similar Coral Gobies probably have similar habits and requirements.

In the wild, only one male and one female are sexually mature in any given coral head, with any other individuals found living therein being sexually immature. Protogynous sex change is the main mode of sex change and occurs when the male is lost or is killed. The functional female will change and assume the male's role, while one of the immature fish will become the functional female. An interesting trait has been described in this species and occurs in situations where the risk of moving to another coral head in search of a mate is high. Bi-directional sex change occurs, allowing a male to revert to its original female function to make spawning successful in female-limited coral heads and the immediate area. Using this knowledge, the breeder can easily form pairs with any two individuals obtained.

Diet: The conditioning diet of this species should contain the typical seafood gelatin paste used for others. Much algae should be provided in the diet as well. Live foods such as *Artemia* and black worms are welcomed.

Spawning: Simple, bare 5 or 10-gallon aquariums make ideal spawning aquariums. The tank should be painted black or covered on the bottom and three sides and supplied with clay flowerpots as spawning sites. The flowerpots should be small with an open-end diameter of no more than 4 inches. It is best to spawn this species as isolated pairs. Small harems of one male and roughly three females are compatible, but only the dominant female will spawn.

Often times, pairs can be picked out of a dealer's aquarium with relative ease. Simply look for two individuals that seem to be compatible with each other, resting close together. Alternately, the largest specimen can be chosen and assumed a male. Next, the smallest and dullest-colored specimen is chosen and hoped to be a female. Given time and their ability to change sexes, the fish should establish a pair. The fish are usually cheap enough that a small group can be purchased and allowed to form their own pairs. Individual pairs can then be removed to isolated spawning aquariums. Live black worms are useful when establishing pairs. It seems to give females the needed metabolic reserves to develop eggs quickly and spawn sooner than they would

Citron Goby (*Gobiodon citrinus*): pairs are easy to spot and will spawn readily if given a good diet including black worms.

when fed normal aquarium fare. This is an important consideration when forming pairs. It is advantageous for females to spawn as soon as possible after being isolated with a male to avoid aggressive advances.

When a heterosexual pair of gobies is present and well fed, it does not take long for the fish to begin spawning. Again, live foods, especially black worms, are useful and recommended to induce the first spawn. They can then be weaned onto a diet of fresh and frozen seafoods.

The eggs are deposited on the roof of the clay flowerpot and guarded by the male. Spawning may occur at any time during the day. Courtship usually begins in early morning and spawning begins shortly thereafter. Spawning is usually cyclical, occurring every 4 days once started. The eggs hatch on the fourth night, soon after the lights have been turned out. The flowerpot that has been used as a spawning receptacle should be removed on the day prior to hatching and transferred to a rearing aquarium. An airstone should be placed near the spawn to keep the eggs well aerated and act as an aid in hatching.

Larval Rearing: The larvae are phototaxic and drawn to any light source. There is no yolk sac present and the larvae begin feeding on small non-elusive prey such as ciliates and small rotifers the following day. Small-strain rotifers with a total length less than 180 μm are necessary for first feeding. Mixed wild plankton fed concurrently with rotifers produce the best results. It takes roughly 5 days for larvae to develop substantially to accept a normal larval diet of large rotifers (~240μm). Larval growth is prolonged, and newly hatched *Artemia* are not usually added to the diet until near day 17. During the first two weeks, greenwater should be added to ensure that feed organisms are of sufficient nutritional value and to aid in feeding success.

Metamorphosis begins on day 33. After completing metamorphosis, the young should be supplied with PVC structures and clay flowerpots to perch on. Coloration begins to appear as a diffuse yellow at day 40.

The most difficult aspect of propagating this species is supplying the first food organism in high enough densities to make feeding successful. Mortalities are highest during this stage, as well as near metamorphosis. Survival rates are often erratic, probably owing to the quality and density of first-feed organisms available.

Gobiodon histrio, *G. unicolor*, and *G. okinawae* are similar species raised in much the same manner. All are commonly available. The Yellow Clown Goby (*G. okinawae*) may prove slightly more difficult to raise than the others.

Neon Goby

Elacatinus oceanops (Jordan, 1904)
Maximumm Length: 3.5 cm (1.4 in.).
Sexual Allocation: Gonochorist.

Neon Gobies are adorned with blue and black horizontal stripes similar to the wrasses of the genus *Labroides*, which warrant their cleaning behavior. These fish are often seen laying eggs in fish shops, proving exactly how easy they are to spawn. The Neon Goby is cheap, easily spawned and reared, making it a perfect beginner fish. Several other related species can be assumed to have the same habits and requirements for breeding. (Some texts use the older name *Gobiosoma* for this genus.)

Neon Goby will spawn readily in small broodstock aquariums.

Habitat & Range: All species mentioned are isolated to the Caribbean from southern Florida to the Bahamas and Bermudas. The so-called Cleaner Gobies (*E. oceanops*, *E. genie*, *E. evelynae*, *E. randalli* and *E. illecebrosum*) occupy vertical holdfasts such as barrel sponges. The other members of the complex are typically found on coral rubble.

Sexual Dimorphism: Few external differences are apparent in any of these species. Monogamous pair bonds are formed and pair recognition has been demonstrated. Since these gobies are inexpensive, retail shops usually have a tank full of them. If you peer into an aquarium containing many individuals, mated pairs are usually evident. Any two fish that remain by each other's side is a good bet to be a pair. Males can often be seen courting females from a cave or pit dug in the substrate. Sometimes, males can be seen guarding eggs on the glass or hard substrate in the aquarium. If no obvious pairs are observed, purchase a group. Females will usually be somewhat larger and plumper than the slim-bodied males. If the fish do not spawn after several weeks of heavy feeding, purchase another individual to add to the pair. Watch their behavior. Males will usually display to one another, although physical contact rarely follows. Females will be approached and courted from a side position forming a T-shape.

Diet: Smaller aquarium fare is important. Chopped squid, shrimp and other seafoods are a good staple. Additional feedings of enriched *Artemia* (either newly hatched or adult), black worms, and prawn eggs should all be added to the diet routinely.

Spawning: A 10-gallon aquarium is all that is needed for a pair of gobies. The fish would probably spawn in aquariums even smaller than this. The aquarium can be bare or decorated with gravel. Spawning caves should be provided with cut lengths of PVC either capped on one end or pushed into the gravel substrate. No live rock should be added, as this is often tempting as a spawning substrate. The male will occupy a cave and dig out a pit in front of it if gravel has been provided. Several caves should be provided as a choice for the breeders. Gray electrical PVC pipe is preferred over white.

There is little preparation involved in inducing a pair of Neon Gobies to spawn. After their introduction, assuming it is a heterosexual pair, the fish will usually spawn in less than a month's time, usually much sooner. If the pair seems reluctant to spawn, temperature should be the first factor considered. A normal maintenance temperature of 75-78°F is usually fine for spawning neon gobies. The temperature can be maintained at the lower end of this temperature range and perhaps even lower (around 72° F) for a few weeks before raising the temperature a few degrees. This will usually induce a spawn. Courtship begins in early morning and involve many different rituals. The now-swollen female will be approached by the male, and games of follow-the-leader are common. The male will swim abruptly up to the female, stop, perform some sort of exaggerated swimming motion and then disappear into the cave. Nest preparation and heightened activity are clues that spawning will soon follow.

One interesting feature of both courtship and nest preparation in the Neon Gobies is their use of the modified pelvic fin. The male will remain stationary with the aid of this fin and appear to swim in place. When he perches on top of the spawning cave, it can attract the female. When inside the spawning cave, he blows gravel and other debris out of the cave. The male will clean the surface of the cave with his mouth and ventral side between episodes of courting the female. If the female is receptive, she will approach the male's cave and the two will move in slow, hopping circles around one another. The male will at this point occasionally nudges the female's abdominal region.

Spawning is accomplished when both fish disappear inside the depths of the tube or cave, where they align their bodies side-by-side upside-down. While pressed tightly together, the female will deposit eggs on the roof of the cave, and the male will then fertilize them. The female may leave the cave several times, but the male rarely leaves. Spawning may last up to two hours with an end result of 50-250 eggs being deposited. The frequency of spawning is usually 7 to 28 days, with an average of every 14 days.

The 2 mm eggs hatch on the 7th to 10th day after spawning, depending on water temperature. The spawning cave should be removed to a rearing aquarium the day prior to hatching. Hatching occurs about an hour after the lights have been turned off. Hatching is often problematic when the eggs are removed from a tending male. A moderate flow of bubbles over the eggs is often sufficient to facilitate hatching, but if eggs fail to hatch on the expected day it may be necessary to induce hatching by artificial means. Hatching *E. oceanops* eggs is accomplished by placing the PVC section containing the spawn into a bowl of water. Without aeration a light is shined on the eggs for roughly 15 minutes. Then, a feather is used to stimulate the egg capsule. Such methods often produce poor hatch rates and some mortality, but yield some larvae with which to experiment.

Larval Rearing: The larvae are phototaxic and measure just over 3mm in length at hatching with fully pigmented eyes and a large mouth. Feeding commences on rotifers until day 10 when newly hatched *Artemia* are added. Growth rates are highly variable, and rotifers should be fed until day 17 or until all larvae are noticeably feeding on *Artemia*. Metamorphosis begins on day 26 and may take as long as 45 days. Coloration begins around the time of metamorphosis, beginning with black stripes and then blue.

Redhead Goby, Red Cap Goby

Elacatinus puncticulatus (Ginsburg, 1938)
Maximum Length: 6 cm (2.3 in.).
Sexual Allocation: Probably protogynous.

Redhead gobies arae often overlooked by aquarists due to their small size and benthic life style, but the growing popularity of nano-reefs and desktop or bookshelf tanks may change all that.

Redheads are excellent fish well suited to life in both peaceful community aquariums and reef aquariums. When viewed in close detail, these are truly beautiful fish blessed with intricate tracings of fluorescent red and orange. The dark blotches toward the rear of the body are the result of pigmentation in the skeletal material. Once difficult to obtain, this species is now readily available for home-based marine breeders. This is a perfect species for those aquarists not willing to dedicate a large amount of space to breeding and raising marines.

Habitat & Range: Redhead Gobies are found in the eastern Pacific along the shores of the Americas, being most common in southern Central America and northern South America. Preferring rubble areas on shallow reefs and lagoons, Redheads are most often found in close vicinity to one another. Typically, the territory of a male is large and encompasses the smaller domains of several females.

Sexual Dimorphism: Although no drastic differences are apparent, this species is easily sexed once several individuals are observed and compared. Males are always larger and have a more robust appearance, especially in the head region. The dark brown blotches present under the skin on the spine are also characteristic of the sexes. Males have fewer blotches that are more elongated than those in the females, which display more, smaller blotches. When maintained under ideal conditions and well-fed, females become quite robust and their abdomens extremely pronounced. During courtship and spawning, males display a charcoal-gray color quite noticeable in the head region fading to a slate gray or almost white near the caudal region.

Social Structure & Reproductive Biology: Like most members of the Gobiidae family, *Elacatinus puncticulatus* is relatively site-attached, as its small size makes long journeys dangerous, with high risk of predation. Males usually maintain a territory within which several females defend smaller domains against other females. Receptive females seek out the tending male to spawn. When maintained in a large species aquarium, this goby is very interesting to watch. In aquariums 125 gallons and up, they have room to display their true antics. Males will stake out territories as large as possible. When 2 or 3 males are present, the territories are equally distributed. When more than 3 males are present, aggression rises and submissive males are driven to the surface. There seems to be a minimum area that male Redheads are willing to accept. Females are very site attached, rarely straying a foot away from a favorite nook.

Diet: Redhead Gobies are adept at taking a wide variety of food morsels. Fresh frozen seafoods such as shrimp, squid, clam and scallop—all finely grated—work well as conditioning diets. Newly hatched *Artemia* is an excellent addition to the diet as is frozen adult *Artemia* and bits of live black worms. Prawn eggs, when available, are a similarly acceptable addition to the conditioning diet.

Spawning: Redhead Gobies are best maintained as isolated pairs in small bare aquaria supplied with PVC shelters as spawning sites. When maintained in groups in smaller tanks, a dominant male will harass other males eventually leading to malnourishment and stress to the submissive males. Similarly, females will quarrel amongst each other and establish a pecking order with the dominant female suppressing other females. Since the sexes are easily identifiable, creating heterosexual pairs is rarely problematic. Pairs can be maintained in aquariums as small as 2.5 gallons. When 2.5-gallon or 5-gallon aquariums are drilled, fitted with bulkheads and plumbed into a central filter system, several pairs can be maintained in a relatively small space while not sacrificing water quality. PVC lengths of 1/2-inch or 3/4-inch should be cut in approximately 3-inch sections to act as spawning sites. At least three or four of these should be present on the bottom of the aquarium. PVC pipe fittings such as elbows and Ts should be avoided

Redhead Goby (*Elacatinus puncticulatus*): small but interesting and perfectly suited to life in a nano-reef aquarium.

as they restricts visual your visual access and confirmation that a spawning has occurred.

After a heterosexual pair of red heads has been established and well-fed at least three times daily, spawning will usually begin within a month. It is typically the female that initiates spawning. Her ovaries will be well swollen at this time, and she will appear to have swallowed a jellybean. At this time, the female becomes increasingly active in approaching the male and his chosen spawning site. This activity may persist all day or for several days, the latter in first spawnings. Males sometimes display a characteristic sexual dichromatism during spawning. The head becomes a dark charcoal-gray that fades to white toward the tail region. In captive males this spawning color often does not develop, and spawning is quite straightforward. In most cases, the male seems to display only modestly, instead waiting for a receptive female to approach.

Spawning occurs on a 7-day cycle with first-spawns producing little more than 50 or so eggs. As females mature, they regularly produce 200 to 300 eggs per spawning. Male Redhead Gobies tend the clutch and rarely eat the eggs. Hatching occurs on the 6th night after spawning at a water temperature of 78° to 80° F. PVC shelters containing the spawn should be removed the day of hatching and placed in a rearing tank. The PVC shelter is held in a vertical position, preferably with a rubber band against the standpipe, and supplied with a steady airflow to mimic the actions of the male. Caution should be exercised when artificially incubating and hatching eggs. The general trend is to offer a weak flow of bubbles so as not to disturb the spawn. When airflow is too restricted, eggs often fail to hatch and will in some cases stagnate and fungus. A modest flow of air will provide agitation and oxygenation of the spawn. Spawns will hatch an hour or so after the lights have been shut off.

Larval Rearing: Larvae are 3.2 mm long at hatching and very slow growing. In my experience, glass rearing aquariums are ill-suited to raising Redheads. Instead, small round (or round-cornered), black rearing vessels should be chosen; utility sinks are ideal. The greenwater method of adding microalgae to the rearing tank to tint the water slightly aids early stage larvae from stacking up in corners.

Rotifers are offered at a density of roughly 10/mL the morning following hatching and maintained at this density until day 20. Rotifers should continue to be offered, albeit at lower densities, until all larvae are visibly feeding on newly hatched *Artemia*. Newly hatched *Artemia* is usually acceptable at day 15. Metamorphosis is delayed until day 36 to 42 in most cases, with some larvae requiring another 10 to 15 days to fully complete the transformation. Larval diet is important, and an increase in HUFAs will often shorten metamorphosis by as much as 10 days, as well as increasing their red coloration.

Greenbanded Goby, Banana Goby

Elacatinus multifasciatus (Steindachner, 1876)
Maximum Length: 3.5 cm (1.4 in.).
Sexual Allocation: Protogynous hermaphrodites.

Greenbanded Gobies, like so many others in the family, have been uncommon in the aquarium trade due to their small size but are now gaining popularity for nano-reef systems. For the aquarist looking for true beauty in a tiny package, Greenbanded Gobies are an ideal candidate. What

Greenbanded Goby (*Elacatinus multifasciatus*): tiny Caribbean species that is rapidly gaining popularity among nano-reef enthusiasts.

Social Structure & Reproductive Biology: Generally, one male Greenband will be found with 2 or 3 females in a very confined space in the surge zone. Typically, these micro niches are centered around small holes in pitted limestone. During the day, Greenbanded Gobies scurry around the base of sea urchins, utilizing the sharp spines as protection. At night these gobies seek out refuge in crevices as the sea urchins are nocturnal and disperse to graze. The dominant female within a social unit will transform sexual function in the absence of a dominant male. When new recruits settle to the reef and enter the social unit, they become functional females and enter the hierarchy at the bottom. Males will court and spawn with any receptive female nearby. The male guards the nest and will not spawn with other females until the eggs from the current clutch have hatched.

Greenbands lack in size, they make up for in coloration and pattern as well as humorous antics. This species is quite popular in Japan and deserves more attention elsewhere.

Habitat & Range: *Elacatinus multifasciatus* is quite common on intertidal, near-shore rocky reefs in the Caribbean, being found from Puerto Rico to the Virgin Islands and south to South America. Preferring limestone pitted rocky shores where wave action is considerably high, this species is difficult to collect in commercial numbers. The pelvic fin is well adapted for this high-surge environment.

Sexual Dimorphism: Greenbanded Gobies lack sexual dichromatism, but are dimorphic in regards to size and behavior. Males are virtually always larger than females, with a more robust cranial profile. Females are smaller, but with a well-rounded abdomen. Males are intolerant of other males, chasing and biting them relentlessly. Females occasionally quarrel with one another, but the severity of these conflicts is quite reduced. Male Greenbands normally do not display aggression toward females.

Diet: Small food morsels must be offered to accommodate the small mouth of this species. Ideal conditioning diets consist of finely grated shrimp, clam, squid and other fresh seafoods as well as newly hatched *Artemia*. Fish should be fed several times daily to induce spawning activity. Fresh frozen seafoods should be offered in the morning and evenings, with newly hatched *Artemia* being added several times throughout the day. This regime is an excellent conditioning diet that should trigger frequent spawns of robust eggs.

Spawning: Spawning is non-problematic, assuming a heterosexual pair is present and well-fed. In a manner similar to *E. puncticulatus,* Greenbanded Gobies will spawn in small quarters. Having a rack of small aquariums plumbed to a central filtration system works well and allows many pairs to be maintained in a confined space. Maintaining multiple pairs off sets the relatively small clutch sizes produced by females. Since pairs will readily spawn in aquariums of 2.5 gallons in capacity, it makes little sense to utilize larger aquariums. Some hobbyists operate large shallow aquariums with multiple breeder baskets hung on the inside for isolated pairs. Both methods produce equal results, and the increased water volume helps in maintaining ideal water conditions. Mesh baskets require regular cleaning to facilitate water exchange through the mesh.

Once pairs are isolated and well-fed, spawning is typically initiated within the first few weeks. The male becomes quite active in courting a receptive female, frantically darting up to the female's side, occasionally nudging her with outstretched fins, and then darting back to his cave. Females become rotund and the urogenital papilla is very evident prior to spawning.

In large aquariums, pairs often choose to spawn in corners, placing eggs on the silicone seams. Eggs placed in such an arrangement are impossible to remove for artificial hatching. Spawning shelters must be supplied throughout the tank bottom to offer a diversity of spawning sites. Straight lengths of 1/2-inch or 3/4-inch PVC are perfect spawning sites as they are easily removed for hatching. If a pair chooses to spawn repeatedly in a tank corner, a thin, clear plastic box, such as packing material, should be cut and fitted to the corner of the aquarium where spawning occurs. The pair will adhere the eggs on this box, thus allowing easy removal for hatching.

Spawning typically occurs in early morning, with as many as 250 eggs being adhered to the inside of the spawning cave. Males remain with the clutch, agitating and oxy-genating them until hatching at night on the 5th or 6th night after spawning. PVC pipes containing spawns should be removed the day hatching is expected and fastened vertically in the rearing tank with a moderate flow of air bubbles passing over the eggs.

Larval Rearing: Rearing tanks for the 3mm long larvae should be small, round, black containers rather than cube or rectangular-style glass aquaria. Microalgae added to the rearing tank helps evenly distribute larvae throughout the rearing chamber. (This is especially important if glass tanks are used with sharp corners.)

High rotifer densities and the addition of microalgae are important due to the small size of the larvae. A small-sized strain of rotifers is especially used with this species, and having reproducing population of these rotifers will provide the first-food needed by this species. Rotifers are added to a density of 10 to 15/mL for the first 10 days, after which they can maintained at approximately 5/mL until day 20. Newly hatched *Artemia* is generally acceptable by day 12 or 14. Larvae begin to settle from the water column and take on adult characteristics and coloration between days 29 and 35. Larval rearing is not particularly problematic, assuming sufficient prey densities and good water quality is maintained throughout the larval period. Mortality is typically highest around metamorphosis. Proper enrichment of rotifers is necessary to reduce mortality during metamorphosis.

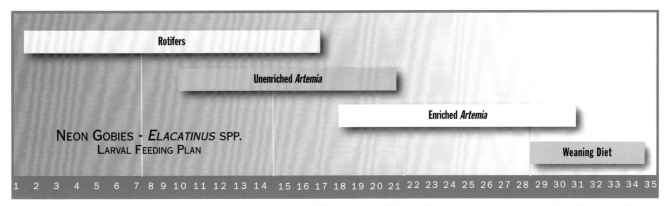

NEON GOBIES - *ELACATINUS* SPP.
LARVAL FEEDING PLAN

Rotifers

Unenriched *Artemia*

Enriched *Artemia*

Weaning Diet

1 2 3 4 5 6 7 8 9 10 11 12 13 14 15 16 17 18 19 20 21 22 23 24 25 26 27 28 29 30 31 32 33 34 35

Guidelines: Feed rotifers at 10/ml; unenriched *Artemia* nauplii less than 12 hrs. old; enriched *Artemia* less than 24 hrs. old.

BLENNIES

FAMILY BLENNIIDAE

No less than six different families are grouped together under "true blenny" banner. We will simply focus on the family Blenniidae, usually referred to as common blennies or combtooth blennies. Resembling gobies, many are elongated almost anguilliform or eel-like, swimming with fluid but sometimes awkward movements. These bottom-hugged fishes can truly seem out of place swimming in open water. With bulbous heads and large eyes and lips, most blennies are adapted to skip and hop over rocky substrates picking at filamentous algae beds and associated microfauna. Blennies, like the gobies, present a wonderful opportunity for an amateur breeder to raise a marine fish species for the first time.

Most blenny species offered for sale around the world make ideal aquarium inhabitants and are easily sustained with minimal effort on the part of the aquarist. Blennies offer many advantages to the would-be breeder. Being small, hardy, and site-attached, they are easily spawned in relatively small aquariums. Although lacking the vibrant colors of some reef fishes, blennies make up for this with comical behaviors and an often humorous appearances.

Blennies have several traits that make their captive propagation so promising. Blenny species produce large demersal eggs that are protected by the male until hatching. Most male blenny species will incubate several clutches of eggs deposited from different females at the same time within the same cavity. This allows a harem to be established and can create an almost-constant supply of larvae.

Sexual Dimorphism: Size dimorphism is common. Males are usually larger than females and remain thin compared to their robust counterparts. Sexing in most species can be reliably identified by the shape of their genital papilla. Similar to gobies, male blennies will exhibit a long tapered, almost pointed papilla. The female's remains short and blunt. A few species display sexual dichromatism.

The larvae of most blennies are quite large and well-advanced in development. Obtaining eggs is not difficult, provided that both sexes are present and well-fed. A species aquarium large enough to accommodate roughly six individuals should yield eggs in no time at all. No monogamous pair bond is established, and will males spawn with several females if they are available. This leads to the deposition of hundreds of eggs spawned by different females in varying stages of development.

I once collected a nest of Seaweed Blennies (*Parablennius marmoreus*) off the coast of Florida. The eggs were roughly two days old, spherical and measured 1 mm in diameter. The eggs of this species are very durable and easily incubated, and the development of the un-hatched larva is easily witnessed through the translucent membrane. The yolk is orange-red and forms a kidney shape around the developing eyes. Fishelson (1975) proposed that this rich orange-red coloration is caused by the presence of carotenoid pigments, which support oxygen metabolism and thus may help protect the spawn from deteriorating in areas devoid of high dissolved oxygen. This theory seems probable due to the placement of the blenny's spawn within the confines of burrows where water exchange is infrequent and oxygen levels below normal. This is a benefit to anyone wishing to rear blennies. Artificial incubation is easy.

I placed the nest in a large volume of filtered seawater with an airstone nearby. The spawn had been laid within the confines of an empty barnacle, so water movement was lacking in the interior. Once a day I used a syringe to pump a burst of fresh seawater into the nest, which was otherwise left unattended.

Hatching in Seaweed Blennies occurs on the 10th night after spawning. The day prior to hatching, the orange-red yolk sac will disappear, leaving a golden sheen and fully pigmented eyes. The larvae are roughly 3.2 mm at hatching with fully pigmented eyes, well-developed pectoral fins and no remnants of a yolk sac. Feeding begins immediately. Since there are usually eggs from multiple spawns present, hatching is sporadic and may stretch out across many days.

A vibrant group of captive-bred Canary Fang Blennies (*M. oualanensis*): this family offers hundreds of possible interesting species for small-scale captive breeders.

Other blenny species make ideal subjects for home breeders. Few of these species of blennies were commercially available just a few years ago. Now, several species have been spawned or reared in scientific laboratories, including *Hypsoblennius, Escsenius* (the so-called Comical Blennies), *Ophioblennius* (Big-lipped Blennies), *Meiacanthus* (Fang Blennies), and *Istiblennius* (Rockskippers) spp.

Recently, the Proaquatix ornamental-marine fish facility in Florida opened its doors to debut several first-time captive-bred blenny species. Commercial production of the Fang Blennies is probably their greatest achievement to date. These blennies possess venomous fangs and associated glands, which they use primarily as a predator deterrent. These fish seem quite comfortable swimming well above the reef structure because many predators know and respect their painful bite. They are very conspicuous on the reef and divers and snorkelers can approach within feet or inches of the unwary fish. This behavior holds in captivity as well, and these fish rarely seek shelter. They boldly swim in the open making them ideal aquarium inhabitants. Most species possess bright colors and intricate patterns and several species develop a forked tail that often grows to half the length of the body.

Reproduction in most blennies follows a common theme, I have included only a few representative species of which I have personal experience.

Striped Fang Blenny (*Meicanthus grammistes*) is an interesting, in-demand species highly appropriate for novice marine breeders. Many similar blennies have the same general breeding requirements and offer great opportunities for small-scale propagation.

Striped Fang Blenny, Black-Banded Blenny

Meiacanthus grammistes (Valenciennes, 1836)
Maximum Length: to 12 cm (4.7 in.).
Sex Allocation: Unknown; probably gonochorist.

Meiacanthus grammistes is a beautiful fish common to shallow reefs throughout its range. Once very common in the aquarium trade, imports are becoming sporadic. Captive breeding should ensure the regular availability of quality stock. As with most fang blennies, *M. grammistes* possess a venomous pair of fangs on the lower jaw. These are used primarily for defense care, but should be taken when handling fish so as to avoid a wasp-like sting.

Perfectly suited to novice marine fish breeders, this species is easily spawned in the confines of smaller tanks and the larvae present little difficulty in hatching and rearing. The young are readily marketable and a welcomed addition to the hobby.

Habitat & Range: Striped Fang Blennies are found over rubble and coral rock on shallow coral reefs and over sand and weeds in coastal lagoons. Distribution includes much of the western Pacific including Indo-China, Philippines, Papua New Guinea, Micronesia and northern Australia including the Great Barrier Reef.

Sexual Dimorphism: Little differences exist between the sexes. Males, as a rule, are somewhat larger than females and often appear much thinner. Large males sometimes appear emaciated. Captive females quickly become rotund with developing eggs. The most reliable method of obtaining captive pairs or harems is to place a group in a 30 gallon or larger aquarium and observe their social interactions. Courting males and those brooding eggs are quite intolerant of other males. Outside the spawning season, males will generally tolerate the presence of other males, but as spawning nears they quickly lose patience for competition. Courting and brooding males darken in coloration, whereas females maintain bright yellow and black stripes.

Spawning: When several to many *M. grammistes* are maintained in a species aquarium and fed a conditioning diet, courtship behavior should be observed rather quickly as long as heterosexual fish are present. The spawning aquarium containing a group of fish should be at least 30 gallons. Isolated pairs or trios can be maintained in smaller tanks of 15 to 20 gallons, assuming proper filtration is employed or the tanks is plumbed to a central system. Several spawning shelters should be provided with cut lengths of 1-inch PVC. Courtship in *Meiacanthus* spp. is initiated by the female. Ripe females signal their readiness to spawn by swimming back and forth in front of the male's shelter. Upon this approach, the male usually leaves the shelter and swims toward the female, stopping some distance away. Hovering above the substrate, the male then darts forward writhing his body side to side and sometimes quivering. Elaborate ballets are often observed, and the male performs underwater twists as he nears the female. Excited males generally nudge the female's abdomen and swim in tight circles around their mid bodies before moving off toward the spawning shelter in an exaggerated manner. Reappearing within seconds, the male sticks only his head from the spawning shelter and bobs in and out, often writhing from side to side. This seductive behavior is performed five or six times before he again darts out from the cave and invites the female from the water column. This display is often repeated several times before the female is successfully lured inside.

Once inside, the female deposits adhesive eggs on the ceiling of the provided shelter. Spawning occurs at roughly 3 to 7 day intervals, with each female depositing from 50 to over 200 eggs. Male *M. grammistes* will spawn with any receptive female, despite the presence of other spawns in the nest. No pair bond is established and multiple spawns from different females are deposited together. Eggs measure slightly over 1 mm and appear as flattened spheres with a flat surface for attachment to the substrate. Eggs are cream to light orange in color and darken within the next few hours or days to a bright orange color. When the eyes of the developing embryos have taken on a golden sheen hatching is imminent. Hatching occurs at 7 to 8 days at 80°F. The pipe containing the eggs is removed to a rearing vessel and fixed in vertically to the standpipe when the oldest spawn reaches 7 days. An air stone is then placed below the pipe to provide a gentle current over the eggs. Hatching occurs an hour or so after the lights have been turned off. The following morning the pipe is removed to a separate rearing tank and incubated until the next spawn hatches out. Typically three spawns are deposited together and the pipe is moved three times to separate rearing tanks.

Larval Rearing: Newly hatched larvae measure just under 3 mm in total length. Larvae congregate on the sides and surface of the rearing tank and lack any remnant yolk but have a large anterior portion of the body. Rotifers are added to a density of 10 to 12/mL on the first day of hatching. At 10 days after hatching, newly hatched *Artemia* is added to the diet. Larvae have grown to roughly 6 mm at this stage and have a well-developed feeding mechanism and exaggerated pectoral fins that aid in feeding efficiency.

Occurrence of metamorphosis is greatest around day 25, when larvae have reached around 10mm in length. Larvae exhibit drastic differences in growth rates and many will complete metamorphosis by day 15 to 20. These large individuals pose a real problem to smaller larvae. Cannibalism will occur if larvae are not well-fed. Many slow-growing larvae will require as much as 40 days to complete metamorphosis. Adult coloration is achieved around day 45. Larvae of this species are quite resilient and not prone to high mortalities during any particular stage of development.

Blackline Fang Blenny

Meiacanthus nigrolineatus (Smith-Vaniz, 1969)
Maximum Length: to 10 cm (3.9 in.).
Sex Allocation: Unknown; probably gonochorist.

Blackline Fang Blenny (*M. nigrolineatus*): an elegant reef fish much sought-after by aquarists and an ideal subject for small-scale marine breeders.

Meiacanthus nigrolineatus is a beautiful and highly sought-after species of fang blenny resembling the Yellow-tail Fang Blenny (*M. atrodorsalis*). Both species display a highly forked tail that often grows to extreme lengths in older males and make a bold impression when swimming high above the reef. The non-venomous blenny *Ecsenius gravieri* has evolved a color pattern resembling *M. nigrolineatus*; a convincing mimic.

Both *M. nigrolineatus* and its relative *M. atrodorsalis* are a real success story in marine aquarium fish production. When captured from the wild, both species are extremely prone to shipping stress, and obtaining quality stock for display or captive propagation can be a real challenge. Often, wild imports would arrive dead or appear extremely stressed and rarely survive the acclimation period. Other fish would arrive in somewhat lively condition, acclimate to tanks and begin feeding only to die mysteriously days or weeks later.

Whenever acquiring breeding stock, try to find captive-raised fish. These should prove disease-resistant and handle stress much better than wild imports. Spawning is generally easier to achieve when captive stock is obtained.

Habitat & Range: These blennies are found on shallow reefs over sand, rubble, rock and coral and in lagoons over sand and weeds in the Red Sea and Gulf of Aden.

Spawning: Being venomous, this species boldly swims over the reef and can usually be found hovering a few inches above some sort of structure. Spawning is relatively simple in home aquariums, and courtship is easily observed in the open. A species tank containing several individuals should be established and each fish provided a length of 1-inch-diameter PVC pipe for shelter. Courtship and spawning is similar to that described for *M. grammistes*, above. The eggs are a semi-spherical with the flat side attached to the substrate with sticky filaments. Hatching occurs on day 8 to 10 at water temperatures of 80 and 76°F respectively.

Larval Rearing: One-day-old larvae measure 3.7 mm in length and have no remnant yolk. Feeding on rotifers begins immediately after hatching. On day two after hatching, the larvae begin to utilize their pectoral fins and become good hunters of rotifers. By day 4 the larvae have reached a size of 4.5 mm in length. The toxic buccal gland which produces venom is developed by day 8, as reported by Fishelson (1975).

Most larvae will be capable of preying on newly hatched *Artemia* near day 10. Metamorphosis is peaks around days 20 to 25 and is accompanied by sedentary behavior. Erratic differences in growth are common and many larvae will require up to 35 days to complete metamorphosis. Adult coloration is reached near day 40.

Mimic Blenny or Striped Fang Blenny Mimic

Petroscirtes breviceps (Valenciennes, 1836)
Maximum Length: 15 cm (5.9 in.), usually to 11 cm (4.3 in.).
Sex Allocation: Unknown; probably gonochorist.
Although poorly represented in the aquarium trade, this

and other members of the genus *Petroscirtes* hold real potential for those interested in marine fish breeding. Reproduction follows the theme previously described for *Meiacanthus* and is generally non-problematic in captivity. Larvae are robust and easily reared with minimal effort.

This and several members of the genus are obvious mimics of the venomous fang blennies. *Petroscirtes breviceps* is said to mimic the Striped Fang Blenny. In the wild, these fish often form loose aggregations and it is difficult to discern the two species. Although non-venomous, *P. breviceps* does exhibit large canine teeth and will bite if trapped in a net or cornered by a keeper's hand. These teeth are used primarily for defense.

The coloration of this species varies widely. When they occur over reefs in association with *M. grammistes,* they exhibit a bright white background coloration with dark brown to black horizontal bands with brilliant yellow on the dorsal. In murky lagoons *P. breviceps* exhibits a mottled color of brown to olive green with a solid or broken vertical line running the length of the body. In captivity the coloration varies as well. Dark substrate will result in a mottled, dark color form, while over white gravel and with *M. grammistes* tankmates, it will typically put on a show of brilliant colors. Other members of the genus follow a similar reproductive scheme, and the similar Deceiver Fang Blenny (*P. fallax)* larvae are similar to those described for *P. breviceps.* A keen eye at a local pet shop will sometimes help if mislabelled as other species of blenny, using the ones they mimic.

Habitat & Range: *Petroscirtes breviceps* is most common on grass flats and sandy areas in the vicinity of coral reefs. Groups of this fish are often observed on shallow reefs throughout its range and can often be found in association with *Meiacanthus grammistes.* This species has a wide distribution stretching from East Africa to Papua New Guinea

Mimic Blenny pair in a broodstock tank, with rotund, egg-filled female, foreground, and male, at rear, awaiting her decision to enter the spawning cave.

including Australia, north to southern Japan and south to New Caledonia. In the Philippines I observed this species on coral reefs, sand flats and murky lagoons.

Sexual Dimorphism: Little differences exist between the sexes outside of the reproductive season. Males as a rule are somewhat larger than females and often appear much thinner. Captive females quickly become rotund with developing eggs. Coloration is useful only when courtship behavior is observed. Males remain dark and turn a bright olive green color at the height of courtship. Females generally turn white to light cream color with distinct horizontal bands. The most useful means of separating sexes is behavior. Males are generally intolerant of other males and will fight relentlessly. When multiple males are housed in the same tank, one will quickly assert dominance and harass all other males present. Unfortunately, the large canine teeth of dominant males can inflict significant damage to submissive males. If not removed, submissive males will perish as these threats continue. When removed to separate tanks, wounded males typically heal quickly.

Social Structure & Reproductive Biology: Very little

is known regarding the biology of this species. They occur over a wide variety of habitats and appear to display no set social unit. Spawning appears to be promiscuous and males maintain a home range centered around a spawning shelter. On coral reefs, these shelters seem to be deep crevices created by corals and rock while on sand flats a depression is usually occupied under rocks or isolated coral heads. In lagoons a preference for empty oyster shells has been noted.

For roughly one month I observed a group of these fish in a lagoon near Bicol, Philippines. Day after day the same fish appeared surrounding a fish cage. This was an interesting observation site as the fish did not occupy territory on the sea bottom. Instead, their habitat consisted of vertical walls and ceilings of net pens and oyster-encrusted bamboo platforms. Males remained stationary and never strayed too far from their oyster-shell nests hanging from submerged ropes. Multiple females were present and seemed remain in the general area of guarding males. At least two spawns were observed at any given time within the cavity of nesting males, suggesting that multiple spawning is not isolated to captive specimens. Only one male was found per rope and each seemed limited to a depth of no more than six feet. Several males were found guarding nests; however, the distance between males was roughly ten feet. On reefs and sand flats, this species is often found singly, in pairs or loose aggregations. Reproduction in these habitats probably follows a similar trend. Males are very resourceful and make use of soda bottles and other human trash as nesting sites. Vacant oyster shells hanging from dock lines seemed a preferred nest site for both *P. breviceps* and *P. fallax.*

Diet: In captivity these fish are not fussy and will accept most aquarium fare. A diet rich in fresh-frozen shrimp and algae material is ideal for initiating spawning. In the wild these fish use a fine row of comb teeth to rasp at solid structures, probably removing macrofauna from the surface. They have also been observed taking zooplankton from the water column.

Spawning: Pairs should be kept as isolated heterosexual pairs or trios consisting of one male and two females in a 20-gallon or larger aquarium. Spawning shelters should be supplied with 1-inch PVC or similar pipe. Spawning in this species is typically initiated by the female, who signals her readiness to spawn by patrolling the entrance to the male's shelter while performing a distinct and exaggerated swimming behavior with outstretched fins. The male rarely leaves the spawning shelter once courtship is initiated. Instead, he waits at the entrance with only his head protruding. From this position he moves his head in and out, sometimes writhing from side to side. The female continues an elaborate dance at the entrance, swimming back and forth to lures the males' attention while alternating between the front and back entrances of the shelter. In instances when the female seems unwilling to enter the spawning shelter, the male becomes excited, leaving his burrow and begins displaying to the female. Darting out from the burrow, the male rapidly approaches the female, pauses with outstretched fins and a slightly arced body posture then darts back to the burrow. If the female is still unreceptive, the male begins nudging her abdomen, often becoming quite vigorous in his efforts. After a lengthy courtship, the female enters and deposits adhesive eggs on the roof and sides of the spawning shelter.

Spawning occurs at roughly 3 to 7 day intervals with each female depositing 50 to over 200 eggs. Male *P. breviceps* will spawn with any receptive female despite the presence of other spawns in the nest. No pair bond is established and multiple spawns from different females are deposited together. Unlike the males of most brooding species that devote constant attention to egg tending, males of this species will often leave the nest to court receptive females.

Eggs measure slightly over 1 mm and appear as oblong circles with a flat surface for attachment to the substrate. Eggs from different spawns at varying stages of development create an interesting mosaic in the spawning shelter. Newly deposited eggs are cream to light orange in color but darken within the next few hours or days to a bright orange color. Hatching occurs in 7 days at 81°F when the eggs take on a characteristic golden color caused by the pigmented eyes of the embryos. When the oldest embryos

Convict Worm Blenny (*Pholidichthys leucotaenia*): a fascinating, eel-like fish with prodigious burrowing abilities that will rather readily form pairs and reproduce in the aquarium. Spawning is unpredictable and usually takes place in deep burrows.

take on this appearance, the pipe containing the eggs should be removed to a rearing vessel and fixed in a vertically the standpipe. An airstone is then placed below the pipe to provide a gentle current over the eggs. Hatching occurs head-first an hour or so after the lights have been turned off. The following morning the pipe is removed to a separate rearing tank and incubated until the next spawn hatches out. Typically three spawns may be deposited together and the pipe is thus each time to separate rearing tank.

Larval Rearing: Newly hatched larvae measure just under 3 mm in total length and resemble tadpoles with large bulbous heads. The larvae congregate on the sides and surface of the rearing tank and lack any remnant yolk. Feeding begins the day after hatching when rotifers are added to a density of 10/mL. After three days the larvae are efficient predators of rotifers and move swiftly in their efforts. After 10 days, newly hatched *Artemia* is added to the diet. Larvae have grown to roughly 6 mm at this stage and have well-developed capacious jaws and large pectoral fins.

About 15 days after hatching the larvae begin to experience erratic differences in growth rates with some larvae double the size of their brethren. Cannibalism will occur if the larvae are not well-fed. Occurrence of metamorphosis is greatest around day 25, but stretches from day 15 to 40 when larvae reach 10 mm. Adult coloration and cirri on the head develop at around days 40 to 45.

Convict Blenny, Convict Worm Blenny

Pholidichthys leucotaenia (Bleeker, 1856)
Maximum Length: 20 cm (7.8 in.).
Sexual Allocation: Unknown, probably gonochorist.

In the aquarium hobby this fish is often mislabeled and unappreciated. It does not belong to the family Blenniidae, but the Pholidichthyidae, of which it is the sole member. As with many marine fish this species has many common names that confuse many hobbyists. Known as snake gobies, eel gobies, engineer gobies, worm gobies and convict blennies in the aquarium trade, these fish are fascinating but notorious for their burrowing tendencies.

The young offered for sale are usually less than 8 cm (3.1 in.) long and are rather drab in comparison to adults. The young are black with a horizontal white line starting at the eye and extending the entire length of the body. Juvenile coloration as well as their habit of forming tight schools that look like balls mimic the color and behavior of juvenile coral catfish. Coral catfish possess venomous spines that offer protection from predators. Within a year Convict Blennies take on drastically different adult coloration—the thin, white horizontal line transforms into numerous yellow vertical stripes that are either continuous or broken, against a dark brown background.

At this size and coloration the fish are quite impressive and make interesting aquarium inhabitants. They are peaceful, very hardy fish that remain hidden in a hole with just Although not for every aquarium, they are much liked by many aquarists and they are not difficult to breed.

Habitat & Range: Western Pacific from the Philippines and Indonesia to the Solomon Islands. Young fish are observed schooling in tight clusters under ledges and overhangs and often in small caves, resembling young coral catfish.

Spawning: There is no sexual dimorphism obvious in this species. The best approach to obtaining compatible pairs is to purchase a group of inexpensive juveniles and place them in a large aquarium. It may take up to a year for the juveniles to become sexually mature and spawn. A single pair can be maintained in a 20-gallon aquarium. A group of adults will require at least a 40-gallon aquarium.

Once compatible pairs have formed, they can be transferred to smaller aquariums. Any two fish that occupy the same burrow can be labeled as a pair. This pair should be provided with rocks or PVC as refuge and spawning sites. Substrate should be crushed aragonite or coral sand. A fine substrate helps the fish with their digging duties.

The pair should be fed with live black worms, mysid shrimp, adult *Artemia* and fresh seafood several times a day. Convict Blennies practice a very unusual mode of reproduction for a marine fish. These unusual fish do not produce pelagic larvae and both parents practice brood care. Spawning occurs infrequently, perhaps once or twice a year, and is usually unnoticed as the eggs are placed deep within a burrow. It is unclear how long it takes for the eggs to hatch.

Usually, the only evidence that spawning has occurred is the presence of free-swimming larvae in the tank. The larvae form a tight school around both parents. The male and female Convict Blennies act like freshwater cichlids and defend the larvae vigorously from any approaching threats.

Larval Rearing: Young are roughly 6 mm long upon emerging from the burrow and still have remnants of a yolk sac (Leis and Trnski 1989). They are large enough to accept newly hatched *Artemia* and already exhibit the typical juvenile coloration. Spawns average 400 to 500 larvae.

The larvae have an adhesive gland on the top of their head, which is used to attach themselves to the substrate or surroundings of their parents during the night. The young should be separated from their parents a week or so after emerging from the burrow. Five hundred fish in the same aquarium is a lot of waste for one tank to handle.

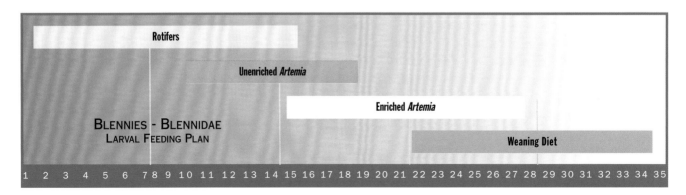

		Rotifers																																
								Unenriched *Artemia*																										
													Enriched *Artemia*																					
BLENNIES - BLENNIDAE LARVAL FEEDING PLAN																					Weaning Diet												
1	2	3	4	5	6	7	8	9	10	11	12	13	14	15	16	17	18	19	20	21	22	23	24	25	26	27	28	29	30	31	32	33	34	35

Guidelines: Feed rotifers at 10/ml; unenriched *Artemia* nauplii less than 12 hrs. old; enriched *Artemia* less than 24 hrs. old.

SEAHORSES

FAMILY SYNGNATHIDAE

Since antiquity, humans have marvelled at seahorses for their curious body plan, equine faces, prehensile tails and the unique ability for males to become pregnant. Along with their larger relatives, the Sea Dragons and the sinuous pipefishes, seahorses in the Family Syngnathidae are viewed by some as mythical aberrations with magical powers. In Chinese herbal medicine, seahorses are used to cure everything from wheezing to impotence. In the aquarium world, they captivate onlookers as symbolic ambassadors to the sea. Seahorses have undeniable appeal and they represent a unique challenge to ambitious (or conservation-minded) aquaculture entrepreneurs.

The family Syngnathidae is comprised of two subfamilies representing the seahorses (Hippocampinae) and pipefishes (Syngnathinae). Of most interest to aquarists, the subfamily Hippocampinae is comprised of roughly 35 species within a single genus. Perhaps fewer than 10 of these species are ever encountered in the aquarium hobby. For years, aquarium enthusiasts have been warned of the delicate nature of seahorses, their seemingly impossible dietary requirements and their intolerance of poor water quality. These warnings were made for good reasons, as few wild seahorses survived captivity for long.

Wild collection of seahorses for the aquarium trade has been severely curtailled, and most available specimens are now captive-raised. While seahorses are still considered difficult to maintain in captivity, their husbandry is much better understood and it is now well within the grasp of dedicated marine enthusiasts to keep healthy animals in the confines of an aquarium.

Wild seahorses that are collected alive still suffer high mortality, which can be attributed to various types of neglect along the transportation chain. If you decide to keep or breed seahorses, start with healthy, captive-raised indi-

Bigbelly Seahorse (*Hippocampus abdominalis*): a breeding male with prominent pouch kept by aquarist Michael Dendler.

viduals. Wild seahorses should be avoided for several good reasons.

Wild seahorse populations are in serious decline worldwide and their situation has drawn the attention of media, business people, ecologists and conservationists. Traditional Chinese medicine uses millions of dried seahorses and their derivatives in healing products each year, as remedies for everything from sexual dysfunction to kidney disorders and high cholesterol. Dried seahorses are also sold as curios throughout the world as Christmas tree ornaments, lamp shade decorations, paper weights and wall hangings. The exact number of seahorses traded annually in the various industries is unknown, but estimated at over 24 million. Sea-horse populations in some areas, such as the Philippines, have declined by as much as 70 percent.

Threats such as development, pollution, curio and medicinal trades collection and unintentional collection in commercial bottom-fishing operations has severely altered the population dynamics of several species throughout the world. The aquarium trade has also shared the blame for the crash of wild seahorse populations. Seahorses are highly specialized feeders (wild specimens often will eat only live foods) with inefficient digestive systems. As such, seahorses are prone to shipping and holding stresses with the vast majority surviving only a few months in captivity, due to malnutrition and diseases from a compromised immune system.

Due to their limited mobility and exaggerated pelagic phase, seahorses are generally limited in geographic distribution. Many tropical species are highly endemic to local hot spots. Certain species in Southeast Asia come from single isolated locations, while others such as the temperate and sub-tropical Lined Seahorse (*Hippocampus erectus)* are widely distributed along the entire eastern seaboard of the United States, into the Gulf of Mexico and south toward Argentina. The mechanisms regulating species distribution are poorly known, but the pelagic phase of larvae is known to be highly variable and influenced by currents, gyres and eddies. Seahorses occur sparsely in any location and their monogamous nature makes mating opportunities difficult once a mate is lost or captured. Anyone who has entered the water with mask and flippers hoping to catch a glimpse of these fishes is surely aware of how elusive and uncommon they are.

On May 15, 2004, all known species of seahorses were listed in Appendix II of the Convention on International Trade in Endangered Species (CITES). Under this appendix, all countries engaged in the collection, use and export of seahorses must prove that the harvest is sustainable and does not threaten existing wild populations. This is a daunting challenge for the Asian countries involved, as no formal data exists to substantiate the sustainability of harvest.

Mated pair of Bigbelly Seahorses (*Hippocampus abdominalis,* formerly *H. bleekeri*) with male in foreground. Finding appropriate broodstock is the first challenge in seahorse propagation.

A minimum size restriction of 10 cm (3.9 in.) was implemented as a first step in seahorse conservation. This size represents the average at the onset of sexual maturity for a number of representative species such as *H. erectus* and *H. kuda.* Culturing and marketing captive-raised specimens is viewed as a positive development both for both seahorse conservation and the growing marine aquaculture industry.

Whatever the cause for the decline of seahorse populations, aquarists who breed these fishes can take some credit for helping counter this loss. Aquaculture is often viewed as a viable tool in the recovery of troubled fish stocks. The advantage of aquaculture typically comes not from stock replenishment, but from creating an alternative supply. Aquaculture can lessen the dependence on wild stocks, provide a consistent supply of seahorses to meet an ever-increasing market demand and expand the hobby by offering healthy specimens with vigorous appetites for frozen foods. The culture of seahorses has been implemented in several countries at the commercial level.

A tremendous amount of literature exists on seahorse reproduction and husbandry and it would be impractical to attempt a detailed account here. For more detail on species accounts, feeding and general knowledge, look to the work of Giwojna 1996, Michael 1998 and Kuiter 2003. (See Bibliography, pages 290-295.) Peter Giwojna is preparing a complete work on this group that will surely be welcomed by seahorse aficionados and newcomers to the hobby. Seahorses have earned a faithful following of naturalists, conservationists, aquaculturists and hobbyists who have created dozens of websites and discussion boards dedicated to their captive care and to reporting advancements in culture. This is a fast-evolving field, and I have limited the scope of this work to include important highlights of reproduction and rearing as it pertains to small-scale enthusiasts. Variations in broodstock maintence, culture methods and rearing protocols are being refined almost daily.

Although the large size of newborn seahorses is encouraging, vexing bottlenecks are common during rearing trials. Many obstacles still exist, and there are surely many paths as yet undiscovered to overcome these tribulations. Small-scale seahorse hatcheries operated by creative aquarists could prove an integral link in the conservation of these remarkable animals. I urge anyone interested in the captive culture of seahorses to join the societies and discussion boards dedicated toward advancing and sharing knowledge.

BROODSTOCK

Perhaps the largest obstacle facing potential breeders of seahorses is the acquisition of healthy broodstock animals. In years past, broodstock supplies were limited to wild-caught specimens with origins in the Caribbean or Southeast Asia, most notably around the Philippines and Indonesia. Shipping and holding-related mortalities were often quite high and attempts at getting these animals into successful breeding projects usually failed. Lacking a true stomach, seahorses must feed almost constantly to remain healthy. Their tissue stores very little fat, and they are intolerant of lengthy fasting. Once collected from reef structures, mangrove roots or seagrass beds seahorses are typically held in floating mesh cages awaiting shipment to wholesale and export facilities. From here, they are jostled in plastic bags, often attaching themselves to one another in daisy chains before reaching an export facility. From this facility to the retail outlet, seahorses are generally starved, stressed and become prone to disease. By the time they reach local aquarium stores, usually some weeks later, they generally exhibit signs of distress and disease. Listless or lethargic seahorses that exhibit pale coloration, grayish blemishes, open lesions, reddening of the gill cover and unusual spots or marks should be avoided.

Once their immune system is compromised seahorses are susceptible to a variety of ailments and pathogens. Protozoans such *Brooklynella hostilis* and *Uronema marinum* and the microsporidean *Glugea heraldi* are common pathogens of wild seahorses and are irritatingly difficult to cure.

Captive seahorses in good condition are inquisitive animals that seem to be highly aware of their surroundings. Healthy seahorses will look alert. Their eyes, capable of rotating independently, will follow a hand in front of the aquarium. Active seahorses that seem to beg at the front glass are ideal candidates for breeding projects. Only purchase seahorses after observing them feeding. Most aquarium stores will offer to feed seahorses upon request. If a seahorse refuses food, do not purchase it. Those that refuse live feeds will surely perish. Weaning wild seahorses onto a diet of frozen and prepared foods is a challenge, but it can be done with a little coaxing. Wild broodstock must be chosen with the greatest of care and quarantined before introduced to systems containing other seahorses. Seahorses are highly polymorphic and species from different locations or habitats are notorious for exhibiting different coloration and morphologies. Behavior is the best indicator of good health.

It is far easier to obtain healthy captive-raised individuals with robust appetites rather than nursing wild seahorses back from the brink of disease and starvation. Wild seahorses are still common in retail outlets and command a hefty price. It is well worth the time and money to locate aquacultured stock. Captive-raised seahorses possess many ideal traits for home aquarists. Like most marine fishes reared in captivity, they are acclimated to confined conditions, feed well on frozen fare and have not been exposed to the stresses associated with wild collection and transport.

Seahorses are highly sexually dimorphic with males exhibiting a characteristic brood pouch. In the wild most species of seahorses are reported to be monogamous, or at least maintain long-term pair bonds. Polygamy has been reported in at least one species (*H. kuda*). In captivity, breeding specimens may swap partners several times. Broodstock should be isolated as individual pairs or small groups containing roughly 4 to 6 heterosexuals in equal numbers. It is generally best to obtain a small group of captive-raised subadults and rear them to adulthood in the same aquarium, allowing them to pair naturally. Once pairs have been identified, it is usually best to isolate them in individual tanks. Many facilities will offer mated pairs for sale. Depending on the species and color morph, the price of these pairs can often be quite high, but buying a known pair significantly reduces the time involved in growing your own.

DIET & CONDITIONING

Broodstock diet is an extremely important consideration in breeding projects aimed at producing high numbers of healthy offspring. As mentioned, adult seahorses possess very little fatty tissue. Without adequate fat reserves, egg maturation is dependant upon a consistent intake of fatty acids and other nutrients that will be incorporated into the

developing eggs as they undergo the process of *vitellogenesis* or "yolking". Live brine shrimp, grass shrimp and newborn livebearers such as guppies and mollies were once the traditional fare of seahorses maintained in aquarium stores and home aquariums. In the wild, seahorses feed almost exclusively on small crustaceans such as copepods, amphipods, mysid shrimps and small caridean shrimps. The feeding response of seahorses is elicited by movement. If a prey item does not move, rarely will a wild seahorse strike. Retail stores and home aquarists were thus limited to common food items that would elicit a feeding response. While seahorses will feed on brine shrimp and livebearer fry, they eventually become malnourished and waste away, becoming susceptible to disease over a period of months.

Live prey items of high quality are an ideal food source for breeding seahorses; however, such live prey is often limited to aquarists living near the coastline. Small live grass shrimp collected from estuaries and bays by use of a dip net will be accepted by most seahorses. Amphipods are similarly eaten with relish, as are myriad other invertebrates collected from plankton tows and within seagrass beds. Swarms of mysid shrimp (a highly nutritious food source) are often locally abundant and make an exceptional diet for captive seahorses. Larval forms of marine fish and shrimp also are ideal. There is always a risk of introducing pathogens from locally collected live prey items and caution should be exercised whenever collecting or utilizing these foods.

An alternative to collecting live prey organisms is to establish closed cultures which reduce or eliminate the problems associated with introducing disease. Mysid shrimp cultures are readily available and not too difficult to maintain longterm. A 20-gallon long aquarium or similar plastic container with a mature sponge filter and fluorescent lighting is typically all that is needed to raise mysids in captivity. Many culture protocols exist for maintaining long term cultures of mysids. Generally, flake or pellet foods are added sporadically every few days to maintain the breeding shrimp. Better results are achieved through the use of live *Artemia* nauplii as a food source for the mysids. Even a

Orangebanded Pipefish (*Doryrhamphus pessuliferus*): male carrying eggs attached to its belly (between arrows). Members of the Syngnathidae family, the pipefishes are related to the seahorses and have similar demands for feeding and, very likely, breeding.

single pair of seahorses will require many mysids daily to sustain reproductive activity and will quickly eat their way through a small culture of mysids. Several culture tanks will be necessary if this food source is relied upon.

Live brine shrimp, commonly available at most pet stores, is a suitable addition to the diet, assuming it is enriched prior to feeding. Products such as Selco or other HUFA supplements are ideal enrichment agents. Brine shrimp should be placed in a gallon container and allowed to 'soak up' the enrichment for a minimum of 12 hours before they are offered as food.

Cleaner Shrimp Larvae: A fantastic and easily supplied food source for juvenile and sub-adult seahorses are the pelagic larval phase of cleaner shrimps. Peppermint Shrimps (Lysmata spp.), various cleaner shrimps (Lysmata amboinensis and L. grabhami), Coral Banded Shrimps (Stenopus hispidus) and Camel Shrimps (Rhynchocinetes spp.) are all readily available and easily spawned. Newly hatched larvae measure roughly 2 mm in length and provide an ideal food for juveniles. If a slight effort is put into raising the larvae to near 4 or 5 mm, they provide an excellent addition to the diet of sub-adult and adult seahorses. The easiest method of obtaining a regular supply of shrimp larvae is to establish a small central system consisting of 2.5 or 5 gallon aquariums fitted with central standpipes lead-

ing to a common sump. Individual pairs of cleaner shrimp can be isolated in each aquarium or small groups of peppermint or camel shrimps can be established. Small ceramic tiles or halved flower pots will provide shelter for the breeding shrimp. Pelleted foods or raw shrimp and squid fed once or twice daily will maintain a reliable spawning cycle. Peppermint Shrimp are simultaneous hermaphrodites that maintain a 10 to 12-day spawning cycle, with each specimen acting as both male and female. This trait proves ideal, as all members of a breeding colony will produce larvae. A system containing a dozen or so pairs of Peppermint Shrimp will produce millions of larvae to be used as food. Collecting larvae in a system such as this calls for the placement of a mesh bag or basket below the central drain pipe in the sump. Each morning the larvae can then be collected and fed out to the mysid cultures accordingly. If the shrimp larvae are to be grown out, they can be stocked into suitable larval tanks and fed newly hatched Artemia until they reach the desired size. Larval rearing of these shrimps often requires mastery of another art, but spawning and obtaining newly hatched larvae is quite simple.

Mysid shrimp: Obtaining live food items is obviously more labor-intensive than using the frozen or prepared fare used to spawn most other species of marine fishes. Seahorses require frequent feedings of quality food containing

Juvenile captive-bred seahorse is a tiny replica of its parents. Some species have pelagic-stage young that need special rearing conditions until they are ready to settle to the bottom.

high levels of Omega-3 fatty acids. Crustacean prey such as mysid shrimp are naturally high in fatty acids and essential nutrient levels and are thus an ideal food source for captive seahorses. One of the major turning points in seahorse aquaculture has been the acceptance of frozen foods by captive seahorses. Healthy, domesticated seahorses will consume frozen foods, often with little coaxing. Frozen mysid shrimp are the most widely used feeds in maintaining and culturing seahorses. Piscine Energetics Inc., a Canadian based company, produces frozen mysids that have been enriched with Omega-3 fatty acids. A slightly smaller mysid shrimp is available from Hikari and is ideally suited to smaller specimens and those undergoing the weaning process. Using frozen mysids is by far the least labor-intensive method of providing a nutritionally sound food to broodstock seahorses. Frozen blocks should be completely thawed and in whole condition before feeding. Broodstock fed a diet solely of enriched mysids have been reported to live and reproduce for over two years.

Frequent feedings of high-quality foods are key to maintaining healthy broodstock willing to spawn on a reliable cycle and also to produce high-quality offspring. Poor survivorship through the juvenile phase can often be linked to an inadequate broodstock diet.

REPRODUCTION

Triggering reproductive behavior in the confines of an aquarium requires little more than healthy heterosexuals kept under ideal conditions with adequate feeding. Little environmental conditioning is necessary to provoke reproductive behavior, but it is useful to maintain the light cycle with 12 to 14 hours of daylight and 10-12 of darkness. Water temperature is not usually critical assuming it is in the normal parameters of the species. While all species require constant conditions to initiate reproduction, temperate species that breed annually should be maintained under summer conditions with slightly warmer water temperatures and increased photoperiod.

While single pairs or small groups can be maintained in isolated aquariums with dedicated sponge filters or outside box filters, for any serious effort to breed seahorses, you will want to establish multiple aquariums connected through a centralized filtration system. This method has the advantage of buffering water quality deterioration and makes the transfer of individuals from one aquarium to another less stressful. It also decreases the time you will have to spend on system maintenance. Broodstock tanks used for seahorses, whether maintained as isolated entities or connected to a central system, are similar to those used for most other marine species. Decorative tanks with gravel and rock are suitable for breeding seahorses but when multiple tanks of broodstock are maintained in a central system, gravel and other decorations tend to prolong maintenance time. Bare tanks facilitate the removal of uneaten food and decaying fecal matter. Acrylic tubing, polypropylene rope or similar artificial material can be used to construct holdfasts where the animals can wrap their tails, or appropriate plastic plants or faux corals can be used. In display tanks, live *Caulerpa* and *Halimeda* macroalgaes are ideal holdfasts, and under ideal light regimes they can help in the absorption of nitrogenous wastes.

The size and shape of broodstock tanks vary widely depending on the species in question. Small groups of the Pygmy Seahorse (*H. zosterae*) can be maintained quite happily in 2.5 gallon tanks, whereas the Potbellied Seahorse, (*H. abdominalis*), grows to almost 14 inches (35 cm) and requires much larger quarters of 50 gallons or more to successfully reproduce. More important than the overall size and surface area, is the depth of the tank. Successful reproduction of seahorses involves a modified spawning assent. After lengthy courtship, the male and female rise off the bottom and entwine their tails. Rising in the water column the female aligns her ovipositor over the male's dilated brood pouch and expels her eggs. In captivity, pairs often fail to complete this sequence due to insufficient tank depth. In shallow tanks, pairs often reach the surface and are separated before successful egg transfer. While the height required to successfully complete egg transfer varies among species it is best to employ broodstock tanks with a minimum vertical height of 50 to 75 cm (20 to 30 in.). The large size of the Potbellied Seahorses warrants the use of tanks with 91 to 122 cm (36 to 48 in.) of vertical height, while smaller seahorses such as *H. barbouri, H. breviceps* and *H. kuda* will successfully spawn in tanks with 38 to 61cm (15 to 24 in.) of vertical height. Glass aquariums are available to fit this profile. Most notably, the so-called extra-tall aquariums produced by some manufacturers work well for seahorses. These tanks are usually around 30 to 40 gallons in capacity with a vertical height of 71 to 91 cm (28 to 36 in.).

These tanks are easily drilled to be plumbed into a central system, and their small footprint allows multiple aquariums to be maintained in a relatively small space. Deep fiberglass and plastic tanks are also available, although the price of these is sometimes prohibitive for small-scale operations. Creative approaches, such as using flat-sided trash cans with acrylic viewing windows, can be successfully utilized. Custom aquariums are ideally suited for breeding seahorses, as they can be made to accommodate the species in culture. The price of these aquariums can be reduced if they are made by the breeder. This can be labor intensive, but does provide an excellent environment for broodstock. Caution should be used when purchasing glass for these aquariums as the relative height of the tank demands thicker glass than conventional display tanks.

Heavy biological filtration is important to eliminate the harmful effects of nitrogenous waste buildups in a seahorse broodstock system. Protein skimming is important to rid the water of dissolved organics. Enriched feeds are loaded with oils and fats that quickly create a nasty film on the surface. A combination of surface skimming and protein skimming is effective at controlling this problem. Central systems possess the distinct advantage of skimming surface waters via a standpipe. Unless a skimmer box is attached to an isolated display aquarium, surface film can create unique problems. Ultraviolet sterilizers are a real asset in controlling disease in seahorse systems and usually worth the initial expense.

SPAWNING RITUALS

The mating game of seahorses is unique and fascinating. Courtship is an almost continuous process in seahorses and starts with morning greetings that reinforce pair bonds and signal the readiness of partners to breed. In captivity, males may compete for the attention of receptive females. Occasionally, these displays will interfere with the actual mating and cause females to drop their eggs. While mating is generally successful in small groups, isolated pairs will tend to have fewer problems. Maintaining isolated pairs often controls the frequency of spawning and eliminates interference episodes associated with group spawning.

Seahorses are reliable spawners, breeding shortly after the previous brood is expelled from the male's pouch. The frequency of spawnings can take a toll on male seahorses, as it is physiologically expensive for the male to brood young. Evidence of this comes when the time between spawns increases. Brood size often decreases and the overall survivorship of newborn seahorse decreases. Males often appear exhausted after repeated spawnings,

Common or Yellow Seahorse (*Hippocampus kuda*): a smaller species that typically produces broods of 250 to 300 offspring with a gestation period of 15 to 18 days.

however, most continue to breed. Some recuperation time is beneficial, as constant mating can prove lethal to sea-horses.

Interrupting the spawning cycle can be accomplished by environmental conditioning or physically separating breeding partners. Environmental conditioning involves using a shorter daylength, accompanied by a drop in water temperature. Reducing the photoperiod to 8 to 10 hours of light and dropping the water temperature by 4 to 8 degrees is often enough to cease reproduction without dissolving the pair bond. Isolated females held under a full photoperiod and warm temperatures will continue to develop eggs which are subsequently expelled.

Following successful mating, male seahorses will typically continue to feed through the gestation period. Gestation typically lasts 16 to 30 days for most popular aquarium seahorses and is strongly influenced by water temperature. Gestation in *H. kuda* and *H. erectus* averages 15 to 18 days, while *H. zosterae* averages 10 to 14 days. These gestation times are typical for water temperatures of 76 to 80°F.

When water temperatures drop to 72 to 74°F gestation time can almost double. During early gestation males continue to be active, however, as gestation nears completion males often become reclusive and may stop feeding. Towards the end of the gestation period, the male's brood pouch often swells to enormous proportions with the developing young.

Large species such as the Pot-bellied (*H. abdominalis*) and Lined Seahorse (*H. erectus*) have been reported to brood as many as 1,500 young, while smaller species such as the Spotted (*H. kuda*), High-crown (*H. procerus*) and Thorny Seahorse (*H. hystrix*) generally produce broods of 250 to 300, with larger and smaller females producing more or less offspring. Pygmy Seahorses (*H. zosterae*) seem limited to a dozen or so young with large broods containing just 16 to 20 newborns.

Moving Pregnant Males: Young seahorses must be raised in a dedicated rearing vessel, not in the broodstock tank. There are two ways to transport young seahorses into the rearing environment. After birth, the newborn seahorses can be removed by means of a shallow bowl or similar water container and transferred to the rearing tank. However, with several hundred to a thousand or so off-spring this can become tiresome. It is therefore best to transfer the brooding male to the rearing tank before he expells the young. In this way, the unborn seahorses are born in the rearing tank without stress and possible transfer loss.

Measures should be taken to minimize stress on the brooding male. Water from the broodstock tank should be used to fill the rearing tank to avoid stress involved with acclimating him to shifts in pH, salinity and other chemical properties of the water. (Again, here is where a centralized water management system can greatly simplify the process.)

Utmost care should be practiced when capturing and transferring the brooding male to the rearing tank. Never use nets and act as slowly and deliberately as possible. A specimen cup capable of holding the male seahorse vertically in the water should be employed. Never expose the brooding male to air. A submerged specimen cup should be brought from underneath and used to capture the male. It is best to avoid detaching the male from his holdfast by grabbing the tail. Wait patiently until the male detaches on his own.

After capturing the male, slowly submerge the specimen cup in the rearing tank and allow the male to swim freely. Transfers such as this are quick and stress-free. The male should be supplied with a simple holdfast constructed of plastic or nylon/polypropylene rope. Live material such as macroalgae should not be used in the rearing tank to avoid bringing in unwanted pests or contributing to the deterioration of water quality.

Expulsion of the young seahorses typically takes place over a period of several consecutive days. Males most commonly birth at night to send newborns in their upward migration in the absence of daytime predators. The male can be removed to a separate rearing tank each morning if one wishes to replicate the rearing process or the male can remain in the rearing tank until all young are expelled. There is always a possibility of the male consuming newborns, but rarely will this take a considerable toll on total sur-

vivorship. After all the young are expelled, the male should be carefully returned to the broodstock tank.

REARING

Much debate surrounds the early life history of seahorses and many claim the existence of a pelagic larval phase is non-existent. It was long thought that most newborns assumed a benthic role similar to the adults immediately upon release from the male's brood pouch. This is one of the key arguments for the limited geographic range of most species.

It is now clear that different species-specific traits exist. A general consensus for most seahorse species is, that upon release from the male's brood pouch, newborn seahorses enter the pelagic zone for a short period of time. Most newborns are attracted to light (the moon in their native habitats) and swim up to the surface. This is a common trait in most demersal spawning reef fish larvae. It is thought that phototaxis evolved to draw larvae away from the predator-filled reef and toward the relative safety of open water. In many newborn broods, young seahorses can be drawn to particular points around the tank by directional lighting. In aquariums with conventional hoods with a single strip light, the entire brood will writh within a thin band below the light. Newborn seahorses commonly entangle one another with their prehensile tails in the water column and most aquarists assume this to be a response of attaching themselves to a benthic structure. Attachment such as this is probably an artifact of the high juvenile densities occurring within the confines of an aquarium.

The number of young seahorses collected in plankton tows and channel nets throughout the world is good evidence of this pelagic larval phase of development. In most species, the duration spent in the upper water column seems to last a few days to a week.

Species such as the Pygmy Seahorse (*H. zosterae*) of Florida seem to lack any pelagic phase, as newborns readily attach to benthic structures and tend to avoid swimming in open water. Some members of the Spotted Seahorse (*H. kuda*) complex and White's Seahorse (*H.*

whitei) also produce benthic juveniles.

However, species like the Lined (*H. erectus*), Brazilian (*H. reidi*), Tiger-tail (*H. comes*), Jayakar's Seahorse (*H. jayakarai*), and others rarely attach themselves to stationary objects during the first few days or weeks of development. Instead, these species orient themselves in the upper water column, free-swimming away from structure. Time spent in the water column seems highly variable among species.

While understanding the early stage of each species is key for protecting wild populations, it is also an essential factor in rearing juvenile seahorses in captivity. In the infancy of the marine aquarium hobby, seahorses were typically reared in rectangular aquariums with very limited water movement and supplied with various plastic plants and other holdfasts. They were fed un-enriched *Artemia* throughout the juvenile period and typically suffered exceptionally high mortality rates.

In recent years, the rearing environment for seahorses has changed dramatically, as have the diets being offered. As a direct result, it is now common for commercial facilities and dedicated home aquarists to achieve upward of 50 to 60 percent survival during the first six months, with many facilities achieving greater than 70 percent survival.

Dozens of seahorse rearing methods have been established and refined over the years. Rearing most marine reef fishes involves little variation from a common theme involving round tanks and airstones. For seahorses, there are two key elements for predictable success: rearing tank design (mainly water circulation) and diet. These two elements stem from the early life history of the various forms of seahorses. In general, those forms that lack a pelagic phase and are immediately benthic and of larger size prove easier to raise than their smaller pelagic brethren.

REARING TANK

The large size of seahorses at birth is often deceptive and has led most aquarists away from traditional conical rearing tanks used. However, any serious attempt to raise a high percentage of offspring should take place in traditional conical, circular or kreisel-type rearing tanks.

Most small-scale hobbyists use rectangular glass aquariums fitted with some form of divider that encases a filter or water pump. In many instances, these rearing tanks work well with survival rates averaging 10 to 30 percent for beginning breeders. Advanced aquarists often attain survivorship as high as 80 percent in these systems but repeated success seems limited. Newborn seahorses are prone to being sucked into filter intakes when housed in traditional tanks. It is necessary to isolate these hazards from the brood. While some aquarists simply wrap the filter intake with fine mesh, the mesh invariably fouls and limits circulation. Often, newborns swimming too close will be pinned to the intake. A tight-fitting aquarium divider drilled with tiny holes works well to form a compartment that excludes the tiny seahorses. The intake pipes of outside box filters or canister filters can be placed within the protected compartment and the exhaust placed in the rearing compartment.

An alternative is to place both the intake and return pipes of the filter in the protected compartment. If the divider is non-permeable, clean water can then be airlifted to the other side. Air lifts are best arranged so the return water shoots gently across the surface of the rearing compartment. Two or more airlifts can create a sufficient surface current that acts as a barrier to newborn seahorses reaching the surface. Water circulation is a key element in raising seahorses and a moderate flow of water should be present throughout the entire rearing tank. Rectangular tanks are poorly suited to creating uniform flow rates because of areas in the tank with extreme high and low currents. In standard 10 and 15-gallon aquariums, flow directions are generally limited to a horizontal plane with quick thrusts towards the surface or bottom glass. Flow rates should be adjusted so newborns are not pushed into glass panes. Newborns should slowly circulate around the tank.

A benefit of conventional smaller tanks is the limited water volume and presence of filtration. It is easier to maintain sufficient prey densities in a small water volume, and the filters lessen the impact of heavy feedings and large bio-loads. The disadvantages of this style rearing tank, how-

Drifting newborn seahorses (*H. reidi*) in a rearing vessel illustrating how they are gently carried by circular water current patterns at this critical stage.

in capacity and are generally taller than they are wide. Tall tanks are ideal as they increase the distance between newborns and the surface. When ideal circulation is maintained, newborns will rarely come in contact with the surface. Aquaculture supply houses and plastics companies offer a wide assortment of such tanks. Tanks of roughly 15-30 gallons are ideally suited to small-scale hobbyists. A bulkhead should be placed in the bottom or side of the tank and a battery of tanks connected through a central system. Biological filtration in the form of a wet–dry or fluidized sandbed filter should dominate the filtration of the system. A protein skimmer and UV sterilizer are important additions, as enrichment products that can quickly foul the water will be an integral part of the rearing protocol.

A simple design is to place a standpipe vertically through the bottom bulkhead of the rearing tank. Incoming water is then directed to the bottom of the rearing tank by means of a continuous PVC pipe to within a half-inch or so of the bottom. The standpipe acts as a surface skimmer to remove oil deposits, but must be fitted with an appropriately sized mesh. Water entering at the bottom of the tank creates an upwelling design that moves in a constant upward motion. A conical bottom helps evenly distribute water flow in these tanks. Centralized systems can often make do without the use of auxiliary airstones or other air-driven devices to maintain high dissolved oxygen. If return water is dripped from above the surface, however, some form of water circulation must be provided or the incoming water will simply be drawn down the standpipe without first circulating throughout the tank. An airstone placed at the bottom of the tank can supply needed water flow. If air must be used to generate water flow, it is advisable to use only rigid airline tubing without an airstone.

ever, are the reduced height that substantially limits water circulation patterns, uneven flow rates created by the rectangular shape and the difficulty of connecting these tanks to a centralized water system. It is generally more desirable to circulate rearing tank water through a large-volume sump with heavy-duty biological filtration and protein skimming. By drilling a hole in the bottom glass pane, behind the tank-divider barrier, and fitting this with a bulkhead and standpipe, a battery of these rearing tanks can be maintained with little effort. A large sump and centralized water return pump can effectively maintain water quality in a dozen or more rearing tanks. Return water can be directed to either the back compartment or to the rearing compartment, based on circulation and flow requirements.

Increasing Survival: For the first few days to weeks, it is advisable to think of newborn seahorses not as the juvenile or adult forms, but as larvae. As such, tall conical or round rearing tanks prove the most suitable for ensuring better survivorship. Most commercial facilities use conical or cylindrical tanks to rear large numbers of offspring. These tanks range in size from roughly 10 to 200 gallons

Bubble Hazards: Large bubbles create sufficient flow and eliminate small bubbles. Many marine aquarists use wooden air diffusers to create gentle currents, but these small bubbles often cling to the body of small juveniles, irritating them to exhaustion. Some feel that small bubbles may present a choking hazard to young seahorses that mistake them for food. Whenever possible it is best to create water circulation with water, not air. Upwelling designs are also beneficial during the weaning process. A constant upwelling of water lessens the settlement of inert foods and keeps them in the water column longer. This helps slow-developing fry and significantly shortens weaning time.

An interesting rearing tank approach being adopted by many private aquarists is a kreisel design. Kreisels can be very complex or very simple, depending on their intended use. Originally designed to keep jellyfish suspended in the water column, kreisels have been used with great success to rear newborn seahorses.

Hippocampus erectus fry in a homemade *Kriesel* fashioned from a plastic goldfish bowl and suspended in a larger aquarium. Air bubbled gently up the rounded side of the bowl creates a circular water flow to keep the tiny seahorses suspended for the first days of larval feeding.

The basics of this design are simple and one can easily be constructed with few materials. Tall glass aquariums such as those used to house broodstock are ideal for use as kreisels. Acrylic sheets or PVC board cut to fit tightly within the inside dimensions of the tank are bent as a half circle or U with the aid of a heat gun. This material is then siliconed in place at the bottom of the tank so that the bottom of the half circle is directly seated on the bottom of the tank. The idea is to eliminate all sharp corners in the main chamber. The simplest of designs then injects a wall of air bubbles starting at the bottom of one of the vertical side panels. When air rises towards the surface it brings water towards the top of the aquarium. Here, it uses the surface tension to force the water towards the opposite side and then down towards the bottom—a weak vortex is created with the most turbulent water patrolling the outside edge. Inert particles are forced to the inside where the water is calmer. This design keeps newborns away from the surface and tank walls or other obstructions.

More elaborate designs can be constructed to create this circular flow with water rather than air. Water pumps and screening are used and bulkheads plumbed to the surface of the tank or in a special compartment can accommodate a surface skimmer and attachment to a central system to maintain water quality. Large fiberglass U-shaped commercial tanks, sometimes as large as 500 gallons, have been developed to rear thousands of seahorses. Water or air creates a similar circular motion in the tank.

Simple mini-kreisels: Home aquarists can create other less complex solutions. For example, breeder David Mulcahy designed a very small kreisel that has been used successfully by many hobbyists and modified in a number of ways. This intuitive design is quite simple and can be created for just a few dollars.

The basic design creates a circular water pattern in a classic goldfish bowl. A plastic, one-gallon goldfish bowl is drilled on one side panel, directly in the middle of the outside curved edge. A barb or nipple is fitted to the drilled hole and supplied with a steady supply of air. The rising air creates the desired circular current and keeps small newborns in rotation.

To keep conditions stable, the mini-kreisel is suspended or placed on a plastic eggcrate rack in a larger tank, with a 2-inch bulkhead in the back of the goldfish bowl covered with 500-micron mesh. This allows water circulation between the rearing vessel and water in the bigger tank, which is in turn filtered and skimmed. The small size of this design makes replication essential and large broods must be split up among several to many of these small chambers. The design and application of this rearing method is an ingenious and inexpensive solution that can easily be duplicated.

Whatever larval rearing vessel is being used, some form of hitching post that will not disrupt the water circular flow is suspended in the calm middle area when the young sea-horses are ready to start clinging to something, usually in about 3-10 days, depending on species. Once the juveniles have oriented themselves toward the hitching post and spend most of their time attached to it, they are removed from this kreisel and reared in grow-out tanks.

Greenwater: Seahorse species with pelagic larvae especially benefit from the addition of greenwater as either live or paste microalgae to the rearing tank. Small volumes of microalgae are added to tint the water a light green or brown color, depending on the algal strain. If paste is used, the tank bottom will need to be siphoned more frequently to remove settled algae cells. Paste forms are ideal to tint the water, but do not facilitate nitrogenous waste removal, an ideal trait in live forms. Greenwater is reported to increase feeding efficiency in early stage seahorses as well as maintaining proper fry and prey dispersion throughout the rearing tank. In clear water, pelagic young often congregate at the surface of the tank and become trapped in oil deposits or seem to drift aimlessly near the surface often whirling their bodies in an exhausting dance. This floating phenomenon observed in young pelagic seahorses can be likened to the crowding effect of early stage marine fish larvae maintained in clear water. Larval dottybacks, gobies, damsels and virtually all other species of marine fish larvae concentrate heavily at the sides of the tank near the surface in clear water. Greenwater is essential in these situations to maintain normal behavior and avoid crowding at the surface. Greenwater should typically be employed until the majority of seahorses in the batch have adopted a benthic mode of attachment. The benefits observed from this method can be applied to any rearing tank design. A central system will require more frequent additions of greenwater to maintain proper shading.

Rearing tanks should be void of decorations and gravel as these will harbor decaying food and fecal matter and increase maintenance time. Attachment sites such as heavy monofilament fishing line fitted with stainless steel weights, strips of plastic gutter guard or strands of thin polypropylene rope should be the only items placed in the rearing tank. Depending on species, newborn seahorses generally begin to settle from the water column and utilize holdfasts within a few days. Growth rates vary significantly and some will settle much faster than others. During the pelagic phase, dense clumps of monofilament or plastic mesh create a hazard for young seahorses. They often become entangled or trapped by these holdfasts and become exhausted trying to free themselves. Only a few vertical strands of rope should be present until the young begin to settle. As juveniles begin to use these attachment sites, add more.

Although newborn seahorses look drastically different from typical marine fish larvae, they can be reared in similar tanks with similar filtration, plumbing and water circulation patterns. Water flow is important to keep both seahorses and their prey suspended and evenly distributed throughout the rearing tank. Stagnant tanks or those with too little circulation will cause serious problems, with newborn seahorses being stuck in the meniscus of the tank, trapped in the surface film, or ingesting air bubbles. Try to create water movement with water and whenever possible increase the total volume of the rearing system by connecting tanks to a large central system. Once weaned onto non-living foods, the juveniles can be relocated to grow out aquariums.

FEEDING NEWBORNS

In all but the rarest instance, there is still no common substitute for the reliance on newly hatched brine shrimp (*Artemia*) as a food source for newborn seahorses. The size of newborn seahorses varies among species and the first foods offered will ultimately depend on their size and state of development upon release.

Hippocampus whitei and *H. erectus* are roughly 9 to 11 mm at birth and are capable of consuming *Artemia* nauplii smaller than 600 microns. *H. reidi* and *H. kuda* release much smaller offspring that measure 5 to 8 mm so require a first food organism smaller than newly hatched *Artemia*, preferably around 250-300 microns.

Traditionally, rotifers followed by *Artemia* have formed the bulk of rearing diets for such species. But in recent years,

the nutritional efficacy of such feeding regimes has been questioned, since survivorship to the juvenile stage is generally quite low. Many investigators have tested the value of incorporating live zooplankton, monocultures of copepods and various inert foods in the rearing diet of seahorses. Also, much work on trying different enrichment regimens for live foods is starting to determine the appropriate ratio and amounts of fatty acids that aid survivorship. Two general procedures apply to feeding newborn seahorses depending on the size of the offspring.

Larger newborns capable of consuming *Artemia* nauplii can be supplied this food source immediately, whether fed exclusively or in combination with a more nutritious organism such as copepods. Smaller newborns will rely on rotifers, copepod nauplii or other small zooplankton species as a main food source until large enough to accept *Artemia* nauplii and larger stages of copepods.

Brine Shrimp Nauplii Tactics: *Artemia* nauplii as an exclusive diet, when properly enriched with commercial HUFAs, can produce sufficient survival to drive economic production of many seahorses. However, because it is difficult to sufficiently enrich early stage *Artemia*, the diet of first-feeding seahorses is typically deficient in Omega-3 fatty acids. *Artemia* less than 12 hours old are notorious for being difficult to enrich. Most commonly available enrichment products are ingested by the food organism, thus delivering the enrichment to whatever consumes them. Since *Artemia* nauplii do not feed for the first 12 to 14 hours after hatching, their nutritional profile is ultimately limited. Mortality of seahorse babies throughout the juvenile phase can often be traced back to the initial diet.

Artemia nauplii past the 12-hour mark are more useful in delivering HUFA enrichments, but are too large for most newborns to properly capture and ingest. When newborns are co-fed with copepods or enriched rotifers during the first feeding stage, mortality rates decrease throughout the entire juvenile phase. By feeding copepod-dominated wild plankton for only the first three days of development, followed abruptly by a diet exclusively of *Artemia*, Gardner (2003) achieved considerably higher survivorship than sim-

Hedgehog Seahorse (*H. spinosissimus*) showing typical feeding behavior, ready to pluck small prey from the substrate.

ilar trials without the addition of wild plankton, which resulted in 100 percent mortality over a two week period. This aspect of feeding is incredibly important. The first feeding stage often proves a pivotal bottleneck to the captive culture of seahorses and can have tremendous impact on the overall survival of a brood.

The first feeding stage of small newborns that cannot successfully capture *Artemia* occurs in a slightly different manner than described above. Since *Artemia* nauplii will not constitute the initial diet in these young, it is important to identify a nutritional stand-in until the young can be successfully weaned onto larger fare. Rotifers are the most commonly used first food for small newborn seahorses. Unlike the small rotifer strains chosen to rear most other reef fishes, newborn seahorses benefit from larger strains. *Brachionus plicatilis* strains are available in a tremendous variety of sizes. An ideal strain for rearing seahorses is the Norwegian strain that typically reaches a lorica length of 250 -290 microns. Most rotifer strains will prove acceptable for rearing seahorses assuming they are properly enriched. It is best to harvest a portion of rotifers the day prior to feeding and soak them in a HUFA enrichment. Prior to feeding,

be sure to rinse the rotifers in seawater to reduce oily deposits and surface film in the rearing tank. Greenwater should be used to tint the rearing water during early development of pelagic young. The gut evacuation rate of rotifers is a mere 8 to 12 hours—after this time the HUFA enrichment is no longer effective, as much of it has been defecated by the rotifer. Greenwater will help sustain the nutritional value of the rotifer population until they are consumed by the seahorses. When available, zooplankton and copepods greatly influence survival during this stage.

When feeding newly hatched *Artemia*, it is useful to maintain the rearing tank as part of a central system to help purge prey organisms that have grown too large to be acceptable as food. By fitting the overflow with an appropriate size mesh, water exchange to the tank can be increased during the night to purge prey. The following morning flow rates can be reduced and the seahorses fed again. When supplied with nutritionally acceptable foods, seahorses grow extremely quickly with most reaching 30 to 40 mm by the third week of development.

As the juvenile seahorses grow, the size of prey should be continually increased. Larval forms of cleaner shrimps can be eaten by many species near the fourth or fifth week, and adult *Artemia* are generally acceptable by the sixth week of development. Eventually, the juveniles must be weaned to accept a suitable prepared food which will greatly reduce the labor involved with culturing *Artemia* and increase the nutritional profile offered to the young. Seahorses are often reluctant to accept non-living prey and should be slowly trained. It is important not to switch diets and abandon live foods abruptly, as mortality will surely ensue from starvation.

A general rule is to wean juveniles when they are large enough to accept whole frozen mysid shrimp, as this is a near-perfect seahorse food and the typical diet of captive adults. For most common species, this occurs by the eighth week of development. Many facilities advocate weaning on chopped mysids near the sixth week. Captive seahorses are voracious predators that always seem to be hungry. In many instances, thawed mysids placed in the rearing tank during the day's first feed will be greedily consumed. It is always best to co-feed with live foods while attempting to wean seahorses. The presence of live prey seems to elicit a feeding response on non-living foods added to the tank. Tanks with upwelling currents help prolong the settlement time of prepared or thawed foods and give them a lifelike action. Be sure that all seahorses are consuming non-living foods before live prey are removed from the menu.

As the number of captive-bred seahorse species increases, the task of choosing potential broodstock candidates becomes more interesting and more demanding. It is important for aquarists to understand the life history of the species they consider for culture and to be prepared for the time and dedication that will be required. Some species are definitely easier than others.

I have loosely described protocols for three species below, each representing a category of seahorse species with different requirements. The Pygmy Seahorse (*H. zosterae*) is considered a great starter species for seahorse breeders, with large, easily reared young. Several other species of *Hippocampus* also produce large benthic offspring and can be reared in a similar manner. The Lined Seahorse (*H. erectus*), produces relatively large offspring with a short pelagic phase and is typical of many species. The Brazilian Seahorse (*H. reidi*) exhibits a longer pelagic phase and much smaller newborn size and makes more demands on the breeder.

Pygmy or Dwarf Seahorse

Hippocampus zosterae (Jordan and Gilbert, 1882)
Maximum Length: 5 cm (2 in.).
Sexual Allocation: Gonochorist.

Here is the guppy of seahorse breeding. I remember ordering a mail-order pair from an ad in the back of a *Boys' Life* magazine during my youth. They arrived in fine shape and seemed perfectly happy in a one-gallon aquarium with some blue gravel and an orange plastic plant. It took only two weeks for this pair to give birth, and the six offspring grew steadily on nothing more than a diet of unenriched *Artemia*.

This species is well-suited to captive conditions and is ideal for budding aquarists to hone their skills and build some confidence before attempting more difficult species. This species reaches a mere 5 cm (2 in.) and groups can be successfully maintained in small desktop aquariums. A breeding project centered on this species can be successful in the smallest footprint possible.

Habitat & Range: Pygmy Seahorses are limited to the subtropical and tropical western Atlantic—from Bermuda and the Bahamas to southern Florida and throughout the entire Gulf of Mexico. Typically, these seahorses are most common in shallow seagrass beds with only a few feet of water.

Breeding & Rearing: *Hippocampus zosterae* is monogamous in the wild, with pairs remaining together throughout the reproductive season. In captivity, however, it is not uncommon for males and females to swap partners. A small group consisting of 15 to 20 individuals can peacefully coexist and breed in tanks as small as 10 gallons. If the goal is simply to maintain a small group of seahorses in the living room and perhaps raise a few newborns to maturity, little more than one or two aquariums is required. Unlike most members of the family, adult *H. zosterae* pose little threat to their benthic newborns. A separate rearing tank is not required and they can be reared in the same tank as the adults.

Individual pairs can also be maintained in 2.5-gallon aquariums or similar containers connected through a central system. In this way numerous pairs can be maintained in the same system with their own synchronized reproductive cycle. This species is easily satisfied by the bare essentials: clean water and something to hold on to. They do, however, benefit from being in a mature aquarium with bio-film or a thin layer of algae along the bottom or back glass. Bio-film and algae tend to support harpacticoid copepods which are a favorite treat for this seahorse. It is a good idea not to scrub all panes of glass, but to leave one or two to support such food items. The main diet of captive Pygmy Seahorses is enriched day-old *Artemia,* and the occasional copepod will greatly benefit the vigor of captive

Pygmy or Dwarf Seahorse (*Hippocampus zosterae*): a diminutive species but perhaps the best for beginning breeders wishing to hone their skills with this sometimes challenging family.

specimens. It is best to feed adult *H. zosterae* live *Artemia* enriched for a full 24 hours.

Little is required to initiate spawning in *H. zosterae* beyond adequate feeding and proper water quality. Temperature should be maintained from 77 to 84°F. A minimum photoperiod of 12 hours light should be provided to simulate the summer reproductive season. After an elaborate courtship lasting several days, the diminutive pair rise into the water column where mating takes place. After a gestation period of roughly 11 days, the male releases 3 to 15 newborns measuring 7 to 8 mm. Newborns are large at release and immediately assume a benthic lifestyle similar to that of the adults. Newly hatched *Artemia* and enriched

rotifers should be offered to newborns. Assuming proper enrichment of prey organisms, few newborns will be lost. Sexual maturity is reached in 2 to 3 months and population doubling can occur very quickly under captive conditions.

Similar species with benthic newborns are usually handled slightly differently. Newborns of species like *H. whitei* and some members of the *H. kuda* complex are best removed to separate rearing tanks, as the adults may consume small offspring. Rearing tanks for benthic newborns can be glass aquariums, fiberglass or conical tanks. Filtration is very important in these tanks; however, creating a circular flow is not essential. Plenty of hitching posts and a sufficiently enriched diet usually result in high survivorship.

Lined Seahorse

Hippocampus erectus (Perry, 1810)
Maximum Length: 15 cm (5.9 in.).
Sexual Allocation: Gonochorist.

This wide-ranging species appeals to experienced aquarists and those new to the hobby. Captive-bred broodstock is easily acquired and easily maintained on frozen mysid shrimp. This species is highly polymorphic with colors ranging from shades of brown and black to orange and gold. Coloration is often a matter of mood and surroundings and can change with age or environment. It is not uncommon for an aquarist to purchase a beautiful gold specimen only to have it turn gray or brown within a few weeks' time. Feeding foods high in carotenoids and maintaining the seahorses in an environment with contrastingly bright surroundings help maintain the long-term coloration of seahorses. As their name suggests, most specimens display an elaborate pattern of fine lines and some specimens develop blotched patterns of alternating light and dark colors. Many specimens develop dermal appendages or cirri. The Lined Seahorse is a large species that spends much time free swimming in the open searching or begging for food.

Habitat & Range: The Lined Seahorse exhibits one of the most far-reaching distributions observed in the family.

Found from Nova Scotia in Canada south along the Atlantic seaboard of the United States to Argentina in South America as well as the east coast of Africa and the entire Gulf of Mexico. Commonly collected in sea grass beds throughout their range, Lined Seahorses are frequently observed clinging to bridge pilings, crab traps and manmade debris. Lined Seahorses commonly associate with dense mats of suspended macroalgae, free-floating sargassum and benthic mats of algae such as *Gracilaria*. Often these specimens develop elaborate cirri or dermal appendages that can become quite long.

Breeding & Rearing: Reproduction in this species is non-problematic and will occur over a wide range of temperatures and salinities. Pairs are best isolated in 16- or 29-gallon high or 36-gallon extra-high aquariums. Custom aquariums often provide more ideal environmental conditions and depth than common display type aquariums. Pairs are easily maintained on frozen mysid shrimp with occasional offerings of enriched live adult *Artemia*, ghost shrimp, and other crustaceans.

Much confusion exists as to whether the offspring of this species are pelagic or benthic. Some have reported that populations from northern latitudes produce pelagic young, whereas those from more southerly locations produce benthic offspring. In my experience, populations from both northern and southern latitudes produce offspring that spend a few days to a week in the pelagic zone.

Many reports of captive breeding exist for this species and it is probably the most commonly reared member of the family. Brood size for an average five-inch fish is around 250 to 300, with numbers up to 600 being quite common. Maximum brood size for this species is around 1,500. Newborns typically hatch around 8 to 11 mm after a gestation period of 14 to 30 days. There is a tradeoff between gestation period and the size of newborns in this and most

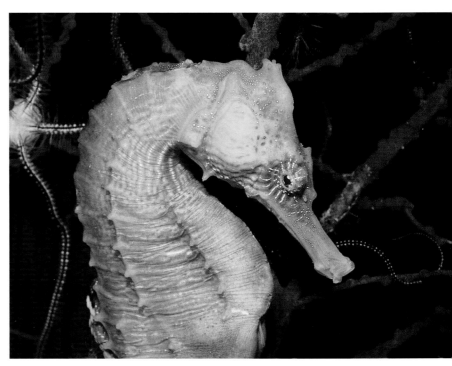

Lined Seahorse (*Hippocamous erectus*): a seahorse of many colors that is justifiably popular and a great subject for small-scale captive breeders,

species in the family. At warmer water temperatures, the gestation period is reduced, but the newborns are slightly smaller. At cooler temperatures, gestation is prolonged with the resulting offspring slightly larger. A temperature near 74 to 76°F produces sufficiently large offspring after a 2 to 3 week gestation period. Water temperature and gestation period also plays a significant role in determining the length of time spent in the pelagic phase. At warmer water temperatures, the pelagic phase is increased to a week or more as the newborns are smaller and less developed compared to those maintained in cooler temperatures.

Owing to the pelagic phase of early juveniles, a rearing tank with a continuous current and no dead spots in the corners or near the surface should be used. Mortality during the early juvenile phase is significantly reduced when offspring are exposed to a circular water pattern so a kreisel or similar design that provides a cross-current near the surface to reduce floaters or those attracted towards the surface film is ideal. Many aquarists, however, have been successful in rearing *H. erectus* broods in compartmentalized aquariums with sufficient flow across the surface. I once reared a batch of Lined Seahorses in a bare 180-gallon aquarium with two single airlines placed on opposite ends of the aquarium. Airstones were not used and the large bubbles created a rocking motion that seemed to suit the newborns. Using this rearing tank and feeding wild plankton and enriched *Artemia*, I was able to record a survival rate of nearly 70 percent. Most of the observed mortality occurring in the juvenile phase can be attributed to water turbulence patterns and feeding during the early pelagic phase.

Although *H. erectus* newborns are capable of consuming *Artemia* nauplii as an initial meal, it is wise to include enriched rotifers during the first week of development. Gut contents analysis performed on newborns reveal that rotifers are ingested in great numbers and may provide adequate HUFA supplementation until enriched *Artemia* is added to the diet a few days later. Copepods added to the diet during the first week can also have a significant affect on survivorship. For the first week of development, enriched rotifers and newly hatched *Artemia* less than 12 hours old should make up the bulk of the diet. Supplemental copepods should be offered when available. A general rule of thumb is to add greenwater as long as rotifers are being fed or until the juveniles have adopted a benthic lifestyle. Settlement from pelagic to benthic modes is usually accomplished within one week, although many will begin hitching to objects within a few days. One-day-old *Artemia* can usually be added to the diet by the end of the first week. When *Artemia* is properly enriched, acceptable survival rates can be achieved. Cleaner shrimp larvae and small live mysids can be added to the diet around the fourth week of age.

Depending on the size and type of rearing tank used, young may need to be separated to larger growout tanks. Large rearing tanks can be used for growout, alleviating the stress involved with transfer to other tanks. In small rearing tanks such as goldfish-bowl kreisels, the young may have to be moved as young as 2 months of age. It is important not to move these young too soon. Growth rates in this species are exceptionally fast and young can grow as much as four or five inches in one year. Sexual maturity is reported by 8 months of age. Major bottlenecks to production involve the design of the rearing tanks used for newborns prior to settlement and supplying a nutritionally rich food during the first feeding stage.

Brazilian or Longsnout Seahorse

Hippocampus reidi (Ginsberg, 1933)
Maximum Length: 15 cm (5.9 in.).
Sexual Allocation: Gonochorist.

The Brazilian Seahorse is a very popular species among aquarists as they often exhibit extreme and variable coloration and are impressively large as adults. The most popular forms are orange, yellows and reds, though colors of green, brown, white and tan are also common. Perhaps one of the most appealing traits of this species is that color patterns are rarely uniform and most sport intricate patterns of two or more colors.

During the breeding season males and females heighten in coloration, taking on an almost fluorescent glow. This species is common in aquarium stores throughout the United States, but prices have recently climbed due to their CITES status and collection restrictions in the wild.

Unfortunately, the Brazilian Seahorse is one of the most difficult species to rear owing to the small size of newborns and an extended pelagic phase. This is a species best suited to advanced aquarists and those willing to invest time and resources in constructing an appropriate rearing tank and providing suitable prey organisms such as copepods.

Habitat & Range: *Hippocampus reidi* appears most commonly throughout the Caribbean Sea from southern Florida to northern South America. The complete range of this species extends northward in the Atlantic to North Carolina, including Bermuda, and the entire Gulf of Mexico. Though not as common as the Lined Seahorse, this species is occasionally sighted by eagle-eyed divers in inlets and on reefscapes clinging to sponges and manmade debris. *Hippocampus reidi* tends to be more common on reef structures than in seagrass beds.

Breeding & Rearing: Pairs should be fed at least three times daily with high-quality mysids appropriately enriched. A spawning tank of at least 20 inches vertical height should be provided and connected to a well-seeded biological filter and protein skimmer. This species seems less tolerant of poor water quality than *H. erectus*. Newly acquired pairs or those paired for the first time may be reluctant to spawn, but spawning is a common affair in healthy, well-fed, well-acclimated individuals. A diet rich in Omega-3 fatty acids and a slight increase in temperature or longer photoperiod usually triggers reproduction. A temperature of 76-80°F is sufficient for spawning. An initial photoperiod of 12 to 14 hours is ideal. If no signs of reproductive behavior are observed within a few months, the photoperiod can be increased to 14 to 16 hours.

Gestation typically lasts 15 to 18 days at a water temperature near 78°F. Typical brood size is around 300 with first-time breeders releasing substantially fewer young. Large broods of around 1,000 or more have been reported. The most difficult aspect of rearing *H. reidi* stems from the small newborn size at release—around 5-7 mm. Young do not initiate settlement and begin hitching to moored objects until they are roughly 10 to 15 mm. This often means young will remain in the pelagic phase for as long as 2 to 3 weeks.

This extended pelagic phase drastically reduces the choices of rearing tanks available to hobbyists. A kreisel-type design is essential for rearing *H. reidi*. Mortality rates in this species will reach near 100 percent in the first few weeks if proper water conditions and feeding are not met. Under less than ideal conditions, at least some newborns may survive the pelagic stage, with a few going on to survive through the juvenile period. Since the pelagic phase of *H. reidi* is double or triple that of *H. erectus,* there is less room for error.

It is possible to split large broods into small kreisel-type rearing tanks, but water quality should remain a major consideration throughout the rearing period. Unless small tanks are connected through a centralized system, it is advisable to

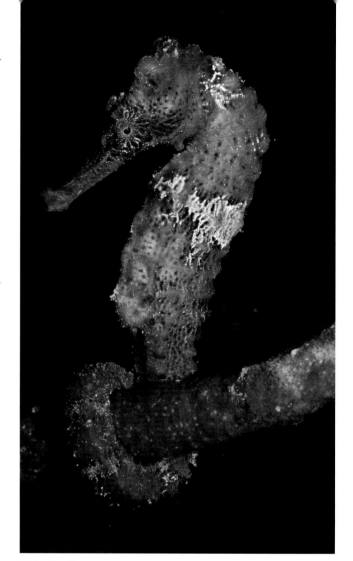

Male Brazlian Seahorse (*H. reidi*) a challenging-to-breed-species whose small newborns go through a pelagic phase.

rear young in one or two larger tanks to control deteriorations in water quality. Although partial water changes can alleviate nitrogenous build-ups, it is much less stressful for delicate newborns if a constant slow water exchange is provided to control water quality continually. Kreisel tanks constructed from 16-gallon high or larger display aquariums work well, as do upwelling conical rearing tanks of 20-or 30-gallons.

It is advisable to use greenwater additions in rearing tanks with access to the surface. Newborn *H. reidi* are highly phototactic and will congregate towards the surface unless access is blocked or light levels reduced. In advanced kreisels, the surface is often blocked with a bent piece of acrylic to facilitate a more uniform circular water flow. This design eliminates the possibility of floaters. It is still advisable to add a small amount of greenwater to these tanks to prevent the young from exhausting themselves trying to reach the surface. Side-illuminated tanks should be avoided. Some breeders advocate the use of low-salinity water (down to 1.018 SG) to make the newborns less bouyant.

Once a proper rearing environment has been established, the next major hurdle is supplying the small pelagic newborns with a nutritionally rich prey organisms small enough to be captured and ingested. Most home-based hobbyists will be limited to a large strain of rotifer enriched with HUFAs. This diet alone is poorly suited to commercial production, as high mortality usually results from malnourishment. Remember, the gut evacuation time of a rotifer enriched with HUFAs is 8 to 12 hours. This means enriched rotifers must be added at least every 8 to 12 hours while purging unenriched rotifers from the system.

Maintaining greenwater in the system ensures that rotifers carry at least some nourishment, but if only microalgae is used as a supplement, newborns rarely survive. For this reason, it is important to establish the rearing tanks on a centralized water system or at least its own independant water exchange system. A constant slow exchange of seawater through the system will purge rotifers from the

rearing tank. The standpipe should be fitted with a 500 micron screen—large enough for rotifers to pass through, but small enough to prevent newborns from entering. Many aquarists prefer a small-mesh screen to prevent the loss of rotifers to the system and reduces the density of prey available for the seahorses. Once rotifers have evacuated their guts and lost the HUFA supplements, they are no longer acceptable prey organisms.

A constant cycle of rotifer culture and enrichment should be maintained while newborn seahorses are pelagic so rotifer enrichment tanks should be run at all times. Rotifers should be enriched for at least 8 hours prior to feeding. A density of 5 to 10 rotifers per mL of water is suitable prey density and will compensate for those lost to water exchange.

If copepods can be made available during the earliest portion of the pelagic phase, significant improvements in survival can usually be observed. Juveniles are usually large enough to accept newly hatched *Artemia* after one week. It is important to co-feed with enriched rotifers during this phase. Once all juveniles are observed feeding on 24-hour enriched *Artemia,* the rotifers can be removed from the feeding regime.

Newly hatched cleaner shrimp larvae and small live mysids should be added to the diet near the fourth week of age. Most juveniles will have settled from the water column by two weeks of age. By this time mortality rates have also usually subsided. Young can be weaned to frozen

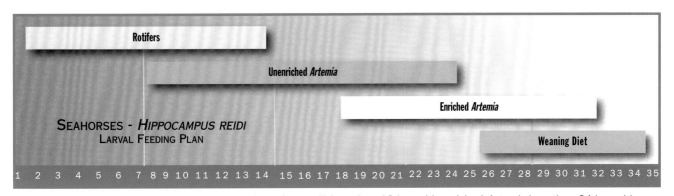

Guidelines: Feed rotifers at 10/ml; unenriched *Artemia* nauplii less than 12 hrs. old; enriched *Artemia* less than 24 hrs. old.

The coveted marine an-
gelfishes, such as this
Earspot Angelfish (*Po-
macanthus chrysurus*)
command high prices
and are beginning to be
bred and reared by ex-
pert aquaculturists.

CHAPTER 12

PELAGIC SPAWNERS

The Ultimate Challenges for Marine Breeding

For many years, the Holy Grail of aquarium breeders, both hobbyists and scientists, has been the successful breeding and rearing of marine angelfishes under artificial conditions. Diverse, incredibly beautiful, and always in demand with price tags to match, saltwater angels make a tempting target for would-be breeding operations.

The problem has not been getting them to spawn in captivity, but raising the larvae. Pelagic spawning fishes such as these pose a drastically different set of challenges than most demersal spawning species. In the early years of commercial aquarium-fish aquaculture, the species of coral reef fishes that were successfully reared in captivity were all demersal spawners. Pioneers in the field faced daunting challenges that they eventually overcame, successfully raising clownfishes, gobies, blennies, basslets and other species that produced demersal eggs.

Spawning in these fishes resembled that in freshwater aquarium species. Demersal spawners usually guard their nests until relatively advanced-stage larvae hatch out and enter the pelagic realm. Once people realized that *Artemia* nauplii were simply too big a first food, and after rotifers were identified as a useable food source, many species of demersal spawners were able to be successfully reared. Many species and groups of demersal spawners continue to resist easy culturing, but dedicated breeders will very likely unlock their secrets.

Pelagic spawners are entirely different to demersal spawners. Their tiny eggs and impossibly tiny larvae have proved extremely difficult to rear using common rearing practices. The vast majority of coral reef fish species are pelagic spawners. Wrasses, reef basslets, anthias, groupers, angels, butterflys, triggers, boxfish—and the list goes

Barred Hamlets (*Hypoplectrus puella*) in classic mid-water spawning act in the water column over a Caribbean reef.

on—all produce small, pelagic eggs at the height of a spawning ascent over the reef.

Pelagic spawning marine fishes with commercial importance for either food or sport are routinely spawned and reared. Snook (*Centropomus undecimalis*), Redfish (*Sciaenops ocellatus*), Pompano (*Trachinotus carolinus*), Cobia (*Rachycentron canadum*), Dolphinfish or Mahi Mahi (*Coryphaena hippurus*), many species of grouper (*Epinephalus* spp.) and many other pelagic spawners have been commercially reared with great success.

So why is it so hard to achieve success with coral reef fish that spawn pelagic eggs?

PRO-LARVAE & POND CULTURE

Pelagic broadcast spawners release thousands to millions of buoyant eggs into the water column. Hatching in an average of 12 to 36 hours, the resulting larvae are very different from those of demersal spawners. Eggs of pelagic spawners average 1 mm in length and contain oil globules that aid in buoyancy. The larvae of pelagic spawners are

roughly half the size of a newly hatched clownfish or dottyback. After working with these larvae, I have gained a new appreciation for the seemingly gigantic larvae of clownfish and similar species. When hatched, a pro-larva does not have eyes or fins—this is a rudimentary fish, a glass thread attached to an enormous yolk sac. Rather than developing within the confines of the egg membrane and protected by adult fishes, pelagic spawners hatch early and develop at sea, a radically different development strategy.

Marine fish that exhibit a pro-larval stage are extremely delicate and exquisitely sensitive to virtually every physical and chemical parameter within the surrounding environment. They are miniscule and require the right-sized live prey organisms for proper nutrition. An environment must be created to offer the larvae good water quality in gentle currents just strong enough to keep them moving without injuring them. Of the many eggs shed by a female broadcast spawner, it is not uncommon to raise less than one percent of the larvae to metamorphosis, if any at all.

Such small larvae are foreign to most newcomers to the hobby and even many experienced culturists continue to experience difficulty dealing with them. It is impossible to stereotype each family of marine fish as having a certain type of pro-larvae, as broad diversity can exist within related genera of fishes.

Many marine food-fish species with small pro-larvae have been raised for years in Southeast Asia. Rabbitfish (Siganidae), many species of groupers (Serranidae), mullets (Mullidae), snappers (Lutjanidae), puffers (Diodontidae), and many more have been captive-spawned and successfully reared. The Panther Grouper (*Chromileptes altivelis*) and Emperor Snapper (*Lutjanus sebae*) are prime examples of food fish co-cultured for the aquarium trade. However, the techniques and systems used in these larviculture protocols differ significantly from those that home aquarists in temperate climates could realistically follow. However, many of these families have representatives in the hobby and existing techniques should have lessons we can use.

In Southeast Asia, pond culture is a popular technique, as is the use of extremely large concrete and fiberglass tanks.

Enormous volumes of seawater are held in rearing tanks and fertilized with microalgae and zooplankton prior to stocking with eggs. Mortality rates are daunting, but stocking densities can be very high. The Red Sea Yellowbar Angelfish (*Pomacanthus maculosus*) is reared in this way in Taiwan. Broodstock are usually injected with hormones (usually HCG) and allowed to spawn in large tanks. Eggs are then collected and stocked into enormous rearing tanks. A few months later, following metamorphosis and a significant growout time, the aquaculturists drop the water level and harvest the progeny.

NEW REARING TECHNIQUES

In Asia, Japan, Europe and the U.S., more sophisticated attempts yield results with a number of economically important food-fish species. Commercial ventures with snapper, grouper, flatfish, pompano, and several other species producing pro-larval forms have achieved success with a variety of different methods. Again, one thing most operations have in common is the size of the rearing tank.

Large water volumes are essential. Larvae are small, easily damaged and affected by uneven water circulation patterns found in smaller tanks. Feeding success is also severely limited in small tanks. Most operations yielding significant results employ some method of maintaining greenwater with the larvae. Rearing water is tinted dark green or brown for the first week or so after first feeding commences.

Most commercial food-fish species are raised with rotifers. Adult rotifers are typically too large to be used as a food source by young pelagic spawners, but in high densities (over 20/mL) the rotifer population produces enough small rotifers to act as a food source for growing larvae. The "*ss strain*" of rotifer is believed by some to be the reason Japanese breeders are having such great success. These

A larval Lookdown (*Selene vomer*) undergoing metamorphosis: a pelagic-spawning success from Proaquatix in Florida. Note dorsal streamers.

rotifers are stocked to over 30/mL in some operations.

So, two problems arise when attempting to raise the vast majority of coral reef fishes: providing a suitable rearing environment and procuring acceptable food items in high enough numbers to act as a reliable source of nutrition.

Several pioneering organizations in Hawaii working collaboratively have made significant headway in finding a suitable food source for pygmy angelfishes, one of the marine aquarium hobby's most challenging pelagic spawner. It was long speculated that rotifers are insufficient feed for smaller, more delicate larvae and that a new food source would have to be discovered and cultured before success could be had.

Accounts from Hawaii illustrate this fact perfectly. Flame Angelfish (*Centropyge loriculus*), Fisher's Angel (*C. fisheri*), and Masked Angel (*Genicanthus personatus*) were all successfully raised at about the same time after the discovery and cultivation of a new zooplanktonic organism. The researchers in Hawaii, of course, have had the benefit of location. Zooplankton, the natural prey for larval fishes, is easily obtained from nearshore and offshore locations. Since

The Wrasse Bass (*Liopropoma eukrines*) is expensive, rare and a perfect species for the experimental pelagic breeder.

the species in question naturally occur in these waters, the natural prey of the larvae must also occur here. With an inquisitive eye and trial and error, a suitable food source was found.

At this writing, these organizations are keeping their secret under wraps, as they currently sit on a proprietary goldmine. Any dedicated hobbyist living on a tropical water way has the opportunity to replicate their efforts. However, staring into a microscope for hours on end, examining gallons of water obtained from plankton tows in search of potential prey organisms is an exhaustive task. Searching for size and movement patterns exhibited by these prey organisms is only half the battle. If a potential prey organism is found, it still has to be mass cultured.

Not all organisms occurring in the plankton have the benefit of asexual reproduction and parthenogenesis that allows massive population explosions as rotifers do. Copepod nauplii have long been cultured, but the life cycle of these crustaceans keeps most breeders from using them successfully. Using size-sorted wild plankton as an experimental food source for captive larvae may not yield economically satisfying results, but gut analysis would indicate what organisms in the plankton were being preyed upon by the tiny larvae. I see this approach alleviating the pressure to find a needle in the planktonic haystack and could allow one to concentrate on culturing the discovered organism to high densities. This is, obviously, an exciting field and we can expect many advances in the coming years.

SMALL-SCALE SYSTEMS

Although delicate pro-larvae have been successfully raised in large water volumes, work is continually being done to improve the hydrology of rearing tanks and decipher water flow patterns that provide the best results. After the problem of first foods, the largest obstacle preventing the average hobbyist from raising these fish is the size of the rearing tank needed. Convincing the person you live with to allow an 800-gallon (3,000 L) tank to be set up in the garage may be more difficult than raising the fish. Success is greater within larger volumes of water. This helps keep delicate larvae away from the sides of the tank so they are not snagged in pits and tangled in filamentous algae. Also avoiding being physically jostled into the sides while at the same time preventing damage to the larvae from air bubbles and strong currents.

Pelagic-Spawning Tanks: The tank chosen to spawn pelagic spawning species is remarkably different from those chosen for demersal spawners. Pelagic spawning species do not produce adhesive eggs for brooding in a nest, in a parental mouth or to be attached to a substrate. Eggs of these fish are small, usually perfect spheres with an oil globule that floats them to the surface of the tank. Hundreds or thousands of these eggs are individually shed into the water column. When spawning occurs in a typical display or broodstock aquarium, these eggs are sure to be lost in the filter intake, over the standpipe and into the sump or stuck to the sides of the tank.

Two factors define an appropriate spawning tank suited to pelagic spawners. First, the reproductive behavior of the fish must be identified. Usually, reef fish practicing broadcast or pelagic spawning rise high into the water column, intertwine their bodies and release eggs at the height of the ascent before dashing back to the protection of the sea floor.

Researcher Phil Geyer and experimental small-scale pelagic spawning tanks in the Florida Institute of Technology breeding lab used by the author. Bouyant Wrasse Bass eggs are spawned at night and skimmed from the surface into egg collectors (arrows).

Many smaller species practice a reduced spawning ascent and can thus be successfully spawned in relatively shallow tanks. Mandarins (*Synchiropus splendidus* and *S. picturatus*) and other dragonets, Belted Sandfish (*Serranus subligarus*) and most small basslets (*Liopropoma* spp.) as well as some dwarf angelfish will successfully spawn in 55 gallon or similar display aquariums with sufficient height. The majority, however, require tall aquariums to complete the reproductive sequence.

I have observed many pairs of angelfish and basslets maintained in standard, shallow aquariums fail to reproduce successfully. These pairs initiate courtship and females release eggs into the ovarian lumen and the pair attempt spawning ascents. While rising into the water column, however, they inevitably run into the surface before eggs are shed. The pair then breaks apart and repeats its efforts. Spawning tanks must be tall.

Egg Collection: The second essential feature of a successful spawning tank is a proper egg collector. Eggs produced in a rectangular aquarium are very difficult to collect. Water flow is poor and unevenly distributed, and the eggs get caught up in the low-flow corners and stick to the meniscus on the sides of the tank. Pelagic spawners also maintain a slightly different spawning rhythm than demersal spawners. Instead of throwing all their eggs into one basket in the manner of demersal egglayers, they generally

School of Yellow Tangs (*Zebrasoma flavescens*) in a large aquarium in Denmark: many open-water species, including the very popular surgeonfish family, may prove to be elusive targets for small-scale marine breeders until new systems are invented.

spawn a portion of their total eggs nightly over a limited spawning season. Smaller species will produce a hundred to a few hundred eggs each evening while larger species may produce thousands to millions. It becomes important with smaller species to have an efficient means of egg collection. If just 100 eggs are produced each night and your collection attempts yield only 50, this immediately reduces your chances of successfully raising larvae.

Pelagic spawning tanks facilitate the spawning of species by providing additional height and a method of collecting the buoyant eggs. Commercial facilities breeding large species use round, fiberglass tanks on the scale of thousands of gallons. A circular water flow is implemented with pumps and often airlifts to move the water toward an egg

collecting apparatus at the surface. A large-diameter PVC pipe is cut in half or a gutter used to direct eggs toward a collector. This bar or gutter is placed at the surface on half the tank with the open side placed toward the direction of water flow. As water circulates in a directional flow, the buoyant eggs are washed into the gutter and transported to an egg collector outside the tank.

This design can be mimicked by small-scale breeders and hobbyists. Typically, pelagic spawning reef fishes of interest to home-based breeders can be successfully spawned in tanks of 50 to 100 gallons. Tall, cylindrical tanks made from fiberglass or various plastics are ideal for such species. The easiest and most inexpensive tanks are plastic drums used for water and food storage. These drums are roughly 50 to 60 gallons in capacity and are available through various aquaculture and plastics supply sources. To convert them into spawning tanks, several modifications must be made. First, the tank must be plumbed to a central sump to allow circulation of water through the tank. Systems can be simple, with a single spawning tank connected to a sump containing the filtration and heating elements or the system can be quite complex linking several to many tanks together through a common sump. Adding tanks to an existing system is easy once the skeleton is created.

Upwelling Water Flow: To concentrate and collect eggs, a circular, upwelling flow of water must be created within the tank. This is most easily accomplished by placing the water inlet angled to the wall near the bottom of the tank. Water is forced in a circular direction and allowed to rise through the tank eventually exiting the top through a one-inch or larger bulkhead. The bulkhead is placed at the desired water level to act as a surface skimmer, removing the eggs as they reach this point.

Next, an egg collector must be rigged for the tank. A collection bar can be placed in the tank to facilitate egg collection, although in smaller spawning tanks this is generally not necessary. If desired, a one-inch length of PVC can be cut in half and inserted in the bulkhead so that the open half is angled toward the direction of flow. As the water and floating eggs reach the bar, they are effectively transported down the length of the gutter and exit the bulkhead.

On the outside of the spawning tank and connected to the bulkhead is a separate, smaller tank used to concentrate the eggs. This is typically no more than 5 gallons (20 L). A bulkhead is then placed on the bottom of this container, with a standpipe, or near the top to maintain a desired level of water in the egg collector. The standpipe or bulkhead is fitted with an overflow screen or banjo filter to keep the eggs from being sucked down.

It is important that such screens offer enough surface area and water flow so that eggs are not pinned tightly to the screen and damaged. Many designs use a wall of air bubbles that constantly wipe the screen of any eggs. In simple egg collectors, the eggs are transported to this tank and later

collected. A series of gates and ball valves control the water from the spawning tank and can be diverted to the sump where the eggs will be harvested. A small beaker or similar glassware as well as a turkey baster can be used to remove the eggs from this collector.

Pelagic eggs are generally water-hardened enough to endure some physical buffeting during transfer. Larger egg collectors feed the water from the spawning tank through a basket made of 240 micron screen. The basket fits into an external box such as that described above and can be lifted out to reduce the amount of water in the basket and concentrate the eggs.

Proper Salinity: Salinity is a major determinant in buoyancy of pelagic eggs and thus the deciding factor as to whether eggs are successfully collected or not. In low-salinity environments, eggs will not float high in the water column and usually evade the most sophisticated egg collectors. Salinity must be maintained at or near ocean strength to facilitate egg collection.

There is a persistent tendency among aquarists to maintain low salinity levels in hopes it will alleviate stress by improving osmoregulation, but fish have evolved in certain habitats under distinct ecological constraints. Salinity must be maintained near normal values.

Pelagic spawning tanks are generally not available and must be built by the aquarist. Any tall plastic, cylindrical container will yield satisfactory results. I prefer to place a viewing window in the tank to monitor the broodstock for signs of reproduction. This is easily accomplished by cutting a hole in the side of the container and inserting a piece of flexible clear plastic sheeting such as Lexan or Makrolon. These are made of polycarbonate, are pliable and will not crack from drilling or being bent to shape. Acrylic or Plexiglas may be used if the bend is not too severe. Silicone is used as a gasket between the polycarbonate window and the sides of the container. Silicone generally does not stick to these types of plastic and thus acts as a simple gasket. Stainless steel or nylon bolts are placed every four inches or so along each axis of the window. Bolts should be covered with silicone once everything is tightened.

SPECIES FOR HOME BREEDERS

Today, these are uncharted waters. Very few pelagic spawning marine aquarium fishes have been raised in small-scale systems at the time of this writing. Conditioning and inducing spawning is a relatively simple task in many species, and egg collection poses few problems in the proper system.

However, first feeding remains a major constraint. I have included a short description of reproduction in some noteworthy species that I feel hold promise to dedicated aquarists ready to devote themselves to pelagic-spawning marine fishes.

Swissguard Basslets (*Liopropoma rubre*) and others in its highly prized genus offer a prime opportunity for home-scale pelagic breeders.

Reef Basslets

This group of highly prized reef fishes (*Liopropoma* spp.) holds tremendous potential for captive propagation. Most species are small and can be successfully housed in aquariums of 15 gallons (57 L) or more. Species of interest include the Candy Basslet (*Liopropoma carmabi*), Swissguard Basslet (*L. rubre*), Wrasse Bass (*L. eukrines*), Swalesi Basslet (*L. swalesi*) and many more that only occasionally turn up in the trade such as the Many-lined Basslet (*L. multilineatum*) and the Ridgeback Basslet (*L. mowbrayi*). These species are rare enough and so well-suited to reef aquarium conditions that they typically fetch tidy sums whenever they are offered for sale to hobbyists.

Few difficulties are encountered when spawning these fishes, assuming a heterosexual pair has been obtained. Although I have observed smaller species such as *L. rubre* and *L. carmabi* spawn in small home aquariums, serious attempts should only be made in tanks with sufficient height to increase total fecundity per spawning.

Pair formation is usually a matter of trial and error. It has been suggested that members of this group display bi-directional juvenile gonads that differentiate terminally upon sexual maturity. Of six attempts to pair adult specimens of *L. eukrines* that I was involved in, four pairs resulted. (The other potential two pairs ended due to death from acrobatic jumpers and poorly covered aquariums.)

Sexual strategies in this group may be more complex than previously thought. These fish are quite rare in aquarium stores and choices are generally limited to adult fish. Random pairing is often the only option. Preferably, one large and one small specimen should be chosen. An alternative is to obtain the smallest individuals possible in hopes of obtaining sexually immature specimens. A prospective pair should be added to the pelagic spawning tank simultaneously to limit aggressive displays. Fortunately, few aggressive displays are observed in most species, with most involving little more than posturing and exaggerated swimming. I have never witnessed actual harm inflicted during one of these encounters.

Conditioning foods include pieces of fresh squid, shrimp, clams and mussels as well as live ghost shrimp and small crabs when available. I have observed Wrasse Basses (*L. eukrines*) develop fatty livers from a diet containing too much squid. A varied diet is important. This group is also particularly sensitive to deterioration in water quality. Heavy filtration, including protein skimming, and frequent water changes are essential to their maintenance and spawning.

Another important factor influencing spawning rhythms is water temperature. Most species of reef basslets occur in deeper, darker habitats with cooler water. The Wrasse Bass (*L. eukrines*) is frequently collected off the east coast of middle Florida where water temperatures routinely drops to 70°F in the winter. A temperature of 74 to 78°F is ideal for most species. If respiratory stress or other physical stresses are observed, a decrease in water temperature accompanied by increasing dissolved oxygen is usually a quick remedy.

Spawning is typically initiated by the male who signals his intentions by swimming toward the female, slowly waving his body erratically side to side. Once he reaches the female, he swims around her in tight circles waving his body. Eventually the male settles under the female and uses his snout to nudge the female upwards. When maintained under a strict daylength, this behavior is usually observed two hours before the lights are due to go out. This behavior lasts an average of 45 minutes to an hour and is thought to initiate final ovulation. Females do not noticeably swell with eggs until an hour before actual spawning is observed.

Successful spawning occurs at the height of a spawning ascent. It is difficult to see the process and keen observers will be hard pressed to see a glimpse of a white fog that is the faint cloud of shed eggs and sperm. Several spawning ascents are observed each evening for weeks at a time. Small species release 50 to 500 eggs each night, while larger species such as the Wrasse Bass have been recorded releasing between 234-1,278 eggs per night.

The morning following successful spawning, the eggs should be harvested from the egg collector and stocked into a rearing tank. Large—20 gal. (76 L) or larger—cylindrical, black-colored rearing tanks should be used with very light aeration or an upwelling flow of water. Eggs measure roughly .5 to .95 mm in diameter and possess a single oil globule that aids in buoyancy. Hatching occurs in 18 to 24 hours resulting in a very simple pro-larva with a large finfold surrounding the body. The finfold is heavily pigmented with white blotches, the eyes are not pigmented, no digestive tract is present, and the larvae possess a very large yolk sac. The oil globule is present in the anterior portion of the yolk and the larvae float in the water column with their heads pointed up. Pro-larvae generally drift motionless with the water current in the tank but erratic swimming movements are often observed. This usually occurs when the larvae sink in the water column. First feeding begins on day 3 after hatching when the larvae have grown to slightly more than 2 mm in total length. The eyes are now pigmented and a filament begins to form from the dorsal finfold. Larval rearing of *Liopropoma* spp. has not been successful beyond 15 days, to my knowledge. Late-stage larvae are very distinctive, adorned with long dorsal and anal filaments that extend beyond the edge of the tail. These filaments are prone to snagging on cuts in plastic side walls or any other minute structure within the rearing tank. First feeding is the major bottleneck to successful culture.

Angelfishes—Family Pomacanthidae

When I first began writing this chapter several years ago I opened with a promising notion: while to date few species of marine angels had been reared past metamorphosis, the future looked bright for their eventual captive propagation in commercial numbers. Several years later, many species have, in fact, been added to the list of captive-raised angelfish, and the future looks brighter than ever for the mass culture of the marine aquarium hobby's most-prized fishes.

The secrets of angelfish reproduction are no longer a total mystery. In fact, with increasing knowledge of the fishes' life history and social structures in captivity, more and more angelfish species are proving to be reliable and productive spawners.

The dream among marine fish culturists is to be the first to spawn and raise various marine angelfish species.

Aquarium pair of Resplendent Pygmy Angelfish (*Centropyge resplendens*): slimmer male is at left, egg-filled female at right.

Angelfishes are found throughout the world's oceans and their diversity attests to their distribution. While it is no longer possible for someone to be the first to raise a *Centropyge* spp., a wealth of opportunity surrounds this group.

Success with this family first began in the 1970s when Martin A. Moe, Jr. raised the first French Angelfish (*Pomacanthus paru*) through metamorphosis. Using common aquaculture techniques, the use of HCG hormone injections and enormous rearing tanks, as well as wild, size-sorted plankton, Moe was successful. Then, decades went by with very little advancement in the field. Fish would continually spawn in hobbyists tanks, but no one could raise the resulting larvae using traditional techniques.

The year 2002 changed all this. Almost simultaneously, three accounts of successful rearing trials involving three different species of angelfish flooded the fish world. The Waikiki Aquarium announced success with the Masked Angelfish (*Genicanthus personatus*) due to the discovery of a new zooplankton food organism by Karen Brittain. Dr. Charles Laidley and Dr. Robin Shields of the Oceanic Institute raised Flame Angelfish (*Centropyge loriculus*) and Frank Baensch, working with Dr. Malia Chow of the Hawaii Institute of Marine Biology, raised Fisher's Angelfish (*Centropyge fisheri*). All three species were raised in Hawaii not by coincidence but because the experimenters collaborated with each other in developing techniques.

In Taiwan, a protocol developed to raise Red Sea Yellowbar Angelfish (*Pomacanthus maculosus*). Although details are lacking, they are presumably spawned using similar techniques employed by Moe to raise French Angelfish. Broodstock are probably maintained in large fiberglass tanks and injected with HCG once oocyte diameter reaches the appropriate size. Eggs from natural spawning are then collected and stocked in pre-established ponds with microalgae and zooplankton blooms. Captive-raised offspring have become available throughout the U.S.

Spawning and raising marine angelfish by home aquarists will be limited, in all but the rarest cases, to dwarf angelfishes of the genera *Centropyge* and *Genicanthus*. Dedicated systems designed for the purpose of raising *Pomacanthus, Holacanthus, Euxiphipops, Chaetodontoplus*, or the monotypic *Pygoplites* will undoubtedly require enormous volumes of water out of the reach of the average home aquarist. For the purpose of this discussion I will limit myself to dwarf angels for dedicated hobbyists.

Spawning angelfish in captivity is relatively easy. Dwarf angels are quite common in the aquarium trade and prove hardy and long-lived when well-kept. Most, if not all, dwarf angels are protogynous hermaphrodites, so obtaining a spawning pair is quite simple and obtaining large numbers of eggs can easily be accomplished by the formation of a harem. The family Pomacanthidae is not unlike most marine fish families in having a wealth of diversity.

Random pairing is the best approach with any species of dwarf angel. Simply placing two random individuals in the same aquarium and cautiously observing their reaction is a simple method. The chance of obtaining a pair can, however, be increased in the favor of the aquarist by bringing one large and one small fish together. It is very difficult to determine the sexual function of any given specimen based on size, color, finnage or other external characteristics. Pairing adult fish is more difficult than pairing juveniles, whose sexual function is still undetermined. It is assumed that male reproductive function is terminal and they cannot revert to the original state of female function. If two large fish are therefore placed in the same tank, vicious attacks may ensue as two males have no chance of spawning and simply view the other as a territorial threat to his harem. If specimen availability is limited, choose only one large fish and assume its reproductive function to be male. Then, find a small specimen to complete the pair. It is very important not to add two specimens to the same aquarium at different times. This would allow one specimen to establish itself in the new environment and most often attack the rival. Instead, the two fish should be added simultaneously to a new aquarium.

When two angelfish of a given species are placed together in the same aquarium, many outcomes are possible. They may ignore one another or attack each other viciously. Those exhibiting extreme, immediate aggression should be separated and assumed to be males. While this may not be the case, pair formation is limited in these situations. Fish

"TANK-RAISED" FISHES

With millions of eggs cast into the ocean and millions of mouths to eat them, fisheries biologists urgently want to know how many pelagic-spawning fish make it back to the reef. At the completion of metamorphosis, juvenile fish are ill-suited to living in the open ocean, where their colors and sizes render them easy targets to keen-eyed predators. During the larval and juvenile stages of development, the immature offspring of many families of marine fishes are attracted to light. Light trapping is a trick originally designed by marine biologists as a way to catch larval fishes and quantify juvenile reef fish recruitment. At night, large acrylic boxes are moored in pre-determined sites with a single, vertically mounted fluorescent bulb inside. Similar to a minnow trap, the lighted box allows juveniles to enter a space with little chance of escape.

Reef fish recruitment seems highest around the new moon and each reef seems to attract different numbers of each family. Entrepreneurs in South Pacific areas have recently begun using this technique to collect settlement-stage reef fish for the aquarium trade.

After capture, juvenile fish are transported to a holding facility consisting of large fiberglass or concrete tubs. Here, they are grown to saleable size and labeled "captive-raised" or "tank-raised".

However, light trapping can be extremely labor-intensive and the traps and trappers are always at the mercy of the seas. In harsh weather, the traps cannot be collected or may be lost or destroyed. Many of the juvenile fish attracted to light traps may be of no commercial appeal and are therefore not saleable. Still, this method does have potential and several companies are now marketing fish captured and grown in this way. Other similar devices such as channel nets prove efficient in capturing settlement-stage fish, but often prove damaging to small fish destined for aquariums. The harvest of pre-settlement stage reef fish is considered a sustainable practice. Juvenile reef fishes undergo extreme mortality shortly after settlement and by removing juvenile fishes before they are exposed to heavy losses reduces the impact on adult populations.

that initially ignore one another are probably females or juveniles of undetermined sex. In this situation, sex change will take place over time, resulting in a heterosexual pair.

At certain times of the year, very small wild-caught specimens are often available. The rules of protogynous hermaphroditism dictate the outcome. If small individuals are available, place two or more in the same aquarium—the smaller the better. As they mature towards adulthood, dominance will be established and the sexes formed accordingly. The dominant fish will assume male reproductive function while a submissive individual will mature to female sexual function. If more than two small angelfish are placed in the same tank, a social hierarchy will form and a harem will be established. One male and several females can be established in this way. Once a pair or harem has been established, they should be kept in a clean tank and fed a basic broodstock diet consisting of fresh shrimp and seafoods in a gelatinous paste. Algae should be a major ingredient in the paste. Fresh algae and romaine lettuce leaves are greatly appreciated by these fish. Feeding should consist of at least three feedings a day. Spawning usually commences within a few months of being isolated, assuming the fish are of reproductive age.

Dwarf angels release individual pelagic eggs into the water column at the height of a spawning ascent. Broodstock tanks should be high, rather than long, to facilitate this behavior. Eggs are roughly .5 to .8 mm in diameter and contain one to several oil droplets that keep them afloat. The spawn may consist of many hundreds of eggs. Spawning occurs daily for many months. Egg collection is difficult as the eggs are not shed in a single mass at one event.

Hatching occurs between 15 to 20 hours in most species, resulting in pro-larvae that lack pigmented eyes, a functional digestive tract, fins, or resemblance to a juvenile. At hatching, pro-larvae measure roughly 1.5 to 2 mm in total length and do not accept food for three days. During this time the yolk reserves provide fuel for their development.

Rearing marine angelfish is no small task. Larvae are small, delicate and exhibit tiny mouth structures. Before long the basics of raising marine angelfish through metamorphosis will be better known, but until then it is up to dedicated and explorative aquarists to deviate from normal protocols. Nothing short of large, round rearing vessels with black sides should be attempted in culturing angels.

Commercially important marine food fish have similarly small pro-larval phases. Eggs are stocked into large round vessels and allowed to develop unmolested until functional digestive tract has formed accompanied by pigmented eyes. At this time the water is tinted with microalgae and the fish fed the appropriate-sized zooplankton. The water remains a pea soup color for the first week. The aquarists forfeit any visual indication of larval survival in these conditions, but the key is finding the right food and getting the pro-larvae through this first critical period.

PELAGIC SPAWNING FUTURES

Whether or not small-scale breeders will achieve widespread success with pelagic spawners remains to be seen. I believe the the lack of progress to date stems from two factors. Firstly, the majority of success with pelagic spawning species occurs in well-funded facilities with academic and scientific expertise or private commercial backing—often both. These facilities deal with species of commercial interest. Until recently, aquarium fishes drew little attention, as money was not available for research. Similarly, competition from wild imports seriously impacts the potential to make a return on investment. Biological data surrounding the life history traits of these fishes is all but absent from literature, while fisheries biologists have long studied the life habits of commercially important food-fish species.

Secondly, the larvae of these species are drastically different than those of demersal spawners that are the mainstay of ornamental or aquarium-fish aquaculture. Incubation is generally highly reduced, resulting in pro-larval forms with yolk sacs that require an additional 2 to 3 days to initiate their first feeding. Egg collection and incubation prior to first feeding remain hurdles in many species that produce pelagic eggs. The miniscule larvae of pelagic

One of the Holy Grails for marine aquarium keepers, the Regal Angelfish (*Pygoplites diacanthus*) is the sort of species that fuels the dreams of breeders hoping to unlock its secrets.

spawners are typically more prone to stress and unable to survive less-than-perfect rearing practices. Perhaps most importantly, traditional foods such as rotifers are often too large for larvae to capture with ease and efficiency.

It is interesting that a number species of pelagic spawning marine aquarium fish are being successfully spawned and reared for the purpose of food including the Panther Grouper (*Chromileptes altivelis*) and the Emperor Snapper (*Lutjanus sebae*). Both have been commercially available for some time. A major difference between these fishes and those of smaller marine species is the size of their eggs and the number produced. Survival rates in these species typically hover at or below 1 percent. When a large female grouper or snapper produces millions of eggs, one-percent survival still yields some 10,000 fish for grow-out. Smaller reef fishes producing hundreds or thousands of eggs typically suffer high mortalities resulting in few to no larvae that survive to juvenile grow-out.

For now, the opportunities for small-scale breeders to find success with many pelagic species is limited, but this may not always be the case. The breeding of marine aquarium fishes is barely out of its infancy, and no one knows what breakthroughs are coming—or what innovative solutions will come from determined hobbyists and small-scale breeders.

Surely many breakthroughs are in store in the coming years, but for anyone ready to try their hands at breeding a pelagic species, this section has been a mere introduction. Many things need to be discovered to successfully induce spawning in pelagic marine aquarium fishes, collect the resulting eggs and get past the critical feeding stages. As more eggs are spawned and successfully collected, the greater the chances of unraveling the secrets of larval rearing.

With continued experience and gained knowledge, more species of pelagic spawners will be successfully reared in captivity for the aquarium trade. Each year hobbyists report surgeonfishes, butterflyfishes, angelfishes, trunkfishes and many others spawning in their community aquariums. As more interest is taken in marine breeding, the number of individual hobbyists and scientists attempting to solve reproductive and rearing problems will increase.

Eventually, commercial culture with high survival will be realized. Whether those who succeed will find adequate financial rewards is an open question. For hobbyists running their small-scale operations primarily as labors of love, the cost of experimentation is relatively low and the potential rewards for being one of the first to achieve success with pelagic-spawning species tantalizing.

A healthy batch of captive-bred Clark's Clownfish (*Amphiprion clarkii*) ready for market. Part of marine breeding is the challenge of finding outlets for your success.

CHAPTER 13

MATH & MOTIVATION

To the Breeder Come the Rewards of Successful Spawns

Astroll through the aisles of marine aquariums at a local pet shop can leave dollar signs dancing in a new breeder's eyes. As you return home to stare into your rearing tanks packed full of colorful juveniles, the mental math puts a smile on your face. Though hardly a get-rich-quick scheme, success in marine breeding can help you reap some financial rewards.

Whether you simply recoup your costs or make a profit will depend on many aspects of both the market and your salesmanship. Early in your endeavors, it is important to make the distinction between profit-driven motivation and self-accomplishment and curiosity. Will you gauge your success in dollars or in knowing you have done something extraordinary?

While commercial marine ornamental aquaculture is a competitive business with a history of financial losses, hobbyists throughout the world continue to document great results in the captive propagation of marine organisms. The reality is that amateurs and basement breeders can record and achieve success in the absence of monetary gain. Curiosity, passion and ambition define the successful small-scale breeder.

While many species are ideal for for commercial propagation, other fishes are economically unprofitable. Species that are too aggressive, ship poorly, exhibit drab color patterns or simply do not draw enough attention, do not make mass production commercially viable. As more home-scale marine breeders are sucessful, a great diversity of fishes should enter the marketplace. Instead of raising the bread-and-butter fishes mass-produced by large aquaculture facilities, a hobbyist can carve a niche with lesser-known and seldom propagated species.

Ready-for-sale Striped Fang Blennies (*Meicanthus grammistes*) at Proaquatix. Marketing fish successfully requires attention to supply, demand and quality.

If we lose 20 juveniles to bad water quality, fighting or disease during the grow-out phase, we end up with 180 offspring. If we then cull any deformed specimens or those with non-marketable characteristics we could lose another 20 specimens.

Now, we have to find a suitable market. One option is to drive our total saleable quantity of 140 fish to local retail shops and beg and barter for profit or trade. If a Pajama Cardinalfish sells locally for $8, a hobbyist can expect to get around $2. Our 140 fish could potentially earn a gross sale of $280.

If, on average, we assume a single aquarium shop would purchase 20 Pajama Cardinals in a month, we would need to find seven shops to unload the whole volume produced in this single spawn. Not bad, but how much money was invested to produce these fish and how long will it take to actually sell all 140 fish?

Consider the electricity it costs to run pumps and heaters, the food required to condition the broodstock and rear the larvae to marketable size and time and transport to deliver the fish to all seven shops. While a few larger shops may take 20 or more cardinals at one time, most would be hard-pressed to accept more than six or so in a week. This means it could take several trips and several months to sell all of the fish produced in this spawn.

Often, the answer to increasing profit is to increase supply. If we raised every single spawn produced by a single broodstock pair or increased the number of broodstock pairs, we could quickly double or triple the number of cardinalfish being produced. A healthy pair of Pajama Cardinalfish spawns on average every 14 days. Using the same assumptions as above, we could expect 140 fish per pair, every two weeks for as long as our broodstock remains together.

So can you really expect to make money selling your coral reef fishes? Rather than a straightforward yes or no answer, let's walk through a mathematical example.

BREEDING MATH

Assume that a single pair of Pajama Cardinals spawns an egg mass containing 1,000 eggs. With a modest hatching and survival rate of 20 percent, we can expect to stock 200 juveniles into our grow-out tanks after a larval period of roughly one month. These juveniles must be grown for 5 to 7 months to a saleable size near 4 cm (about 1.5 in.) long.

With two breeding pairs, in a single month we could produce 560 Pajama Cardinals and potentially earn $1,120. In three months 1,680 fish could be produced and be worth $3,360—at least on paper.

While the math sounds enticing, simply increasing the number of fish produced for sale does not guarantee greater returns. The reality of increased production is that more money will be invested in grow-out and it could take many months to sell 1,600 fish to local retailers, especially with the danger of saturating local markets. Increasing the market distance you cover can help distribute more fish, but in time these markets, too, may become saturated. You have become the PJ Cardinal king or queen of your area, but your growout tanks are brimming with unsold stock.

Different species will have different bottom-line scenarios, but the principle is the same: local markets are ultimately limited in the number of fish they can sell. A single spawn from an adult pair of Steene's Dottybacks or Maroon Clownfish can supply a local market for more than a year. Large fish such as these are very prolific and a single spawn can result in more than 1,000 juveniles.

Other species such as Mimic Blennies or Olive Dottybacks can saturate a market within days as their plain colors make them difficult for retailers to sell in any appreciable quantity.

Two options exist for hobbyists who have produced a large number of offspring. Selling locally will increase the price paid per fish, but if it takes months or years to sell your offspring, you may end up investing more in keeping the fish healthy than will ever be recouped. Selling wholesale is an option available to home-based breeders who want to sell large numbers fast.

Packing fish for shipping at ORA: whether to sell locally or long-distance, to retail or wholesale buyers or direct to hobbyists, are decisions all breeders face.

WHOLESALE OPTIONS

Although the wholesale price may range from 25 to 50 percent of what a local retailer would pay, bulk quantities can make this a worthwhile option. If a single spawn from an adult pair of Maroon Clownfish containing 1,500 eggs is reared and with a 70 percent survival rate to the juvenile stage, 1,050 juveniles remain. If 5 percent are culled, we are left with 997 fish to sell. This would likely be too many for a local market to handle, but it would be worth selling a few locally and the rest wholesale. If Maroon Clowns are selling to consumers for $16 and we sell 100 to local retail markets at $4 each, we could earn $400. A large wholesaler should be capable of taking 100 or more every week. A wholesale price of $2 each would yield $1,794. Selling the offspring from this single spawn could result in over $2,000 and take about 2 to 3 months to sell.

The Internet has become a fantastic tool available to small-scale breeders. Websites and discussion boards quickly disseminate information about breeders and the species they produce. They can generate sales both locally and nationally. If you decide to offer your captive fishes on the Internet, you must properly pack and ship them and handle all customer service chores. Direct sales to consumers typically yields better prices, but the time invested in establishing and maintaining the website and time spent packing and shipping small orders (and dealing with dead arrivals and other complaints) can be a burden for small-scale breeders.

It is important to keep the scale of operation realistic. Time and resources devoted to rearing fish can translate to more expense and less return if you get too ambitious. Understand your local markets and know the popular species. Determine how many stores constitute your local market and approximately how many fish of a particular species they are able to take each month. This will help determine the number of fish you could raise without getting stuck with crowded tanks of unsold fish. Following are a few tips to help you sell more fish.

Raise a diversity of species: Becoming proficient at raising a single species is a remarkable personal accomplishment, but it is a surefire way to limit your sales. There is only enough space dedicated to one species in most local retail outlets. Raise multiple species and your sales should grow. It is demand that drives sales. Your appeal as a source for captive-raised fishes is greatly influenced by the number of species you can supply. Most retail shops are more than happy to purchase locally raised fish even when wild imports are less expensive, but they will prefer breeders with a variety of choices.

The author examining a group of Orchid Dottybacks: working with popular species assures ready markets for captive breds.

Raise a popular species: Popular species sell. The faster a retail store sells them, the faster they will buy more. Species such as Royal Grammas, Orchid Dottybacks and Ocellaris Clownfish are mainstay species in the hobby. They are ubiquitous in pet shops all around the world and raising such species would ensure a continuous market. If you choose a species with less desirable traits, you should be prepared to offer them wholesale or to keep them healthy until the market manages to absorb your stock.

Raise a species not raised anywhere else: Demand for captive-bred fish has never been higher, but many species are of no interest to large commercial breeders. There are dozens and dozens of breedable species that fall into this category.

Distributing these fishes locally may be more challenging, but selling them wholesale or through the Internet will secure a future for both the species being raised and your continued sales.

Raise expensive species: Expensive fish are always good candidates for breeding projects. Popular dottybacks that retail for $40 can sell to retailers for $12 to $15. Most clownfishes will earn less, around $2 to $6. If you can sell a number of expensive fish in a single week to several aquarium shops your hobby may fund itself. There is one trade-off with expensive fishes: as the price increases, the number you can sell typically decreases. It is safest to stay somewhere in the middle. You want to sell all the fish you produce.

Don't raise more than you can sell: Whether you plan to sell to local retail shops or to national wholesalers, determine how many fish you can sell each month. Raising every spawn produced by a productive pair will quickly crowd your rearing tanks with too many fish.

Produce quality: The quality of fish you produce and sell will quickly become your stamp. If you sell only the highest-quality specimens displaying vigor and the attributes that make the species desirable, you will earn respect and expanding business opportunities. If, however, you routinely offer pale-colored or sickly looking specimens with torn fins or physical deformities, your sales will quickly sour. Crowding fish is a sure fire way to kill sales. Water quality deteriorations and disease will quickly ruin the appeal of your fish. Cull mercilessly. This is a very difficult act for most aquarists, but it is vital to the long-term sustainability of captive propagation efforts. Deformed fishes and those straying from the natural appearance do not enhance the field of captive propagation. Consumers can misinterpret these deformities as a common result of aquaculture.

Do it because you love it: Someone once told me that curiosity is the best motivator in the world. Do it because you love it. You will be rewarded every day. Let's face it, the majority of money generated from selling your fishes will be put right back into your hobby. Broodstock food, HUFA enrichments, and algae paste are constant necessities. When we find success with one species, it makes us more confident to try others. Acquiring new broodstock can be expensive. Building new systems and gathering all the required material to tackle a new species can quickly drain the profit from selling your offspring.

Why not trade your offspring for broodstock, filters, food or whatever a local aquarium shop can offer you in return? If your breeding projects can pay for themselves, you have succeeded in creating a self-sustaining hobby. I can think of few pasttimes that offer comparable returns.

BREEDING FOR CONSERVATION

In 1997 author John Tullock wrote, "What mankind can foolishly destroy, we can sometimes wisely rebuild."

The sustainability of harvesting millions of reef fishes every year for the aquarium trade has aroused increased concerns from some observers.

In the absence of biological knowledge surrounding adult population dynamics and connectivity among distinct geographic regions, it is difficult to ascertain the affects of collection on coral reef fish populations. Reef populations were long viewed as open systems with passive exchange of larvae occurring between geographically distant reefs. The pelagic larval period of most marine species was thought of as a dispersal phase, because, at least in theory, they were capable of traveling hundreds or thousands of miles from their natal reef during their month or more riding in the plankton.

Recent evidence suggests larvae may not disperse as widely as previously thought and some scientists think they may settle on the very reefs where they were conceived. Population connectivity can have huge implications on the sustainability of reef fish populations, and it is important to determine how many fishes are produced and where they end up. When eggs or larvae are cast into the ocean do they return to the natal reef, a nearby reef, or a very distant reef? In pandemic species with wide geographic distributions, this can be a very difficult question to answer. If the genetics of a population remain homogenous throughout the range is it implied that many fishes are exchanged among metapopulations or does it mean a few stray larvae bridged the gap in the gene pool? This question is more easily answered in endemic species with a limited distribution. The Banggai Cardinalfish, for example, lacks a pelagic larval phase and the juveniles settle quite near the parental population. If we heavily collect a certain species from one location or several are they vulnerable to exploitation?

PRESERVING BIODIVERSITY

It is no secret that coral reefs throughout the world are in various states of decline. Particularly in developing countries, many areas that had diverse and pristine coral reefs are now little more than rubble fields of dead coral and limestone rock. Now overgrown with macroalgae, these habitats lack the diversity of corals and fishes present on healthier reefs and beg the question why? Surely in a system as large as the ocean, fishes and corals could rebuild. Is it simply a question of inappropriate habitat? Are fish spawned at distant reefs settling in these areas and simply not surviving? Or are there no fishes because there are no parental populations to produce them? The answer to these questions may lie in environmental threats such as coastal development, agriculture runoff and destructive fishing practices including the use of dynamite.

In many overfished and otherwise depleted areas, local governments and scientists have urged the implementation of Marine Protected Areas (MPAs)—no-take zones where fish and coral populations have a chance to grow and thrive without human threats. Excess healthy populations act as a source to supply depleted sinks. When properly sited and protected, MPAs are proving to be important as a fisheries management tool. However, whether MPAs act as sources or sinks or simply preserve the biodiversity of a small selected area remains to be seen in many areas.

A large, prolific species, the Maroon Clownfish can produce single broods yielding 1,000 or more marketable fish.

Throughout the world there is great motivation to preserve the biodiversity found on coral reefs. Traditional tools of preservation include biological research, experimentation and the active involvement of people whose lives depend on the reefs for daily survival.

As aquarists, especially as breeders of marine organisms, we stand to contribute by preserving bio-diversity through captive propagation. By spawning and rearing coral reef fishes in captivity we can learn important aspects of the early life history of reef fishes that could prove vital to understanding population dynamics in the wild. The techniques and methods used to raise reef fishes in captivity may one day preserve a species from extinction. If it were not for the aquarium trade, how many species of Victorian cichlids and American pupfish would have been lost forever?

Captive propagation techniques also hold promise to restock depleted reefs. Experimental placements of captive-grown corals on depleted reefs have shown success and may one day prove an invaluable tool in the restoration of reefs. Stock enhancement has been used to replenish populations of food fishes such as red drum, snook, red snapper, sea trout and salmon, and pilot projects have more recently aimed to replenish seahorses and clownfishes.

Aquariums are an amazing world that have the power to captivate and to educate. Though the trade in live reef fishes has very little impact on the threats facing coral reefs, it can be difficult to counter stereotypes of collectors as "raiders of the reefs," as *Audubon* magazine called them.

Before the scientific community and government legislation enforce collection bans, it is important for the aquarium hobby to demonstrate passion by committing to raising species of concern in captivity.

In my view, while marine aquaculture will play a vital role in the future of the hobby, it will never wholly replace wild collections. It is important that we stand together and let our biological and technological knowledge change the profile of the marine aquarium industry while we help secure future bio-diversity in the wild.

Sources & Contacts

Aquaculture Supplies & Larval Foods

Algagen LLC
www.algagen.com
PO Box 1734
Vero Beach, FL 32961
772-978-1395
Live microalgae, rotifers and copepod cultures & resting eggs.

Aquatic–EcoSystems Inc.
www.aquaticeco.com
2395 Apopka Blvd
Apopka, FL 32703
877-347-4788.
Aquaculture equipment, live feed cultures and most essentials needed by fish breeders.

Argent Chemicals Laboratories
www.argent-labs.com
8702 152nd Avenue NE
Redmond, WA 98052
425-885-3777
Chemicals, equipment and supplies for aquaculture.

Brine Shrimp Direct
www.brineshrimpdirect.com
PO Box 13147
Ogden, UT 84412-3147
800-303-7914
Source for Artemia cysts of all types and sizes.

Carolina Biological Supply Company
www.carolina.com
2700 York Road
Burlington, NC 27215-339
800-334-5551
Laboratory equipment and live food cultures.

Culture Collection of Algae and Protozoa (CCAP)
Dunstaffnage Marine Laboratory
P.O.Box 3
Oban, Scotland
Argyll PA 34 4AD UK
01-631-565518
Starter cultures of microalgae and protozoa.

Florida Aquafarms Inc.
www.florida-aqua-farms.com
33418 Old Saint Joe Road
Dade City, FL 33525
352-567-0226
Microalgae and rotifer cultures, aquarium equipment, aquaculture supplies.

Doctors Fosters and Smith
www.drsfostersmith.com
800-381-7179
Online aquarium supplies and fish, including a wide selection of Caribbean fish and livestock from their etropicals.com site.

INVE Americas, Inc.
www.inve.com
3528 W 500 S
Salt Lake City, UT 84104
801-876-2500
Live feeds enrichments, Artemia cysts and a range of inert weaning diets.

Reeds Mariculture Inc.
www.Reed-Mariculture.com
520 East McGlincy Lane, #1
Campbell, CA 95008
877-SEA-FARM
Algae paste, live microalgae, rotifer, mysid shrimp and copepod cultures.

Piscine Energetics Inc.
www.mysis.com
1355 Parker Street
Vancouver, BC
V5L 2J9, CANADA
1-888-220-2238
Enriched mysid shrimp—a must for seahorse aquaculture.

Sea-Gear Corp.
www.sea-gear.net
700-B1 S. John Rodes Blvd.
Melbourne, FL 32904
321-728-9116
Plankton nets and micron mesh.

Slic Dive Inc.
www.slicdive.com
304 Green Hills Dr.
Gilbert, SC 29054
803-892-3982 / 800-343-7542
Professional collecting nets and gear to collect broodstock.

Captive-Raised Broodstock

Oceans, Reefs and Aquariums (ORA)
5600 US 1 North,
Fort Pierce, FL 34946
Telephone: 772- 468-7008
Toll Free:1-888-317-3276
Fax: 772- 468-7353.
Email: sales@orafarm.com
Website: www.orafarm.com/
Captive-bred clownfishes, dottybacks, gobies, cardinalfishes, corals and clams are among many. Wholesale only.

Proaquatix
6020 99th Street
Sebastian, FL 32958
Telephone: 772-581-8066
Toll Free: 888-725-8420
Fax: 772-581-2693
Email: info@proaquatix.com
Website: www.proaquatix.com/
Captive-bred clownfishes, dottybacks, gobies and blennies. Wholesale Only.

C-Quest
Telephone: 787-845-2160 / 787-845-3909
Fax: 787-845-3929
Email: cquest@prtc.net
Captive-bred clownfishes, dottybacks and gobies. Wholesale.

Tropic Marine Centre (TMC)
Solesbridge Lane
Chorleywood Hertforshire
WD3 5SX England
Website: www.tmc-ltd.co.uk/
Captive-bred clownfishes, gobies, dottybacks, seahorses. Aquarium supplies and books.

Inland Aquatics
10 Ohio Street
Terre Haute, IN
Telephone: 812-232-9000
Fax: 928-395-9434
Email: InlandAquatics@aol.com
Website: www.inlandaquatics.com/
Captive-bred clownfishes, dottybacks, gobies etc.
Aquarium supplies. Retail.

Seahorse Australia
PO Box 363
Beauty Point
Tasmania 7270
Australia
Telephone: +61 3 6383 4811
Fax: +61 3 6383 4812
E-mail:info@seahorse-australia.com.au
Website: www.seahorse-australia.com.au/
Several species of captive-bred seahorses.

Seahorse Source
914 Delaware Ave.
Ft. Pierce, FL 34950
Telephone: 877-465-2401, 772-462-2401
Fax: 772-462-2402
Website: www.seahorsesource.com/
Several species of captive-bred seahorses.

South Australian Seahorse Marine Services
Tracy Warland, Port Lincoln, South Australia
Email: tracy@saseahorse.com
Website: http://www.saseahorse.com/default.htm
Several species of captive-bred seahorses.

Ocean Rider, Inc.
734460 Quen Kaahumauna, Suite 118
Kailua Kona
Hawaii 96740
Telephone: 808-329-6840
Fax: 808-329-6841
Email: info@oceanrider.com
Website: http://www.oceanrider.com/
Several species of captive-bred seahorses.

Online Forums and Societies

Breeders Registry
5541 Columbia Drive North
Fresno, CA 93727
Email: tlang@aquariusaquarium.org
Website: http://www.breedersregistry.org/
Nonprofit association for marine ornamental propagators, mostly hobbyists. Database on reproduction events and requirements of aquarium species.

Seahorse.Org
Website: www.seahorse.org
Database of articles, information and forums on seahorse care and reproduction.

Reef Central
Website: www.reefcentral.com
Online community of hobbyists and professionals. Database of articles, information and forums on captive care and culture of marine fishes and invertebrates. Publishers of Advanced Aquarist's Online Magazine.

Photography & Illustration Credits

All photographs by Matthew L. Wittenrich
unless otherwise indicated.

Photographers

Alf Jacob Nilsen (Bioquatic Photo: *biophoto.net*): 13, 14, 20, 22, 24, 27, 31, 32, 35, 51, 52, 53, 55, 56, 57, 78, 130, 132, 137, 144, 145, 148, 151, 164, 168, 169(TL, TR, BL), 175, 177, 199, 200, 203, 209, 213, 217, 226, 227, 232, 236, 241, 243, 264, 270, 272, 274, 277

Scott Michael (Reef Impressions: *coralrealm.com*): 5(C), 92, 96, 106, 107, 156, 167, 169(BR), 173, 185, 178, 184, 187, 188, 189, 191, 194, 197, 198, 210, 211, 215, 219, 221, 222(L), 226, 228, 238, 247, 244, 250, 257, 259, 262

Roger Steene: 176, 182, 186(BR), 206, 214, 231

Proaquatix: 163, 267, 284

Alexandra Didoha: 17, 186, 282, 304

Stephen Moe: 70, 142

Stephen Simpson, Ph.d.: 62

Rudy Kuiter: 178, 190

Dr. Howard Browman: 177

Barbara Moe: 71, 142

Martin A. Moe, Jr.: 222 (R)

Horsman Digital Photo: 128

Reed Mariculture: 127

NASA (Chlorophyll concentration in a Moderate Resolution Imaging Spectroradiometer [MODIS] image taken by NASA's AQUA Satellite. Courtesy NASA Earth Observatory, *earthobservatory.nasa.gov*): 120

NIWA (Courtesy National Institute of Water & Atmospheric Research, New Zealand, *niwa.co.nz*): 147

Fenton Walsh: 193

WikiCommons (Haeckel Copepoda Illustration, in public domain): 141

Illustrations

All illustrations by **Joshua Highter**

SELECTED BIBLIOGRAPHY

Allen, G.R. 2000. *Marine Fishes of Tropical Australia and South-east Asia.* Western Australian Museum, Perth.

Andrews, C. A. Exell & N. Carrington. 1988. *The Manual of Fish Health.* Tetra Press, Blacksburg, VA.

Asoh, K. and D.Y. Shapiro. 1997. Bisexual juvenile gonad and gonochorism in the fairy basslet, *Gramma loreto. Copeia.* 1: 22-31.

Axelrod, H.R., W. E. Burgess and R. Hunziker. 1990. *Dr. Burgess's Atlas of Marine Aquarium Fishes.* Tropical Fish Hobbyist Publications, Neptune City, NJ.

Baensch, H.A. and H. Debelius. 1994. *Marine Atlas.* Vol.1. Mergus, Melle, Germany.

Baez, J. 1998. Breeding the Marine Comet: a challenge for the best. *SeaScope.* Vol. 15.

Bailey, K.M. and E.D. Houde. 1989. Predation on eggs and larvae of marine fishes and the recruitment problem. *Adv. Mar. Biol.* 25: 1-83.

Battaglene, S.C. and R.B. Talbot. 1992. Induced spawning and larval rearing of snapper, *Pagrus auratus* (Pisces: Sparidae), from Australian waters. *New Zeal. J. Mar. Fresh. Res.* 26: 179-183.

Beck, J.L. and R.B. Turingan, in review. The effects of zooplankton swimming behavior on prey-capture kinematics of red drum larvae, *Sciaenops ocellatus.*

Bromage, N.R. and R.J. Roberts, eds. 1995. *Broodstock Management and Egg and Larval Quality.* Blackwell Science, Cambridge, MA.

Cato, J.C. and C.L. Brown, eds. 2003. *Marine Ornamental Species: Collection, Culture, and Conservation.* Iowa State Press, Ames, Iowa State Press, Blackwell Publishing, Ames, IO, pp. 297-303.

Checkley, D.M. 1982. Selective feeding by Atlantic herring (*Clupea harengus*) larvae on zooplankton in natural assemblages. *Mar. Ecol. Prog.* Ser. 9: 245-253.

Cole, K.S and D. Y. Shapiro. 1990. Gonad structure and hermaphroditism in the Gobiid genus *Coryphopterus* (Teleostei: Gobiidae). *Copeia.* 4:996-1003.

Cole, K.S. 1983. Protogynous hermaphroditism in a temperate zone territorial marine goby, *Coryphopterus nicholisi. Copeia.* 3:809-812.

Cole, K.S. and R.R. Robertson. 1988. Protogyny in the Caribbean reef goby, *Coryphopterus personatus*: gonad ontogeny and social influences on sex-change. *Bull. Mar. Sci.* 42(2): 317-333.

Connel, S.D. and G.P. Jones. 1991. The influence of habitat complexity on postrecruitment processes in a temperate reef fish population. *J. Exp. Mar. Biol. Ecol.* 151: 271-294.

Cushing, D.H. 1975. *Marine Ecology and Fisheries.* Cambridge University Press, Cambridge.

Cushing, D.H. 1981. *Fisheries Biology, a Study in Population Dynamics.* University of Wisconsin Press, Madison. 296. pp.

Dakin, N. 1992. *The Book of the Marine Aquarium.* Tetra Press, Blacksburg, VA.

Doi, M., A. Ohno, H. Kohno, Y. Taki, T. Singhagraiwan, 1997. Development of feeding ability in red snapper (*Lutjanus argentimaculatus*) early larvae. *Fish. Sci.* 63: 845-853.

Delbeek, J.C. and J. Sprung. 1994. *The Reef Aquarium Vol. 1.* Ricordea Publishing, Coconut Grove, FL.

Ebert, E.E. and C.H. Turner. 1962. The nesting behavior, eggs and larvae of the bluespot goby. *California Fish and Game.* pp. 249-252.

Fisher, R., D. R. Bellwood and S. D. Job. 2000. Development of swimming abilities in reef fish larvae. *Mar. Ecol. Prog. Ser.* 202: 163-173.

Fuiman, L.A. and A.E. Magurran. 1994. Development of predator defenses in fish. *Rev. Fish Biol. Fish.* 4: 145-183.

Fuiman, L.A. and D. Higgs. 1997. Ontogeny, growth and the recruitment process. *Early Life History and Recruitment in Fish Populations.* Chapman and Hall, London, UK. pp. 225-249.

Fowler, J. and L. Cohen. 1990. *Practical Statistics for Field Biology.* Open University Press, Berkshire, UK.

Fishelson, L. 1976. Spawning and Larval Development of the Blenniid Fish, *Meiacanthus nigrolineatus*, from the Red Sea. *Copeia.* 4: 79 8-800.

Fenner, R.M. 1998. *The Conscientious Marine Aquarist.* Microcosm Ltd./TFH, Shelburne, VT.

Ferrell, D.G. 1987. Population ecology of the Queensland dottyback (*Pseudochromis queenslandica*). *Unpublished master's thesis.* University of Sydney. NSW, Australia.

Gardner, T. 1999. Breeding the masked goby. *SeaScope.* Vol. 17.

Gardner, T. 2003. The copepod/*Artemia* tradeoff in the captive culture of *Hippocampus erectus*, vulnerable species in lower New York state. In: Marine Ornamentals: Collection, Culture and Conservation, eds.

Gill, A.C. and G.R. Allen. 2004. *Pseudochromis lugibris* and *P. tonozukai*, two new dottyback fish species from the Indo-Australian Archipelago (Perciformes: Pseudochromidae: Pseudochrominae). *Zootaxa.* 604: 1-12.

Gill, A.C., K. Shao and J. Chen. 1995. *Pseudochromis striatus*, a new species of pseudochromine dottyback from Taiwan and the northern Philippines (Teleostei: Perciformes: Pseudochromidae). *Revue fr. Aquariol.* 21(10): 3-4.

Gill, A.C. and J.B. Hutchins. 1997. *Assiculoides desmonotus*, new genus and species of dottyback from the Kimberley coast of Western Australia (Telostei: Perciformes: Pseudochromidae). *Revue fr. Aquario.* 24(20): 1-2.

Gill, A.C., and J.K.L. Mee. 1993. Notes on dottybacks of the genus *Pseudochromis* of Oman, with description of a new species (Perciformes: Pseudochromidae). *Revue fr. Aquariol.* 20(30):2.

Gill, A.C., Allen, G.R. 1996. *Pseudochromis viridis*, a new species of dottyback from Christmas Island, Indian Ocean (Teleostei: Perciformes, Pseudochromidae). *Revue fr. Aquariol.* 23(30):1-2.

Gill, A.C. and J.E. Randall. 1998. Five new species of the dottybacks *Pseudochromis* from Indonesia (Teleostei: Pseudochromidae). *Revue fr. Aquariol.* 25(22): 1-2.

Gill, A.C. 1992. *Pseudochromis steenei*, a new sexually dimorphic species of dottyback fish from Indonesia (Perciformes: Pseudochromidae). *Revue fr. Aquariol.* 19(31): 1 et 2.

——1995. Identification of the primary types of Pseudochrominae species described by Pieter Bleeker, with lectotype designations for *Pseudochromis tapeinosoma* and *P. xanthochir* (Perciformes: Pseudochromidae). *Copeia.* 1: 243-246.

Gill, A.C., R.L. Pyle and J.L. Earle. 1996. *Pseudochromis ephippiatus*, new species of dottyback from southeastern Papua New Guinea (Teleostei: Perciformes: Pseudochromdiae). *Revue fr. Aquariol.* 23(20): 3-4.

Gill, A.C. and R. Winterbottom. 1993. *Pseudochromis kolythrus*, a new species of dottyback from New Caledonia, with comments on its relationships (Teleostei: Perciformes: Pseudochromidae). *Amer. Mus. Novit.* 3082: 7pp.

Gill, A.C. and D.J. Woodland. 1992. Description of a new dottyback of the genus *Pseudochromis* (Pisces: Pseudochromidae) from Western Australia. *Rec. Aust. Mus.* 44: 247-251.

Giwojna, P. 1996. Seahorse nutrition, Part 1: live food for adults. *Freshwat. Mar. Aquar.* 19 (10): 40-56.

——1996. Seahorse nutrition, Part 2: frozen foods for adults. *Freshwat. Mar. Aquar.* 19(11): 72-78.

——1996. Seahorse nutrition, Part 3: hand-feeding adults. *Freshwat. Mar. Aquar.* 19(12): 30-46.

——1996. Seahorse nutrition, Part 4: feeding juveniles and dwarf seahorses. *Freshwat. Mar. Aquar.* 20(2): 30-48.

Gratzek, J.B. ed. 1992. *Aquariology: The Science of Fish Health Management.* Tetra Press, Morris Plains, NJ.

Green, E. 2003. International trade in marine aquarium species: using the global marine aquarium database.

Marine Ornamental Species: Collection, Culture, and Conservation. Iowa State Press, Ames, Iowa.

Green, B.S. and M.I. McCormick. 2001. Ontogeny of the digestive and feeding systems in the anemonefish *Amphiprion melanopus*. *Env. Biol. Fish.* 61(1): 73-83.

Grier, H.J. 1981. Cellular organization of the testis and spermatogenesis in fishes. *Amer. Zool.* 21: 345-357.

Govoni, J.J., P.B. Ortner, F. Al-Yamani, and L.C. Hill. 1986. Selective feeding of spot, *Leiostomus xanthurus*, and Atlantic croaker, *Micropogonias undulates*, larvae in the northern Gulf of Mexico. *Mar. Ecol. Prog.* Ser. 28: 175-183.

Halver, J.E. ed. 1989. *Fish Nutrition.* Academic Press, London.

Harding, J.M. 1999. Selective feeding behavior of larval naked gobies *Gobiosoma bosc* and blennies *Chasmodes bosquianus* and *Hypsoblennius hentzi*: preferences for bivalve veligers. *Mar. Ecol. Prog. Ser.* 179: 145-153.

Heath, M.R. 1992. Field investigations of the early life stages of marine fish. *Adv. Mar. Biol.* 28: 1-174.

Heath, M.R. 1993. An evaluation and review of the ICES herring larval surveys in the North Sea and adjacent waters. *Bull. Mar. Sci.* 53: 795-817.

Hjort, J. 1914. Fluctuations in the great fisheries of northern Europe viewed in light of biological research. *Rap. Proc. Reun. Con. Int. Expl. Mer.* 20: 1-228.

Hoff, F.H. 1996. Conditioning, spawning and rearing of fish with emphasis on marine clownfish. *Aquaculture Consultants Inc.*, Dade City, FL.

Houde, E.D. and R.C. Schekter. 1980. Feeding by marine fish larvae: developmental and functional responses. *Env. Biol. Fish.* 5 (4): 315-334.

Hunter, J.R. 1981. Feeding ecology and predation of marine fish larvae. *Marine Fish Larvae: Morphology, Ecology and Relation to Fisheries.* Seattle, WA. p. 33 -77

Hunter, J.R. 1976. Report of a colloquium on larval fish mortality studies and their relation of fishery research. *NOAA Tech. Rep. NMFS Cir.* 395: 1-5.

Hunter, J.R. and C.A. Kimbrell. 1980. Egg cannibalism in the northern anchovy *Engraulis mordax. Fish. Bull.* 78: 811-816.

Hunt von Herbing, I., T. Miyake, B.K. Hall and R.G. Boutilier. 1996. Ontogeny of feeding and respiration in larval Atlantic cod (*Gadus morhua*) (Teleostei: Gladiformes): *I. Morphology. J. Morph.* 227:15-35.

Hunt von Herbing, I. 2001. Development of feeding structures in larval fish with different life histories: winter flounder and Atlantic cod. *J. Fish.* Biol. 59: 767-782.

Iwasa, Y. 1991. Sex change evolution and cost of reproduction. *Behav. Ecol.* 2(1): 56-68.

Job, S.D. and D.R. Bellwood. 1996. Visual acuity and feeding in larval *Premnas biaculeatus. J. Fish. Biol.* 48:952-1002.

Korringa, P. 1976. *Farming Marine Fishes and Shrimp*s. Elsevier Scientific Publishing Co., New York.

Kohno, H.R. Ordonio-Aguilar, A. Ohno and Y. Taki. 1996. Osteological development of the feeding apparatus in early stage larvae of the seabass, *Lates calcarifer. Ichthyol. Res.* 43: 1-9.

——1997. Morphological aspects of feeding and improvement in feeding ability in early stage larvae of milkfish, *Chanos chanos. Ichthyol. Res.* 43: 133-140.

——1997. Why is grouper larval rearing difficult? An approach from the development of the feeding apparatus in early stage larvae of the grouper, *Epinephelus coioides. Ichthyol. Res.* 44:267-274.

Kiorboe, T.K., P. Munk and J.G. Stottrup. 1985. First feeding by larval herring (*Clupea harengus*). *Dana.* 5: 95-107.

Krebs, J.M. and R.G. Turingan. 2003. Intraspecific variation in gape-prey size relationships and feeding success during early ontogeny in red drum, *Sciaenops ocellatus. Env. Biol. Fish.* 66: 75-84.

Kuiter, R.H. 1996. *Guide to Sea Fishes of Australia.* New Holland Publishers, Sydney.

——2003. *Seahorses, Pipefishes and Their Relatives: A Comprehensive Guide to Syngnathiformes.* TMC Publishing, UK.

Kuwamura, T. and Y. Nakashima. 1998. New aspects of sex change among reef fishes: recent studies in Japan. *Env. Biol. Fish.* 52: 125-135.

Kuwamura, T. and Y. Nakashima. 2000. Male morphological characteristics and mating success in a protogynous coral reef fish, *Halichoeres melanurus. J. Ethol.* 18:17-23.

Kuwamura, T., Y. Nakashima and Y. Yogo. 1994. Sex change in either direction by growth-rate advantage in the, monogamous coral goby, *Paragobiodon echinocephalus. Behav. Ecol.* 5(4): 434-438.

Langsdale, J.R.M. 1993. Developmental changes in the opacity of larval herring, *Clupea harengus*, and their implications for vulnerability to predation. *J. Mar. Biol. Assoc. UK.* 73: 225-232.

Lasker, R. 1975. Field criteria for survival of anchovy larvae: the relation between inshore chlorophyll maximum layers and successful first feeding. *U.S. Fish. Bull.* 73: 453-462.

——1978. The relation between oceanographic conditions and larval anchovy food in the California Current: identification of factors contributing to recruitment failure. *Rapp. P.V. Reun. Cons. Int. Explor. Mer.* 173: 212-230.

——1981. The role of a stable ocean in larval fish survival and subsequent recruitment. *Marine Fish Larvae: Morphology, Ecology and Relation to Fisheries*, Washington Sea Grant Program, Seattle. pp.80-87.

Lazo, J.P., M.T. Dinis, G.J. Holt, C. Faulk, and C.R. Arnold. 2000. Co-feeding microparticulate diets with algae: toward eliminating the need of zooplankton at first feeding in larval red drum (*Scieanops ocellatus*). *Aqua.* 188: 339-351.

Leis, J.M. & T. Trnski. 1989. *The Larvae of Indo-Pacific Shorefishes.* University of Hawaii Press, Honolulu, HI.

Lieske, E. and R. Myers. 2001. *Coral Reef Fishes.* Princeton University Press, Princeton, NJ.

MacKenzie, B.R. and T. Kiorboe. 1995. Encounter rates and swimming behavior of pause-travel and cruise larval fish predators in calm and turbulent laboratory environments. *Limnol. Oceanogr.* 40(7): 1278-1289.

Michael, S.W. 1998. *Reef Fishes, Volume 1.* Microcosm, Ltd./TFH. Shelburne, VT.

Michael, S.W. 1999. *The PocketExpert Guide: Marine Fishes.* Microcosm Ltd./TFH. Shelburne, VT.

Mills, D. 1987. *Tetra Encyclopedia of the Marine Aquarium.* Tetra Press, Blacksburg, VA.

Miyazaki, T., R. Masuda, S. Furuta and K. Tsukamoto. 2000. Feeding behavior of hatchery-reared juveniles of the Japanese flounder following a period of starvation. *Aquacul.* 190: 129-138.

Moe, M.A. 1992. *The Marine Aquarium Handbook: Beginner to Breeder.* Green Turtle Publications, Plantation, FL.

——1997. *Breeding the Orchid Dottyback.* Green Turtle Publications, Plantation, FL.

Mooi, R.D. 1990. Egg surface morphology of Pseudochromoids (Perciformes: Percoidei) with comments on its phylogenetic implications. *Copeia.* 2:455-475.

Mooi, R.D., R. Winterbottom and M. Burridge. 1990. Egg surface morphology, development, and evolution in the Congrogadinae (Pisces: Perciformes: Pseudochromidae). *Can. J. Zool.* 68:923 – 934.

Moteki, M. 2002. Morphological aspects of feeding and improvement in feeding ability in the early larval stages of red sea bream Pagrus major. *Fish. Sci* .68: 996-1003.

Munday, P.L., M.J. Caley and G.P. Jones. 1998. Bi-directional sex change in a coral-dwelling goby. *Behav. Ecol. Sociobiol.* 43(6): 371-377.

Munk, P. 1992. Foraging behaviour and prey size spectra of larval herring *Clupea harengus. Mar. Ecol. Prog. Ser.* 80: 149-158.

Nakashima, Y. T. Kuwamura and Y. Yogo. 1996. Both-ways sex change in monogamous coral gobies, *Gobiodon* spp. *Env. Biol. Fish.*

Norman, J.R. 1958. *A History of Fishes.* Hill and Wang, N.Y.

Sunobe, T. and A. Nakazono. Sex change in both directions by alteration of social dominance in *Trimma okinawae* (Pisces: Gobiidae). *Ethology* 94: 339 – 345.

Ostrowski, A.C. and C.W. Laidley. 2001. Application of marine foodfish techniques in ornamental aquaculture: reproduction and larval first feeding. *Aquar. Sci. Cons.* 3: 191-204.

Paletta, M.S. 1999. *The New Marine Aquarium.* Microcosm Ltd. Shelburne, VT.

Peterson, W.T. and S.J. Ausubel. 1984. Diets and selective feeding by larvae of Atlantic mackerel *Scomber scombrus* on zooplankton. *Mar. Ecol. Prog. Ser.* 17: 65-75.

Pepin, P. and R.W. Penney. 1997. Patterns of prey size and taxonomic composition in larval fish: are there general size dependant models? *J. Fish. Biol.* 51:84-100.

Pillay, T.V.R. 1990. *Aquaculture: Principles and Practices.* Fishing New Books, Cambridge, MA.

Pothoff, T. 1984. Clearing and staining techniques. American Society of Ichthyologists and Herpetologists (eds.). Ontogeny and Systematics of Fishes. Special *Publication, No. 1. Amer. Soc. Ichthyol. Herpet.* Allen, New York. pp. 35-37.

Pryor, V.K. and C.E. Epifanio. 1993. Prey selection by larval weakfish (*Cynoscion regalis*): the effects of prey size, speed, and abundance. *Mar. Biol.* 116: 31-37.

Robertson, D.R. 1972. Social control of sex reversal in a coral-reef fish. *Science.* 15(177):1007-1009.

Sadovy, Y. and D.Y. Shapiro. 1987. Criteria for the diagnosis of hermaphroditism in fishes. *Copeia.* 1: 136-156.

Sadovy, Y. and T.J. Donaldson. 1995. Sexual pattern of *Neocirrhites armatus* (Cirrhitidae) with notes on other hawkfish species. *Env. Biol. Fish.* 42:143-150.

Shirota, A. 1970. Studies of mouth size of fish larvae. *Bull. Jap. Soc. Fish.(translation of the Fisheries Research Board of Canada No. 1978)* 36: 353-368.

Spotte, S. 1992. *Captive Seawater Fishes: Science and Technology.* John Wiley and Sons, Inc. New York.

Stoecker, D.K. and J.J. Govoni. 1984. Food selection by young larval gulf menhaden (*Brevoortia patronus*). *Mar. Biol.* 80: 299-306.

Sugama, K., S. Ismi, S. Kawahara and M. Rimmer. 2003. Improvement of larval rearing technique for humphead grouper, *Chromliptes altivelis. Aqua. Asia.* 8(3): 34-37.

Thresher, R.E. 1984. *Reproduction in Reef Fishes.* Tropical Fish Hobbyist Publications, Neptune City, N.J.

Turingan, R.G. and P.C. Wainwright. 1993. Functional and morphological basis of durophagy in the queen triggerfish, *Balistes vetula* (Pisces: Tetraodontiformes). *J. Morph.* 215: 101-118.

Turingan, R.G. 1999. Two-stage development of the feeding mechanism in larval marine fishes: consequences for feeding performance. *Amer. Zool.* 39(5): 85A.

Turingan, R.G., J.L. Beck and J.M. Krebs. 2005. Development of feeding mechanics in marine fish larvae and the swimming behavior of zooplankton prey: implications for rearing marine fishes. *Copepods in Aquaculture.* Blackwell Publishing, Ames, Iowa, USA.

Wallace, R.A. and K. Selman.ß 1981. Cellular and dynamic aspects of oocyte growth in teleosts. *Ameri. Zool.* 21: 325-343.

Warner, R.R. 1975. The adaptive significance of sequential hermaphroditism in animals. *Amer. Natural.* 109(965):61-81.

Warner, R.R., D.R. Robertson and E.G. Leigh. 1975. Sex change and sexual selection. *Science.* 14(190):633-638.

Watanabe, T. and V. Kiron. 1994. Prospects in larval fish dietetics. *Aquacul.* 124: 223-251.

Westneat, M.W. and P.C. Wainwright. 1989. Feeding mechanism of *Epibulus insidiator* (Labridae, Teleostei): evolution of a novel function. *J. Morph.* 202:129-150.

Wilkerson, Joyce D. 1998. *Clownfishes: A Guide to Their Captive Care, Breeding and Natural History.* Microcosm Ltd., Shelburne, VT.

Wittenrich, M.L. and P.L. Munday. 2005. Bi-directional sex change in coral reef fishes from the family Pseudochromidae: an experimental evaluation. *Zool. Sci.* 22: 797-803.

Wuenschel, M.J. and R.G. Werner. 2004. Consumption and gut evacuation rate of laboratory-reared spotted seatrout (Sciaenidae) larvae and juveniles. *J. Fish. Biol.* 65: 723-743.

Zupanc, G.K.H. 1988. *Fish and Their Behavior.* Tetra Press, Melle.

FURTHER READING

MICROCOSM/TFH PROFESSIONAL SERIES TITLES

REEF FISHES
A Guide to Their Identification, Behavior & Captive Care
BY SCOTT W. MICHAEL

VOLUME I: MORAY EELS, SEAHORSES & ANTHIAS
VOLUME II: BASSLETS, DOTTYBACKS & HAWKFISHES
VOLUME III: ANGELFISHES & BUTTERFLYFISHES
VOLUME IV: WRASSES, DAMSELFISHES & BLENNIES (2007)
VOLUME V: GOBIES, TRIGGERFISHES & SURGEONFISHES (2008)
THE REEF FISHES ENCYCLOPEDIA (2009)

CLOWNFISHES
A Guide to Their Captive Care, Breeding & Natural History
BY JOYCE D. WILKERSON

POCKETEXPERT GUIDE: MARINE FISHES
500+ Essential-to-Know Species
BY SCOTT W. MICHAEL

POCKETEXPERT GUIDE: REEF AQUARIUM FISHES
500+ Essential-to-Know Species
BY SCOTT W. MICHAEL

AQUARIUM SHARKS & RAYS
An Essential Guide to their Selection, Keeping & Natural History
SCOTT W. MICHAEL

FURTHER INFORMATION: WWW.MICROCOSM-BOOKS.COM

REEF SECRETS
Reef Aquariums Made Simpler: Expert Advice, Selecting Fishes & Invertebrates
BY ALF JACOB NILSEN & SVEIN A. FOSSÅ

THE CONSCIENTIOUS MARINE AQUARIST
A Commonsense Handbook for Successful Saltwater Hobbyists
BY ROBERT M. FENNER

NATURAL REEF AQUARIUMS
Simplified Approaches to Creating Living Saltwater Microcosms
BY JOHN H. TULLOCK

AQUARIUM KEEPING & RESCUE
The Essential Saltwater Handbook & Log
BY CARL DELFAVERO

POCKETEXPERT GUIDE: MARINE INVERTEBRATES
500+ Essential-to-Know Species
BY RONALD L. SHIMEK, PH.D.

THE NEW MARINE AQUARIUM
Step-by-Step Setup & Stocking Guide
BY MICHAEL S. PALETTA

AQUARIUM CORALS
Selection, Husbandry & Natural History
BY ERIC H. BORNEMAN

REEF LIFE
Natural History and Behaviors of Marine Aquarium Fishes & Invertebrates
BY DENISE NIELSEN TACKETT & LARRY TACKETT

FURTHER INFORMATION: WWW.MICROCOSM-BOOKS.COM

About the Author

MATTHEW L. WITTENRICH is a marine biologist who has been deeply involved with the aquarium world since the age of 15. Working in various capacities as a researcher, consultant, and hobbyist, his work has taken him to the Philippines, Australia, Fiji, Solomon Islands and throughout the Caribbean and Central America studying coral reef fishes. After graduating with a Bachelor's degree in Marine Biology from Long Island University, Southampton College, he worked in various facets of commercial finfish aquaculture and collaborated on various research projects throughout the United States and Australia. He is currently pursuing his doctorate at Florida Institute of Technology in Melbourne, Florida, with research projects centered in the Philippines. A native of western New York, he began breeding saltwater fish in his parent's basement, successfully raising more than 56 species of marine fish and shrimp. His research focuses on the development of feeding abilities in early stage larvae of coral reef fishes.